And the View from the Shore

10 april 1998

Dear Art and Helene —
   This is the second time
I'm signing this book, but
everything is worth it!
Thanks very much for the
years of friendship and
wonderful talks. I hope
we'll have many more
times together.
                   aloha,
                   Steve Sumida

And the View from the Shore
Literary Traditions of Hawai'i

Stephen H. Sumida

Stephen H. Sumida

A SAMUEL AND ALTHEA STROUM BOOK

University of Washington Press
Seattle and London

This book is published with the assistance of a grant from the Stroum Book Fund, established through the generosity of Samuel and Althea Stroum. An additional grant was provided through the generosity of Bamboo Ridge Press, Honolulu.

Library of Congress Cataloging in Publication Data

Sumida, Stephen H.
  And the view from the shore : literary traditions of
Hawai'i / Stephen H. Sumida.
      p.   cm.
  Includes bibliographical references and index.
  ISBN 0–295–97078–2 (alk. paper)
  1. American literature—Hawaii—History and criticism.
  2. American literature—Asian American authors—History and
  criticism.   3. American literature—Oceanian American authors
  —History and criticism.   4. Oceanian Americans in literature.
  5. Asian Americans in literature.   6. Hawaii—intellectual life.
  7. Hawaii in literature.   I. Title.
PS283.H3S86   1991   90-46127
810.9'9969—dc20   CIP

The paper used in this publication meets the minimum requirements of American National Standard for Information Sciences—Permanence of Paper for Printed Library Materials, ANSI Z39.48–1984. ∞

Title page and chapter ornaments are from a detail of a Polynesian *tapa* cloth.

In memory of
NORMA FUMIKO YAMAMOTO SUMIDA
28 February 1918–18 July 1987

Contents

Preface

This book is intended as a catalyst. I hope it will cause readers to take a fresh look at the vivid and various patterns within Hawaii's pastoral and heroic literary traditions. As a literary history, the book covers two centuries of Hawaii's culture since Captain James Cook's arrival in 1778. The approach is multicultural, ranging through and relating together the spectrum of native Hawaiian, colonial, tourist, and polyethnic local literatures. Analysis of these broadly representative works invites the reader to explore further in the literature itself and to reconsider the present and future direction of Hawaii's writers.

I hope that my comments are inclusive, but a synthesis does not purport to be the final word. In the *kaona*, or subtext, of what I say here, please read this. I am glad that the creation of Hawaii's literatures continues today, and that critical studies of it, my own and others', will continue as well. Indeed, rather than close with the conventional *pau*, meaning finished and final, I conclude my book with the Hawaiian word *lawa*, implying sufficient for the moment and for the task at hand.

While this book is unprecedented in its scope and theme, the lack of prior full-length studies of the kind may be surprising, especially when the image of Hawai'i as paradise—the simple pastoral view—is so predominant worldwide that it loudly begs that opposite, heroic aspects of the islands' arts and cultures be considered as well. Hawaii's isolation, not merely perceived but promoted, has tended to keep humanists in particular away from undertaking such a task, perhaps out of fear that in one's interpreting and in one's teaching, without an adequate guide, one is bound to violate a supposedly unique and exotic culture.

Explicit historical, social, political, and linguistic contexts of Hawai'i, and to a smaller extent literary theory, inform my analyses and explications of texts, which in turn reinterpret the nonfictional contexts themselves. These "texts" include poems, song lyrics, novels and short fiction, drama, and certain historical writings and events that epitomize cultural milieux and sensibilities. Though the texts are necessarily selected, the book is thus comprehensive in important ways. While it is extensive, however, the work also serves as an introduction to the literature, its history, and its most salient concepts. I hope that my study of particular texts presents paradigms that will prove useful in interpreting and evaluating works and authors that I have not specifically covered.

Hawaii's writers and artists are a diverse group of people who have been devoting lifetimes to articulating their cultures and who continue to contribute to them. In this book, analysis of specific contemporary works is carried up to the 1980s, including in the closing chapter a discussion of the Hawaiian Renaissance and the Talk Story Writers' Conferences of 1978 and 1979. Hawaii's writers are notably productive today in several literary genres, as are scholars of numerous disciplines and specialties; I would like to think that the literary groundwork and events of the late 1970s as well as earlier writers in the traditions recalled here have helped make possible such a literary life in and for Hawai'i. For the interested reader, I note the following selected writers, in alphabetical order, who have published major works during the 1980s, each in some way or another representative of serious literary activity in Hawai'i. Their publications are listed in the Bibliography: Keith S. Abe, Nell Altizer, Joseph Balaz, John Charlot, Steven Goldsberry, Garrett Hongo, Dean Honma, Doris Kawano, Juliet S. Kono, Wing Tek Lum, Michael McPherson, Pat Matsueda, W. S. Merwin, Rodney Morales, Susan Nunes, Leialoha Apo Perkins, Tony Quagliano, Marjorie Sinclair, Michelle Cruz Skinner, Cathy Song, and Frank Stewart.

In another category entirely are Ken Goring, whose *Gone to Maui* (1983) is so egregiously a potboiler that it must be a parody of the kind, and Hunter S. Thompson and Ralph Steadman, whose *The Curse of Lono* (1983) simply repeats stereotypes about primitive peoples and their gods in a conventional way uncharacteristic of Thompson's usually acid (to put it mildly) words and views.

Locally published literary journals and anthologies since 1980 include *Bamboo Ridge: The Hawaii Writers' Quarterly*, *Hawaii Review*, and *Literary Arts Hawaii* (formerly the *Hawaii Literary Arts Council Newsletter*), which continue from earlier years to publish local and other writers, and since 1987 the *Chaminade Literary Review* has joined them. *Hapa, The Paper, Hanai, Ramrod,* and *Hawaii Pacific Review*, some of these newly, not regularly, or no longer published, have also featured local writers in this decade. A new literary journal, *Mānoa*, covers Hawai'i and other Pacific islands. One of its founders, Frank Stewart, has also edited another of his valued anthologies, *Passages to the Dream Shore: Short Stories of Contemporary Hawaii* (1987), a groundbreaking collection that presents many new voices. In general, literary activity in Hawai'i seems strengthened since the 1970s and certainly since the 1950s and early 1960s, an especially lethargic era for literary periodicals locally. But it is also true that journals have come and gone in such a fashion that the number I have just listed is greater than the number active at any given time in the 1980s, and over time the repetition of editors' and contributors' names from one journal to another shows how tight is the circle of Hawaii's literary net.

I should note at this point that native Hawaiian literary works, written in the Hawaiian language, occasionally appear in newspapers such as *Ka Wai Ola*, the monthly publication of the Office of Hawaiian Affairs (OHA); *The Native Hawaiian*, published by the Hawaiian rights group Alu Like; and *'Āha'i 'Ōlelo*, a quarterly publication of 'Ahahui 'Ōlelo Hawai'i. As few as these may seem, they carry on a rich and prolific tradition of newspaper writing by native Hawaiians in the nineteenth century, when Hawaiians quickly numbered among the most literate peoples in the world and filled the pages of many local newspapers with poetry, chants, and historical narratives in addition to news and opinions. Individual journals or anthologies in Hawai'i such as *Mana* and *A Pacific Islands Collection* also concentrate on publishing literary works of native peoples of the Pacific, and Topgallant Publishing Company, with its emphasis on native Hawaiian scholarship and arts, continues under its new name of Ku Pa'a, Incorporated, to publish books on topics in Hawaii's polyethnic history and culture. It is important to acknowledge these and other Hawaiian sources in my text because, with the exception of the pages I devote to John Dominis Holt and his Hawaiian novel *Waimea Summer*, my use of native Hawaiian studies is mainly illustrative. I myself do not read the Hawaiian language. In certain matters, I trust my expert colleagues whose words I hear, scholars I read, and our *kūpuna* (elders) with knowledge of the past and, therefore, a view of the present.

Various American authors have contributed to the long and continuing effort of interpreting dynamics of race, class, gender, and ethnicity; and while in my book I focus on Hawaii's writers, in both thought and practice I find myself drawing comparisons and relationships with writers from throughout the United States. I am heartened, for instance, by Toni Morrison's 1989 lecture at the University of Michigan, where she demonstrates how a point of view and method derived from ethnic American literary studies can illuminate standard authors of the American canon such as Melville.[1] Morrison's reading of *whiteness* in *Moby Dick*, which she explicates within a framework of ethnic literary studies and fine points of closely reading the opening lines of her own novels, shocked me with what (perhaps only to me) seemed its resemblance in principle to my view of Melville's criticism of ethnocentrism in his *Typee*. However dim my own sight may be in comparison to Morrison's vision, I am convinced that the main reason for any such resemblance of my efforts—whether to Morrison, say, or to John Dominis Holt of Hawai'i —is owing to these authors' having taught me certain ideas, feelings, and ways of seeing in the first place.

Throughout my study I refer to a variety of traditions; this method proved useful at the 1979 Talk Story Conference, where our morning seminars typically ranged through impromptu allusions to Greek classics, Asian literature, the Anglo American canon, Asian American literature of Hawai'i and the mainland, and native Hawaiian culture—even while we also talked story from the daily life of yesterday and today— in our free discussions of themes, forms, and symbols in the literature of the island of Hawai'i. Here I need to explain as briefly as possible— because I would hope my discussion itself demonstrates my point— that in citing authors other than Hawaii's in my study, I am trying to employ what to me is part of my method and my view. I aim to imply or subsume an idea, a relationship, which the cited writer or scholar has in some way already made current. I do not feel I need explicitly to reinvent the idea or its relationships with other literary principles. For example, there are resemblances, as well as differences, among authors and works of America's various nonwhite races and their communities in how they view people in power and, in what I consider to be Morrison's very apt example of reading Melville, how they view the established, empowered canon of American literature. Hawaii's authors and their communities share to some degree or another Morrison's awareness of the workings of power and empowerment. Personally and collectively they know something about social, cultural, political, and economic inequalities, owing in part to their situation in life as residents of these islands. In trying not to treat my subjects with inequality or to insulate them within a precious uniqueness, I aim instead to view Hawaii's literary works in explicit and implicit terms of *difference*, where appropriate: in

other words, *to relate* Hawaii's literature and its creators with writers elsewhere and of other eras.

Different from my reference to Morrison but parallel to it by
method, some of my allusions to authors of an established Anglo male
canon, such as Marlowe, Shakespeare, Wordsworth, Keats, Faulkner, or
Hemingway, apply specifically within the context of a particular discussion. It is not that I am trying to validate Hawaii's writers by having
them thus rub elbows with presumed greatness; the assumptions behind
such an idea are abhorrent to me. Whether I am right or wrong, and
whether the Hawai'i author being discussed is conscious of it in the way
I am, at these moments I believe there is a useful underlying comparison,
contrast, or influence at work which I have reason to assume is part of
the Hawai'i writer's or, in some cases, my readers' own study, casual
reading, or breathing the air, so to speak, of such authors in the established
canons of an Anglo culture we have all been required to learn. Part of
my job as a critic is to discern and point out such possible layers of
influence, certainly to do so before we presume to judge by standards
which are themselves influenced by literatures of the world. Again I stress
one of my principles: Hawaii's writers in their thoughts and expression
are not isolated from the world's cultural currents; to discuss them within
a larger context helps, at the very least, to keep American literary history
accurate.

I also neither believe nor want to allow that only Anglo literary
references are relevant in a discussion of Hawaii's literature, much of it
by Asian Americans. Being a researcher and teacher in Asian/Pacific
American studies, I taste the bitterness of seeing new works of Asian
American literature and scholarship written, marketed, or reviewed as
if none existed before. This taste is rank, however distinctive a contribution a work may make or relationship it may bring to an already existing
body of art and knowledge. I try to indicate and explain some literary,
historical, and other kinds of works in Asian/Pacific American studies
that my discussion may echo.[2] Because I consider Asian American literatures of Hawai'i and the mainland related often more significantly to each
other than to other sources of references outside Hawai'i, I do not treat
Hawaii's by simple contrast with Asian American culture of the mainland.

The nature of the relationship and comparison changes from one
generation and era to the next and varies as well by individuals. On
the one hand, the writer Darrell H. Y. Lum may see himself, his work,
and his part in a Local literary tradition to be distinctly of Hawai'i in

diction, form, and theme. On the other, the poet Wing Tek Lum himself sees in his own and in certain others' works of Hawai'i some cultural values that stem directly but neither obviously nor simplistically from Chinese laboring immigrants and their histories in both Hawai'i and the mainland. Just as the *issei*, Japanese immigrants, generally shared a common cultural origin whether they settled in Canada, the mainland United States, Brazil, or Hawai'i, so also Wing Tek Lum consciously brings to his literary work a certain interest in history which ties him with Asian American writers of the mainland, such as Frank Chin. At the same time, Darrell and Wing Tek Lum work together in the production of the journal *Bamboo Ridge*, and in numerous other literary projects, without conflict over their different sensibilities. Darrell Lum considers his own views to be distinctive yet consonant with Wing Tek's and Chin's, like three lines spiraling toward and away from a common center, even while Chin may criticize an aspect of Lum's work for reasons with which Lum disagrees. Meanwhile my work involves bringing such larger cultural relations to light insofar as I can discern them and as they are germane to what I am trying to say.

In contrast to what I have been claiming here, the most isolating term in my discussion is "local." The term "local," as in "local-style" food, culture, T-shirts, or "whatevah," has been used so much that a backlash has developed against it and the people it describes—a backlash that is still loudly evident. Race is partly at issue—but not exactly, not truly. A "local" (meaning here a certain kind of person) is usually thought of as nonwhite, for instance a native Hawaiian, Asian American, Samoan, or Puerto Rican; or a local may be someone historically, ethnically originating in the working classes of Hawai'i, such as a Portuguese American or a Spanish American with a family history on the sugar plantations or the ranches of *paniolo* country. A *haole*, "foreigner" in the Hawaiian tongue and nowadays meaning Caucasian, is not usually assumed to be a local. But once he or she turns out to be a "local haole," someone brought up amongst locals in Hawai'i and who knows something about the weave of his or her own ethnicity (not "just haole" but, say, Irish, Norwegian, and English) then the usual assumptions disappear. African American locals similarly have a special place, which includes more insistently the need to be introduced by the personal histories of their families' arrival in Hawai'i (i.e., perhaps to work on the sugar plantations), their upbringing, their neighborhoods, their schools, their circles of friends and family. Most *hapa haole*, "half whites," and other kinds of racially mixed "hapas" are assumed to be local. As I have tried to suggest, this involves far more than a racist arithmetic of what fraction of this race, what fraction of that, an individual claims. Rather, it concerns the rich complications and diverse tributaries of family and ethnic histories that continue to course through the hapa individual and into the generations to come, particularly in a local culture that values an elaborate yet clearcut family history. Furthermore, the term "Hawaiian" is not a synonym for "local." In Hawaiʻi, "Hawaiian" is commonly taken to mean "native Hawaiian" and is usually reserved for that use in order to avoid ambiguity among those who speak these terms—that is, among locals. A Hawaiian is quintessentially a local, but a local is not necessarily a Hawaiian. Thus the term "local" does not itself denote race. It is some speakers of the term who do that, sometimes indeed in bigoted ways on whatever sides of conflicts involving the assertion of localism in Hawaiʻi.

So yet again the term "local" by all appearances *does* have everything to do with race, in precisely and disturbingly the way countless social, cultural, class, and ethnic identities in the United States involve racial issues, whether in perpetuating or in resisting racism. Of course there are exceptions: I like to think that calling a person a "New Yorker" ought to have nothing to do with race, especially since I know from experience (nowadays as a visitor who never has enough time there to take its sights, sounds, and smells for granted) that a walk down a New York City block is a multiracial, polyethnic, and international adventure. Today the New York City television dial is quite as much a spin around the world as Honolulu's is, as far as broadcasts of New York's local programs in languages—and races—in addition to Anglo are concerned. But for many in this country, many among New Yorkers and Hawaii's locals as well, the restrictive implications of the term "American" are racist, despite what should be the powerful example of such numerically pluralist societies as New York City's, California's, and Hawaii's. Indeed, despite the racial and ethnic kaleidoscope of that city, those states, and our nation, yesterday and today "New Yorkers" fight among themselves along virulent racial and ethnic battlelines over contested turf in the name of one group's considering itself more "American" than another by right of race. Whether we prefer to see ourselves as, say, "locals," as "New Yorkers," or as "Americans," none of these terms is free from the reality of racist baggage.

But ethnicity and localism, like being a New Yorker, are still somewhat different from race, which is never one's to choose. For a "white ethnic" can indeed choose to assimilate and pass for Anglo, as when some German Americans in the years surrounding World War I took refuge by changing their names—from James Gatz to Jay Gatsby.[3] In Hawai'i it would appear that being of Asian stock may work in one's favor if one aims to "assimilate." An Asian American newcomer, for instance a person in local pidgin called a "katonk," a Japanese American from the mainland, could choose to blend into a local ethnicity—that is, to pass for being local-born.

Gatsby's and the katonk's ploys "work" as long as it is possible to avoid talking truly about one's past and heritage, which, ironically, other locals of Hawai'i (though perhaps not of the Long Island of Tom and Daisy Buchanan) would probably respect if one would only treat one's history without shame. The choice by definition limits the pretender to the confines of how he or she preconceives the ethnicity chosen. In an odd sense, Fitzgerald's hero "Great" Gatsby reduces himself to being less than the sum of his history, less an embodiment of humanity than his father, who comes from rural Minnesota with hat in hand to the son's funeral in West Egg, Long Island. In Frank Chin's tragedy *The Year of the Dragon*, Pa has shaped himself, his son Fred, and his American-born wife Hyacinth into the image of a Chinese American family required by American law and his longtime desire to settle here, trying to fit into roles Chinese are allowed. Now one of his many problems is that the image cannot contain the fullness of his life and history and heart, when he brings his first wife, Fred's natural mother, from China to San Francisco. He thus unwittingly exposes the lies that their American family has been living, by the mandate of racist laws smothering the conception and birth of Chinese American families before World War II. These characters' responses to racist assumptions again show how pervasive these assumptions are. When the term "local" is thus used to alienate people by race, an attempt is being made to rationalize a cruelty which cannot be rationalized; and that is *not* how I use or define the term "local" in my discussion, though I know I am contending against such an alienation throughout my text.

In the following chapters, "local" is today's shorthand by which people in Hawai'i—whether local or not, whether in pride or in derision —label a culture, a sensibility, an identity, and, often forgotten despite how strongly it is valued, a personal, family, and community history. Local culture in Hawai'i has its own rituals, codes, and sensibilities. These undergo continual change. The ethos and the changes have roots not always known to locals themselves. The local poet Phyllis Thompson, a migrant teacher from the mainland in the 1960s, once told me that in the native Hawaiian way, personal introductions include these questions:

What are you called (i.e., your given name)? Who is your family (i.e., your surname and genealogy)? Where are you from (i.e., your neighborhood or district)? And who is your teacher (i.e., your school or the way of thought to which you are loyal)? It occurs to me that, without their knowing its Hawaiian origins, locals expect this genealogical exchange, this fine ritual of personal introductions, not for judging the superiority of one person over another, but for learning facts that relate somehow to inner values of the individual, on the one hand, and to already existing social and cultural connections on the other. This local ritual is expressively a way for two people to begin discovering their relationships with each other, however distant, in order to talk stories that sprout on common ground. It is a way to begin weaving their histories together—and this defines friendship, or an aspect of it, local style.

I need to add, finally, that Hawaii's locals know very well that they are members of American society, because Hawai'i is a state of the Union. By itself the term "local" does not imply a desire for separatism from America; it is indeed quintessentially American to assert one's individualism within a representative group, to enjoy, for instance, eating noisily with one's family in a local chop suey house without feeling that one is partaking in something alien. The term is thus inherently pluralistic in concept—it abhors assimilation even though there is plenty of evidence of assimilation too in Hawai'i, where many still think that the "melting pot" preserves racial and cultural diversity, which it expressly does not. Assimilation is opposite the concept of pluralism. With its inherent value on history and the processes by which a community comes to be, pluralism implies that the kaleidoscopic (not melted) local sensibility continually changes, for instance by the influence of current events and the introductions of new groups of people, of individuals to established groups of friends, and certainly of new fads that with astonishing speed come to be identified by word of mouth with locals in Hawai'i.

A newcomer to Hawai'i can change his or her behavior to be "accepted" as if a local; but I am told it is neither easy nor always desired, because *acceptance*, implying one person or group is in a superior position to judge the other, is not the point, which rather ought to be *recognition* of equal worth and self-respect.[4] Newcomers who ape what they perceive to be local behavior worsen the very problem they wish to avoid. No one likes to be aped, because this implies not only that the imitator must have a low self-image, or more likely is being downright condescending, but also that the one being imitated is an ape in the imitator's eyes; and this is painfully evident when people act as if being local only means conforming to a narrow, bigoted, and crude behavior. In my definition of the term, a newcomer to Hawai'i becomes a "local" when he or she considers him or herself a participating member of Hawaii's society. These considerations directly affect how locals see America as a supposedly pluralistic entity, even while Hawaii's history has made all locals, in whatever terms, familiar with and generally wise to a colonial power which uses pluralism, or ethnic and racial diversity, against itself. While I have been addressing here my interpretation of the term in popular uses and misuses, in my discussion I also note some of what I understand to be merits of and objections against use of the term in literary matters.

Acknowledgments

Socially, life in Hawai'i is tough and tricky. Locals are as unforgiving about failures to thank people as they are about lapses in humility.

For their direct help in my work on this book, I wish first of all to thank people who do not otherwise appear in the following chapters. Roger Sale, Robert Schulman, Harold Simonson, and, especially, Robert D. Stevick of the University of Washington offered useful criticism and suggestions in the early stages of this project, as did Martha Banta of the University of California, Los Angeles.

T. Foster Teevan and Richard Foster in their different ways helped the rest of us who call ourselves Talk Story, Inc., during the year or two before they each passed away. With their experience in observing literary activists—or perhaps outlaws—came their encouraging insights into what we were doing.

The late Dorothy Ritsuko Yoshimori McDonald of Michigan State University for years told me she knew the value of my work better than I; and I can only hope somehow to repay her and others for such faith in me.

Mark Wilson, Larene Despain, Joseph Backus, Ann Rayson, Richard Lessa, and Lorraine Nagata and her staff, of the University of Hawaii at Manoa, are among those who individually supported my work in distinct ways. Of the University of Hawaii at Hilo, Glenn (Kalena) Silva, as a doctoral candidate (now with with a Ph.D. to his name) in ethnomusicology, twice visited Washington State University to speak about and perform *mele* and *hula*. Together with Pila Wilson and Kauanoe Kamanā of the University of Hawaii at Hilo, these scholars presented pilot programs on native Hawaiian literature at the 1987 and 1988 annual conventions of the Modern Language Association of America (MLA).

And with Ofelia Zepeda of the University of Arizona, in 1988 to 1989 they proposed and secured the passage of an MLA resolution to recognize the value of studying native American tongues among the languages of America.

At Washington State University, Alex Kuo, Albert von Frank, William Willard, Julia Cruz, Joan Burbick, F. S. Schwarzbach, Paul Brians, Susan Armitage, Richard Law, and Alexander Hammond, among my colleagues in Comparative American Cultures, American Studies, and English, have helped me in specific ways.

Since 1975, I have been supported by a patchwork of institutional help, beginning with the local, regional, and national sources of funds for the Pacific Northwest Asian American Writers' Conference, which I coordinated after the groundwork had been dug by the enterprising Garrett Hongo. Afterwards, in Hawai'i, notable early support for my and my colleagues' work in Local literatures came from the Hawaii Committee for the Humanities (HCH), which to me still means, from the old days, Annette Lew, Laurie Lee Bell, and Phil Brossert. The HCH helped to fund the two Talk Story conferences in which I directly participated, 1978 and 1979, and for part of that time Travis Summersgill, chair of the co-sponsoring Department of English, University of Hawaii at Manoa, offered us an office where we coordinated our project. A year-long grant came from the Ethnic Heritage Studies Program of the former United States Office of Education, 1978–79, during which time Seymour Lutzky, chair of the Department of American Studies of the University of Hawaii at Manoa made generous room for Arnold Hiura and me to work and, it should not be taken for granted, the Hawaii and Pacific Collection of the University's Hamilton Library proved to be a genuine treasury. From 1980 to 1981, the Asian American Studies Program of the University of Washington provided me a study desk, with Gordon Hirabayashi for an officemate. In 1982 the University of Washington awarded me a Lockwood Dissertation Fellowship in the Humanities; my project being the one recipient in this category of the award for the year, I was both elated and astonished by the institution's recognition of my subject's merits. Furthermore, having at times been without, I know a steady job is a most basic form of support. Since 1981 I have had a steady job at Washington State University; then, after the spring of 1990, I will move with my family and my work to the University of Michigan. The Office of Grant and Research Development of Washington State University occasionally enabled me to travel to conferences and to conduct specific projects in research. The Washington State University Foundation granted seed money for a lecture series that, matched with funds from the Washington Commission for the Humanities and from Asian/Pacific American student groups on campus, lasted three years and brought us at least three dozen major speakers and events which we called "Living Treasures of Asian/Pacific American Cultures," that is, of the mainland and Hawai'i. In 1983 the Hawaii Literary Arts Council and co-sponsors invited me to lecture in the islands; and in 1984 the Washington Commission for the Humanities assigned Gail Nomura and me co-leadership of a cultural study tour of Hawai'i, which, with two dozen Washingtonians who trusted me to point things out under the Hawaiian sun and sky, gave me the renewed opportunity to compare literary references with actual peoples, historical sites, and settings. It also showed me firsthand that touring Hawai'i need not be a mindless and dehumanizing experience focused predominantly on serving and being served.

Also responsible in a real and important sense for prolonging the process of revising this work are my programs and departments, which have most generously provided travel funds, meeting and research facilities, the freedom of courses I want to teach, and much more: the Asian/Pacific American Studies Program of the Department of Comparative American Cultures, the American Studies Program, and the Department of English of Washington State University have enabled me regularly to conduct research and to teach undergraduate and graduate courses in Asian American and Hawai'i/Pacific American literatures. Given the demographics of the university, 95% of my students in these subjects are usually other than Asian/Pacific American. Our studies are therefore based not on personal experience of being Asian/Pacific American, not, that is, on confirming what the students already know, but on reading and interpreting texts and contexts which may thereby illuminate, change, enrich, or complicate the individual student's sensibility; and this goes, too, for the Asian/Pacific Americans enrolled. This experience in the classroom has allowed me never to be satisfied with my written assertions about these literatures, for my students have been an active, questioning, vocal audience directing me endlessly to rework my inchoate thoughts and wordings about our subjects. I thank my students, so many of whom I cannot help but remember, whether they would want me to or not.

Elsewhere, too, institutional support and personal or professional friendships are indistinguishable to me: I thank with special warmth my colleagues and advisers on the Modern Language Association's Committee on the Literatures and Languages of America. I likewise thank the scholars with whom I have worked in the American Studies Association, the Association for Asian American Studies, and MELUS (the Society for the Study of the Multi-Ethnic Literature of the United States). These colleagues of many locales have sharpened my awareness of our common grounds as we argue over concerns within and among our different literary traditions of America.

I wish also to thank the writers, scholars, and other sources of information named in the pages of this book. Whether I myself think their works and ideas individually good or bad, their scholarship valuable or weak, we are indebted to them for participating actively in literary traditions of or relevant to Hawai'i and for making it possible for us to see Hawaii's relationships with worlds of literature at large. My ulterior motive for not repeating everyone's name here is that the writers and scholars will now have to read the book to find out whether, where, and why I mention them. And I thank the Study Group, now ten years old, not only for giving me some of my earliest opportunities to try out ideas about specific works of Hawaii's literatures but also for critiquing portions of my manuscript, for which I of course am nonetheless solely responsible.

Work on this book could not have proceeded without a debt to Hawaii's polyethnic communities, and although specific people and their deeds are right now in my thoughts, they are far too numerous to name individually. Likewise, Asian and Pacific American individuals and communities throughout Washington, but notably of Spokane, Yakima, and Pullman, contribute directly to the very existence of such studies, including the study of Hawai'i, and courses such as mine at Washington State University; and they have opened their homes and territories to those of us pressuring them heavily for historical and cultural subjects and artifacts. I hope that those of you of Hawai'i and the Northwest who remember me will know that I am thinking of you as well while I write this. Connections between the two locales are evocative to me and to others who know of them. It is more than coincidence—a kind of historical truth, I think,—that in the Pacific Northwest in 1787, Kaiona, a chief of Kaua'i, became the first Hawaiian to see North America. Thereafter, following a route they quickly established, Hawaiians arrived to work in nearly every walk of pioneering life of the region until the middle of the nineteenth century, when the gold rush lured most of them to California and, at the same time, they and other nonwhites were barred from United States citizenship in the newly organized Territory. The

Hawaiian genealogy—Northwest branch—of their descendants is known particularly in the American Indian communities where they once settled and some lived out their lives.

Insofar as I can distinguish extraliterary and nonacademic assistance from the rest, I thank too my friend Wilfred Hasegawa, who was generous beyond repaying in welcoming me to stay with him when I desperately needed a place to live and work in Seattle. Norman and Julie Izumo, Norman's parents Satoshi (Soapy) and Yuki, Mitsunari and Sharon Akaki, Karen Fung, Faith Matsuwaka, Barbara Tanabe and Roy Kawaguchi, Mariko Miho, Linda Menton, Frank and the late Michiko Fujii, Bill and E. B. Proctor, Ben and Sally Tsutsumoto, David Ishii, Karen Yamamoto, Mark Kaya, MiBy Kim, Penny Choy, Eddie Hirata, Judy Owyang, Tritia Toyota, Masako Notoji, Hubert Sakai, and Evelyn Horiuchi (who helped materially in the production of my manuscript) at various times during this project have been of deep personal support to me. Mel and Karen Masuda likewise put me in touch with Kahu Edward Kealanahele, an expert in certain aspects of Hawaiian culture. He now has a somehow superfluous but joyously hard-earned Ph.D. in religion and Hawaiian studies. I am glad however that the friendship and guidance Kahu and the others have given me go far beyond the provinces of our classrooms and the disciplines of our professions.

These people I thank, as I do their families whose time, energies, food, and drink we heroically consumed usually in overabundance in our meetings and gatherings.

My own family or *'ohana* of parents, brother, sisters, clans, and in-laws has over the years given much to my enthusiasms, and for their support I am deeply grateful. Besides those with whom I grew up idyllically or not on the watercress farm in 'Aiea, I especially thank both my wife, Gail Mieko Nomura, who as an Asian/Pacific American historian understands my drift even when I have to yell at her in order to catch it myself, and our daughter Emi Fumiyo Nomura Sumida, for love.

S. H. S.
'Aiea, Hawai'i

About Spelling and Capitalization

The word *can't* without the apostrophe would not be the same word at all. Necessary to the spelling of Hawaiian words are the *'okina*, or glottal stop, which appears thus as a single inverted comma ('), and the *kahakō* or macron (−) to indicate elongated vowel duration. Though I quote Hawaiian words as printed in any text at hand, in my own text I spell Hawaiian names and words with these diacritical marks. When Hawaiian words are Anglicized, these marks are generally not used: for instance, I do not use the 'okina in the word "Hawaiian," or in the possessive, "Hawaii's," both derived in English from "Hawai'i."

Words from other languages are generally spelled as in the texts being discussed. "Foreign" terms are generally italicized on first usage. Once incorporated, the term is no longer foreign to the discussion and, more important, whether Hawaiian or Asian American, these terms are indeed integral to the lexicon of the whole American language of the peoples whose cultures are my subjects.

Throughout my discussion I reserve the word "Hawaiian" to identify native Hawaiian (i.e., Polynesian) people and culture. For a non-Polynesian, I refer to a "Hawai'i" person. Thus, in the shorthand I employ, Samuel Kamakau is a Hawaiian historian while Patsy Saiki is a Hawai'i writer.

I capitalize "Local" when I am referring to "Local literature"—that is, a "Local literary tradition" or culture. I do not do so when I am simply identifying, say, a local writer as such. I do this for two reasons: first, to be consistent, since I similarly emphasize the terms "Colonial" and "Tourist" only when they identify a literary tradition. And second, the word "local" appears often enough to seem rather monolithic, were it always capitalized like some allegorical Vice or Virtue.

And the View from the Shore

Myths at First Sight

I

Mai Kahiki ka wahine, o Pele,
Mai ka aina i Pola-pola
Mai ka punohu ula a Kane,
Mai keo ao lalapa i ka lani,
Mai ka opua lapa i Kahiki.

From Kahiki came the woman, Pele,
From the land of Pola-pola,
From the red cloud of Kane,
Cloud blazing in the heavens,
Fiery cloud-pile in Kahiki.
                    —from *He Oli—O Ka mele mua keia o ka hula Pele,*
                    A Song—The first song of the hula Pele[1]

For as far back as memory can recall, the pastoral and the heroic have been inseparable in Hawaii's oral and written literatures, in the literatures' underlying myths and mythologies, in popular images of Hawai'i, and in Hawaii's actual history. From one point of view, the Hawai'i pastoral, an idealization of a simple life free of strife, necessarily begins with the heroic. For this island "paradise," this hospitable retreat, was first of all discovered and rediscovered by voyagers undertaking arduous and perilous journeys across the open ocean.

"Eager desire for Hawaii seized the woman, Pele," continues the chant narrating the fire and volcano goddess's expulsion from Pola-pola (Bora Bora) of Kahiki (Tahiti) to the new land far to the north. A fiery reflection perhaps of political conflicts that drove Hawaii's Polynesian discoverers from their home in the South Seas, the chant sings of how "The tides swirl . . . / . . . The splash of the paddles dashes o'er the canoe," until Pele and her divine retinue "Disembark on solid land; / They alight on a shoal" to stay at the new house of Pele. Even today, advertisements for Hawaiian vacations serving a main course of indolence also hint at adventure, exploration, and encounters with the exotic. The contrasting ideas of repose and adventure embrace somewhere deep in our dream of these Hawaiian Islands.[2]

Whatever their heritages, in Hawaii's literatures European and North American concepts of the pastoral bear peculiar force and substance. These concepts were ready-made well before the arrival of James Cook's expedition in 1778. In Western annals for half a millennium, interesting confusions and blurred relationships have occurred between the pastoral as literary mode (the *concept* of a simpler and truer life) and the pastoral as literal fact (the supposed *reality* of an earthly paradise come true). Possibly seeking to persuade his sovereigns to grant him another voyage, Columbus once claimed that he had found the Biblical Eden among the islands he explored off the New World coast.[3] For complex reasons, the New England Puritans recorded themselves as living examples of their Christian ideals in the world's eyes. During the journey westward across the Atlantic by some two thousand Puritans, beginning with the Great Migration that Pilgrims had pioneered a decade earlier, John Winthrop in 1630 enjoined the fleet of voyagers to "consider that we shall be as a City upon a Hill, the eyes of all people are upon us." Notwithstanding the convention (i.e., the "city" as a symbol that the pastoral opposes), Winthrop's thrust is not to deny the main work of cultivating the land, but to get his flock to put their words into action, in the "good land," the New England "plantation" they are to make into "a model of Christian charity"—and good Puritan profit. "That which the most in their churches maintain as a truth in profession only," preached Winthrop, "we must bring into familiar and constant practice."[4] In other words, with their unique dispensation, they alone must make the Good Book come true in everyday life, in every way. Though Winthrop does not say so explicitly, behind his call for heroic efforts is the hope of peace and comfort through the guidance of that supreme pastoral figure, the Good Shepherd, and his pastors in the potentially good, new land.

These visionaries who established footholds for their civilization on the eastern edges of the stupendously vast continent christened their newly claimed lands with such names as "Providence," "New Canaan," indeed "New England," names laden with cultural and political implications, and with allusions to the literary pastoral land of Theocritus, which Virgil immortalized as Arcadia. In French Canada, for instance, the name "Acadia" is no less than a version of "Arcadia." The Louisiana "Cajun," after the eighteenth-century diaspora of the Acadians from Canada, is a direct outgrowth of that name and culture made local in the bayous, and both the name and the myth of the European pastoral land have spread to new worlds since the time of Columbus, as did the name "Hawaiki," or "Hawai'i," throughout Polynesia in the centuries before him. When Christian missionaries set out from Connecticut in 1820 to convert the Sandwich Islanders, they did not assume that paradise already lay before them. It was instead a heathen land to be worked—a wilderness not of nature but of the spirit to be tamed in the natives and in themselves, much as Winthrop had preached nearly two hundred years earlier on the approach to a different shore. "City Upon a Hill," "Arcadia," and, in Polynesia, "Hawaiki" symbolized ideas rather than actualities already achieved on earth. And at least in the case of the Christian myth and mission, the idea included an aim of making its rich pastoral elements come true.

The notion of the European pastoral coming true has also played an important part culturally and historically in Hawai'i. In the eighteenth and early nineteenth centuries, to Western seafarers needing mainly a place to refresh their supplies of drinking water and food, and to hire crew members, Hawai'i was a haven nicely situated at a crossroads for far-ranging commerce. Shortly after his first arrival there in January of 1778, Captain James Cook noted in his journal that his ships once more had found refreshment in a "land of plenty."[5] Despite occasional bad press, notions of Hawai'i as paradise have blossomed ever since 1778, along with an imagined, romanticized, idyllic, ahistorical timelessness predating Cook's arrival. Yet, to use Leo Marx's symbol for the processes of "civilizing" the pastoral landscape and transforming a simple American pastoral ideal into a complex cultural myth and reality, Cook's ships, the *Resolution* and the *Discovery*, humble, refitted colliers though they were, represented the European marine technology of their time: from one point of view, they themselves were the machines in the garden, as they sailed ominously and imperiously into Hawaii's calm, blue bays.[6]

The differences between the simple and the complex pastorals of Hawai'i turn upon the idea of Hawai'i as a dream come true. In "simple" or "simplistic" pastoral, Hawaii's paradise image is taken literally, and distinctions between myth and fact are obliterated, ambiguities washed away by single-minded interpretations of complex pastoral designs.[7] Here, the external reality, whatever it is, reflects the viewer's own simplistic thoughts, or else the viewer's words are simply incapable of expressing anything more. The simple pastoral of Hawai'i includes instances where the writer—that is, the civilized man or woman—believes that the primitives he or she encounters take their own primitive myths literally. In Hawaii's simple pastoral, the identification of fact with myth is unquestioned: Hawai'i *is* paradise; the native Hawaiians *believe* that Captain Cook *is* their god Lono.

In Hawaii's "complex" pastoral, images of Hawai'i as paradise and of Hawaiians as noble savages are used metaphorically or symbolically. While tacitly recognizing the imaginative and sentimental powers of these images, the complex pastoral often satirizes and even parodies simplistic claims about earthly paradises come true. Moreover, the complex pastoral of Hawai'i often gives a major role to intercultural encounters and interactions in the Hawai'i setting, where differences between cultures, perspectives, and values are considered important. In effect, the complex pastoral questions the melting-pot symbol for race relations in Hawai'i and America. Rather than cultural diversity, the melting pot implies, in its origins and its effects, the annihilation of cultural differences in the heat of assimilation. And, as in the mainland American pastoral examined by Leo Marx, the Hawai'i complex pastoral takes into account, rather than evades, the intrusion of the machine into the garden, of civilization into rural stasis, of history into a timeless dream.

What then of the heroic? I have suggested that the heroic and the pastoral are joined in some dynamic way in a much broader context to which Hawaii's literature belongs. But whereas the *pastoral* is a state of mind and of sentiment represented by a host of elements coming together to sculpt a figure of repose, the *heroic* depicts actions, actions of and bearing upon the hero. In Hawaii's literature, the hero typically enacts a drama against an idyllic backdrop on a pastoral stage. Heroes in Hawaii's modern history (i.e., since 1778), but not all of them already heroes in literary works, include, for example, the Hawaiian King Kamehameha I, his Queen Ka'ahumanu, Captain Cook, Father Damien of the Kalaupapa leper settlement, King David Kalākaua, Queen Lili'uokalani, and immigrants from the East and from the West who arrived in Hawai'i to work, to settle, and to cultivate an island civilization. Among these heroes are American missionaries, whose influence in Hawaii's development may be recognized, but who are surrounded still with controversy and misunderstanding. All these as yet are historical and not mythological heroes. They did exist, and they did contribute to changes Hawai'i has undergone in the past two centuries. This point is important, for how a Hawai'i writer creates a hero out of such figures is still affected by lively debate over such matters as accuracy and decorum: is it true and is it proper to write of these people and their deeds in this way or that? Accuracy and decorum often clash in this relatively young and certainly close-knit polyethnic culture that sometimes would like to see parts of its own past buried. Working with socially sensitive materials in a community that is quick to censure insensitivity toward ethnic distinctions, the Hawai'i writer—a native or a settler, rather than a transient—may undergo harrowing self-examination before the writing will come. As if the heroic literary work itself were a metaphor for the writing of it, the individual and cultural difficulties are enough to make the writer, too, a hero, for his or her very act of writing a vision of the truth. This is the situation today for the writer of the Hawai'i heroic.

Although it is rarely found unaccompanied by the pastoral, Hawaii's heroic offers an entirely different outlook on the Paradise of the Pacific. Because of the pervasiveness of Hawaii's paradise image, the heroic must stretch its way out of a sleepy assumption that binds the development of a serious literature. The assumption is that heroic action is somehow incongruous with Hawai'i. Thus, when heroic action is set in Hawai'i, the typical result in popular culture is a gimmick and a spectacle: the TV detective series. This contemporary genre set in Hawai'i dates back at least as far as the earliest Charlie Chan movies, the stereotypical Chan being based on a Chinese American detective of Honolulu. Western epics conventionally contain "pastoral interludes" where heroes recuperate from the wounds suffered on their quests. But in Hawaii's literature, the pastoral is the norm, the heroic the interlude. Or so it often seems.

2

The pastoral and the heroic are inseparable in living accounts of the discoveries of Hawai'i recorded in written and in oral sources. Some also reveal the mixture, identity, confusion, or interplay of fact and myth that contributes to the persistence of the simple pastoral notion of Hawai'i, even while the central event or drama described is heroic. Fact and myth coalesce in the earliest surviving written reports of Hawaiians and Europeans coming face to face; that is, in the deeds and the tragedy of Captain Cook.

The "dream of islands" was apparently not confined to European and American views of Hawai'i. A dream perhaps also guided the first settlers to Hawaii's shores. Anthropologists tell us how people of the Society Islands, of which Tahiti and Raiatea are members, originally populated these new islands lying under unfamiliar stars north of the Equator and called the islands "Hawaiki." This was a name Polynesians gave to successive South Pacific settlements where the people came to stay for a while in their gradual migration toward the east.[8] Hawaiki thus also signifies a gateway toward a new home; and the name further connotes that next home itself, undiscovered but envisioned, a new Hawaiki waiting to be found and settled. Indeed, the name prophesies a fabled land, even a paradise. This version of a Polynesian pastoral filled the seafarers' visions as they launched their long double-hulled canoes—sleek technological wonders in their own right—and directed them toward the north. So from the beginning of known human habitation on the islands, the very name of Hawai'i—Hawaiki—has represented both the notion of paradise and the awesome adventure of getting there.

It is not surprising that the Hawaiians' mythology deeply underlies this human history of voyaging as well. In the song of the fire goddess Pele, from which I quote above, the story of Hawaii's gods and goddesses goes back to their origins in Tahiti. At the poem's conclusion, where the voyagers look back at Tahiti, it is as if their connection with their old home were burned out of them: "Lo, an eruption in Kahiki! / A flashing of lightning, O Pele! / Belch forth, O Pele!" (*Hua hua'i Kahiki, lapa uila, e Pele. / E hua'i, e!*, Emerson, 188). The goddesses and gods are forerunners to the people who thus followed them to Hawai'i, broke political and economic ties with Tahiti, suspended the traffic of ocean-going canoes that voyaged between Hawai'i and the old home islands 2,300 miles to the south-southeast, and continued the life of their Polynesian culture by adapting it to the conditions (such as the active volcanoes, metaphorically applied to Tahiti in the verse above), genealogies, and history of the Hawaiian Islands that had become their home.

A pattern of heroic journey resulting in the discovery of a paradise was repeated when Captain James Cook, on his fateful third Pacific voyage, found himself once more approaching what promised by its rain clouds and mass to be a "land of plenty." Probing northward from Christmas Island, which he had just named, in search of the Northwest Passage and needing to replenish his expedition's provisions, Cook sighted Hawaii's "high land" on 18 January 1778. The next day he first encountered a people who spoke a language Cook was "agreeably surprised" to find was close to Tahitian, which he and others aboard the *Resolution* and the *Discovery* knew. The natives pulled alongside with their canoes to barter for iron, at Cook's first stop off Waimea on the southern shore of Kauaʻi. Thus began the Western traffic through Hawaiʻi.

Like the Polynesians who discovered Hawaiʻi before them, the Europeans shaped their understandings of their Pacific island observations and experiences with their own imported mythologies. Cook himself was not prone to hyperbole and was scarcely likely to describe the natives and their islands in mythological terms.[9] Others who had explored the Pacific, however, sang their enthusiasm over their discoveries; and all subsequent European explorers of the Pacific, including Cook and his crew, no doubt have carried with them venerable myths and clichés that the earlier explorers spontaneously applied to these islands. The French explorer Bougainville, for one, in 1768 exuberantly proclaimed Tahiti to be "Nouvel-Cythère, New Cythera, after the Greek island where Aphrodite . . . had been born out of the sea."[10] For Bougainville and his crew, and certainly even for Captain Cook's men despite his stringent, clinical precautions and rules to stall the spread of venereal disease, Tahiti and the other hospitable Polynesian islands were fabled, mythical paradises, especially sexual ones. While Tahiti was both in deed and in word a Nouvel-Cythère to the French, the British names for these havens were rather more restrained, suggesting current history rather than myth, but a British history at that. Captain Samuel Wallis, whose "discovery" of Tahiti in 1767 preceded Bougainville's by a year, named the lovely island "King George III"; and Cook named Hawaiʻi the "Sandwich Islands" after a patron of his expedition. But beneath the decorous surface of the British names, the myth of an island paradise on earth grew abundantly to feed both an insatiable popular appetite for the exotic and the erotic and also the curiosities and imaginations of a sizable crew of Western writers and artists in the ensuing two hundred years.

How literally did Hawaii's Polynesian and European discoverers take their identification of the islands with one or another myth of paradise? How seriously do we—that is, we modern-day Americans who are inheritors of these myths? When acted upon, the identification has proved to be not only potent but also dangerous. The beginning of Hawaii's written history two centuries ago demonstrates the danger. The power of confusing history with myth, actual facts with literary or mythological truths, is compounded by an idea that is handed down to us as a matter of revered fact. It is said that in 1778–79, the Hawaiians welcomed Captain Cook as their mythical god Lono, returning to them now as he had promised in some distant past. Here is an archetypal instance—an especially compelling and tragic one—where distinctions between facts and myths are obliterated, with great consequence to Hawaii's history.

For a reliable report on the beginning of the story of Cook as the god Lono, let us hear from Cook himself. A reader of Cook's log of the events of Monday, 19 January 1778, would be disappointed if he or she expected to find, gushing from Cook's pen, explicit descriptions of noble savages living in a paradise. One cannot imagine a more matter-of-fact account than Cook's of his momentous first encounter with Hawaiians. Neither Cook nor the natives appeared awed. It is as though Cook sensed an ambiguity, but without urgency, about whether the Hawaiians had ever before seen such ships and faces. He soon found that here was a stone-age people who already recognized iron and its uses, however vaguely. Cook's account suggests, moreover, that the natives treated the meeting as a commercial transaction from the start. When he saw canoes launched from the nearest shore, Cook gave the paddlers time to reach his ships. The canoes pulled alongside Cook's *Resolution*. Immediately the barter commenced. Speaking the language of Otaheiti, Tahiti, which the men in the canoe understood, Cook entreated the natives to board his ship. They refused. Instead "they exchanged a few fish they had in the Canoes for any thing we offered them, but valued nails, or iron above every other thing" (264). One can conjecture that Cook judged these men to be friendly, on first impression, for he notes that "the only weapons they had were a few stones in some of the Canoes and these they threw overboard when they found they were not wanted" (264). With a second, better-supplied fleet of canoes that replaced the first alongside the *Resolution*, the basic bargains were struck:

> Others came off from the shore and brought with them roast-ing pigs and some very fine potatoes, which they exchanged, as the others had done, for whatever was offered them; several small pigs were got for a sixpenny nail or two apiece, so that we again found our selves in the land of plenty, just as the turtle we had taken aboard at the last island (Christmas Island) was nearly expended. (P.264)

For the plain-writing Cook, the phrase "land of plenty" is poetry. Indeed his restrained tone makes his view of the Hawaiians sound gracious, and this perhaps would suggest to early editors of Cook's journals that the natives not merely disarmed themselves of "a few stones," but saw iron as material for domestic implements, not weapons.

This fabled pastoral calm, however, lasted through only one

night's sleep. On the following morning, the commerce increased frantically. Now Hawaiians actually boarded the ships and were astonished by what Cook calls "the several new objects before them." The very first Hawaiian aboard attempted to paddle off with "the first moveable thing that came his way," in his case a lead and line, but was dissuaded by his companions from taking it. At the end of the morning's trade aboard the *Resolution*, "an Indian stole the Butcher['s] cleaver, leaped overboard with it, got into his canoe and made for shore, the boats pursued him but to no effect" (265). And by the end of the day, a shore party scouting for a landing place and fresh water source had rashly killed a hapless man who had crowded too close to Cook's sailors while trying perhaps to help them to land by pulling on the barrel of a musket. In hindsight, we might well say that this day foreshadowed the tragic events of the following year.

It was, after all, an eventful first two days among the Hawaiians. Yet Cook himself left much to be told by others. His concerns over his lean writing and his subject were certainly neither a dramatist's nor a novelist's. Yet so compelling a drama was actually to unfold that writers began amplifying the story as soon as the journals were published; and the story is rewritten even in our day.[11] With Cook's journals as a sober standard of fact and reliability, others—for instance, by James King, Charles Clerke, and even by Cook's editor, John Douglas—seem at times to contain literary liberties.[12] And compared with any European or American account, the native Hawaiian ones, whether authentic or fabricated by Westerners mimicking Hawaiian idioms of expression, seem to be told or written in and for another world entirely—not the world of Cook's facts or Bougainville's fancies, but of the natives' history and mythologies.

What did the Hawaiians see in their first encounter with Europeans? We are accustomed to reading Pacific literature or viewing films and television romances that give us views of approaching islands, that is, the view from a ship's deck. But what of the view from the shore?

Drawing from some Hawaiian sources dating close to Cook's time and calling upon resources of the Hawaiian oral tradition he inherited, the Hawaiian scholar Samuel Manaiakalani Kamakau explains the appearance—the "apparition," the translation calls it—of the *Resolution* and the *Discovery* off Hawaii's shores, not in Cook's European terms of "the land of plenty" and all that the Christian expression implies, but in the terms of the native history and mythology. Thus in 1866, compiling his *Ruling Chiefs of Hawaii*, Kamakau recounts the Hawaiians' first sighting

and welcome of Cook and his men. Whereas to Cook the historical context of his voyage is understood to be the reign of King George III,
such that in 1776 Cook's departure on his third voyage to the Pacific
coincided with the outbreak of trouble in the American colonies, to
Kamakau the historical context of Cook's arrival looks the following way:

> It was eighty-eight years ago, in January, 1778, that Captain
> Cook first came to Hawai'i. Ka-'eo was ruling chief of Kauai,
> Ka-hahana of Oahu and Molokai, and Ka-hekili of Maui,
> Lanai, and Kahoolawe. The ship was first sighted from Waialua
> and Wai-anae on Oahu sailing to the north. It anchored at night
> at Waimea, Kauai, that place being nearest at hand. A man
> named Moapu and his companions who were out fishing with
> heavy lines, saw this strange thing move by and saw the lights
> on board. Abandoning their fishing gear, no doubt through
> fright, they hurried ashore and hastened to tell Ka-'eo and the
> other chiefs of Kauai about the strange apparition. The next
> morning this ship lay outside Ka'ahe at Waimea. Chiefs and
> commoners saw the wonderful sight and marveled at it. Some
> were terrified and shrieked with fear. The valley of Waimea
> rang with the shouts of the excited people as they saw the boat
> with its masts and its sails shaped like a gigantic sting ray.
> One asked another, "What are those branching things?" and
> the other answered, "They are trees moving about on the sea."
> Still another thought, "A double canoe of the hairless ones
> of Mana!" A certain kahuna named Ku-'ohu declared, "That
> thing can be nothing else than the heiau of Lono, the tower
> of Ke-o-lewa, and the place of sacrifice at the altar." ("*A'hoe
> kela he mea'e, o ka heiau no kela o Lono, o ka'anu'unu'u no kela
> o Keolewa, a o na lele kela o ke kuahu.*") The excitement became
> more intense, and louder grew the shouting.[13]

Kamakau then tells how the chief ordered several men to board
the ship, among them the *kahuna* (priest) Ku-'ohu, "wearing a whaletooth
ornament to show his rank." This is the kahuna who had already declared
the ship to be "the heiau of Lono," that is to say, the temple of "the
god Lono who had gone away promising to return." In Kamakau's telling
of the story, the kahuna swiftly identifies Cook and acts assuredly as
if his own signs of office—the ornament (*palaoa*) shaped as a tongue
poised in the midst of speech, for instance—would be understood.

But apparently not everyone among the Hawaiian party was concerned with mythologies and Cook's place in their pantheon. While with

high dignity and authority the kahuna spoke in comfortingly familiar terms to his people about how these ships must be the heiau of Lono, most of his companions marveled incredulously at how much iron was evident on the ship. The men "said excitedly to each other, 'Oh, how much dagger material (*pahoa*) there is here!' for they called iron *pahoa* because that is what they used in the old days for their fighting daggers," which were called *pahoa* (92–93). So it was, from these Hawaiians' point of view, that iron was somehow already known to be best for fashioning weapons, not only pans and awls. But while some natives harbored valorous and possibly murderous thoughts of how to procure iron and what to do with it, they encouraged the European visitors to think that these apparently gentle and peaceful people treasured iron for its usefulness in domestic arts and crafts. The Hawaiians communicated to Captain James King that "of Iron they only knew its use for boring & to make Tòès (Hatchets) & wanted them large" (Cook, *Journals*, 265 n. 1).

By the time Kamakau wrote his history in 1866, the story of Cook's identification with the Hawaiian god Lono had become established not only as an extension of an ancient Hawaiian mythology but also as historical fact. Yet Kamakau's version of this first encounter, as well as accounts by other important Hawaiian historians during the nineteenth century, suggests something other than this usual literal interpretation. Already we see in Kamakau's narration, embellished though it is, that the kahuna and the others in the canoes focused on two different points of interest: while the priest seemed to ponder Cook and his religious significance, the others were spellbound by the ships' iron. Might not still others have been contriving to procure some metal—or power— by flattering Cook with treatment befitting a god?

When on that Tuesday morning, 20 January 1778, the Hawaiians actually boarded the *Resolution* and met the strangers on deck, this according to Kamakau is what transpired:

> One . . . went on board and saw many men on the ship with white foreheads, sparkling eyes, wrinkled skins, and angular heads, who spoke a strange language and breathed fire from their mouths. The chief Ki'ikiki and the kahuna Ku-'ohu, each clothed in a fine girdle of tapa cloth about the loins and a red tapa garment caught about the neck, stepped forward with the left fist clenched and, advancing before Captain Cook, stepped back a pace and bowed as they murmured a prayer; then, seizing his hands, they knelt down and the tabu was freed. Captain Cook gave Ku-'ohu a knife, and it was after this incident

that Ku-'ohu named his daughter Changed-into-a-dagger (Ku-a-pahoa) and The-feather- that-went-about-the-ship (Ka-hulu-ka'a-moku). This was the first gift given by Captain Cook to any native of Hawaii. (P.93)

Kamakau says nothing about another incident that occupied Cook's attention: a native's attempt to snatch away a lead and line. (Cook, of course, was keeping a journal; Kamakau was writing with the historical perspective of hindsight.) Kamakau implies that these are what are worth remembering; the kahuna freed the ship from tabu; Ku-'ohu subsequently gave his daughter a name that would commemorate the event and tell its story in a genealogy that is presumed to last for ages; and this knife that Cook gave Ku-'ohu was the *first* gift he gave to any Hawaiian native. The attempted theft is forgotten, an unpleasant and somehow irrelevant detail, we might infer. In spite of the rather solemn dignity of Kamakau's chantlike narration, however, it should be mentioned that Kamakau was himself hardly pleased by other gifts left by the *Resolution's* and *Discovery's* crews. He and others, Hawaiian and European, especially abhorred the crews' giving of venereal disease to Hawai'i. That "first" gift of a knife connotes a profound tragedy to follow.

And again, not everyone shared the priest's lofty view of the scene's religious, mythological, and historical importance. Kamakau describes how the Hawaiians who accompanied the kahuna Ku-'ohu gave their own fanciful names and epithets to the fearsome marvels aboard that temple-like apparition, the *Resolution*:

> They called Captain Cook Lono (after the god Lono who had gone away promising to return). A man hoisting a flag they called Ku-of-the-colored-flag (Ku-ka-lepa-'oni-'oni'o) after the image that stood against the outer wall of the heiau. A lighted pipe in the mouth of another gave him the name of Lono-of-the-volcanic-fire (Lono-pele). (P.93)

Clearly, the names serve simply to describe these strange men. There is no suggestion here that calling the pipe smoker "Lono-pele" deifies him.

But then the names begin to assume another function. They suggest explanations for who these men are and how they arrived:

> When the Hawaiians saw a heap of coconuts they said, "These are the fruits of Traveling-coconut (Nui-ola-hiki), they must

have killed the mischief-maker of the sea." Of a bullock's hide
they said, "They must also have killed Ku-long-dog, (Ku-
'ilio'loa)! Perhaps they have come here to kill all the mischief
makers of the sea." (P.93)

The Hawaiians in Kamakau's account thus began immediately to incorporate their visitors into their mythologies, even as the European visitors
were mythologizing their islands as "a land of plenty" and "paradise."

It appears from Kamakau's heroic narrative that the boarding
party seemed satisfied with their identification of the visitors, or at least
with such names as they had given the white men. When these first official
envoys reported to the people ashore, "both chiefs and commoners, hearing this report, said to each other, 'This is indeed Lono, and this is his
heiau come across the sea from Moa-'ula-nui-akea across Mano-wai-nui-
kai-o'o'" (93).[14] When a chief asked the priest Ku-'ohu if there would
be any harm in visiting the floating temple of Lono, the kahuna replied
reassuringly and proudly, "No harm at all, for I did my work well,"
and, perhaps warned after all by Cook's treatment of the would-be thief,
Ku-'ohu cautioned, "Only do not meddle with the things belonging to
the god"(94).

Whether because of his mid-nineteenth-century influences or his
oral sources themselves, Kamakau's Hawaiian version of Cook's arrival
rides on a strong undercurrent. The kahuna Ku-'ohu, as Kamakau sees
him, was fulfilling his official role in Hawaiian theocracy and was doing
a good job of appropriating political power for himself (a priest of Lono)
and for his party.

It may be impossible to determine with certainty how the Hawaiians regarded this return of the god Lono—that is, apart from what
has been written through hindsight after Cook's death and the establishment of his reputation as a tragic, mythic, Promethean hero. The written
accounts themselves disagree. And why should they agree? Why should
it be expected that the Hawaiians' assessments of Cook were unanimous,
any more than that European and Hawaiian accounts should match? Was
Cook greeted with pleasure in his seeming fulfillment of the god's promise to return? Or were the Hawaiians skeptical of these visitors' intentions? Was the association of Cook with Lono simply the most convenient
way to describe him under the circumstances? Did the Hawaiians consider
Cook still to be a man? Or was he in their eyes a god, and if so, then
what could that have meant to them, in their culture? And which European view is the more true—that the natives were peaceful, domestic

sorts, noble inhabitants of a paradise; or that the natives, although useful for replenishing the ships' stores, were depraved and were to be shot at the first threat of harm to the visitors?

One of Kamakau's predecessors, David Malo, was the first Hawaiian historian to compile his written knowledge of Hawaiian antiquities and culture. In his best known work, Malo writes surprisingly little about Cook. He simply points out a nowadays well-known but still myth-shrouded detail that the Hawaiians called Cook "Lono" because the sails of Cook's ships happened to look like Lono's banners: broad tapa swathes hanging from a tall mast and crosstree.[15] As far as I have been able to find in the English translation by Nathaniel Emerson, one sentence is all Malo provides about Cook in *Moolelo Hawaii, Hawaiian Antiquities* (ca. 1838). Malo makes it appear that in naming Cook "Lono," the Hawaiians were being descriptive, possibly metaphorical, not literal.

But other citations and readings of Malo and Kamakau tell still different stories. In 1879 Abraham Fornander, circuit judge of the island of Maui and Knight Companion of the Royal Order of Kalākaua, provided variant quotations and interpretations of the historians Malo and Kamakau themselves. In *An Account of the Polynesian Race*, Fornander first considers evidence that there had been Spanish and perhaps other foreign visits to or near-discoveries of the Hawaiian Island.[16] But "However that may be," Fornander writes, "the astonishment and excitement of the Hawaiians as Cook's vessels approached the coast of Kauai were thoroughly genuine and extravagant." Fornander goes on to quote what he cites as David Malo's 1838 account of Cook's arrival, an account Malo wove out of "the account . . . from actual eye-witnesses" (167).[17] The narrative Fornander thus quotes is essentially the one provided by Kamakau, with perhaps an even greater prominence placed on the quantity of iron that awed the Hawaiians during their visits aboard Cook's ships. Some details differ, however, owing perhaps to variant translations from Malo's and Kamakau's original Hawaiian into English. In Fornander's version Malo notes, for instance, that the Europeans were first thought to have "corner-shaped heads" (cf. Kamakau, "angular heads") because of the tricorn hats they wore. The Hawaiians wondered too, whether perhaps these were "all women, because their heads were so like the women's heads of that period" (168), an observation not noted by Kamakau.

Beyond these small differences, an important distinction separates Malo's and Kamakau's accounts in Fornander's text: Malo's account lacks mention of the priest, Ku-'ohu and the rites he performed. I cannot say why this discrepancy occurs—whether, for instance, it is simply because Fornander's quoting of Malo is thus incomplete; or whether, say, David Malo as an ordained Christian minister skirted a sensitive issue by avoiding mention of the service Ku-'ohu performed. This latter possibility, however, contradicts the fact that Malo's *Moolelo Hawaii* describes precisely just such rites and customs. Perhaps Kamakau, also a devout Christian, enriched his own account by dramatizing the priest and his role in the oral histories. More than Malo, who reports "antiquities," or Fornander, who compares what these others have written before him, Kamakau uses dialogue and points of view to interpret events and their actors, somewhat like a writer of fiction or drama. Fornander, in his own way, further complicates the matter of the kahuna's role. Fornander's version of Kamakau is very brief and is pocketed in a footnote. His reading differs substantially from what I have given above, in my reading of Kamakau's *Ruling Chiefs of Hawaii*. According to Fornander,

> Kamakau relates that *Kuohu*, the priest, had his doubts whether the newcomers were gods or mortal men, and that having tried to ascertain by means of the sacred cup (*Ka ipu Aumakua*), he came to the conclusion that "they were not gods but Haole (foreigners), from the country whence *Kaekae* and *Kukanaloa* came; but the young people and the majority looked upon Cook as the god Lono." (Pp. 168–69 n. 3)

So it appears here, *haole* men, not gods, were already known to the Hawaiians, who did not all believe their visitors divine. Cook's presumed forerunners Kaekae and Kukanaloa were known to the Hawaiians as two of the white men shipwrecked in the islands in earlier days. In his next note, Fornander says that, according to Kamakau, "the high priest of *Kahahana*" interpreted these visitors to be people, the foreigners (haole) whose arrival was foretold in prophecy and chant (169 n. 1).

At another point where accounts differ—and this includes Cook's —according to Fornander, Malo tells of how the warrior Kapupuu, with the consent of the chiefs, boarded the ship and "took away some iron, and he was shot and killed" by "a ball from a squirt-gun." Kamakau, according again to Fornander, adds that the people urged that Kapupuu's death be avenged, but the priest Ku-'ohu dissuaded them because of the dangers involved. The real dangers were soon made clear, for that night "guns were fired and rockets thrown up. They (the natives) thought it was a god, and they called his name *Lonomakua*, and they thought there would be war" (Fornander, 168).

Quoting Malo, Fornander recounts how the Hawaiians then propitiated their angered visitor, man or god:

> Then a chiefess named *Kamakahelei*, mother of *Kaumualii* [later
> to become the great chief of Kauai] said, 'Let us not fight
> against our god; let us please him that he may be favourable
> to us.' Then *Kamakahelei* gave her own daughter as woman
> to *Lono*; *Lelemahoalani* was her name; she was older sister of
> *Kaumualii*. And *Lono* slept with that woman, and the Kauai
> women prostituted themselves to the foreigners for iron. (Pp.
> 168–69)

Here the tone is of Malo speaking from the pulpit of his church, and
the incident he describes, Cook's being thought to have violated his own
tabu against sex with the natives, was to play a central part in what
happened when Cook returned months later to Hawai'i. With the women
went ample gifts of "hogs, vegetables, and kapa," and in return, it is
bitterly said, Cook and his men left venereal disease in their wake (Fornander, 162).

This welter of views from the shore demonstrates a lack of single-
or literal-mindedness about who the visitors were and how they were
to be treated by the Hawaiians.[18] Also, the accounts tend to underscore
the continuity rather than the disruption of native Hawaiian political and
indeed military activity through Cook's visit.

On Monday, 2 February 1778, the *Resolution* and the *Discovery*
departed Hawai'i for far-northern waters, to Alaska, where Cook sought
the fabled Northwest Passage and, making his way down the coast, studied the natives of the Pacific Northwest. Some ten months later Cook
would return to Hawai'i, by which time news of Cook's first stop in
Hawai'i had spread throughout the island chain. The Europeans' sight
of the islands this second time would be grim; the shores would prove
eventually to be inhospitable.

Perhaps the real surprise ought long ago to have been over how
some among Cook's men, for instance William Bligh, took as fact that
the natives with one primitive mind *believed* Cook to *be* Lono and that
Cook foolishly pretended to be the god, with fatal consequences. Bligh
became captain of the *Bounty* not long after his voyage as master of Cook's
Resolution. And though most people would take issue with Bligh's tyrannical, narrow fundamentalism, his literal-minded conviction that the Hawaiians identified Cook with Lono is widespread.

But perhaps some natives called Cook "Lono" in the same way

one called a pipe-smoking crewman "Lono-of-the-volcanic-fire"—that is, named him descriptively, by metaphor, in an imaginative and not a literal comparison. Perhaps the Hawaiians did *not* confuse the idol for the god, or the symbol for the concepts that he, Cook, represented to the Hawaiians. Perhaps Lono's priest Ku-'ohu and (presiding like a local counterpart to King George III in the background of the tale) the chief Ka'eo set out deliberately, with the advice and aid of Kamakahelei and their daughter Lelemahoalani, to exploit Cook for political reasons: that is, to gain control of the visitors in order to strengthen the chief's power over his people.

Consider then a further idea. Suppose that from the Hawaiians' point of view, it was these strange, white-foreheaded visitors themselves, having arrived aboard their primitive, clumsy ships, who seemed child-like in their apparently literal belief that Hawai'i was their mythological "paradise" and these Hawaiians, their "noble savages." Except in superficial ways, the idea that the people of Hawai'i for more than two hundred years now may have been scrutinizing and judging—not worshiping —their European visitors is almost entirely foreign to usual notions of what it means for civilized people to meet savage and primitive others for the first time. Yet to see the islands' natives in this way, not as simple primitives but as human equals staring back at us like mirror images gaping at the sight, makes these, in startling moments, our islands of self-discovery.[19]

Paradise of the Pacific?

Nineteenth-Century Prototypes
in American Literature

I

In its century and well into ours, Herman Melville's *Typee* (1846) has stood as the most prominent early novel of the South Seas written by one who actually explored Pacific island valleys and lived among its inhabitants. Fashioning a mix of fact, adventure narrative, parody, and myth, Melville gave his contemporary audience the exotic tale they wanted. While Hawai'i is an actual setting for Melville's subsequent tale, *Omoo*, it is the unprecedented *Typee* that did much to shape Western nineteenth-century art and literary works set in the Pacific far beyond the shores of *Typee*'s Nukuhiva. In it Hawai'i is the object of Melville's most pointed criticisms, not of a simple life but of civilization and how it has ruined a paradise. That is, in *Typee* Melville examines its narrator's view of an idyllic world such as Hawai'i is thought to have been before the arrival of outsiders. Part of the marvel is that Melville did so while doubting and indeed mocking his readers' fantasies about Pacific islands and their peoples.

Melville based *Typee* on fact and experience. This set *Typee* significantly apart from earlier and contemporary works in a long tradition of literary "island" creations, as can be shown in a brief comparison with James Fenimore Cooper's *The Crater: Or, Vulcan's Peak* (1847).[1]

While Melville was gaining his first fame with *Typee*, the veteran novelist Cooper wrote his own Pacific island tale. Though in writing *The Crater* he drew upon his extensive knowledge of sailing the seas,

Cooper himself never visited any Pacific islands; nor did he make any pretense of basing his novel on actual experience. *The Crater* falls into the tradition of utopian works such as More's *Utopia* and Bacon's *The New Atlantis*; and, at the same time, it is clearly reminiscent of Defoe's adventure story of Robinson Crusoe, a prototypical pioneer who, alone, must create a habitation in an island wilderness. To eke out a subsistence that is sufficient only in contrast to starvation, Cooper's protagonist, Mark Woolston, stranded on a barren volcanic island, must start from scratch, manufacturing the very soil in which to plant seeds saved from the shipwreck. Cooper uses this Pacific desert island setting as an imagined ecological experiment—and as a vehicle for his critique of contemporary American society. He makes little or no claim to be uncovering truths about actual Pacific islands and their inhabitants, since, in the first place, there are no "natives." Indeed, after a fellow shipwrecked sailor disappears in a violent storm, Woolston has no companions other than his pigs and goat. Rather, the novel concerns the building of a life free of superfluities and governed by intelligence, self-discipline, and the need to maintain sturdy health.

Furthermore, when Woolston discovers and moves to a lush, fertile island, where he is subsequently joined by other people, he colonizes this new "Garden of Eden," this "earthly paradise," as a utopian experiment. The colony did not exist as a prior condition on the tropical isle but is created as Woolston had earlier created his garden on desert land, from scratch. And, as often happens in such island or oceanic fictions, the colony is lost. It is destroyed by a volcanic earthquake that sinks the island's shores deep beneath the sea. One of course is reminded of the fabled Atlantis, but Cooper's island arises out of the Pacific, in some ways a vaster, far more exotic sea in the nineteenth-century Westerner's imagination.

Something quite different from Cooper's *The Crater* happens in Melville's *Typee*. Melville's treatment of Tommo, or Tommy, the first-person narrator, is clearly meant to convince us that the tale tells of an actual experience. And it was indeed Melville's actual experience, or close to it. When in 1842 the *Acushnet*, a whaler that Melville shipped aboard under a tyrannical captain, called at the Marquesan island of Nukuhiva, Melville jumped ship with a crewmate, Richard Tobias Greene.[2] The pair of deserters evaded capture and hoped to find refuge among the Happar people residing in one of the island's valleys. But a dangerous escape over a mountain ridge and down into a treacherously steep valley—or so the trek is described in *Typee*—led the deserters instead to the most feared of the Marquesan natives, the Typee. Though Melville and Toby stumbled into the wrong valley, and though Melville had badly injured his leg, they received good treatment from these reputedly fierce and hungry cannibals. Melville left the Typee after a few weeks, Toby having already departed the valley in search of help for Melville's slow-healing leg.

Even readers of *Typee* unfamiliar with Melville's claims for the story's authenticity can recognize in Melville's actual experience the subsequent plot of his first best seller, which Howard Mumford Jones calls "the first full length evocation of the actual [i.e., as contrasted with the imaginary] exotic" in American literature.[3] What Melville's publishers wanted was no less and no more than a convincingly true Pacific island adventure to satisfy the reading public's tastes. Harper Brothers declined buying the manuscript because "it was impossible that it could be true and therefore was without real value" (Daws, *Dream of Islands*, 81), so incredible was Melville's tale and so much did Harper want it to be "true." Melville had better luck with a London publisher, John Murray, "whose Colonial and Home Library," Gavan Daws notes, "specialized in the experiences of white men in exotic places" (*Dream of Islands*, 82). Still, Melville had to add more authenticating material to satisfy his publisher. As a result, *Typee* contains expository passages and nearly entire chapters he lifted from various sources explaining native customs and providing factual information about Taipivai, the valley, apart from the narrative line itself. As in *Moby Dick*, where Melville would further employ his technique of interspersing among the narrative chapters the facts and the lore of whales and whaling, *Typee* swings between fact and fiction, actual experience and imagined adventure story. This swing indeed contributes to the peculiar force of these works, as if the factual element were persistently pounding against a resilient imagination until the two elements fit and fuse, in order that Melville might introduce to the world an insight perhaps never before glimpsed or experienced. Yet in *Typee* the exoticism that Jones describes thematically as a "pagan . . . amoral . . . lazy . . . languid . . . special variety of experience" (Jones, 284) masks some disturbing ideas that counter those exotic pastoral notions which the narrator, in his inexperience, initially applies to the Typee and their valley. But Melville, by his own actual experience, was not himself confined to such popular notions in interpreting his subject, and this fact alone should caution us not to trust our reading of the exotic in *Typee*.

In Melville's novel, we find the protagonist learning progressively that the people and things surrounding him may not be what they seem.

Seen from the distance of the whaling ship, the seagoing factory Tommo hates, the green mountains of Nukuhiva are paradise. But when he and Toby escape into those same mountains, the jungle and the sublimely steep and green mountainsides prove all but impassable to them. Tommo begins by fearing the Typee because of their nasty reputation. He then briefly admires them as embodiments of the noble savage, becoming familiar with them in all the moments of his own daily life of indolence. Increasingly and by turns, he feels contempt, bewilderment, sympathy, and eventually fright and terror during his time in their valley. It is a process of disillusionment, or of stripping away the exotic elements and their lush yet simplistic appeal. The difference between *Typee* as autobiography and as fiction centers in Melville's role as the critic and interpreter, rather than the ego, of Tommo's perception of his experience.

The sloughing of Tommo's illusions about the Typee is in some ways an endless process, one that begins with his assertion of admiration for the Typee as noble savages living within a congenial paradise. Tommo first encounters the Typee chief, Mehevi, in the full regalia of his noble rank:

> A superb-looking warrior stooped the towering plumes of his headdress beneath the low portal, and entered the house. I saw at once that he was some distinguished personage, the natives regarding him with the utmost deference. . . . His aspect was imposing. The splendid long drooping tail-feathers of the tropical bird, thickly interspersed with the gaudy plumage of the cock, were disposed in an immense upright semicircle upon his head, their lower extremities being fixed in a crescent of guineabeads which spanned the forehead. (P. 77)

Tommo describes the chief's ceremonial garments in exquisite detail, with expressions of wonder and appreciation, literally down to "little streamers of the thinnest tapa" that flutter from the tobacco pipe hanging from Mehevi's waist. And the decoration of the chief extends beneath his garments to "that which was most remarkable in the appearance of the splendid islander . . . the elaborated tattooing displayed on every noble limb." Like his fellow Polynesian Queequeg in *Moby Dick,* Mehevi is covered with an elaborate, intricate, and profuse lacework of tattoos indelibly marking him as a chief and, in Tommo's eyes, a savage. Tracing the decoration covering Mehevi's body and face, Tommo concludes: "The warrior, from the excellence of his physical proportions, might certainly have been regarded as one of Nature's noblemen, and

the lines drawn upon his face may possibly have denoted his exalted rank"
(78). Having thus read and interpreted Mehevi's appearance, Tommo later
refers explicitly to him as the "noble savage." Though appearing here
in a local, native form perhaps rather new to Melville's American contemporaries, the figure is the familiar, conventional noble savage nonetheless,
seen in Tommo's only ready terms for conceptualizing the chief Mehevi.

   If Melville's suggestion of this, Tommo's ethnocentrism, is not
strong enough in Tommo's talk of Mehevi and others as noble savages,
then the depiction of Fayaway, unabashedly the incarnation of a sailor's
dreams, should circle the point in red. Fayaway sails Tommo's canoe
across the Taipivai lake by untying "her ample robe of tapa" and holding
it out to catch the breeze, her body a lovely mast naked to his eyes (134).
Yet just how different could this woman be from accustomed female
beauty and behavior, to Melville's audience, and still be alluring rather
than strange and alienating? Melville couches his sketch of Fayaway in
a familiar form, the prototypical Western pastoral love song, The Song
of Solomon: "Her full lips, when parted with a smile, disclosed teeth
of a dazzling whiteness, and when her rosy mouth opened with a burst
of merriment, they looked like the milk-white seeds of the 'arta,' a fruit
of the valley, which, when cleft in twain, shows them reposing on either
side, imbedded in the red and juicy pulp" (85). And at the same time,
references to an exotic local fruit aside, how familiar this astonishing
Fayaway is, this "very perfection of female grace and beauty": for Fayaway has deep blue eyes! Small wonder that John La Farge's portrait of
Fayaway, drawn from fantasy, sailing in her unique manner across
Melville's imaginary Taipivai lake shows her not with the emphatic Polynesian features of Tahitian women painted by Paul Gauguin, but with
European features, the perfect complement to her blue eyes.[4] By his
use of the conventionally familiar, by Tommo's openly admiring "the
European cast of their features" (184), Melville shows us a profound problem: we experience the Typee as versions of our own selves, a reflection
of our own projected desires and yearnings, rather than as distinctively
themselves.

   Much of what Tommo sees reflects a contemporary American
taste for pastoral self- and communal sufficiency. With fact and with fancy
Melville creates the setting in which the Typee live in natural harmony.
For example, he carefully describes a typical Typee dwelling made of
grass, palm leaves, and fibers. No doubt such authenticating, factual material that Melville took from other sources impressed his nineteenth-
century readers, especially when set in the context of Melville's romance.

The description of the thatched houses impresses not only because of the primitive materials used in building the perfect house but even more because of the resourceful self-sufficiency that such a house implies. Imagine fashioning a dwelling using only the material found in Taipivai, a single, narrow valley of a Pacific isle, severely limited in area yet wholly sufficient for the natives' needs. Such is, of course, one of the pastoral appeals of Cooper's fictional *The Crater* and Thoreau's supposedly nonfictional *Walden*, published eight years after *Typee*.[5] And what more than a house of palm thatch could any Typee desire? After all, Tommo marvels, "a more commodious and appropriate dwelling for the climate and the people could not possibly be devised. It was cool, free to admit the air, scrupulously clean, and elevated above the dampness and impurities of the ground" (82).

Like its predecessors in a pastoral tradition, *Typee* allows the author to criticize, by unfavorable comparison with his Golden World, the civilization from which he is temporarily divorced during his sojourn.[6] Tommo considers at one point that there is no escape for him from the valley, but seeing no alternatives and feeling no urgency about the matter, he drives such disconcerting thoughts away. Instead he takes pleasure in Taipivai, judging it preferable to the civilized world from which he is now insulated. "When I looked around the verdant recess in which I was buried," Tommo muses, "and gazed up to the summits of the lofty eminence that hemmed me in, I was well disposed to think that I was in the 'Happy Valley,' and that beyond those heights there was nought but a world of care and anxiety" (124). He speaks as if he were already dead, "buried," and happy in a Christian heaven. And the pleasantness of the valley is matched by the good temper of the natives: "As I extended my wanderings in the valley and grew more familiar with the habits of its inmates, I was fain to confess that, despite the disadvantages of his condition, the Polynesian savage, surrounded by all the luxurious provisions of nature, enjoyed an infinitely happier, though certainly less intellectual, existence than the self-complacent European" (124). These thoughts lead Tommo to a sardonic observation:

> The term "savage" is, I conceive, often misapplied, and indeed
> when I consider vices, cruelties, and enormities of every kind
> that spring up in the tainted atmosphere of a feverish civiliza-
> tion, I am inclined to think that so far as the relative wickedness
> of the parties are concerned, four or five Marquesan Islanders
> sent to the United States as missionaries might be quite as

useful as an equal number of Americans dispatched to the islands in a similar capacity. (Pp. 125–26)

By contrast, whenever Melville pauses to consider the fate of
another group of Polynesian islands and their people—Hawai'i—his tone
is no longer musing, certainly not idle: He asks—what does the "Indian"
desire of "Civilization"? "She may 'cultivate his mind'—may 'elevate his
thoughts'—these I believe are the established phrases—but will he be the
happier? Let the once smiling and populous Hawaiian Islands, with their
now diseased, starving, and dying natives, answer the question" (124).

But while conforming closely to pastoral, exoticist, and cultural
primitivist patterns of thought, sentiment, expression, and purpose,
Typee also molds primitivism in a peculiar way. Because of the setting
and Tommo's way of perceiving it, life for him in Taipivai is seemingly
without conventional "tension" between the pleasures and the limitations
of primitive life (the tension that, in this literary tradition, is the wit
of the reply from Raleigh's Nymph to Marlowe's Passionate Shepherd).
Melville's *Typee*—and indeed much of the Pacific literature that extols the
islands' simple ways of life and fulfillment of one's basic needs—exemplifies what A.O. Lovejoy calls the "soft" type of cultural primitivism,
where the featured attraction is "the alluring dream, or the hope, of a
life with little or no toil or strain of body or mind," opposite the "hard"
primitivism in the life of Vikings in winter (Lovejoy, 9). Once Tommo
gets to the valley, Nature is more than benign; it is benevolent. He scarcely
recognizes, however, that Nature feeds and beds him mainly because
the Typee spend their days working and cultivating it. Meanwhile Tommo's chief activity, if it can be called that, is indolence, both because
his injured leg at first prevents him from moving far and because, even
after the pain stops, he enjoys the luxury of having to do nothing but
what little he fancies.

Thus Tommo spends hours swimming with Typee maidens and
sailing a canoe around the lake, with Fayaway at the bow. Otherwise
he eats and naps the day's warm hours away among the Typee men in
the pavilion, "a sort of Bachelor's Hall" reserved for their exclusive use,
where the chief Mehevi could usually "be found enjoying his 'otium cum
dignitate' upon the luxurious mats which covered the floor" (158). But
gradually this soft life itself—and not Nature—limits Tommo's movements and horizons. Having grown accustomed to his indolence yet still
critical of it as a "civilized man" would be, Tommo complains peevishly
about both indolence and toil, in one breath, when the Typee inexplicably

and suddenly busy themselves to prepare an enormous feast and thus disturb his rest. Often not knowing the purpose of the Typees' labor, Tommo complains that "seldom do they ever exert themselves," yet "when they do work they seem determined that so meritorious an action shall not escape the observation of those around." He goes on to compare the Typee at work with "an infinity of black ants clustering about and dragging away to some hole the leg of a deceased fly," while he himself luxuriates in having to do nothing, not even to feed himself (159). Sloth dulls his appreciation for what he earlier saw as his paradise. Living his own idea of the life of a savage means, for Tommo, a heedless committal of Christianity's deadly sins: thus is Tommo's supposed pleasure self-consuming yet never satisfied.

Given his blindness to how the Typee must work to support life in their valley, Tommo's story generates little meaningful tension between its "soft" and "hard" aspects of Nature. So Melville finds conflict between tribes of people. Neglected through most of Tommo's autobiography of indolence, as it were, is the infamous enmity between the Typee and their enemies, the Happars. Moreover, as we learn explicitly rather late in the tale, the Typee guard the gateways into their valley not only to repel the Happars but, in those times, even more to prevent the intrusion of another tribe, the Europeans, who have already spoiled the port town of Nukuhiva for Tommo (205). In the Edenic Typee landscape we find the imminent clash of cultures, a clash that signifies the encroachment of "civilization" upon the primitive and savage.

And Tommo himself represents that civilization against which the Typee stand guard. The central conflict in Tommo's adventure turns out to be between the Typee and himself, between the supposedly primitive and the civilized, despite the fact that Tommo is a fugitive from civilized authority and despite the stress on his unlicensed enjoyment of the harmonious life in the valley. We have to wonder with Tommo why he should be indulged by the Typee, in view of his possible threat to them. Might not the foreign authorities seek Tommo by marching up the valley from its shores? Might not Tommo and Toby have been sent from Nukuhiva to report on the Typee, for whatever purposes the Frenchmen might be devising? Just as Tommo and Toby wonder immediately whether these are Happar or Typee, safe or dangerous; ought not the Typee be expected to ask the same basic question of Tommo? From the Typee point of view, Tommo is the mysterious stranger who has come to town, a likely threat to their morals and their lives.

Tommo's blindness to certain roles he plays among the Typee

involves a major self-deception, one which occupies most of the narrative. His seemingly growing understanding of the Typee is really illusory. How deeply can this escapee from civilization understand the "savage"? It pleases and must suffice Tommo to learn solely by experience, by living with them. But what does this mean when he lives as an *exception* to the Typee rules?[7]

Having lived briefly among the Typee, Melville knew something about the terrible force of their tabus. He did not presume to understand the system's complexities or even its fundamentals (*Typee*, 221, 224). By revealing Tommo's complacency about Typee laws, Melville exposes the Westerner's presumption of knowing the Typee. It is nothing more than a mask for ignorance. From the Westerner's point of view, these Typee primitives may seem joyfully free from certain constraints—for example, regarding sex. And from the point of view of strict Christian morals, the Typee may seem not merely free but licentious and, in some lurid respects, depraved.

But in surprising, ironic contrast that is evident everywhere in Tommo's tale, it is not so much the Typee as it is Tommo himself who is emphatically freed from constraints by his residency in Taipivai. It is Tommo who has escaped the sexual tabus and the toil imposed by the moral codes and necessities of his Northeastern American origins. In the entire narrative, with the exception of an elderly couple obviously devoted to each other, the only pairing at all between man and woman is between Tommo and Fayaway. The Typee are not actually depicted as being sexually free or unusual at all. And it is Tommo alone who is free, not only from Christian commandments but from some of the tabus that normally constrain the Typee themselves. An outsider to Typee law, he cajoles the chief and priests into giving his Fayaway a special dispensation, requiring them to lift from her the tabu that forbids women to board a canoe, which, at any rate, he uses not to perform tasks but to idle away his hours. Fayaway is thus allowed to accompany Tommo on his languorous canoe rides. In this way, Tommo rejects local laws and customs in order to satisfy a whim, with impunity. In short, like no one else in the tale, Tommo himself is the classic primitive, when he acts the part of one set free in a paradise where he thinks himself "relatively exempt from constraint," as Lovejoy puts it.

Changes in Tommo's attitudes toward the Typee and toward himself and the civilization he represents are a result partly of the complexity of—the contradictory impulses of harmony and discord within—the pastoral that still underlies much of the tale, while the plot and conflicts introduce turmoil into his life of contemplation. Using the pastoral convention of satirizing civilization, Melville not only contrasts primitive and civilized people but also implies similarities between them. For example, Tommo learns how a native might feel to be hounded by Christian missionaries, when the Typee attempt to tattoo him with their religious symbols (218–20). What frightens him, in addition to his terror of being marked indelibly a savage, is that he, the Ariel, cannot guess whether they, the Calibans, are merely playing a joke on him. The abrupt, physical threat of "conversion" by sacred ritual is quite another matter from musing about Typee "missionaries" redeeming a civilized country. Melville's distaste for missionaries is no secret, and here the reversal of roles, with the Typee trying to "convert" a distressed Tommo, acts as yet another of Melville's satirical attacks on the missionaries' overbearing ways. The reflection, in the Typee, of his own race and culture is as right hand to left, at once the opposite of and identical to Tommo himself. No matter how much sympathy and humane understanding Tommo gains for the Typee, his illusion is still so pristine, hard, and brittle that its exposure comes as all the more horrid a shock.

Shrouded in enough uncertainty to intensify Tommo's fears, the specter of cannibalism grins hideously at Tommo at his narrative's climax. Tommo glimpses all too clearly, despite the Typee's attempts to hide it, a preserved Happar's head, a perversion of the conventional, mocking skull that reminds us of death's presence even in Arcadia. The sight warns him not merely of death, but of a horrific death, one that possibly faces him (232–33). Outside Tommo's view, a battle with the Happars follows shortly after this shock. What appear to be bundles of slain enemies are carried like slaughtered pigs into the Typee village. A feast follows from which Tommo is barred. Before all remnants of the feast have been cleared, however, Tommo steals a sight of the disarrayed bones of a human skeleton, "the bones still fresh with moisture, and with particles of flesh clinging to them here and there!" (238). The image Tommo has been tailoring for the Typee as civilized, virtuous people in their own right is shattered. Agitated far more deeply than when he was nearly tattooed, Tommo cannot possibly accept or fathom all the values of these people, to whom he likewise is an alien, no matter how breezily he could excuse their cannibalism in the abstract (205). Lonely, homesick, fearing for his life, suddenly unsure of the Typees' intentions in fattening him with food and sloth, Tommo makes a violent escape from Taipivai, exiting by way of the valley's beach and the sea beyond. His Fayaway— for *whatever* her reasons—sobs a farewell on the shore. Her point of view is never made clear, in that Tommo never questions his assumptions about Fayaway's motives for acting as she does, there on the beach or anywhere during their weeks together.

In its way, Melville's plot is archetypal. It is characteristic of many novels based on initial assumptions of a simple pastoral and set in some paradise of the Pacific or another. In the Christian world, the basic use of this pattern lies in the story of the original Garden and its inhabitants. But one lesson in *Typee* is that this is already a fallen world, including these Pacific islands, fallen before the story even begins, a world where innocence and Edenic pleasures are illusory or are transient at best; or else such pleasures still exist wholly and solely in the imagination and the intellect, where the literary pastoral once had its true life. And precisely because in Christian mythology ours is a fallen world, human imperfection makes it impossible to understand the cultural *other* even when such understanding seems most assured or most urgent. Tommo's myths of noble savages and pastoral sufficiency prove to be walls that, like the sperm whale's blunt brow, conceal who the Typee and their culture really are. The Edenic myth is not enough, to know these people. The plot itself suggests that something considerably more substantial is needed— and, moreover, is yet possible in Pacific literature—than the simple pastoral with its evocations of cultural primitivism. In its movement toward self-understanding through instances of self-discovery among "primitive," "savage" people, Melville's *Typee* is the prototypical Pacific novel, pointing toward the heroic in the unfolding or discovery of character through deeds and experience.

2

By the time Melville wrote *Typee* and marketed it as authentic, such a tale would have been unlikely to originate in contemporary Hawai'i. Hawai'i in 1846 was in places already modern or was at any rate a frontier poised, Melville put it, between "barbarism and civilization" (*Typee*, Appendix, 255).

In Hawai'i, certain events of international adventurism provoked Melville to add his hot and stinging Appendix to *Typee*. At issue were circumstances surrounding the provisional cession of Hawai'i to the British Lord George Paulet by the Hawaiian monarch Kamehameha III in 1843. Melville considered this king to be profligate and he viewed the five months of Lord Paulet's stewardship as the sanest or at any rate the least debauched in recent Hawaiian history. But the restoration of Hawaiian rule to King Kamehameha III by Rear Admiral Richard Thomas, Captain Paulet's commanding officer in the British Pacific Squadron, was followed by "ten memorable days . . . of universal broad-day debauchery." The spectacle beggared description, fumed Melville: "It was a sort of Polynesian saturnalia" (258). Melville sternly admonished that "the history of these ten days reveals in their true colors the character of the Sandwich islanders" (258). Without subtlety or equivocation, he squarely blamed "the labors of the missionaries" for the sordid state of affairs that not only led to the Paulet hiatus but that afterward resumed in even greater perniciousness. In Melville's view, the Hawaiian government's maltreatment of British merchants and residents in Hawai'i, and the "iniquitous maladministration of affairs" in general, both of which prompted the takeover, were a direct result of the influence wielded by American missionaries acting for American interests, among whom he singled out as especially odious Dr. Gerrit P. Judd, to Melville "a sanctimonious apothecary-adventurer" and no lover of the British presence in the islands (255).

Not many shared Melville's approval of what Lord Paulet had done, whose own British government repudiated the takeover. When the restored Kamehameha III spoke at a thanksgiving service raising the Hawaiian flag once more over his kingdom, he uttered the words: *Ua mau ke ea o ka 'aina i ka pono*; "The life of the land is perpetuated in righteousness." These words are now the motto of the State of Hawai'i. How galled Melville would be to know this.

Whatever the judgments passed on this 1843 affair, however, this storm center of controversy was the Hawai'i of Melville's time. Though calm at moments, it was certainly not blessed with an endless summer of warm human sentiments. Hawai'i and the missionaries, as Melville saw them, were the embodiment of "civilized" hypocrisies, vices, and extravagances that the pastoral Taipivai and the Marquesan noble savages put to shame. In *Typee*, he recounts a grotesque instance of missionary bigotry, describing a "robust," red-faced wife of a missionary, her cart drawn by two islanders who have for months taken her on such daily airings. She explodes in rage when the elder of her draft pair falters, unable to pull the cart up a small, sandy hill. Refusing or not even thinking to lighten the old man's load by dismounting from her cart, the woman screeches out her order, *Hookee! Hookee!* (Pull! Pull!), punctuating her words with blows of her huge fan's handle on the unprotected head of the "old savage" (196–97). By such undependable conveyance, Melville bristles, these good Christians suffered themselves to ride to and from church on humid Hawaiian Sabbaths.

Boston-born James Jackson Jarves lived in Honolulu during this same period. Despite being a journalist and historian responsive to events of his own time, Jarves wrote nonetheless a pastoral novel of Hawai'i. Melville had scarcely embarked on his actual South Seas adventure, in 1841, when Jarves began the serial publication of what was to become the first novel in English to be set in Hawai'i.[8] Six installments ran in *The Polynesian*, Jarves's own weekly newspaper, of that year. It was not until 1857, however, by which time Jarves—publisher and editor of Hawaii's first newspaper, a historian of Hawai'i, and an art historian and collector of note as well—had moved to Florence, Italy, that his *Kiana: A Tradition of Hawaii* was published as a complete novel.[9]

Jarves wrote his novel of a noble Hawaiian people not by writing a romance like Melville's of contemporary primitive life in a land as if forgotten by time, but by writing a pseudohistorical novel set in prehistory, some two and a half centuries before the arrival of Cook. *Kiana* is based on a sort of chronological primitivism, an imaginative re-creation of a time pictured as being more simple, a Golden Age. Yet it does have contemporary significance. Like *Typee*, it may "be seen as a plea for tolerance and understanding among conflicting religions, cultures, and peoples in the Islands, the United States, and the world at large."[10] Indeed Jarves himself, in his preface to *Kiana*, suggests the allegorical, didactic application of his fiction: "Every tale is based upon certain ideas, which are its life-blood" and "which bear directly upon" the "welfare" of the present age (8–9).

In a setting envisioned as more simple than the Hawai'i of the mid-nineteenth century, and beginning about the year 1530, Jarves's narrative introduces and establishes in Hawaii's fiction the twofold theme of the mixture of cultures and races that contributes to Hawaii's unique social and cultural characteristics. His prefatory words set the framework:

> Eighteen generations of kings previous to Kamehameha I, during the reign of Kahoukapa, or Kiana, there arrived in Hawaii, a white priest, bringing with him an idol, which, by his persuasion, was enrolled in the calendar of the Hawaiian gods, and a temple erected for its service. The stranger priest acquired great influence, and left a reputation for goodness that was green in the memories of the people of Hawaii three centuries later. Another statement adds that a vessel was wrecked on

the island, and the captain and his sister reached the shore,
where they were kindly received and adopted into the families
of the chiefs. (P. 6)

Jarves goes on to note that he has become convinced that these
white strangers were Spaniards, in the time of Cortez and in the conquistador's service, who not only carried with them their own religion but
"for a while were even regarded as gods" by the Hawaiians. Blown by
a storm far off course on a caravelle journey from Mexico to California,
Jarves's Spaniards are saved by being shipwrecked on the island of Hawai'i. Intermarriage introduces their foreign blood into the Polynesian
veins and heart; and Jarves claims that this blood "still exists (or did
recently) among certain families, who pride themselves greatly upon their
foreign origin" (6).

In Jarves's preface, his Spaniards are recognizably the forerunners
of Captain James Cook, seen as the god Lono—like Cortez among the
Aztecs, a *white* god, in Western mythologizing.[11] Nowhere does Jarves
explicitly state it, but it would be safe to suggest that the "idol" the white
priest contributed to the Hawaiian pantheon was a crucifix, as Samuel
Kamakau asserts (*Ruling Chiefs*, 324). It is not much more of a leap to
see that the crucifix, introduced in the midsixteenth century, by Jarves's
reckoning, evolved into the god Lono's staff, the pole with a crosstree
from which banners depend and fly. In fact the pole itself was topped
by a carved face, perhaps originally Christ's, as pictured in *Kiana*. In
Jarves's conjectured prehistory of Hawai'i, it is uncertain whether any
other foreigners preceded the Spaniards. In any case, the leader of the
Spaniard group, Juan Alvirez, is greeted as the god Lono by the Hawaiian
Chief Kiana and his people, expressly since the shipwreck occurs while
the people sport and celebrate in Lono's honor, observing Lono's festival
season (Makahiki). Similarly, Cook arrived in Hawai'i during two
Makahiki seasons—first, in his January 1778 stopover on Kaua'i; and
second, at the end of that year and into February of the next, upon his
return from far-northern Pacific waters and the North American coast.

Jarves attempts to meld his historiography, his assuredly good
knowledge of Hawaiian history and prehistory according to oral sources,
and his respect for compelling myths into a single, imaginative whole.
The myths that inspire him include not only the identification of Cook
with Lono but also explanations of what appear to have been accidental
landings in Hawai'i by "superior" civilized people who, prior to Cook,
left artifacts and influences not indigenous to the Polynesians.[12] While

the setting may be otherwise idyllic—both in time and in place, Kiana's reign being in Jarves's view "the Golden Age of Hawaii"—Jarves's tale is pastoral in design, but not simply so (78). Although the novel is implicitly nostalgic about that prehistoric past, it is not a quieting of the heroic ambitions, desires, and energies of the Spanish and Mexican voyagers; and *Kiana* concerns the elevation of the natives to the strangers' presumably superior level. It should be noted explicitly that Jarves's view of European superiority over the Polynesian noble savage, whether in religion, in knowledge, or in arms, was more to be expected in a white writer of his time than was Melville's contemporaneous, subversive critique of the frightening inadequacy of Tommo's view of the Typee. There is also, however, Jarves's evident ambiguity about European cultural superiority: the humane nobility of Kiana, who is chosen over Alvirez as the title character, and the very name of Jarves's newspaper, *The Polynesian*, indicate his desire to avoid Eurocentrism.

The Spaniards' superiority, such as it is in the novel, is concentrated in Beatriz, Juan Alvirez's blond sister. Jarves appears to have used the medium of fiction to test his ideas of how a white woman of culture and breeding would fare among savages. He states in the preface: "Especially have I always been curious to trace the fate of the solitary white woman,—a waif of refinement cast thus on a barbarous shore,—and of the priest, too,—to learn how far their joint influence tempered the heathenism into which they were thrown, or whether they were finally overcome by paganism" (7–8).

The priest is Olmedo, a Dominican monk and a man of great compassion who spurns some of the harsher strictures of the Church and repudiates the cruelties inflicted by the Spaniards on the Mexicans they crush, but who is indefatigable in his unexpected mission to convert the Hawaiians. It is not a cultural difference between the Spaniards and the Hawaiians, however, that most bothers Beatriz and Olmedo. Rather, the central conflict is between their love and their religion. Their story might have occurred anywhere, except perhaps that being stranded together on a tropic island where their survival is threatened heightens their passions. Both Olmedo and Beatriz adhere so firmly to certain Catholic doctrines and vows that, when they confess to each other their mutual romantic love, they immediately recoil from any thought of Olmedo's breaking his vows of celibacy or abandoning his responsibility for his spiritual daughter Beatriz. Earlier, because her love for Olmedo prevents any other from entering her heart, Beatriz declines the love offered her by the noble Kiana. But far more trying is the love—portrayed as lust

—of the Aztec captive among them, Tolta. The spurned Tolta kidnaps the woman and her priest for delivery to Kiana's brutal rival, Pohaku. Beatriz is weakened by the great physical exertion required to cross the entire island of Hawai'i, to escape the lava rushing from Mauna Loa's side, and to flee Tolta's and Pohaku's clutches by undertaking another arduous hike, this time through wet jungles. Her health gradually declines, though she grows more ethereally beautiful even through the moment of her death in Olmedo's arms. Aside from her ordeal, from which her companions vigorously recover, why Beatriz dies is uncertain, except that her malady has something to do with her impossible love for Olmedo. This, then, is what happens to Jarves's white woman in a barbarous setting.

In love, reason, and faith Jarves's Spaniards live on an elevated plane. It is not the Hawaiians with their beliefs in Lono, Pele, and other gods and goddesses, but the Catholic maiden and priest whom Jarves makes the most blindly faithful. Beatriz's religious "influence," moreover, is strong enough to reach farther than her too brief life. Olmedo plants a cross on her grave and prays there daily for years to come. In a somewhat similar gesture, Jarves concludes his novel by weaving these imagined characters into the warp of his modern Hawaiian history. Juan, a staunch conquistador, recovers quickly from grief over his sister's death and marries her new-found companion, the beautiful fourteen-year-old Princess Liliha. This princess is the daughter of Hewahewa, a prudent, politically shrewd high priest of Pele, the volcano and fire goddess worshipped by Pohaku's people. Aided by Hewahewa's love for his daughter, Olmedo influences the Hawaiian priest with Christianity. In due time the Hawaiian people depart from demonology, and Hewahewa abolishes the crueler rites of the Pele mythology. Meanwhile, so intent is Olmedo in his solitary gazing toward heaven, where Beatriz awaits him, that the people call him *Kapiolani*, the captive of heaven. Another Kapiolani, presumably his namesake, was a chiefess who in 1824 defied Pele's wrath by publicly breaking the goddess's *kapu* (tabu) at the rim of Kīlauea Crater. She was an important early convert to Christianity in written historical times.[13] Kiana, meanwhile, also faithful to the memory of his beloved Beatriz, grows solitary as well, gaining even deeper popular respect in the remainder of his reign. The people call him *Kamehameha*, the lonely one. In time, one with this name will play a larger role than Cook's in establishing the groundwork for nineteenth- and twentieth-century Hawai'i. A descendant and namesake of Hewahewa, just before American missionaries' arrival in Hawai'i in 1820, will be instrumental in abolishing the old religion's kapu system. Juan Alvirez (Lono) will be thought to return as Cook, although it must be noted that Juan never leaves Hawai'i alive, promising to return, as the god Lono is supposed to have done. According to Jarves's narrative, several noted chiefs will be descendants of Juan and Liliha.

Thus Jarves ends rather than begins his narrative with a genealogy of sorts, invoking names that ring a familiar note to his contemporary Hawai'i readers. This, the placement of the genealogy tells us, is the beginning of modern Hawai'i. Today, these names—Kamehameha, Liliha, and Kapi'olani, though the Kapi'olani alluded to is not the more famous Queen Kapi'olani, consort of King David Kalākaua, who reigned some four decades after Jarves wrote his novel—are still familiar ones, and Hawaiian names of other characters were certainly well known locally in Jarves's time.

But far more significantly, certain elements of plot, characterization, and theme established in *Kiana* recur in some important later novels of Hawai'i. Three of these elements are especially noteworthy in this first novel of Hawai'i: first, Jarves's attempt to root contemporary people of Hawai'i in ancient times through genealogy, to exploit, that is, the ancient qualities of the indigenous heritage; second, a parallel treatment of the land itself through descriptions of its geological and biological growth through the eons, a process which Jarves describes in chapter 3; and third, the elevation of the Hawaiian race and culture though intermarriage and, despite the assumption of Western superiority, the salubrious cross-fertilization of diverse cultures. We later find various of these elements at work in Hawai'i novels by authors as disparate as Mark Twain, James Michener, and O. A. Bushnell.

The most important of these elements in *Kiana* is the intercultural. But Jarves's skepticism about the nature of the cultural mix developing in Hawaii's "transitional" society can be seen in his novel's most interesting character, the Mexican captive Tolta. Son of an Aztec high priest killed by the Spaniards, Tolta himself is saved from slaughter but is taken captive and forcibly baptized by Olmedo. As victim and witness of the conquistadors' atrocities, he plots vengeance with never a moment's rest. When the few survivors of the shipwreck first enter Kiana's village, deserted because the celebration for the god Lono is being held some distance away, Tolta senses immediately that the Spaniards may well do to the inhabitants of this unknown place what they did to the Aztecs. He is angered by Juan Alvirez's wary comparison of the dead silence of the Hawaiian village with the silence of "La Noche Triste," the night when Spaniards were fiercely ambushed during their attempt to march from Mexico. Tolta's people suffered much greater losses than did the Spaniards. But Tolta's vengefulness is confused by his personal love and loyalties for the captors who nonetheless saved him from slaughter at the point of Spanish steel:

> In him love to the individual and hate to the Spanish race were so interwoven, that it would have been impossible for himself to foresee how he should act on any occasion which might afford scope for either passion. He was an Aztec by birth, of the race of the priesthood, young, accustomed to arms, and learned in the lore of his race; at heart a worshipper of [Aztec] idols, though a forced baptism, and the necessities of a captive, made him nominally a Christian. (P. 44)

This remarkable, alternately glaring and apathetic character is both "a tiger in rage, and a lamb in sentiment; in short, combining in his own breast the instincts of brute and man, with no harmonizing principle to keep him in permanent peaceful relations with himself or his kind" (45). Jarves seems to take a special, increasingly unsympathetic interest in this prodigy of newly mixed—violently mixed—cultures. At heart, Jarves seems unable to understand the likes of Tolta, who must have appeared in various incarnations among people Jarves actually saw and perhaps even knew in the Hawai'i of his own time. Whether intended or not, Tolta is Jarves's prototype for a multicultural Hawaiian under increasingly colonial rule. In contrast to Tolta's case, practically no manner of contradiction, complexity, or duality of nature seems incomprehensible to the novelist in drawing the characters of a Juan Alvirez, a Beatriz even with her heart cloven by her love for a priest, an Olmedo, or a Kiana, all pure representatives of their races. Tolta becomes the villain of the novel. But Tolta is also a victim of Spanish conquest, and though Jarves tries to use this as a reason for the character's violence, he seems himself unconvinced of the truth or adequacy of this motivation. Doubly treacherous, Tolta plots and sets into motion a plan to destroy not only Kiana and his guests, the Spaniards, but also Pohaku, Tolta's evil ally. Utterly possessed by desire for this purest of white women, Tolta aims to have Beatriz all to himself. But he dies in agony when, escaping from combat with an enraged, double-crossed Pohaku, he leaps into a river but lands in quicksand. Even after such a death, Tolta deserves only to be exploited, since Jarves makes Tolta's violence serve a purpose; it climaxes then tempers the conflicts between hostile districts; and this mitigation of hostilities helps make it possible for the priest Olmedo to teach the rudiments of his religion peacefully. Thus Juan Alvirez's usually fervent thirst for heathen blood is slaked, and the Hawaiians are spared further slaughter by Juan and his troop, the foreigners' own savagery just barely veiled.

In the mythology that Jarves consciously fashions, the sword of Juan Alvirez is a motif. "Eighteen generations of kings" later, in 1778, Captain Cook was to see its scant remnants in the Hawaiians' possession. This vestige and memory, this *pohaku* or *pahoa* (stone, iron, or dagger) cuts across the peaceful image others may have fancied for the Hawaiians in their earthly paradise. Cook's arrival in Hawai'i and the return of his ships to England, along with the politics and leadership borne by King Kamehameha I through the entire island chain, set in motion processes of cultural change on a scale probably never before experienced by Hawai'i since the first arrival of the Polynesians, a process that continues unabated through our time.

3

The facile image of Hawai'i as paradise, everywhere associated with pop literature, music, film, and travel-poster graphics of Hawai'i, is contradicted by nonfictional and fictional works that may serve as prototypes in the development of Hawaii's literature beyond the simple pastoral. But, for Melville and Jarves, despite their concerns that it was dehumanizing and untrue, the *illusion* of a Hawaiian paradise in the middle of their century was a powerful marvel, then and now. The illusion affected Mark Twain after them, though his words on the subject have to some extent been misconstrued.

In 1884, while Twain was seeing *Adventures of Huckleberry Finn* through the press, he was also completing another novel, one set in Hawai'i and based on what he had learned during and after his 1866 visit to the islands. Extant fragments and his own comments about the never-published work suggest that Twain saw it as a complex and somehow troubling project combining the idyllic, the heroic, and the tragic in ways that contradicted contemporary simplistic conventions of a Hawaiian paradise. Twain's Hawai'i novel has not survived intact, and so it cannot be said to have influenced the course of American literary traditions concerning Hawai'i and the Pacific. But however obliquely and humorously he addressed certain issues in his writings about "the loveliest fleet of islands that lies anchored in any ocean," vestiges of the novel suggest that in composing it, Twain thought very seriously about Hawai'i, the island kingdom sitting in the path of America's Manifest Destiny.

Thanks mainly to *Roughing It* (1872), readers of Twain know that earlier in his writing career he visited Hawai'i. Yet while he satirized certain popular views of Hawai'i, Hawaiians, and their place in the Western imagination, his remarks have typically been taken, even by scholars, as endorsements of the conventional paradise image promoted by the Hawai'i tourist industry.[14] Contrary to its apparent breeziness, Twain's total published contribution to Hawaii's literature is rather substantial and embodies a complex pastoral view masked, however, by the allure of the very clichés Twain first parodied, then pondered, yet failed to subvert in a fully consistent way.

If Twain's intended book had matched in keenness the double-edged satire of *A Connecticut Yankee in King Arthur's Court* (1889), with which the earlier, abandoned novel has been compared, it would have shared in a literary tradition developed by Western colonials and visiting writers alongside the continuing native Hawaiian and the relatively new, polyethnic, "Local" literary tradition begun by laboring immigrants. In *A Connecticut Yankee*, the plot—an initial retreat from what is considered a brutally complex, urban, technological society to an ostensibly simple, even primitive world which itself becomes an object of satire—matches a pattern Twain had uncovered and traced not only in *Huckleberry Finn* but also, it may well be, in his novel of the Sandwich Islands. Here, in this pattern, and not in any notions of Hawaiian indolence, was room for Twain's imagination to work. Had the novel survived intact, Twain's fictional treatment of racial and intercultural issues might at the very least have been the basis for the sort of serious reputation Twain has not been accorded in Hawaii's literature. But more important, the novel might have contributed to an understanding of the growth of an especially diverse culture of Hawai'i in the course of a century. Extant fragments of the novel, Twain's written comments about the work, and the historical context in which he set it suggest a point of view that subverts the monocultural and racial assumptions of the colonizers and tourists whom Twain, with his charming words and his white suit, has mistakenly been made to symbolize in Hawai'i.

That Twain adopted a pastoral, paradisiacal view of Hawai'i is obvious nearly everywhere in the writings that resulted from his visit. But equally obvious, yet somehow obscured, is the fact that Twain greatly complicated this view—indeed, made it incompatible with the pastoral.

He seemed both to experience in his visit and to evoke in literary ways the notion of a retreat to a pastoral setting, followed by a return (the sojourner now wiser and refreshed) to an urban, civilized world. But the whole pattern is never made explicit in Twain's published writings on Hawai'i, though other elements of a complex pastoral certainly are. Most obviously a contravention of the usual pattern of retreat and return is that Twain was assigned as a professional journalist to report on the Hawaiian sugar industry and to observe prospects for increased trade between California and the Hawaiian Kingdom. Twain's visit was no escape from daily work. Indeed he shipped aboard the *Ajax* on the very first commercial steamship crossing of the eastern Pacific, and he emphatically noted the ship's value to Pacific trade. The *Ajax* and the nature of Twain's assignment characterize the entire visit as the capitalist antithesis of the pastoral: Twain saw himself as a passenger aboard a kind of history-making machine in the garden, and everywhere he looked in the island paradise, he saw consequences of the machine's arrival.

Without the novel as a centerpiece, Twain's Hawai'i writings appear scattered across the decades from 1866, when he spent his four months on the Sandwich Islands, to 1910, the year of his death. His surviving contribution to Hawaii's literature consists mainly of his letters to the Sacramento *Union* in 1866 together with portions of *Roughing It* and *Following the Equator*. By their very nature, Twain's twenty-five *Union* letters do not compose a unified narrative description or report. Still, they contain the raw material on which he drew in later work. About a third of what he reported in the letters, for example, was fashioned into a coherent narrative in the Hawai'i chapters of *Roughing It*. Besides being briefer and more coherent as a narrative than the letters upon which they are based, however, these chapters are considerably less exuberant, a change resulting in part from the deletion of the recurring low-comic figure, Mr. Brown, the imaginary fellow traveler and stock type of the laughably boorish American tourist, who serves as a foil for Twain's busy and relatively sober persona of the *Union* correspondent. Also in the canon is the famous lecture called "Our Fellow Savages of the Sandwich Islands," with which he entertained audiences on both sides of the Atlantic from 1866 to 1873. Twain's last important published treatment of Hawai'i in a book came in 1897 with a chapter devoted to Hawai'i in *Following the Equator*, another travel account, this one based on a world lecture tour he undertook in 1895 and 1896.[15]

The abandoned Hawai'i novel of 1884 marks the height of Twain's drive to contrast what he saw as two divergent aspects of Hawai'i and his experience there and to bring together two ways of writing and of viewing the island world. On the one hand there was the "poetic," the idyllic or romantic evocation of a world fragrant with blossoms; on the other, the "unvarnished truth" of life in islands where mosquitoes bite and centipedes sting and where history is ever running its course. Twain's comic realism enlivens his reports to the *Union*, beginning with the very first, where the correspondent notes: "There are a good many mosquitoes around tonight and they are rather troublesome; but it is a source of unalloyed satisfaction to me to know that the two millions I sat down on a minute ago will never sing again."[16] The contrasts seem to die away after 1884 in Twain's increasingly sentimental vision of the islands. A simplistic, timeless Hawaiian paradise comes to dominate his reminiscences, even as his concerns about American military and political adventures in Hawai'i and the Philippines grow more pronounced.

We know enough about Twain's Hawai'i novel to regret that only fragments survive. On 7 January 1884, he wrote to William Dean Howells:

> My billiard-table is stacked up with books relating to the Sandwich Islands; the walls are upholstered with scraps of paper penciled with notes drawn from them. I have saturated myself with knowledge of that unimaginably beautiful land & that most strange & fascinating people. And I have begun a story. Its hidden motive will illustrate a but-little considered fact in human nature: that the religious folly you are born in you will *die* in, no matter what apparently reasonabler religious folly may seem to have taken its place meanwhile & abolished & obliterated it. I start with Bill Ragsdale at 12 years of age, & the heroine at 4, in the midst of the ancient idolatrous system, with its picturesque & amazing customs and superstitions, 3 months before the arrival of the missionaries & the erection of a shallow Christianity upon the ruins of the old paganism. Then these two will become educated Christians, & highly civilized. And then I will jump 15 years, & do Ragsdale's leper business. When we come to dramatize, we can draw a deal of matter from the story, all ready to our hand.[17]

In spite of his own claim in other correspondence, there is some question as to whether the story thus outlined was ever completed. Paine asserts without explanation in his edition of the letters that it was not.[18] There is no evidence that Twain and Howells ever succeeded in dramatizing the Sandwich Islands tale, although their correspondence through Jan-

uary and February of 1884 frequently mentions both the story and the
projected play. But Howells was not the only one to whom Twain wrote
that the novel was done. Twice in January he wrote his friend Mary
Mason Fairbanks that he had indeed finished the novel and would soon
be sending it to press. Thereafter his Hawai'i novel disappears from his
correspondence and notebooks. What survives are three fragments at and
near the manuscript's beginning.

As for the Bill Ragsdale mentioned in the letter of 7 January,
Twain had in 1866 reported briefly on the real-life, "half-white" (i.e.,
also half-Hawaiian) figure with fun and admiration—but with nothing
to hint of his possibly becoming the hero of a serious novel. Ragsdale
was a lawyer and an English-Hawaiian interpreter in the Hawaiian legislature. Twain delightedly calls him a "rascal," and Ragsdale was in fact
known throughout the islands as a capable politician and flamboyant rake
from Hilo.[19] When he reappears as Twain's fictional hero eighteen years
later, Ragsdale is characterized not now as a dandy in the Hawaiian court
but pathetically as a victim of leprosy. Twain's remarks to Mrs. Fairbanks
reveal that if there was anything he wanted to impress upon her, in this
year that *Huckleberry Finn* was to have been published, it was the seriousness of the Hawai'i story. On 24 January 1884 Twain wrote her that
"this book is not humorous but a serious book, & may damn me, tho'
Livy says *No*. I do wish you would come & read it in MS & judge
it, before it goes to the printers. Will you? You shall have till March
1st—5 weeks."[20] Mrs. Fairbanks apparently had some doubts about
the book's seriousness, though it seems she had not read the manuscript. Twain wrote her again on 30 January: "The novel? Yes, it's serious
. . . ," then went on to specify that its setting was the Sandwich Islands
beginning "65 years ago" (256). And as he had informed Howells in
more detail, he noted to Mrs. Fairbanks that the novel consisted of two
parts separated by a chronological gap. His repeated insistence on the
novel's seriousness suggests how differently Twain wanted this work to
be seen among his usually humorous books and, perhaps, among popular
accounts which were anything but serious on the subject of Hawai'i and
the South Seas.

The surviving pages of Twain's manuscripts attest to the temper
of his intent and to the likelihood that his humor played a nonetheless
important part in the novel. In nine of the seventeen extant pages, he
presents a description of the islands which resembles nothing so much
as his own earlier parodies of paradise of the Pacific clichés.[21] In another
fragment the king questions a boy about a girl condemned for some trans-

gression.[22] In reply, the boy states that the girl "is no kin" to him: "She is Aloha; her mother . . . was Kalama; her father was Mainly the Boston sailor; they . . . are dead." Over the objections of an obviously powerful priest, the king orders the girl and the boy released. A third fragment concerns the theft of the king's spittoon which, in the hands of his enemies, could serve as the instrument by which the king may be prayed to death. Twain describes the great hubbub of the search for the royal spittoon. A final fragment, evidently describing a Hawaiian house, hints at the admirably simple comfort of the native dwelling, much as in the prototypical American narrative of Polynesian life, Melville's *Typee*.

The first and largest fragment shows that the conventions of the Pacific paradise were to be important as a thematic framing device for the novel:

> The date is 1840. Scene, the true Isles of the Blest; that is to say, the Sandwich Islands—to this day the peacfulest, restfulest, sunniest, balmiest, dreamiest haven of refuge for a worn and weary spirit the surface of the earth can offer. Away out there in the mid-solitudes of the vast Pacific, and far down in the edge of the tropics, they lie asleep on the waves, perpetually green and beautiful, remote from the work-day world and its frets and worries, a bloomy, fragrant paradise, where the troubled may go and find peace, and the sick and tired find strength and rest. There they lie, the divine islands, forever shining in the sun, forever smiling out on the sparkling sea, with its soft mottlings of drifting cloud-shadows and vagrant cat's-paws of wind; forever inviting you, never repulsing you; and whosoever looks upon them once, will never more get the picture out of his memory till he die. With him it will stay, and be always present; always present and always fresh; neither time nor distance can dim its features, or dull their charm, or reconcile him to the thought that he will never see that picture with his eyes of flesh again.
>
> The Islands are so beautiful! The richest fancy cannot imagine their beauty, and no brush can adequately paint it . . . .The skies do weep, there, but the leaves never fade—because the skies weep.

Here is the full-blown, explicit, stylized expression of Twain's Hawaiian paradise of memory and rather distant vision. But whereas in his original Sacramento *Union* letters Twain usually joked about the narrowness of this picturesque view, here he seems to espouse it. The quality of the writing prompts Henry Nash Smith and William M. Gibson to note that these fragments "may have been omitted from the MS in revision," and "the indications are that Clemens was right in deciding not to publish the book."[23] Certainly this rhapsody soars away from all the information, history, and actual observations which anchor his nonfictional works about Hawai'i. Whether deflating the island paradise cliché with complaints about the stings of tropical insects or marveling firsthand at the magnificent and awesome Kīlauea volcano and a sublime sunrise viewed from atop Haleakalā, Twain in his non-fiction writes prose that is both freshly detailed and animated. By contrast, the beginning of his Hawai'i novel is scarcely a description of what "eyes of flesh" see. Not only are the envisioned islands "a very paradise" but they are also "the true Isles of the Blest," a phrase which locates them squarely in the ocean of Western mythology. Thus situated, "always present and always fresh" nowhere but in the imagination, the islands float outside of history and the reach of historical time.

The novel begins, however, with a single stated fact which is not an impression: "The date is 1840." In specifying the date Twain implies that what is to occur is not timeless but historical. By 1840 Hawai'i had been ruled by three successive kings of the dynasty secured in 1795 with Hawaiian spears, European cannon, and a warrior genius, Kamehameha the Great.[24] In 1819, this venerable hero's greatest widow, Ka'ahumanu, successfully maneuvered Kamehameha II into abolishing the ancient *'ai kapu* (literally, tabu on eating), an act which, while based upon a history of changes instituted by the first Kamehameha and his generation, radically altered the religious, cultural, and political systems of Hawai'i. The abolition allowed women to eat with men, to eat the foods once allowed only to men, and, in a larger sense, to share in governance in new ways. The need was urgent for a wider franchise, since exotic diseases had reduced the Hawaiian population from three or four hundred thousand, and perhaps a good many more, at Captain Cook's arrival in 1778 to some 140,000 by the time the Hawaiians dismantled the kapu system. Liholiho (Kamehameha II) and his Queen Kamāmalu themselves died of measles while on a state visit to England in 1824. By the 1840 of Twain's novel, the total native Hawaiian population of only 90,000 was being reduced still further by the sterilizing or fatal effects of measles, venereal disease, influenza, and now leprosy, which reportedly appeared in Hawai'i as early as 1830. On 30 March 1820, the First Company of New England missionaries arrived and began their very busy careers within a political context prepared by the Hawaiians. At the time of the novel's idyllic opening, Hawai'i was vital to Pacific and, indeed, global commerce. First the sandalwood, then the whaling trades flourished in their times, and sugar was beginning to attract colonizers. Churches associated with American and European powers competed for converts—and visitors began arriving, hungering to test the ancient Western dream of an earthly paradise. Sacred and profane joined hands in a pattern and process typical of colonialism. Although the sovereignty that Kamehameha established was to last for a hundred years, the Kingdom, Twain saw, was treated in effect like a colony by outsiders competing to become master. In 1843, the year Jarves, Twain's chief historical source, published his *History of the Hawaiian or Sandwich Islands*, Hawai'i was the setting for the short-lived British takeover sparked by a land dispute raised by a resident British diplomat.[25] The object of "civilization" scorned in *Typee*, Hawai'i in 1840 was not asleep. It was certainly not the "dreamiest haven of refuge" for any weary travelers who were to stay for a while.

So at the very beginning of his novel, Twain introduces two contrasting senses of time, the timeless and the historical, a set of contrasts inherent in his earlier writings on Hawai'i but not until now brought into sharp and sustained focus. He must have placed his story within a historical context he had carefully researched and selected. He wrote to Mrs. Fairbanks in 1884 that the novel's chronological beginning was "65 years ago," and to Howells that that was "3 months before the arrival of the missionaries," which places it in late 1819 or early 1820, a time near the Christmas which fell between the abolition of the *'ai kapu* and the Christian invasion of Hawai'i. Up to that historical moment, it may be said that the Hawaiians were still the shapers of their own destinies, while the newcomers—whether Cook, or the soldiers of fortune, or the diseases they brought—were still being subsumed under cultural changes the Hawaiians themselves had initiated. The year 1819 was a turning point for Hawai'i.

Meanwhile, the novel's first sentence—"The date is 1840."—foreshadows a time when, according to Twain's statements, the hero must already be dying of leprosy. The fictional Bill Ragsdale would then be thirty-three years of age, and leprosy would historically have begun its awful march through the islands. The picturesque description of the "Isles of the Blest" may well be ironic, painting pastoral scenery for some opening action *in medias res*, as in the epic convention, contrary to the idyllic manner of the rest of the opening paragraph. Or perhaps the beginning explicitly foretells the end, the beautiful islands arrayed like flowers at the hero's funeral.

The other fragments (about the half-Hawaiian, half-American boy and girl, and set in the royal court) evidently jump back in time to establish the story's chronological beginning, late 1819, with "Bill Ragsdale at 12 years of age, & the heroine at 4," about to be adopted by King Kamehameha II. The three characters are as yet in good health and humor. To mark the beginning of the hero's tragedy with the Hawaiians' breaking of the *kapu* system and the arrival of the missionaries shortly afterward (and, four years later, the deaths of Kamehameha II and Kamāmalu by measles), Twain departs from the dates of the real Bill Ragsdale's life (183?–77). In choosing the year 1819 as the beginning of his fictional hero's story, Twain seizes a pivotal moment of high historical drama in and between the two cultures, to be explored in Ragsdale's character and in nineteenth-century Hawai'i.

We might reconstruct, then, how the rest of Twain's novel, involving suffering and presumably death by a loathsome disease in a supposed paradise, may have compassed the dichotomies he witnessed in his travels through Hawai'i. The opening passage itself, with its cloying jargon, redolent with sentimentality, insinuates that its dream of the islands is vain: "There they lie, the divine islands, forever inviting you, never repulsing you . . . ." Implicitly, the islands are forever unattainable, contrary to what the words promise. This is so, at least, of the ideal of refuge they represent. Twain evokes a yearning that could not be satisfied in fact and that he would not satisfy in fiction, for he knew the tragic course of Hawaii's history in his century.

But why was the Sandwich Islands novel never published? Twain's fiction at the time was rooted in his own local upbringing. Hawai'i was perhaps more alien to him than, say, the British Isles or even the Holy Land had ever seemed. As sensitive as Twain was to his native locale and region—and likewise to the lands he avidly visited—might he have questioned whether he had the understanding needed to write a Hawai'i novel? But Twain never mentions any such difficulty in his correspondence. His 24 January 1884 letter to Mrs. Fairbanks intimates instead his concern that he himself might be misunderstood and maligned. The work might "damn" him, he thought, although his wife Livy reassured him that it would not. Still, he was evidently seeking further assurance by asking Mrs. Fairbanks to read the manuscript. What troubled him?

The first trouble may have been "Ragsdale's leper business," judging from what several commentators on Twain's Hawaiian works imply. In the novel, the disease itself would bring an awful testimony to bear against the image of paradise. Possibly, too, since the disease was introduced after the coming of the whites, leprosy might have symbolized for Twain the destruction of paradise by exotic elements planted in a vulnerable Hawaiian soil—an obvious possibility in a novel informed by Christian concepts of sin, guilt, and the myth of Eden, where outsiders play the serpent, rather than by a contrasting vision of the Hawaiians' own control over great cultural and political changes prior to the missionaries' arrival from Connecticut.

Let us consider how unreceptive his audiences would have been to Twain's exposure of leprosy in his Hawai'i novel. Rather than draw upon documents of medical history and trace the course of people's beliefs and attitudes toward the disease through the centuries, we need only turn to literary commentators' attempts to explain why Twain fails to mention leprosy in either his Sacramento *Union* letters or *Roughing It*. These commentaries suggest that readers would have been repelled by any mention of the disease. Specifically, in the case of Twain's letters from Hawai'i, the reason usually adduced for Twain's silence is that any mention of leprosy would have caused the *Union*'s business readers to balk at its earnest attempts to promote a California-Hawai'i commerce.[26] But the historical context and Twain's own words raise questions about his explanation. Who among his seriously business-minded readers in 1866 could have been ignorant of the presence of leprosy in Hawai'i? Who was trying to hide it completely, and who could have done so? In 1884, Twain would hardly suppress his own novel because of leprosy, when he himself sometimes began his Sandwich Islands lecture by describing his first memorable sight in Hawai'i—a victim of the so-called Oriental leprosy was looking his way on the dock as he disembarked, as if the pitiful figure were there to greet him.[27] In the year of Twain's visit, the Hawaiian government had begun shipping lepers from that very dock to the newly designated leper settlement on the island of Moloka'i. The scourge was great. Twain had seen the horror firsthand and had been intensely moved by what he saw. Whatever the case with his *Union* letters, he was not interested in concealing it from his lecture audience.

A second possibility is that Twain might have been anxious about the issue of mixed race integral to his Hawai'i novel. Unlike *A Connecticut Yankee* or *Huckleberry Finn*, the racial issue in the Hawai'i novel was embodied in a single character, Bill Ragsdale, who also embodied the conjunction and conflict of *cultures* that Twain planned to dramatize. The question Twain posed about Ragsdale's childhood, his inherited or his native beliefs and his conversion to Christianity, echoed questions raised by Jarves in *Kiana* and foreshadowed the mystery of *Pudd'nhead Wilson* (first published as a book in 1894), where Twain enacted the same principle he asserted to Howells regarding the Hawai'i novel: when tested in crisis, one cannot escape the circumstances of one's birth. It was a question for Twain of whether the main factors are environmental, or racially inherited, or both. And in the Hawai'i novel, everything would seem to have some intercultural significance. Even the spittoon in the humorous fragment symbolizes Western culture and a new age, if not of gold, then of brass among a people who only yesterday were wielders of stone and wood. In such a mosaic, Ragsdale's character may have integrated the two cultures, but not in any simple way. As Twain indicated to Howells, Ragsdale's ancient Hawaiian religion, in which he was born and trained until at least the age of twelve, probably reasserted itself under great duress, shattering his "shallow Christianity."[28] Unavoidably, too, the struggle was not only between two religions but also between two races, represented by the white Christian missionaries on one side of Ragsdale and the brown-skinned native Hawaiians on the other—and by Ragsdale in and of himself.

So the racial issue peculiar to it placed a heavy burden on Twain's Hawai'i novel. Might it have been too mechanical a way of analyzing and developing a human character, for instance, to base Ragsdale on the premise that he was ever warring within himself on account of his racial mix? Twain had evidently observed no such inner conflict in the actual Ragsdale: rather, when watching Ragsdale at work he marveled at the man's adroit act of interpreting between two cultures. Clearly, however, it would have been dishonest to avoid race as an important element in characterizing Ragsdale and as an issue in Hawaii's cultural dynamics; and it seems unlikely in the face of Ragdale's tragedy that Twain would simply resort to the cliché that Hawaii's racial blending melts all these issues away. Seen in Twain's report of Ragsdale at work in the Commons of the legislature, the essence of his vitality was the singularity of an identity and sensibility forged of two cultures. The possibilities for wit, irony, tricksterism, and duplicity in the multicultural Hawaiian setting were not lost on Twain, who saw the bicultural Ragsdale both as knowing more than a person of one culture and as able to exploit his ironical position:

Bill Ragsdale stands up in front of the Speaker's pulpit . . .
and fastens his quick black eye upon any member who rises,
lets him say half a dozen sentences, and then interrupts him,
and repeats his speech in a loud, rapid voice, turning every
Kanaka speech into English and every English speech into Kanaka, with a readiness and felicity of language that are remarkable . . . . His tongue is in constant motion from eleven in
the forenoon till four in the afternoon, and why it does not
wear out is the affair of Providence, not mine. There is a spice
of deviltry in the fellow's nature, and it crops out every now
and then when he is translating the speeches of slow old Ka-
nakas who do not understand English. Without departing from
the spirit of a member's remarks, he will, with apparent uncon-
sciousness, drop in a little voluntary contribution occasionally
in the way of a word or two that will make the gravest speech
utterly ridiculous. . . . The rascal.[29]

Twain wrote this report in 1866, well before anyone knew Ragsdale's
fate. Ragsdale's death by leprosy in 1877 perhaps moved Twain to attempt
the novel. While the novel, if published, might have strengthened a tourist
literary tradition weakened by clichés, it might conceivably have distinguished itself more in exploring questions of racial and cultural relations
pertinent to an American society where race is a sensitive and deeply
established issue.

To speculate upon Twain's intent with regard to these issues is
to come up against an insistently narrow "misreading" as to Twain's missionary bias. Insofar as such readings have both reflected and shaped a
Hawai'i literary tradition, they are worth noting here. Twain himself
may have been derailed by the dilemma, which he could not adequately
address through the third-person narrative of his projected Hawai'i novel.
At the crux of this argument, Fred W. Lorch and, following him, A.
Grove Day assert that Twain would have sided with the New England
missionaries in the novel, who would in effect battle the Hawaiian priests
as the Yankee battles Merlin, with, presumably, Ragsdale's soul as a prize.
To support his assumption about Twain's missionary allegiance, Lorch
points to the historian Jarves's abhorrence of certain aspects of Hawaii's
ancient religion and to Twain's agreement with Jarves about the savagery
of Hawaii's history prior to the rise of Christianity.[30] But Lorch omits
to note that both writers also found great virtues in Hawaiian history
and culture: in general their judgments of events in Hawaiian history seem

not to be based on race. For instance, Twain repeats Jarves's harsh, hu-morless attack, not against the Hawaiians as savage hosts but against Cap-tain Cook as an ungrateful guest who overstayed his welcome. And un-derlying the humor of his satire in most other instances, one of the remarkable qualities of Twain's observations of Hawai'i is his circumspec-tion in judging the Hawaiians and their islands. When viewing the Hale-akalā sunrise, he locates himself metaphorically between disparate points of view, "pinnacled in mid-heaven" and situated between the heavenly and the earthly of his Hawaiian experience. It is very difficult to see this duality of Twain's vision if one reductively assumes that he must be taking sides between the missionaries and the natives. To be sure, reminiscent of Tommo's far more immediate horror of cannibalism in *Typee*, Twain in the *Union* letters and *Roughing It* abhors the human sacrifice the ancients used to perform on the long stone of the temple, a ritual that had occurred right through Kamehameha's conquests of the 1790s, and perhaps more recently. Twain seems to credit the missionaries for helping to end such practices. But he is nonetheless angered that the Hawaiians may once have been happy, peaceful, sad, and warlike in their own way, as their own occasions required and their own aspirations guided them, doing well enough by themselves, enjoying and suffering their share in life in sufficient measure—until the missionaries "braved a thousand privations" to come to this paradise and make these na-tives "permanently miserable by telling them how beautiful and bliss-ful . . . heaven is, and how nearly impossible to get there," especially with the pagan sins of the natives' past.[31]

Lorch acknowledges Twain's ambivalence but chooses sides just the same. His support comes in part from his reading of *A Connecticut Yankee*, which he argues is strongly influenced by Twain's never-published novel of Hawai'i. That Twain is on the Yankee's side against the savage Britons, as Lorch reads the novel, is further evidence that Twain sides with the missionaries against the unconverted or backsliding Sandwich Island natives.[32] In either case, these alliances are highly sus-pect. How would Twain deal with readers' applause for the victory of either side, when both sides lose in the death of even one good person —who belongs to both sides to begin with—the Bill Ragsdale who in-trigued Twain for decades?

It is highly unlikely that Twain's novel of the Sandwich Islands departed radically from the social consciousness expressed in his other works based upon comparable plots, characterizations, settings, genres, and themes. Here a parallel between Twain's Hawai'i writings and *A*

Connecticut Yankee is useful—not to demonstrate a direct influence, as Lorch argues, but to suggest how Twain's way of handling a novel ostensibly about a primitive people of a faraway island visited by a modern man who finds he has a mission can illuminate the author's strategy in the earlier Hawai'i novel. While the protagonists of the two works are in a sense opposites—Hank Morgan being the missionary, and Bill Ragsdale, the convert—Twain in his moral vision and manner of expression has a consistent way of examining such characters and their situations.

There is, for instance, a phrase that recurs in Twain's descriptions of the Hawaiian and the Arthurian settings, matching a setting and mood found at moments in other works as well. In his lecture "Our Fellow Savages of the Sandwich Islands," he would sometimes end with these words of tribute to Hawai'i: "It is a Sunday land. The land of indolence and dreams, where the air is drowsy and things tend to repose and peace, and to emancipation from the labor, and turmoil, and weariness, and anxiety of life."[33] Elsewhere in his works, Twain's evocation of "a Sunday land" signals a conflict soon to come. The Yankee's description of Camelot's environs, shortly after he awakens there, resembles Twain's dream of Hawai'i both in wording and consequently in the feelings evoked: "It was a soft, reposeful summer landscape," Hank Morgan says, "as lovely as a dream, and as lonesome as Sunday."[34] The Connecticut Yankee's sojourn in King Arthur's realm thus begins as an idyll. It is an illusory retreat from a complex, technologically advanced, urban world, the West Hartford of the 1880s with its Colt gun works, to what appears to be a simple, backward, rural setting ruled by noble though primitive and savage men. Set loose in an unspoiled landscape and among a people who appear to be simpletons on excursions from an asylum, as far as the disoriented Yankee can at first tell, the machine-age foreigner sets out zealously to reform both man and nature. He considers the field his for the exploiting.

What then does *Connecticut Yankee* show us about how "primitive" people are to be judged, in Twain's view? He pits Hank Morgan and his nineteenth-century technology against Merlin and the Britons under his sway. But the *values* Twain upholds in the novel tell another story. In tone, the novel is a satire of the brutalities within both societies: the sixth-century feudal Britain and the nineteenth-century Republican America. Among the ironies pervading *Connecticut Yankee* is that Hank Morgan is happily trapped within his own self-assurance, his own point of view, his own ethnocentrism, as it were. He considers himself morally and intellectually superior to the Britons, a highly questionable stance in light of the havoc he wreaks and the many lives he numbers as victims of his power and technology. Jousting and all the martial requirements of knighthood may have been bloody and savage; but the Yankee himself prances through the lists triumphant with his six-guns smoking. Whether by gunfire or by electrocution, he kills as if magically, apparently without shedding blood; but that can hardly be a testament to the Yankee's moral superiority, no matter how vocal he himself is in condemning such violence when others inflict it. The similarities between Morgan and the primitives he finds himself among are evident from the start. He lands in sixth-century Britain by losing his wits in the nineteenth-century American equivalent of a joust. One day in the Colt factory, where he is a superintendent with a "couple of thousand men under me," as he complacently puts it, he is dealt a blow as crude and effective as any knight's: "It was during a misunderstanding conducted with crowbars with a fellow we used to call Hercules. He laid me out with a crusher alongside the head that made everything crack" (5). Using a narrator, the Yankee himself, who is sensitive to and compassionately critical of the suffering that the feudal savages inflict upon one another, but who is utterly unaware of his own moral shortcomings and how others must suffer on his account, Twain does not state the matter explicitly, nor does he need to: the industrial world that the Yankee gets knocked from by Hercules's crowbar is, in some deep-seated respects, like the feudal world he lands in—because in the first place he is an inheritor of Arthur's culture. But the Yankee cannot appreciate the similarity because he is quite simply blind to it.

Against such a reading, and arguing instead from the premise of Hank Morgan's moral superiority, Lorch concludes that the Hawai'i novel championed the Connecticut missionaries and condemned the Hawaiian natives on account of their ancient idolatry and feudalism. The evidence of Twain's own words, meanwhile, as well as of his other works containing intercultural and interracial themes, shows otherwise. The Hawai'i novel presumably ends with Ragsdale's death by leprosy, his only "apparently reasonabler" Christian faith—or "folly"—powerless to help him, and the ancient Hawaiian religious "folly he was born in" once more in charge. Twain's words to Howells shows his cynicism about aspects of the missionaries' work. It is difficult to grant Lorch's premise that, in effect, Twain, of all writers, would be so narrowly evangelical as to devote an entire novel to punishing his hero with death by leprosy and damning him ever after for abandoning his adopted Christian faith or even possibly for being abandoned and thus being victimized by that faith. Twain's comments commit him to neither side in the religious and cultural drama he describes. It is more likely that, given the evidence of the 1884 letter to Howells, Twain intended to end the novel as a somehow balanced elegy for all that had passed away: for the virtues of the ancient Hawaiian religion and culture, for the good works and intentions of the missionaries, as well as for Bill Ragsdale himself and the contemporary, lively, and tragic Hawai'i he embodied. With perhaps a somewhat lighter load of moral cargo to bear and somewhat more familiar seas to sail in, it may be that *Connecticut Yankee* in a sense enabled Twain to have his great island novel after all. Perhaps he had somehow anticipated the severe misreading to which his Hawai'i novel was vulnerable and to which it has indeed been subjected. How strangely contradictory it would have seemed, had the work been published and misread as anti-Hawaiian, pro-missionary propaganda, when Twain came at the turn of the century to be a symbol for bitter opposition to American imperialism in the Pacific.

In yet another respect, what survives of Twain's Hawai'i novel implies how critically different it is from *Huckleberry Finn* and *A Connecticut Yankee,* and this element may also have influenced Twain to abandon the project. It may be that from his own experience—or lack of it—Twain could not adequately realize the Ragsdale character. Twain did visit Hawai'i for a very active four months. But he may have found it difficult to enter, so to speak, the nature of a Bill Ragsdale as he could a Huck Finn or a Hank Morgan. Unlike the other two works, but like the later *Pudd'nhead Wilson,* the Hawai'i novel is narrated in the third person, not by a central character acting as both participant and observer. It appears that Twain tried to instill, then perhaps to reverse, certain moral changes in the character of Ragsdale. Whether he could draw a pattern of moral changes satisfactorily in the third person is uncertain; and even in Twain's more customary use of first-person narrators to explore moral issues, fundamental changes rarely happen convincingly. Indeed, moral changes fail to occur in Huck Finn and Hank Morgan at the most crucial levels. Moreover, Ragsdale's situation is unlike Huck Finn's, Hank Morgan's, or that of typical male protagonists of complex pastorals in this American literary tradition. Like Andrew Marvell's Fairfax in "Upon Appleton House" or his Cromwell in "An Horatian Ode," the American protagonists in the tradition retreat to a supposed pastoral setting and, having learned from or become vitally renewed through that experience, they return to a life of social action. In his own way, Thoreau lived this pattern.

Melville's Ishmael rehearsed it on the epic stage of *Pequod*'s decks and the seven seas. The pattern is clear in *Typee*, and in both these works by Melville, the resulting social action includes the surviving narrator's first-person story that he has lived to tell. While in some ways Twain seems to play on the dream of an island retreat, he might finally have come to a dead end on account of it. His third-person narrative about a man exiled into the world of lepers would allow for no return to urban society, no way to test, within the novel, what the experience may have meant not only to Ragsdale but also to his outside world. It indeed is no pastoral romance at all, not even in some literary form of primitivism. With death at its center and not in the background, where the conventional *memento mori* of pastorals is expected to remain, the story is of another genre entirely, a tragedy—not only of Ragsdale but of Hawai'i as well. And in the fragments of the novel, there appears no character—no fellow shepherd, as it were—to bear witness to Ragsdale's life and death and to sing his elegy.

　　Twain's 1884 correspondence is his last surviving, explicit mention of the novel. Still, it is remarkable how the story and the facts underlying it appear to have haunted him for at least another decade. Quite naturally, by the 1890s Twain's actual visit to Hawai'i was not much more than the stuff of memories. In 1895–96 Twain undertook a worldwide lecture tour and wrote about it in *Following the Equator*. Near the tour's beginning he had a chance to see Hawai'i again for the second and last time in his life. But on arriving in Hawaiian waters, he and his shipmates learned that the islands were quarantined because of cholera. He had to resign himself to viewing O'ahu from offshore: "Thus did my dream of twenty-nine years go to ruin," writes Twain of his disappointment.[35] Still, he spent hours on deck gazing at the island and revolving the matter of Hawai'i in his mind. What he saw now was a result of his distance from shore and the distance of his memories from the Hawai'i of what he considered his day, 1866. His view of Hawai'i in *Following the Equator* is largely idyllic and nostalgic—regretful that Hawai'i had encountered rough sailing in the intervening decades of economic and political spoliation.

　　The Hawai'i chapter of *Following the Equator* concludes, however, not with the picturesque, not with the idyllic, not with an elegy simply for times past. Twain instead raises a subject he seemed earlier to have buried: leprosy and the fate of Bill Ragsdale. Although in 1884 he referred knowingly to "Ragsdale's leper business," he writes about it in *Following the Equator* as if he only now had learned of it and the man's "case of self-sacrifice." "I asked after him," he writes, "and was told that his prosperous career was cut short in a sudden and unexpected way, just as he was about to marry a beautiful half-caste girl." Twain recounts how, having discovered by "some early invisible sign" that he was afflicted with leprosy, Ragsdale turned himself in to be shipped to the leper settlement on Moloka'i. Had he kept his secret, Ragsdale could have married and carried on his career for a while longer. But he had sacrificed temporary fulfillment of these aspirations in order to prevent dooming his beloved with the disease.[36] On Moloka'i, the noble Ragsdale "died the loathsome and lingering death that all lepers die" (63).

Twenty-nine years after a delighted and admiring Twain actually saw the "rascal" Ragsdale holding forth on the floor of the Hawaiian legislature, and eleven years since he attempted a novel with Ragsdale as hero, the story still tugged at his imagination and sympathies. It is curious that here, in *Following the Equator*, Twain publishes a synopsis of the plot of his abandoned novel, and that he tells it now as the nonfictional story of Ragsdale. He provides further observations that make the Ragsdale story even more poignant. Leprosy, Twain believed, was transmitted to the "innocent" victim from ancestors guilty of "sins" that incurred the "curse" of leprosy, though the guilty ancestors themselves escaped unharmed (64). It appears that Twain thought the disease both physical and spiritual. One wonders to which ancestors, of New England, or of Hawai'i, Twain might have imputed the guilt—and guilt for what?

Twain closes the chapter by telling of an "inexpressibly touching and beautiful" custom at the leper settlement: "When death sets open the prison door of life there, the band salutes the freed soul with a burst of music!" Remarkably Twain thus takes his leave of Hawai'i with a strong image of escape—not an escape from a corrupt world to the paradise island, but from the island prison to the paradise and freedom of the afterlife.

In Hawai'i today, a century after one of the islands' most famous visiting writers struggled with the problems of writing a great Hawaiian novel, Twain's best-known piece of writing about Hawai'i is the phrase, "the loveliest fleet of islands that lies anchored in any ocean."[37] Generations who have seen this advertisement of Hawai'i have ignored the fact that Twain's expression itself is couched in the metaphor of ships—oceanic symbols of progress, commerce, the American Navy in the Pacific, and civilization in general. His remark has come to stand for a vacation away from all of that. Meanwhile, his projected novel of Hawai'i and the nature of that work are virtually unknown. This highly selective exploitation of the idyllic, where snatches of Twain's Hawai'i works are put to use by promoters of tourism, mistakenly isolates him not only from the writers of Hawaii's literature who came before him—such as Jarves and Melville, or the artists in a tradition of native Hawaiian chant and poetry—but from those who have followed in the century since, whether these writers be visitors or locals. Whatever the qualities of their treatments of the subject, Robert Louis Stevenson, Jack London, James Michener, and other visitors since 1866 have written about the dark side of Hawai'i as symbolized by the leper settlement. So have Hawaii's own historical novelist O. A. Bushnell (*Molokai*, 1963, a work resembling Twain's novel in several interesting respects) and dramatist Aldyth Morris (*Damien*, 1980).[38] Twain alone is interpreted as writing only of the light side of a light subject.

As it is, however, Twain did face the dark side of a supposed earthly paradise. His sympathy, pity, and fear were deeply moved by what he saw and learned of the leprosy victims. Maybe through them Twain came to see the humanity of Hawaiians, quite apart from their stock comic use, their noble-savage or hula-girl image, or the parodies of these stereotypes in literature. In his Hawai'i novel, with what appears to be its insistent dialectic between heaven and hell, Twain apparently struggled to deal with an extreme of human suffering and to map a middle ground between what he called the "romantic" idealization and the "unvarnished truth" of Hawai'i. Despite his effort to slice through the conventional, simplistic rapture over the islands' natural charms, Twain—and the very thought of a "literature" of Hawai'i—have unfortunately been bound to a simple pastoral illusion.

Hawaii's Pastoral

From *Mele Hula* to the Childhood Idyll

I

Whether their natures be understood or misunderstood, whether they be respected or considered frivolous, Hawaii's songs form the literary and cultural bases for Hawaii's pastoral today. In the popular imagination, Hawaii's songs embody the love, the loveliness, and the simple sentiments attributed to Hawaii's people and their paradisiacal island home. This embodiment is especially evident when the songs are set to movement in the "modern" hula dance. The hula dancer, her dance, and her song are the pastoral dream incarnate, whether in Hawai'i or abroad.

Hawaiians themselves, however, know the hula to be but one part of a cultural, political, and indeed commercial life of much greater scope. Current revivals of *hula kahiko*, the ancient forms of hula, demonstrate anew the extent and profundity of the art of hula itself, which goes far beyond the informal modern hula (*hula 'auana*) familiar to tourists and non–Polynesian residents of Hawai'i alike through much of this century. When Charles Warren Stoddard recorded in 1873 his fortunate observation of the ancient hula, the art was barely reemerging from underground; and Stoddard, the tourist in quest of the idyllic, had scarcely the means for interpreting these vigorous, heroic dances.[1] Judging Hawai'i by its modern hula and love songs is like judging the European Renaissance by its sonnets alone, or the American mainland exclusively by its country and western music and lyrics. (Indeed, Hawaiian music of the past hundred years has from time to time been compared in scope, in certain musical characteristics, and in cultural function with country and western.) But no matter how enjoyable and significant one may find popular Hawaiian lyrical song and dance to be, to assess the entire culture by these modes of artistry alone is to view it narrowly and to miss out on available riches.[2]

Hawaiian music and lyrics have a deceptive simplicity unless one understands the language of *nā mele*—the songs, lyrics, or poetry. Today poets in the Hawaiian language still compose highly complex lyrics following poetic requirements and conventions and using technical skills stemming from ancient times. Those listeners who are unfamiliar with the language—its limited sounds—and therefore the value of its poetic stresses, repetition, assonance, and other features—are inclined to praise or to ridicule the language of Hawaii's songs for a primitive charm that babbles ever on the edge of self-parody, as in a "Wicky Wacky Hula." The problem is that this very quality is considered all the more charming because it fits the island paradise dream.

Hawaii's most renowned song worldwide, "Aloha 'Oe," illustrates not only the simplistic uses to which the song has been put but also the actual complexity of the song itself and its genre. In the account provided by Samuel H. Elbert and Noelani Mahoe in their collection and study of *Nā Mele o Hawai'i Nei: 101 Hawaiian Songs*, the young woman who in 1891 was to succeed her brother David Kalākaua to the throne and become Hawaii's last reigning monarch, Lili'uokalani wrote "Aloha 'Oe" when inspired by an incident she witnessed in 1877.[3] One of Hawaii's greatest songwriters, Lili'u is said to have seen two lovers parting with a final embrace while she rode on horseback through forests near the Nu'uanu Pali. She wrote the song while at Maunawili, in Kailua, O'ahu, to which the song refers at the end. Elbert and Mahoe further recount that Queen Lili'uokalani once heard her "Aloha 'Oe" "sung at the funeral of a missionary friend. She was shocked, for 'This is a love song,' she said afterwards, but was told that the song would live forever as a song of farewell" (Elbert and Mahoe, 35). Eminently well versed in Hawaiian poetry, Lili'uokalani had a sense of decorum based on knowledge of diverse poetic types and functions, a sense that her audiences generally have lacked, particularly in approaching the Hawaiian song. "Aloha 'Oe," in its popular reception, was transformed from a love song into something quasi-elegiac—"that soft farewell with a dying fall," as Gavan Daws echoes the usual sentiment.[4] And, especially in the tourist industry, the song now evokes a visitor's sweetly sad departure from Hawai'i and promotes the obvious wish that the visitor will return, as the singer promises.

This is Lili'uokalani's "Aloha 'Oe," with a translation by Elbert and Mahoe:

Ha'aheo'ē ka ua i nā pali	Proudly the rain on the cliffs
Ke nihi a'ela i ka nahele	Creeps into the forest
E uhai ana paha i ka liko	Seeking the buds
Pua 'āhihi lehua o uka.	And miniature *lehua* flowers of the uplands.

Hui	*Chorus*
Aloha 'oe, aloha 'oe,	Farewell to you, farewell to you,
E ke onaona noho i ka lipo.	O fragrance in the blue depths.
One fond embrace, a ho'i a'e au	One fond embrace and I leave
A hui hou aku.	To meet again.

'O ka hali'a aloha ka i hiki mai	Sweet memories come
Ke hone a'e nei i ku'u manawa.	Sound softly in my heart.
'O 'oe nō ka'u ipo aloha	You are my beloved sweetheart
A loko e hana nei.	Felt within.

Maopopo ku'u 'ike i ka nani	I understand the beauty
Nā pua rose o Mauna-wili	Of rose blossoms at Mauna-wili
I laila ho'ohie nā manu,	There the birds delight,
Miki'ala i ka nani o ia pua.	Alert the beauty of this flower.
	(Pp. 35–36)

What, in terms of Hawaiian poetics, is noteworthy about this composition? In the opening stanza the rain on the cliffs creeping into the forest and seeking the buds refers not only to the actual setting described (in this case, the wet uplands of Nu'uanu), but also to the approach and the embrace of the two lovers. In this poetic tradition, flowers and birds usually refer to women, sometimes to both women and men. Like the flowers, the rain metaphor of the poem carries a strong sexual connotation. Both the indirectness and presence of *kaona* (inner or underlying meaning) are poetic attributes and are generally to be appreciated in "Aloha 'Oe." The final stanza takes up the incipient narrative at the time of the poem's actual composition: the woman embracing her lover in the misty forest is said to have been the poet's sister, Likelike, one of the beautiful "rose blossoms at Mauna-wili," one of the "birds" taking further "delight," now on the windward side of the Nuʻuanu Pali. The missionaries, both the dead and the living, would no doubt have been as shocked as Liliʻu had they known these playful and joyous, amorous and sexual meanings when the song was performed at that funeral.

It must be cautioned, however, that features of the Hawaiian language and poetic art, promoting ambiguity and indirection, make it easy to read too much into the Hawaiian song's kaona. Elbert and Mahoe cite the example of the Irish poet Padraic Colum who, commissioned by the territorial legislature in the early 1920s, wrote a book on Hawaiian legends, but "rewrote them in an Irish vein" (Elbert and Mahoe, 17): "He did not know the language, but saw hidden meanings everywhere, and he claimed . . . that every Hawaiian poem had at least four meanings —an ostensible meaning, a vulgar meaning, a mythicohistorial-topographical meaning, and a deeply hidden meaning." The Hawaiian scholar Mary Kawena Pukui responded to Colum's observation by pointing out that "there are but two meanings: the literal and the *kaona*, or inner meaning. The literal is like the body, and the inner meaning is like the spirit of the poem. . . . There are some poems that have no inner meaning, and to read such meanings into them is folly" (quoted in Elbert and Mahoe, 17). Elbert and Mahoe add, "To say that every poem has a vulgar meaning sounds like a comment by some of the more extreme nineteenth-century missionaries" (Elbert and Mahoe, 17). I have nonetheless heard a panel of Hawaiian lyricists discuss their art in terms familiar to Western literary analysis and exegesis, where as many as *five* levels of meaning, including of course the "vulgar," also called the "sexual" or "procreative," were postulated for the best compositions.[5]

Part of the point here is that the art of Hawaiian poetry in the Hawaiian language is not a traditional practice frozen long ago like an old lava flow. In today's Hawaiian Renaissance, literary issues are subject to and indeed are subjected to much lively debate between those who try to preserve tradition as it *was*, at its best and purest, and those who innovate, adapting tradition as a continually growing and changing body. In some way or another every practitioner of native Hawaiian arts today must deal creatively with both these pulls. Similarly, in the Hawaiian Renaissance we find renewed enthusiasm for and controversies over languages, both the native Hawaiian and Hawaii's vernacular pidgins and creoles—and the relationships of these with the rough equivalent of Medieval Europe's Latin standard, today's "standard English," in Hawaii's rich linguistic milieu.

As a representative Hawaiian song, "Aloha 'Oe" demonstrates the desired formal parallelism between the literal meaning and the kaona, between the actual witnessed incident and the poet's interpretation of it. The manner of expression thus admired in this and other Hawaiian songs is in some ways comparable to the manner, say, of the Japanese courtiers and ladies who communicate through poems at once both allusive and direct in Lady Murasaki's *The Tale of Genji*. In other ways, Hawaiian songs resemble both Japanese haiku and medieval European lyrics in the former's concentration of a particular moment of inspiration and the circumstances that sparked it, and the latter's serene assumption of the interrelatedness of things natural, human, and divine. But the songs still have their strict or proper limitations.

One limitation is thematic. This limitation is basically related to the kind of poetry appropriate to any given occasion or situation. Aside from the impropriety of using a non-Christian poetic form to accompany a Christian missionary to his paradise, Queen Lili'uokalani's shock on hearing "Aloha 'Oe" (a *mele hula*) sung at a funeral was because the occasion would have called for poetry not meant for hula: either a dirge (a type of *oli*) or a conventional Hawaiian Christian hymn (*hīmeni*). In Hawaiian poetics, sounding a dirge would mean offering a solemn chant, or oli, of the kind called *kanikau*, performed in the style of lamentation (*ho'ouwēuwē*). A mele or song like "Aloha 'Oe" was especially inappropriate since the rank of the deceased warranted some gravity. Although a very few mele, rather than chants, are considered to be dirges, and a number are clearly elegies, songs in general are not the vehicles for directly expressing grief, hardship, or the heroic, epic, and tragic aspects of life, history, and the Hawaiian culture. These themes fall into the realm of specific kinds of *oli*, chants often of great seriousness for narrating mythological and historical epics, for eulogizing, for praying, for the recitation of genealogy, or for the paying of tribute to the deceased by means of a dirge. This basic, conventional distinction between mele hula (song to be danced) and certain kinds of oli (sacred and historical chants) has no doubt reinforced the image of Hawai'i as a romantic paradise, for it is the mele hula that has been popularized around the world.[6] This may be because the lyrics of the mele, as distinct from those of the oli, seem somewhat closer to romantic Western sentiments about Hawai'i and appear to be more easily translatable into simple terms. To cite one analogy, Wordsworth's "lyrical ballads" are on the surface easier to understand than Spenser's *Faerie Queen* or Milton's *Paradise Lost*. So too, the more

easily accessible romantic side of Hawaii's own culture has received dis-
proportionate emphasis through deceptively simple songs that are only
partly understood.

Yet sometimes, too, the performance of songs disguises somber
aspects of their meanings with the appearance of happiness. This is obviously a difficulty for the audience ignorant of the song's words. Nowadays
it is quite usual that a performer will introduce a song by telling the
audience in English what the song means in Hawaiian. Song collections
and translations such as Elbert's and Mahoe's and those often provided
on Hawaiian record albums and liners serve a valuable purpose. Recently
Hawaii's general audiences have been surprised to learn, for instance, the
meaning of "Kaulana nā Pua" (famous are the flowers, i.e., the people),
sung and danced by performers wreathed in great smiles, plying hand
gestures that, no matter how accurately expressive to those in the know,
could not possibly convey meaning to the uninitiated. It is just possible,
however, that the exuberance of this mele was ironically meant to disguise its dangerous political theme from those authorities who may have
been truly ignorant of the native Hawaiians' point of view. Far from
being cheerful, "Kaulana nā Pua" is a bitter song of protest and rebellion
against the imminent annexation of Hawai'i by the United States. When
in 1893 an American band of businessmen led by Sanford Dole dethroned
Queen Lili'uokalani, Ellen Wright Prendergast wrote the patriotic Hawaiian song and gave it the title, "Mele 'Ai Pōhaku," the stone-eating
song. This enigmatic title alludes to a fundamental value called *aloha 'āina*
(love of the land) and is best explained by the central stanzas:

A'ole a'e kau i ka pūlima	No one will fix a signature
Ma luna o ke pepa o ka 'enemi	To the paper of the enemy
Ho'ohui 'āina kū'ai hewa	With its sin of annexation
I ka pono sivila a'o ke kanaka.	And sale of native civil rights.
'A'ole mākou a'e minamina	We do not value
I ka pu'ukālā a ke aupuni.	The government's sums of money.
Ua lawa makou i ka pōhaku	We are satisfied with the stones,
I ka 'ai kamaha'o o ka 'āina.	Astonishing food of the land.
	(Elbert and Mahoe, 62–64).

According to Elbert and Mahoe, the song, powerfully invoking
the names and the territories of Hawaii's ancient chiefs in its opening

stanzas, "was considered sacred and not for dancing" (Elbert and Mahoe, 63). Not understanding the song's words, I grew up hearing and seeing the song danced at lūʻaus without suspecting that it was anything other than a song in praise of flowers. To my knowledge, "Kaulana nā Pua" is the only bitter song among the one hundred others selected for the Elbert and Mahoe compilation. I recall hearing and watching it performed years ago, when probably no one in the audience knew its meaning. I have to wonder what those performers must have felt about our blissful ignorance of the song's real subject, and about the smiles on our faces —and theirs.

Something similar occurs in an old song, "Lā ʻElima," recently brought to public light from the fishing village of Miloliʻi, on Hawaii's Kona Coast. Sung by Diana Aki with The Sons of Hawaii, "Lā ʻElima" concerns a tragedy that occurred in the mid-nineteenth century—certainly neither the first nor the last time—when a tsunami swept over the village. The girls of the village, Aki explains before singing the mele, ran to the highlands with their elders when the receding of the ocean warned them of danger. Upon reaching a safe elevation, the fleeing people turned to watch the oncoming seismic wave and were horrified to see the village boys lagging far behind, playing where the waters had receded only for an awful moment. Massively the sea returned. The village's boys perished. Yet precisely in the spirit of mele, after thus introducing "Lā ʻElima" (meaning "the fifth day," the tragedy having occurred on the fifth of February), Aki breaks into an incredibly radiant and simply understated song passed down for a hundred years by the people of Miloliʻi. To see and hear her sing it and dance it, one might very well think it a love song.[7]

How close together love and grief can be in Hawaii's songs is again illustrated by "Ipo Lei Manu" (my cherished sweetheart who is like a bird). Queen Kapiʻolani, consort to King David Kalākaua, composed the mele for the king in his absence. Kalākaua had sailed for San Francisco in November of 1890 in an attempt to recover his failing health. There, in January 1891, Kalākaua suffered a stroke and subsequently was diagnosed to have Bright's disease.[8] On 20 January he died. What was to have been Kapiʻolani's love song for her husband the king became an elegy instead:

He manaʻo he aloha, ʻea   I have a feeling of love
No ka ipo lei manu.   For my cherished birdlike
[He] manu kuʻu hoa, ʻea   sweetheart.

Noho mai i ka nahele.   My companion is a bird
'I'iwi a'o uka   Who dwells in the forest.
Polena i ka ua.   The 'i'iwi bird of the uplands
Ha'ina ka puana   Appears yellow in the rain.
                            Tell the refrain
No ka lani hele loa.   For the chief gone forever.[9]

I cannot document my interpretation of a symbol appropriate to, though not explicit in, "Ipo Lei Manu" and some others I have used so far in this discussion to illustrate various complexities of the art of mele. That symbol is the rainbow, which marks the presence of simultaneous sunshine and rain. It is explicitly named, usually as an identifying characteristic of Hawai'i, in some newer English language Hawaiian song lyrics such as the Cazimero brothers' "Where I Live, There are Rainbows." Besides being a daily natural phenomenon and a traditional Hawaiian symbol for royalty, the rainbow is generally a good omen in Hawaiian culture, as its appearance is noted and remembered for a blessing, say, at the funerals of royalty and on other occasions when auspicious signs are sought. It would seem also that in consonance with this belief, the rainbow symbolizes some goodness radiating through the rain, as if an inner sun were shining through a veil of tears. The songs I have just discussed—again, selected not to be representative of the entire range of Hawaiian mele but to illustrate specific points—implicitly bear this quality of mixed sunshine and rain. In this way, some especially fine Hawaiian songs are not so much denials of grief and hardship as they are expressions uttered and sung in the aftermath of triumph over these adversaries, recollected in tranquility, if not forever, at least for now.[10]

Lighthearted songs on other motifs surprise listeners when they learn what these themes are. A whole body of Hawaiian songs is about machines, from another point of view the archetypal machines in America's garden. But in the Hawaiian garden, machines are sometimes transformed from an intrusion like a death's head in paradise into symbols for lovemaking or expressions of wonder. Machines in mele may be put to use in the way flowers, birds, the rain, and the beneficent landscape are. In performing the song "Maunaloa," Robert and Roland Cazimero introduce this former inter-island steamship, "supposedly with wide sides" and named after the Big Island's actively volcanic, southern mountain mass, by joking that "it would be difficult for us not to see a big woman with wide hips" when hearing the song.[11] *'Auhea wale 'oe Maunaloa lā / Kīkala nui / Ho'iho'i mai'oe i ku'u aloha lā / Ē . . . /*

Ka'awaloa nei, the mele begins (This I say to you *Maunaloa* / Ship with a broad stern / Bring my love back / E . . . / Here to Ka'awaloa). Of course not merely concerned with comparing the ship with a person, the lyrics of the song, composed by Helen Lindsey Parker perhaps in the 1920s, are spoken by a woman of Ka'awaloa, the village on Kealakekua Bay where Captain Cook was killed. She sings to her lover, a crewman or officer aboard the *Maunaloa,* about his romantic calls at island ports. This mele in particular contrasts the urban and the rural, so to speak, by means of two sharp images: the speaker refers to her lover's "tattered handkerchief," as though the finery of his being from the distant city has worn out somewhat, and to his "pointed-toe shoes," an image intimating that the speaker, unlike her more sophisticated lover, is herself barefoot on the sands. And at a deeper level, Parker, using the conceit or device of the inter-island steamship, presents a view from the shore that recalls the story of Cook's first historical arrival and the affairs of his crew in their comings and goings—the point of view *this* time, however, being the island woman's.[12]

While other songs of this kind, using machines to represent human stories, may not be as historically evocative as "Maunaloa," in general they commemorate occasions and events. The foundering of an inter-island steamer, the *Makee,* is the unlikely donnée for a love story in disguise, when the valiant ship *Malulani* seeks her out in "the swaying seas" of the channel, in the "Hula o Makee." Mele sometimes resemble mainland truckers' songs in the way they celebrate machines. Palani Vaughan sings onomatopoeic praises of the "Lahaina-Ka'anapali Train" and other machines in the garden, never once with the plaint that these locomotives violate the pastoral repose of the Hawaiian landscape. His train whistle is echoed by the Hui Ohana singing of another Maui train, "Ka'a Ahi Kahului." Eddie Kamae and the Sons of Hawaii sing with joy, humor, and energy about "Kela Mea Whiffa," the sweet breath or whiff of love, in this instance the sulfurous fumes emitted by the Lahaina Sugar Mill on Maui, a desecration that assaults the purity of Hawaii's atmosphere of love but is in turn hungrily inhaled by the wit that relishes such incongruities.[13] The machine, too, has its place in the garden of Hawaiian songs, within limits.

Even the natural imagery of the love songs can surprise. One of the most beautiful and hauntingly enigmatic Hawaiian love songs heard today is "Ku'u Ipo i ka He'e Pu'e One," probably by Princess Likelike, sister of Lili'uokalani, Kalākaua, and Leleiohoku. Ruth Leilani Tyau and S. H. Elbert translate the song's title and first line, "My sweetheart in

the rippling hills of sand" (Elbert and Mahoe, 70). Somewhat less deli-
cately, and apparently as an outright joke, the performers Robert and
Roland Cazimero translate the title, "My love is the octopus on the sand
dunes," since the *he'e* (octopus), Robert begins to explain, "is a great
delicacy here in the islands."[14] This, however, turns out to be a probably
false pun in the poem's first line. With a crude term in the first stanza,
however, the song in Hawaiian explicitly, and thus unconventionally,
mentions lovemaking. Thereafter Likelike's mele turns stanza by stanza
upon a contrast between the sea and "the forest where we delighted,"
in a way I do not profess fully to understand. And yet again, this multi-
faceted, enigmatic "Ku'u Ipo i ka He'e Pu'e One," with snatches of
English embedded in the Hawaiian, is a beautiful song:

Ku'u ipo i ka he'e pu'e one	My sweetheard in the rippling hills of sand
Me ke kai nehe i ka 'ili'ili,	With the sea rustling the pebbles,
Nipo aku i laila ka mana'o	There, the memory is impassioned
Ua kili-opu māua i ka nahele.	In the forest where we delighted.
Ka owē nenehe a ke kai	The gentle rustle of the sea
Hone ana i ka piko wai'olu	Softly in the pleasant center
I laila au la 'ike	Where I looked
Kili'opu māua i ka nahele.	We delighted in the forest.
Hiki 'ē mai ana ka makani	The wind came first.
Ua hala 'ē aku e ka Pu'ulena.	The Pu'ulena wind passed by.
Ua lose kou chance e ke hoa:	You've lost your chance, O friend:
Ua kili'opu māua i ka nahele.	She and I delighted in the forest.
Eia la e maliu mai,	Here, please listen,
Eia kō aloha i 'ane'i.	Here, your lover is here.
Hiki mai ana i ka pō nei.	He came last night.
Ua kili'opu māua i ka nahele.	We delighted in the forest. (Elbert and Mahoe, 70–71).

As far as I know, although "authentic," post-missionary Hawaiian mele thus have a greater scope of imagery and theme than commonly

expected, they neither celebrate nor value indolence. As surprising as this may seem in contrast to a popular image of Hawai'i, it makes sense. Indolence in all forms is basic to the vacationer's song, where laziness, languor, infatuation without consequence, and utter relaxation may be found, excused, catered to, but certainly not taken seriously to be the sum of what life in the islands is all about. Conversely, in the view that comes from experience of those who live and work in Hawai'i, the authentic Hawai'i pastoral reflects certain aspects of life as it is, *not* an escape from life. The Hawaiian *haku mele* (weaver of songs, or poet) is like a Thoreau at Walden, who finds abundant life and rewards not in indolence but in reflection on social affairs, in contemplation, and especially in the active examination of the pond. Although one of the most common tourist images is of a romantic Hawaiian sunset, many native songs celebrate sunrise, as in Larry Lindsey Kimura's mele to Eddie Kamae's inspired meleody, "E Ku'u Morning Dew" (beloved morning dew), which is not alone among mele in singing of the day's awakening.

According to some, as is universally true of artistic expressions of a culture, the mele helps to preserve and, more than that, to keep green the memory and value of what is. "Words bind, and words set free," a Hawaiian proverb proclaims, recognizing that poetry has certain powers over life. Translator Alfons L. Korn notes the inherent vitality of Hawaiian mele:

> Native poets of the immediate Hawaiian past . . . celebrated not only their land but also the life in and of the land: as if simply by naming and "placing" old scenes and sites of Hawai'i's familiar landscape, redeeming it as it were, the potential fierceness of the world might come to be gentled, so that sky, ocean, shore, inland forest, volcanic heap, sunburnt plain, and winding stream might go on forever, just as in the past, as man's proper and potentially friendly habitat.[15]

It is to this spirit of the Hawai'i pastoral as both an examination and a preservation of certain aspects of real life that our discussion will return after a consideration of one version of the simple pastoral that, despite the subtle complexities of mele and the broad *subversion* of the paradise theme by Melville and Twain, has dominated a narrowly construed literature of Hawai'i.

2

James A. Michener's novel *Hawaii* depends upon taking seriously the simplistic view of island pleasures, in spite of the novel's overt heroic themes. In certain respects, Michener's novel is a simple pastoral in the guise of the heroic.

It is important to discuss *Hawaii* alongside certain contemporary examples of Hawaii's literature, because Michener's work, it has been asserted, has posed a formidable barrier to the recognition and development of an indigenous literature in Hawai'i. Writing about the 1978 Talk Story Conference devoted to polyethnic literatures of Hawai'i and Asian American literatures of the mainland as well, Katherine Newman rightly observes that Michener's *Hawaii* "was very conspicuous during Talk Story—by never being mentioned at all."[16] She judges that because of its overwhelming celebrity, "*Hawaii* is clearly an obstacle to the recognition of any indigenous, synthesized, Hawaiian-American literature." I would add that *Hawaii*, because of its masked yet effective support of the simple Hawai'i pastoral, incorporates a view not likely to be shared by a local writer. How can the local writer's view of Hawai'i gain recognition when it differs from Michener's and is judged unfavorably on that account?

Michener's *Hawaii* is not overtly idyllic. It even debunks the Hawai'i paradise myths. By 1959, when Michener wrote and published the book, the ridiculing of naive Western clichés of Pacific islands was well established in Western literature, as in T. S. Eliot's crabbed parody in 1932 of the South Sea isle pastoral convention. His *Sweeney Agonistes* crew, mimicking a minstrel show, sings of life on a "cannibal isle":

> *Where the breadfruit fall*
> *And the penguin call*
> *And the sound is the sound of the sea*
> *Under the bam*
> *Under the boo*
> *Under the bamboo tree*
>
> *Where the Gauguin maids*
> *In the banyan shades*
> *Wear palmleaf drapery*
> *Under the bam . . .*[17]

Sweeney's companion and intended "little island girl" Doris objects: "That's not life, that's no life / Why I'd just as soon be dead."

"That's what life is," Sweeney slides in, "Just as is . . . Life is death" (26–27). After all, Tommo, too, finds that for the likes of himself, indolence is awfully deadly. That Sweeney's song is not about Hawai'i but about a South Seas isle hardly matters: neither does the lack of penguins on South Seas islands matter to one singing ridiculously of the Pacific from a great distance away.

There are ways other than parody to debunk the simple paradise myth. Eliot's parody suggests what the South Seas isle is *not*: it is not the clichés associated with it. But because they cannot provide insight into the islands, clichés keep us wondering what Hawai'i really is. The parody refuses to supply simple answers and mocks any attempt to do so. Other writers closer to the island scene itself wipe the glow from the myths by offering readers a presumed look into the "true" or "real" Hawai'i. Melville and Twain, each in his own way, do this in their Pacific writings.

But Melville and Twain show us the need to question myths that cloak all—the land and the people, including the narrator—in illusory fables of an earthly paradise inhabited by noble savages. The myth of Hawaii's physical beauty, too, is stripped away in some rather sensational works, among them Michener's, which thus seem to offer a realistic view yet one layer deeper into the subject than popular literature has shown us before.

Michener is not the first among authors of major works to describe Hawai'i in harsh terms of bare rock in salt water. Describing the arid volcanic wasteland in the saddle between snow-topped Mauna Kea and Mauna Loa, James Jarves in 1857 made it clear that not all of Hawaii's land is lush; and even the green land of Kiana's people takes skillful cultivation and constant toil to be made and kept productive. Echoing Jarves, Michener recounts Hawaii's geological formation, describing how, after eons of developing barely enough mass to rise above the waves, and after further eons of natural processes and events that create soil on the "new" islet where now a bird deposits a single seed, another cataclysm shakes and submerges the projecting rock yet once more in the ocean depths. Geologically and topologically, Michener shows, the islands have been barren for most of their existence. Indeed, marine biologists explain that even the seas of the islands are a clear, luminescent blue because they are relatively sterile.

Yet despite the *in*hospitable nature of the Hawaiian islands, Michener's immigrant settlers, through the centuries, heroically wrest a home in Hawai'i. Now their descendants, the "Golden Men" of

Michener's *Hawaii*, are building a utopia out of the islands' culturally mixed civilization. This is the basic plot of Michener's novel, and it is heroic.[18]

So Michener's *Hawaii* seems to incorporate the literary pastoral tradition only in part. As in epics of the European Renaissance, Michener's pastoral dreams and interludes occur in the midst of heroic action. But its plot is directed nevertheless toward a kind of simple pastoral —envisioned ultimately to lie not in Hawaii's natural or human history but in its social, cultural future. Unlike the great literary epics of the world, moreover, Michener's *Hawaii* does comparatively little to illuminate the dark, Dantean, underworld passages of the imagination and the psyche. It is difficult to imagine a blind bard at work on Michener's "epic." Not that this is necessarily a flaw. It is one of the features that distinguishes a modern, realistic genre from the literary epics of the seventeenth and prior centuries.

Michener's emphasis on action suggests an emphasis on historical narrative and, with it, faithfulness to history or to the interpreting of history truly. Yet the history which he presents, "fictionalized" from factual materials, is a kind of crafty pretense of history, the veracity of which we are invited to trust, though it does not hold up under questioning. Deliberately or not, whether anticipating criticism of the novel as being historically inaccurate or *too* accurate in exposing scandals closeted in the histories of prominent families of Hawai'i, Michener prefaces his novel with a paradoxical disclaimer: the novel is "true," but it is "imaginary"; it is fictional, yet it has the authority of scholarship. "This is a novel," Michener warns; "It is true to the spirit and history of Hawaii, but the characters, the families, the institutions and most of the events are imaginary—except that the English schoolteacher Uliassutai Karakoram Blake is founded upon a historical person who accomplished much in Hawaii."[19] Defending Michener from the criticisms that some among Hawaii's people have thrown at the book, A. Grove Day finds it necessary to caution the reader in *Books About Hawaii: Fifty Basic Authors:* "Too often its fictional treatment of a social scene is taken as gospel, even by those aware of the actual historical sequence of events."[20] In other words, what Michener asserts as the novel's underlying historicity ought not to be trusted.

The problem of veracity can also be seen in Michener's device of using one of the main characters as a narrator, yet not divulging his identity until the novel's end. This is the reverse of Melville's forthright introduction of his narrator in *Moby Dick:* "Call me Ishmael." Through nearly his entire novel, Michener's narrator is ostensibly omniscient. The impression is that the narrative voice is indeed Michener's, or close to his, bearing whatever authority Michener has gained from his research as well as biasing the story—that is, interpreting his subjects—as Michener himself may incline. Moreover, it is assumed that such an omniscient narrator undergoes no change or development affecting the novel's course, because he is uninvolved with the novel's plot. But, like Michener's perplexing opening disclaimer, the final disclosure that the narrator is Hoxworth Hale confuses rather than illuminates, because it is by then impossible to tell what difference, if any, there is between the "truth" of Hawai'i expressed by the narrator and the "truth" as seen by the author. The device of the surprise narrator, in short, hides rather than reveals what Michener himself believes, and the device is itself a disclaimer.

More obvious stylistic and structural features, however, do illuminate the grand idea behind the novel. The novel's chapters may be said to resemble epic cantos. But rather than begin *in medias res*, in the epic convention, Michener begins at the beginning of time, with the Hawaiian Islands' geological creation, a process spanning eons. It is reminiscent not only of Jarves's description of Hawaii's creation but also of the infinitely drawn out description of hell in James Joyce's *Portrait of the Artist As a Young Man*, where the priest impresses his pupils with an idea of how long and tedious an eternity spent in hell must be. The opening chapter establishes the heroic character of Hawai'i itself through the ages to come. The ensuing chapters in turn narrate the arrivals and the settlings in Hawai'i by the Polynesians, the New England missionaries, the Chinese, and the Japanese, beginning with the lives of each in their native lands. The final chapter, titled "The Golden Men," shows the modern-day interaction of these people and offers a vision (Michener's? Hoxworth Hale's?) for Hawaii's future.

Especially with reference to the Chinese, the Japanese, and the modern Polynesians in Michener's novel, it is clear that the main characters symbolize their entire races; as such, they risk being mere "prototypes" rather than "people," the characters being subservient, as one reviewer felt, to Michener's allegorical scheme of history.[21] The division of chapters by nationality reflects Michener's (the narrator's?) vision of a people whose ethnically differentiated values interact, though their bloods need not necessarily mingle: even when racially separate, the Golden Men are culturally mixed. Thus, each main character symbolizes not only his or her race but also a quality necessary to the creation of a new "race" of Golden Men. Michener's *Hawaii* is an allegory in which the Polynesian represents Nobility and Aloha; the Chinese represents Tenacity and Shrewdness in Business; the Japanese represents Loyalty and Competence; the haole, that is, the Caucasian, represents Technological Power, Ambition, and, somehow, Godliness.

A character in Michener's short story, "Povenaaa's Daughter," prefigures Michener at his own work of writing his Hawai'i epic.[22] The young French sailor Victor de la Foret aches to write an epic of Raiatea. The first and only canto resulting from his efforts "was superb and was published with distinction. It dealt with Polynesia as a physical world: the sky, the stars, the lonely islands. It was when people were introduced that the poem turned to rot" (84). Implicit in Victor's sad experience is the idea of a once-noble race, and, farther back still, of an Edenic island setting.

Unlike the pitiable and ironically named "Victor" in that story, Michener spends little time lamenting any loss of a Hawaiian paradise.[23] Far from pining for restoration of times and conditions of their past, Michener's heroes stand for progress, most conspicuously in material wealth. They stand also for progress in education, in health care, and in race relations, as the narrator reminds his readers in the final chapter. In the last analysis, the main characters of Michener's *Hawaii* prefigure the completing of a circle of grand scale. Along its curve, Michener envisions the restoration of a Euro-American vision of paradise, something his Hawai'i as a physical setting never was. He does not invoke Victor de la Foret's Raiatea, a paradise only until people arrive; this time, paradise is populous. As a version of regaining paradise, Michener's *Hawaii* is pastoral in its aim, though the impression is that once that aim has been met, the real and insatiable work of American empire-building in the Pacific is to proceed, with Hawai'i for a base.

In the novel's present, the quintessence of Michener's pastoral dream is sex. We can, for our purposes, begin in the middle of things, then work outward. Hoxworth Hale is given furlough from the business empire he and other descendants of American missionaries and merchants have built in Hawai'i. Coming in the midst of World War II, this break from all the worries of civilization is, in short, a conventional pastoral interlude.

The interlude takes place not in Hawai'i but on Bora Bora, the fabled island, the Pola-pola in the first song of the Pele cycle, from which Hawaii's original Polynesians ventured northward some twelve centuries ago. Bora Bora has an allure and promise of satisfaction that Hawai'i has lost and must henceforth recover through the good example of the land of its people's origin: this is the premise behind the episode to come.

Hoxworth Hale, forty-four-years old, head of the H & H conglomerate dominating Hawaii's economy, is asked by the U.S. Army Air Corps to join a group whose mission is to scout the South Pacific for potential airstrip sites early in 1942.

Hale's group of senior officers visits a variety of South Pacific islands, and Hale experiences something rare to him. That is, he remembers his part-Polynesian ancestry:

> When he first stepped upon an atoll reef he had the peculiar sensation that he had come home, and although for years he had forgotten the fact that he was part-Polynesian, that ancient ancestry came flooding back upon him, and often while the other officers were inspecting possible landing areas, he would remain upon the reef, looking out to sea, and long-submerged components of his blood came surging before his eyes, and he could see canoes and voyagers. (P. 746)

What more subtly influences Hale in this wartime mission into the South Pacific is his realization of how humane and prosperous Hawai'i is in comparison with the islands he now visits, where he encounters racism in many forms as well as poverty and general shabbiness. Not even Tahiti, "that Mecca of the South Seas," offers anything to delight him. That is not surprising. As yet, by no stretch of the imagination can Hoxworth Hale be considered a hedonist. He has been identified mainly as an upright descendant of stern and sturdy New England missionaries. But "he was disappointed in the legendary girls of the island, . . . for few of them had teeth" (751), the ruinous result of a recently introduced diet of Australian canned goods. Hale's disappointment betrays his latent expectations about physical pleasures.

In a PBY seaplane, Hale becomes "the first part-Hawaiian ever to see his ancestral island of Bora Bora from the air" (752), although no real attention is paid to expressing and understanding a view from the shore. The symbolism grows heavy, when clear contrasts are implied between the mechanical and the natural and between the other officers and Hale. While Hale gasps at the "sheer physical delight of this fabled island" below and proceeds "to chant fragments of a passage his great-great-great-grandfather Abner Hale had transcribed about Bora Bora," the PBY's other occupants are equally impressed—but by Bora Bora's suitability for an airstrip. "Throw a couple of bulldozers there for three days," one of them remarks about the outer reef, "and a plane could land right now" (752). Juxtaposed with Hale's own rapt musings, the engineer's remark raises the threat of the island's desecration by the machine, that ubiquitous spoiler of many an idle pastoral dream.

Yet Hale is so engrossed in his observations that he is momentarily oblivious to their war mission. "How marvelous that island was, how like a sacred home in a turbulent sea," he delights. And as the PBY approaches and settles onto the waters of Bora Bora's lagoon, Hale imagines the seaplane to be one of those "first great beasts on earth who mastered flight. They must have risen from the sea and landed on it, as the PBY now prepared to do" (753). At touchdown, Hale imagines himself as the bird/machine:

> As it reached down with its underbelly step to find the waves, he caught himself straining with his buttocks, adjusting them to insure level flight, and then seeking to let down into the waves, and he flew his bottom so well that soon the plane was rushing along the tiptop particles of the sea, half bird, half fish, and then it lost its flight and subsided into the primordial element, a plane that had conquered the Pacific and come at last to rest upon it. (P. 753)

Michener adroitly neutralizes the threat of conflict between bulldozer and reef by thus identifying man, machine, and the primordial bird. Hale never again questions the bulldozing of the island. Hale's "return" to his ancestral island of Bora Bora strangely echoes the song of Pele's expulsion from that same island, but played in reverse. This reverse echo seems exactly Michener's intended effect.

Like Melville's Taipivai, Michener's Bora Bora puts Hawai'i to shame. One way Bora Bora excels is made clear from the start. The village headman offers the group the same hospitality presumably extended to Western male explorers in those islands for two centuries. "While your flying boat sleeps in the lagoon, you will have some place to sleep on shore," the headman offers. (Note that the bird/machine metaphor sounds oddly primitive issuing from the islander's mouth, though its kindred usage is, by implication, civilized, eloquent, and imaginative in Hale's own narration, above). Despite their chaste protests, the seven Americans are to be housed individually, the headman insists— and are to be made comfortable by "seven of our young girls" who will be asked to "take care of everything" (754). At this moment the larger share of Hale's ancestral blood wells up and balks at the offer, and the "son of missionaries began to blush, and when the maidens were brought forth, clean, shapely, dark-haired, barefoot girls in sarongs and flowers, he began to protest, but when the headman actually stared apportioning the girls, the tallest and prettiest to the general, and a shy, slim creature of fifteen to him, Hale quite broke up" (754). Even as Cook failed to prevent sexual intercourse between his crewmen and South Seas and Hawaiian women, so Hale and company cannot reject the living arrangements they have been offered.

For nine days Hale is served by Tehani. He and the others in the surveying party find that they can indeed be sexually active, refuting expectations that are shown as being culture-bound: "I am amazed at what a man of forty-nine can do," remarks the general, aided by his two-hour naps thrice daily. This is the American group's only explicit mention of sex. While these men are made to feel rejuvenated, Tehani and her peers consider them to be in their prime: "She had been taught that men of Colonel Hale's age were those who enjoyed sex most, and who were often most proficient in it; and whereas she had been wrong in both guesses about Hale, for he was both afraid and unskilled, she had never known a man who could learn so fast." Thus two cultures' expectations about sex are made to align, with supposedly mutual benefit. Needless to say, for Hale, as a descendent of *both* cultures, the one slow to age and the other quick to learn, these were "days of listless joy" (756).

Oddly, though, while Hale submits passively to the idyll come true, Tehani displays a competitive flair, which runs as an undercurrent through the interlude: "Knowing that she was the envy of all the others for her man could dance," Tehani thinks, "'I got the best one of the group, and I was smart enough to ask for him'" (756). But this zeal is evident only sporadically, in the budding characterization of Tehani as a young woman of ambition. Hale (or Michener?) takes the dream literally. He prefers to think of Tehani "as not even a real person," high spirited and ambitious as she really is (757). It is essentially the same dream as Tommo's in *Typee*, now updated to the era of flying boats exactly a century later. But this time the narrator, unlike Tommo, never awakens from the dream.

The contrast between the simple and the complex pastorals of the islands is the contrast between the responses to the dream of sexual escape by the respective narrators of Michener's ostensibly heroic *Hawaii* and Milton Murayama's ostensibly pastoral and quintessentially local novel, *All I Asking for Is My Body*. The comparison is ironic because one would expect the pastoral to be carefree, but here the reverse is true. During World War II, in Michener's epic, Hale blindly lives the simple pastoral on Bora Bora. But Murayama's narrator Kiyo, brimming with desire as a young, working-class man on a sugar plantation on Maui, pinches himself and rejects that very dream as nothing but a caveman's illusion, a self-deluding, one-night's refuge from the war and from history.[24]

One way to examine this difference is through the literary tradition in which Michener writes. His Bora Bora interlude conforms to a popular literary convention that Earl Miner calls "the novel of desertion."[25] Writing not mainly about the South Seas but about Japan's impact on Western literature, Miner names the Frenchman Louis Marie Julien Viaud, whose pseudonym was "Pierre Loti," as having the "dubious honor" of originating the desertion theme in his *Madame Chrysantheme* (published in 1888). The theme is latent, too, in earlier works, as when Tommo forsakes Fayaway upon fleeing from Taipivai; and, indeed, the theme is legendary in sailors' yarns and songs. In Viaud's novel, "the pleasures of exoticism and imperialism permit moral indifference and forms of spiritual brutality," where the "marriages" between the French naval officers and Japanese women "are only a joke." "It is an ugly novel," Miner makes clear, "but basic reading to understand what imperialism means to the Orient today"; "if America and its women were to be judged by 'quaint' prostitutes at the docksides of New Orleans the effect would be much the same" (48). The basic theme of the novel of desertion "usually revolves around Europeans, especially naval officers, who visit Japan, acquire 'wives,' and desert them. Moral issues are often obscured, as in *Madam Chrysantheme*, behind the exotic mist, although later novels in this form usually soften the theme by making the woman something other than a prostitute and by attributing reluctance to the man who leaves her" (48). Giacomo Puccini's *Madama Butterfly* is the most famous piece in this genre.

Michener's aptly titled *Sayonara* (published in 1954) is the most recent novel of desertion Miner discusses. Of Michener's postwar version of *Madama Butterfly*, Miner writes: "The lightly exotic and erotic treatment of the Japanese woman has now made her incredibly superior to the American women on the scene." The novel's hero changes from the deliberately portrayed embodiment of racial prejudice at *Sayonara*'s beginning to the apparently unintended portrait of racial, racist self-hatred, disguised as tolerance, as the end nears, where the American protagonist discovers and acts out his contempt for American women. Miner adds as a final but mild remark on Michener's *Sayonara* and the postwar novel of desertion: "The unfortunate result is, as usual in do-gooding novels, that the story has more good will than credibility" (49).

The theme of desertion, the result of the "lightly exotic and erotic" encounters such as Hoxworth Hale finds on Bora Bora, is a familiar one in Michener's South Pacific works. The theme is central, for example, to the rather lengthy short story, "Povenaaa's Daughter," which casts light on the cynicism lurking in the heart of the desertion theme. It should not be necessary to stress that the view of island women and men offered by works of this genre can hardly be expected to fit the way islanders see themselves and their visitors. Teuru, the title character, is pregnant by Johnny Winchester, her third successive white lover, a beach bum of wealthy California pedigree. Teuru is confronted by his mother, who has come to fetch her son home and who now takes pity on Teuru, soon to be deserted. Mrs. Winchester is the butt of Michener's ridicule, with her conventional, patronizing, condescending sentiments about the "classic island tragedy" while Teuru smiles bravely. Mrs. Winchester is shocked out of her stock response to what she thinks is a stock situation when Teuru explains that she will give the baby to her boss, the vanilla planter Kim Sing, who has won the unborn child of Teuru and Johnny at the customary game of dice that decides such matters.

There is no ambiguity about Teuru's disclosure of the deal, in Michener's telling of the story. By his style and treatment of character he is saying that in Teuru's and her culture's eyes, she is right. There is no tragedy, for there is no moral issue. Nothing is wrong. Far from being damaged by her transient affairs, the pretty, clever, spirited, and lucky island girl profits from the traffic of white lovers. In effect, she is a prostitute who in addition sells her babies, and Michener implicitly praises her for it. He does this by stripping Mrs. Winchester of her conventional responses, as though, then, what is uncovered, the laughing Teuru at the story's rock bottom, is not merely the reality but is the utter truth. We are asked to believe that it would be foolish to take Johnny's desertion of Teuru moralistically, for carefree sex and selling the resulting babies are simply the islanders' ages-old business, their way of handling one of life's blithe occurrences.

It appears that Hoxworth Hale learned from Johnny, as there is no indication that the narrator of *Hawaii* is in any way circumspect about either deserting Tehani or betraying his wife. A very savvy narrator intimates to us that these are the customary and expected island ways of love, of dance, of preparing food, and of being blessed with babies.

Hale departs having provided, without yet knowing it, for Tehani's happiness at least for a while to come. Some months or perhaps years after the interlude, in some smoke-thick bar where he meets a Navy man who also knew Tehani, Hale learns that has had a baby, a boy, the first American baby of Bora Bora. Hale learns, too, that Tehani (rather like Povenaaa's daughter) gave the infant to a family on another island, since "girls there had no chance to produce American babies, and the island wanted one" (760). Thus Michener repeats his theme of love with no serious consequences, no lasting responsibilities, with the baby treated like some kind of commodity.

If anything, however, *Hawaii* is a hair more complicated than "Povenaaa's Daughter," though still dependent heavily on the conventions of desertion and the simple pastoral. In a recurring dream Hale "saw a young girl dancing beside a lagoon, and he saw on the blue waters an ancient double-hulled canoe and he thought: 'I am forever a part of Bora Bora, and my son lives on in the islands.' Then the memory vanished and he heard a girl's voice lamenting: 'The years go by very fast, and soon we play no more games'" (760). Michener thus concludes the interlude with his expression of the *carpe diem* theme basic to all visions of the pastoral in a mortal world: seize the day, for youth and life are short.

At the conclusion of the novel's section containing the Bora Bora interlude, we find Hale putting Tehani—and sex—from his mind and contemplating Hawaii's progress since the coming of his missionary ancestors. Sex aside, "in every respect but one" Hawai'i under American dominion has progressed farther than Fiji under the English and Tahiti under the French, Hale sees (760–61). The exception: "But in the way we have allowed our Hawaiians to lose their land, their language, and their culture, we have been terribly remiss," Hale senses a collective guilt (761). The assumption is that Hawai'i was a relative social paradise before "we," the haole, arrived. It is a deeply Christian assumption, based on the story of the serpent in Eden. It is also an arrogant assumption, for it assigns to the white race something like sole and total power to change history, despite the author's portrayal of fictional characters of other races and cultures, including the native Hawaiian and the changes they, too, effect.

A perverse semblance of a Hawaiian paradise does exist in the novel's modern Hawaiian times in spite of the unfavorable comparison with Bora Bora. The modern Hawaiian is represented by the beachboy

Kelly Kanakoa. He is a mid-twentieth-century version of the noble savage, the male counterpart to Tehani of Bora Bora, although in apparent crudeness he reminds us more of Povenaaa's daughter Teuru. Just as Tehani entertained her eminent male visitor to Bora Bora, Kanakoa of Waikīkī performs for his female visitors services which are world renowned. As his sidekick Florsheim notes, the Hawai'i travel posters hanging in New York City tour offices always show sensuous hula girls swaying their hips against the blue sky and gesturing a welcome, as if these women were what Hawai'i offered. Yet there are few women so available. Instead, the beachboys Kelly and Florsheim lie in the invisible undertow of the posters, pulling in the New York City women (841). In the narrowly male point of view from which *Hawaii* is narrated, it is small wonder that Hawai'i is a paradise no longer. Hawaii's swain is indeed a swain and not a sweet nymph like Tehani. Kelly Kanakoa, Florsheim, their visitors, Waikīkī, and the whole tourist package of Hawai'i in the final chapter of the novel seem grotesque caricatures of whatever was truly noble and beautiful in Hawaii's past.

The following instance in Michener's *Hawaii* is a remarkable moment in Hawaii's literature. It is Kelly Kanakoa at his best: that is, his most charming and suave. The episode contrasts with Hoxworth Hale's earlier episode on Bora Bora.

It is early 1948 and the beginning of a tourist boom. Kelly and Florsheim board the *Moana Loa*, a transpacific passenger liner that has just arrived from the mainland. A cable from a former but forgotten client instructs Kelly to meet a Mrs. Dale Henderson, arriving aboard the ship. Such referrals being common in his trade, Kelly routinely finds and greets Mrs. Henderson—Elinor Henderson, a New Englander, a Smith College instructor, a woman with a steady air of self-assurance. Kelly speaks an atrocious variety of pidgin English, Michener's own invention, yet Elinor never stumbles in their initial verbal exchange while Kelly tries frantically to recall the "Rennie" who sent him the cable of referral. Elinor is so self-assured that she even mimics Kelly's strange idioms:

> He was irritated with this secure woman and said, "S'pose one year pass, bimeby I say Florsheim, 'Cable here speak Elinor Henderson. Who dat one wahine?' Florsheim doan' collect. I doan' collect."
>
> "Who's Florsheim?" Elinor asked.

"Da kine beachboy yonder 'longside tall wahine," Kelly explained. Mrs. Henderson laughed merrily and said "Rennie told
me you were the best beachboy in the business, but you must
promise me one thing."

"Wha' dat?"

"You aren't required to talk pidgin to me any longer. I'll
bet you graduated with honors from Hewlett Hall. You can
probably speak English better than I can." She smiled warmly
and asked, "Aren't you going to give me the lei?"

"I'm afraid to kiss you, Mrs. Henderson," he laughed, and
handed her the flowers, but Florsheim saw this and rushed
up, protesting, "Jeezus Crisss! Kanaka handin' wahine flowers
like New York?" He grabbed the lei, plopped it around Elinor's
head and kissed her powerfully.

"Florsheim's been in New York," Kelly joked. "He knows
how to act like a Hawaiian." (Pp. 827–28)

Thus Kelolo (Kelly) Kanakoa is suddenly conferred a great deal
of dignity by his ability to speak the English of an educated American,
while poor Florsheim is at best pitied for speaking nothing but pidgin.
Up to this point Kelly, who soon reveals himself to Elinor to be a descendant of the leaders of the first Polynesian settlers of Hawai'i, appears
to illustrate Hoxworth Hale's guilt-laden concern that the Hawaiians,
stripped of all their dignity, have fared very badly under the islands'
American control. But now we find that the noble savage still lives, under-
cover. He wears his crude beachboy life by choice because no one would
believe in a dignified, noble young Hawaiian any more. So guarded is
Kelolo Kanakoa's nobility that even to his stately, indeed regal, Vassar-
educated mother he speaks pidgin. He, too, like Florsheim, "knows how
to act like a Hawaiian" in order to get by. Yet, as Michener's treatment
of Kelly implies, his true nature can be revealed not even to his family,
not to his Waikīkī cohorts, but only to Elinor Henderson, the most deeply
conservative, modern-day Puritan among Kelly's many haole women visitors. It is she, it seems, who must validate Kelly's true nature, as if
he were powerless to attest to his own, usually hidden worth.

　　　Despite Michener's claim, repeated through his long career, that
his characters and the cultures they represent stand and "clash on equal
footing" (937), the scene where Kelly Kanakoa shifts from pidgin to standard English at Elinor's command enforces a contrary idea that only one
culture, one language, is supreme in the novel: the one directly descendant
from the American missionaries. And it strongly suggests that Michener,

whether knowingly or not, in his creation of the scene supports that idea of so-called white superiority.

For one thing, Michener's contrived pidgin English serves to *disguise* rather than to express the character's identity. It also serves to denigrate: the inference is that Hawaii's pidgin vernacular is the identifying mark of a savage, a fool, or a simpleton such as Florsheim is flatly depicted to be. Kelly's pidgin is like the image of a Hawai'i paradise pictured on the travel poster: his pidgin-speaking world itself is one of deception and cynicism. Also, as anyone who has grown up with Hawaii's pidgin recognizes, Michener's pidgin is not only atrocious when judged by standards of English but is even more abominable when measured by the language it is supposed to imitate. The matter is both ludicrous and serious. When Hoxworth Hale notes that the missionaries were guilty of "allowing" the Hawaiians to lose their language, he might just as well be referring to the moment when the pidgin vernacular of Hawai'i is implicitly and powerfully ridiculed in the scene between Kelly and Elinor. The scene is the most succinct single illustration, in Hawaii's literature, of both the plundering and the shaming of Hawaii's vernacular.

The episode played by these two characters is evidently in deliberate contrast to Hale's and Tehani's Bora Bora interlude from beginning to end. At the end of the affair, nothing less than a tsunami catches Kelly and Elinor in another fine and sincere discussion. The inexorable wave carries them into a narrowing valley, and Elinor is dragged seaward in the wave's rip. Michener thus concludes the entire affair: "As the last stones whipped past she thought: 'This cursed island!' And she thought no more" (840). It is difficult to say why it takes a monstrous tsunami for Michener to deal ultimately with the hapless Elinor of Smith College. But for Kelly, the drowsy beachboy, life blithely resumes. For him and the race he represents, there seems to be no better future: this is what has become of fruitless love. His life can only grow worse with age. The tourist trade in Michener's *Hawaii* capitalizes on the *carpe florem* (gather the flowers) pastoral theme that used to lead poets to far more sober thoughts than Kelly's. The "flower" in Hawaii's songs, Kelly is himself being plucked by visitors in their dreams of islands.

Considering narrator Hoxworth Hale's professed sympathies for the Hawaiians, author Michener leaves the Hawaiians in his novel with curiously dismal prospects. But perhaps Michener was of a mind with A. Grove Day, who wrote of his own conversation with one of the script writers for the film version of *Hawaii*. The writer agreed with a criticism —not Day's—that the novel's outcome is "a libel on the noble Polynesian voyagers who first found and possessed" Hawai'i: "Here you have every-body else winning what he wants, . . . but Kelly Kanakoa, descendant of generations of kings, remains sitting in a loincloth on the beach, strumming a ukelele." Day offered an incredible rejoinder to the script writer's complaint:

> I tried to point out that Kelly not only was marrying a beautiful heiress to a Chinese fortune, but that he also was a golden-voiced idol among residents and tourists alike, and nobody could desire more than that. . . . Kelly Kanakoa makes music and fun, he offers love and welcome, he voices the spirit that most of all makes Hawaii a paradise—the spirit of aloha. (*Michener*, 118–19)

It is a great pity that the strength of the conventional paradise image prevents most readers from taking seriously Michener's potentially insightful social criticisms in *Hawaii*. Michener's treatment of the Kelly Kanakoa anti-pastoral serves, oddly enough, to intensify the flames of popular curiosity about the Hawaiian Islands. It somehow strengthens the paradise image—at least the tourist's version of paradise. For one thing, the unfavorable comparisons of Bora Bora with Waikīkī, and Tehani with Kelly, suggest that someday Hawai'i will be restored to the paradise it once was, just as, say, Hale's Polynesian blood returns to invigorate him when he steps ashore at Bora Bora, or when Kelly obeys Elinor's order to stop speaking pidgin. In other words, despite heroic devices to the contrary, Michener still seems to assume the validity of the Paradise-of-the-Pacific concept in his criticism of that paradise's destruction and his depiction of the islands' supposed pleasures of life. Second, Michener's fiction at the same time pretends to be showing us what is "real" beneath the façades of island life, as when Kelly drops his pidgin to please Elinor. Like Elinor, readers are apparently expected to think that the book provides a moderately penetrating and very readable look at Hawaii's molten social core. Thus satisfied that Michener is not dispensing the usual tiresome clichés about a *romantic* Hawaiian paradise, the reader may be predisposed to accept the ways in which Hawai'i is *really* a paradise in Michener's view. The author has one especially grand way of showing this—namely, his Golden Man.

Michener's Golden Man embodies the idea of a racial paradise, of Hawaii's "cross-fertilization" of cultures. The symbol is an interesting one in the context of a discussion of the pastoral; and, significantly, it is also the title of the novel's final chapter with its prospect of Hawaii's

future. Michener's composite Golden Man is reminiscent of several symbols that figure in the garden world of Western pastorals: there was once
a Golden Age which, when translated from time and timelessness into
imaginary space, became various Golden Worlds; for instance, the Isles
of the Blest. Inhabiting this once Golden World was the noble savage,
discovered by Westerners successively in Africa, the Americas, and the
Pacific and lavished, in each instance, with attention and curiosity, until
each in time proved to be a disappointment, a mere human being, then
a subhuman in the discoverer's eyes. Many such related ideas are conjured
up by Michener's Golden Man. This Golden Man himself is able to envi-
sion a utopian future, to be realized on islands where newly regenerated
qualities and values are guarded by an ocean moat. The Golden Man,
moreover, is to be a composite of the noble savage of the Pacific, the
noble sage of Asia, and even, one might say, the noble American of the
Golden West.

The literal and the literary truths of the Hawai'i paradise image
are sometimes conflated, and Michener himself is ambivalent about
whether the term "Golden Man" refers to the actual or to the ideal. His
sixth chapter, "The Golden Men," explains that the term was invented
by sociologists not necessarily to refer to men of racially mixed parentage
but to "a way of thought." The narrator introduces the idea: the Golden
Man "was influenced by both the west and the east, a man at home
in either the business councils of New York or the philosophical retreats
of Kyoto, a man wholly modern and American yet in tune with the
ancient and the Oriental." He continues: "His awareness of the future
and his rare ability to stand at the conflux of the world he owed to his
understanding of the movements around him." The narrator, in this chapter, has become intrusive; here he shows his actual familiarity with the
Golden Men: "His was a way of thought, and not of birth, and one
day I discovered, with some joy I may add, that for several years I had
known the archetypes of the Golden Man"(807). For in addition to
Shigeo Sakagawa, Hong Kong Kee, and Kelolo (Kelly) Kanakoa,the narrator Hoxworth Hale is himself a Golden Man. Hale states the purpose
of his fraternity: "In an age of Golden Men it is not required that their
bloodstreams mingle, but only that their ideas 'clash on equal footing
and remain free to cross-fertilize and bear new fruit" (937).

If not a "racial paradise" where differences are eliminated through
intermarriage, Michener's might be called a "cultural" one, where cultures—various and disparate—coalesce to form a new hybrid fruit. Perhaps the narrator's repeated stress against intermarriage is one way the

author distances himself from Hoxworth Hale. His South Seas stories and essays and his own marriage attest to Michener's positive view of interracial marriages and children of mixed blood.[26] Perhaps the insistence that the Golden Man represents "a way of thought" and not a skin coloration, an exchange of ideas between cultures and not the children of interracial marriage, reflects Michener's desire to elevate *Hawaii* above the raw and rowdy, the indulgence in sensationalism and gut reactions that make up so much of its mass. The concept, the "way of thought" adds yet one more layer of abstraction to the already stereotypic characterizations of the Japanese, the Chinese, the Hawaiian, the *kamaʻāina* haole, long resident in the land, representatives of their respective races. And as Hoxworth Hale's words imply at the novel's end, the interaction between Hawaii's Golden Men is based on competition, more the basis for business and commerce than for marriage: it is, Hale says, the "clash" of ideas that is crucial.

Then what will be the fruit, so to speak, of this cultural clash and cross-fertilization? What does the novel posit? Will a single colonial culture emerge, dominated by the victors of the clash, as standard English triumphs over the vernacular pidgin and creole and the Hawaiian language? We find in "The Golden Men" and throughout *Hawaii* a message running contrary to the voiced support of cultural diversity. We find preachments about the common origin of various races, delivered in a tone that discourages any emphasis on cultural differences among the world's peoples. Although the social usefulness of the Golden Men is attributed to their individual differences, what is ultimately important, somehow, to Michener (or Hale?) is that men's ancient blood origins are said to be the same. Their differences seem to be meaningless and indeed to be annihilated in the big picture.

The following is one of several similar passages where Michener makes his point that all people are one, and that in this essential sameness lie equality and value. Captain Sakagawa is a returning World War II hero, a *nisei* or second-generation Japanese American, born and educated in the United States:

> When Captain Sakagawa climbed aboard the transport he felt completely American. He had proved his courage, had been accepted by Honolulu, and now he was wanted by someone. In a sense, he was already a Golden Man, knowledgeable both in western and eastern values, for although he reveled in his newly won Americanism, he also took pride in being a pure-

blooded Japanese. Of course this latter was ridiculous, for he contained inheritances from all those nameless predecessors who had once inhabited Japan: some of his genes came from the hairy Ainu to the north, from Siberian invaders, from the Chinese, from the Koreans amongst whom his ancestors had lived, and more particularly from that venturesome Indo-Malayan stock, half of whom had journeyed eastward to become Hawaiians while their brothers had moved northward along different islands to merge with the Japanese. Thus, of two ancient Malayan brothers starting from a point near Singapore, the northern traveler had become the ancestor of Shigeo Sakagawa, while the other had served as the progenitor of Kelly Kanakoa, the Hawaiian beachboy who now stood with a pretty girl watching the end of the parade.

Or, if one preferred looking north, of three ancient Siberian brothers, one bravely crossed the sea to Japan, where his genes found ultimate refuge in the body of Shigeo Sakagawa. Another crept along the Aleutian bridge towards Massachusetts, where his descendants wound up as Indian progenitors of Hoxworth Hale; while a third, less venturesome than his brothers, drifted southward along established land routes to central China, where he helped form the Hakka, thus serving as an ancestor to Hong Kong Kee. In truth, all men are brothers, but as generations pass, it is differences that matter and not similarities. (P. 817)

This novel was not well received in Hawai'i, where even a reader of little sensitivity would sense that the narrator—and probably Michener—is ultimately denying the value of ethnic diversity. To a Japanese American, and because the particular passage I have chosen to quote is about one of Michener's Japanese American characters, the assimilationist message would be especially evident, though it may remain buried in the passage and in a Japanese American reader's simmering defenses against being bothered for a lifetime by such things. The narrator speaks apparently without irony, but his words imply approval of Sakagawa's feeling of having been "accepted," of reveling in his "newly won" Americanism. The nisei's Americanism is, to the contrary, his birthright, yet he had to fight to win it, to be "accepted" by fellow citizens of Hawai'i and the United States who had rejected him—because he was racially different—as if these others were a higher class of citizen, culture, and race. But racial difference is not the problem. The problem is racism, bigotry. Although the narrator elsewhere speaks (however qualifying his remarks) against the injustices of the American treatment of Japanese Americans on account of racial, social, and cultural differences, here the narrator implicitly congratulates Captain Sakagawa for his *conformity*, his assimilation—in all but race—into "Americanism," whatever that is. On the other side of Michener's ambivalence on this point is the thought that, when Hawai'i became part of America, whether in 1898 or in 1959, the very definition of what is *American* necessarily changed, as it changes by the birth or naturalization or residence of every new arrival. But this idea again raises the question: how can a Captain Sakagawa feel "completely American" in a "newly won Americanism" if, indeed, his Americanism itself was already complete, was *already defined by* the fact of his birth in an American territory? Can cultural differences really matter so much in the concept of the Golden Men if, after all, one's being born a Japanese American in Hawai'i still requires becoming "completely American" in the way Michener requires of Sakagawa?

When James A. Michener's *Hawaii* was published in 1959, Hawai'i was celebrating its recent status as America's fiftieth state. The utopian dream of an island paradise evoked by this novel—in its way recalling the entirely fictional Eden of James Fenimore Cooper's *The Crater* —was pertinent to Hawaii's position on the brink of great new developments. Statehood culminated years of effort stretching back into the nineteenth century by those who fervently believed in the greatness of Hawaii's economic prospects at a potentially busy global crossroads, the image of Hawai'i as the busy Crossroads of the Pacific contrasting and balancing its momentarily overshadowed image as the lazy Paradise of the Pacific. The statehood effort and debate stretched, too, through the first fifty-nine years of the twentieth century. With mounting virulence, critics in many camps charged that Hawaii's Asian Americans, though born into American citizenship, could never be assimilated and would in fact become a political threat. Countless proofs of Americanism literally took a deadly toll—in the battlefields of Europe, for instance, where Japanese Americans, soldiers in the U. S. Army, are said to have fought to prove their American loyalties—but still yielded little understanding of the diversity and the integrity of Hawaii's cultures.

I have tried to suggest some reasons for judgments of Michener's *Hawaii* as an "entertaining" but certainly "not great" example of literature about Hawai'i. The novel nonetheless has been a formidable bone in the Hawai'i writer's gullet.[27] Although some people advise against treating Michener's work seriously in my study, if readers uninitiated in Hawaii's literary traditions ask about any work at all, that work is Michener's.

Paradoxically, Michener's *Hawaii* makes pretensions of "greatness," in its sheer size and grandeur, while implicitly denying that the subject itself is great or deserves the honesty, not the disclaimers, needed to articulate its worth and significance. While many readers in Hawai'i, too, have been entertained by *Hawaii*, as by the TV series *Hawaii Five-O* and *Magnum PI*, scarcely anyone can consider such productions to be authentic with respect to Hawai'i. But the question remains: what is "authentic" literature of Hawai'i?

In that same year of statehood and Michener's *Hawaii*, an anthology of selections from Hawaii's literature, edited by A. Grove Day and Carl Stroven, was also published. *A Hawaiian Reader* carries an introduction by Michener.[28] All three responsible for the anthology—if Michener may be so described—weighted the volume with authority, since Professors Day and Stroven were already considered experts in the still sparsely growing field of Hawaii's literature and of Pacific literature as well, and Michener could by then be considered an expert by virtue of his reputedly having read every available piece of Hawaii's literature in order to write *Hawaii*.

The anthology is somewhat biased toward selections derived from the simple pastoral idyll of Hawai'i, although, like Michener's novel, the anthology's selections also include narratives whose stress on action rather than vacation may seem heightened against the island backdrop. Besides the editors' having to select from a known canon of literature whose rationale in the first place was a paradisiacal view of Hawai'i, and besides their own inclinations to favor the idyllic in certain aspects of Hawaii's literature, the anthology expressly seeks to show off Hawai'i and its literature at their shining best. Mark Twain's "Prose Poem" extolling Hawaii's deeply breathed charms serves as an epigram for *A Hawaiian Reader* and strikes the familiar, effulgent gong that sounds thereafter in even the darkest moments of the selections. Finally, five ancient Hawaiian passages conclude the book, not as afterthought but, according to Michener, in order that "the casual reader" might not be "alienated" at the outset by the Hawaiian works' "language," "so alien to the modern world." "It was advisable to start with some selection more in the modern mood," Michener further explains, "like that written by Captain Cook" (*A Hawaiian Reader*, 14). To many readers today, especially Hawaii's readers, the condescension in such remarks is so readily obvious as to be egregious.

Indigenous Hawaiian lyrics and chants play integral parts in Hawaii's cultural history and current life, contrary to Michener's constraint that they are alien and alienating. The same is true of creations by writers of Hawai'i of other races and ethnicities besides native Hawaiian, because to most people of Hawai'i these authors and their works are not alien but are native born. The works and their authors have no other *ke one hānau* (sands of their birth) but Hawai'i, no matter what race they are. Still further, many writers who have settled in Hawai'i from elsewhere include themselves as contributors to the pluralistic, multicultural life of the islands, whether or not they identify themselves and their art with the local and the native. The Hawai'i-born and the newly settled alike generally write in English, knowing that other languages and vernaculars exist all about them in Hawai'i. Hawaii's writers are typically most influenced by their American literary education (which includes native Hawaiian) and are fundamentally versed in Western modes and forms, while the cultural diversity that defines this part of America also encourages interests in Asian and Pacific literatures. This would seem to belabor the obvious until one recalls that the usual authors cited as central to a Hawai'i literary tradition—among them Twain, Stevenson, Stoddard, London, and Michener—are *visitors* to Hawai'i, every one of them a sojourner, a traveler or a tourist. Ironically, a criticism of Hawaii's writers has been that their being of the islands diminishes their value, for by definition they are insular; or else it is they, not the Londons and other mainland visitors, who are considered racially or culturally exotic, revolving eccentrically outside American audiences' presumed cultural interests. The very existence of elements of Hawaii's literary traditions not only went unrecognized but in 1959 actively denied by Michener who, publishing a commonplace falsehood, asserted in his introduction to *A Hawaiian Reader* not only that native Hawaiian voices are "alien" but also that Hawaii's people who are "Oriental in ancestry," "having arrived in the islands as laboring peasants, . . . did not produce a literature of their own" (*A Hawaiian Reader*, 12). His own research into the literature of Hawai'i ought to have overturned rather than promulgated this falsehood.

3

The mele in their popularity and their varieties of style, theme, and tone (here meaning attitude toward the song's subject), provide a context that encourages the writing of complex pastorals of Hawai'i. And mele concommitantly present a somewhat hostile context for simplistic pastorals now that Hawaiian poetry is again being taken seriously. Whether or not a local Hawai'i writer draws inspiration directly from the tradition of mele, the Hawaiian art and its pervasiveness teach a common lesson, a double consciousness, as it were, that what the tourist sees and hears is not how a child of the land views the life of the islands. A child who grows up with the varieties of hula and mele—and not with a view of these arts as reductions of life and culture to the simplest of terms—learns their values and knows well that the "Little Grass Shack in Kealakekua, Hawaii" is nothing less than a deliberately crafted tourist trap.

Those Hawai'i writers who are unable directly to use the island's ancient language as a way to identify with a revered ancient Hawaiian past and literary traditions have often turned instead to their own pasts, their childhoods and the languages of their childhoods, to set the groundwork for their idylls. In general, the resulting imaginative, literary childhood idylls of Hawai'i in their various forms are often meant to be enjoyed as somehow humorous, whimsical reminders of what we once were. Yet at the same time the writer's motivation is serious: true to the complex elements that compose the pastoral, Hawaii's childhood idylls stand as implicit critiques of a present-day Hawai'i already vastly changed since the time of even a young writer's childhood. The idylls are critiques, too, of adulthood; for the idylls sometimes are implicitly about the loss of the ability to take pleasure in small things, as do the child's "mosquito fish" minnows, living in their old mayonnaise jar and apparently doing just fine. Tacitly, these idylls are about the loss of innocence, both personal and communal, when along with the *keiki o ka 'āina* (the child of the land), the State of Hawai'i, too, continues to grow up.

Characteristics of Hawaii's childhood idylls appear across genres of fiction, drama, and poetry. They are evident in a song by Jerry Santos of the duo, Olomana. Santos and the late Robert Beaumont are among those whose compositions and performances, in both Hawaiian and English, are considered representative within a rather wide range of contemporary Hawaiian music. In "Ku'u Home 'o Kahalu'u" (my beloved home Kahalu'u), with stanzas in English and a refrain line in Hawaiian, Olomana voices sentiments felt by many in Hawai'i, especially during the 1970s, a time of change and of reflection upon changes during what already seemed like the many long years since statehood:

> I remember days when we were younger
> We used to catch 'o'opu in the mountain stream.
> 'Round the Ko'olau hills we'd ride on horseback
> So long ago it seems it was a dream.

Last night I dreamt I was returning,
And my heart called out to you.
But I fear you won't be like I left you,
Me kealoha ku'u home'o Kahalu'u.

I remember the days when we were wiser,
When our world was small enough for dreams.
And you have lingered there, my sister,
And I no longer can it seems.
Last night I dreamt I was returning,
And my heart called out to you.
But I fear I am not as I left you,
Me kealoha ku'u home'o Kahalu'u.

Change is a strange thing,
It cannot be denied.
It can help you find yourself,
Or make you lose your pride.
Move with it slowly
As on the road we go.
Please do not hold on to me
For I must go alone.

I remember the days when we were smiling,
When we laughed and sang the whole night long.
And I will greet you as I find you
With the sharing of a brand new song.
Last night I dreamt I was returning,
And my heart called out to you
To please accept me as you find me,
Me kealoha ku'u home'o Kahalu'u.[29]

The themes of change and of loss have long been current in and about Hawai'i. Central to Olomana's song is the recognition that both the child and the paradise homeland have changed over the years: a sense of loss is complicated by recognition of maturity gained. The theme is old, everywhere. Three decades after his first visit to Hawai'i, Twain mourned the passing of the Hawai'i he once knew. On another level, King David Kalākaua was enough alarmed about the loss of the Hawaiian culture that he instituted a Hawaiian Renaissance during his reign (1874–91), a rebirth that may be said to continue today. Such rebirths do not just happen. They are created by men and women who lead their communities at times of need. The patriotic mele of that era of the 1870s and 1880s exhibit a twofold intent and function: they extol the glory of Hawai'i while conveying an urgent call for restoration of the life of the land.[30] This desire to reconnect to one's own youth and to Hawaii's history and cultures, for the shared welfare not merely of one's self but of the community, finds common and widespread expression in Hawaii's literature.

So the Hawai'i novelist Armine von Tempski writes at the beginning of her autobiography, *Born in Paradise* (1940): "Attaining Paradise in the hereafter does not concern me greatly. I was born in Paradise."[31] From the moment of such a birth any change in the setting, or in one's perception of it, can only be for the worse. And von Tempski was even further blessed. She was born not simply in Paradise but also into the gentry class, granddaughter of a Polish nobleman and the daughter of the "king" of the sixty-thousand-acre Haleakala Ranch on the cool, green slopes of the great Maui mountain. To her father, von Tempski dedicated each of her eight novels; he had died when she was still a youth but stood taller than life in her memory. The already rich and unbroken history of a class, therefore, plays as great a role as does the setting in making von Tempski's remembered childhood paradisiacal and never to be recovered.

For Hawaii's Asian American writers, the situation is very different from that of the Hawaiian *haku mele* (weaver of songs) or of the haole and hapa haole gentry. Compared with these—compared even with the castaway following Robinson Crusoe's deeply planted footsteps on the world's island shores—Hawaii's Asian Americans may seem still to lack deep historical roots in the islands, although it seems that nearly every year in the 1980s one ethnic community of Hawai'i after another celebrates a significant anniversary of its settlement and publishes histories to go along with it (1989 being, for instance, the bicentennial of Chinese history in Hawai'i). These are usually immigration, sociopolitical, and labor histories, as is to be expected, but cultural history is somewhat scarcer, with the possible exception of the strong cultural output during *Ho'olako*, the state's designation of 1987 as the "Year of the [Native] Hawaiian." From one point of view, the situation is paradoxical. While people outside the Asian American groups tend to venerate the antiquity of what is presumed to be these people's Asian cultural heritage, this same veneration tends to ignore or belittle contemporary Asian *American* cultures. It thus contributes to a denial that such cultures, quite distinct from Asian ones, have been developing for more than four generations in Hawai'i and elsewhere in America.[32]

It is impossible to conceive of genuinely heroic literature that lacks any historical contexts for the events narrated. It is difficult, moreover, for anything but the most simplistic of idylls to be written without some useful conception of the experiences and social conditions that a pastoral work is to depict, or to contrast and criticize. Since in theory the pastoral is written by an urban poet about an imagined rural or simple life, and in criticism of the "civilized" and sophisticated, the pastoral work is presumably informed by the writer's thoughts of a highly complex reality—which includes historical contexts and views, however broad and inchoate, of the rise and fall of the writer's own "civilization." Nonetheless, despite the fact that the social and cultural histories of Hawaii's Asian Americans are only just reemerging and are still grossly misunderstood in present times, Asian American writers in Hawai'i—identifying themselves along with an ethnically mixed group of others as together comprising local Hawai'i writers—began as early as the 1920s to publish their discoveries of their personal, family, and community experiences in a number of literary forms and modes, including the childhood idyll in a variety of formal genres.

But local Asian American literary history itself has not until recently been researched. In consequence, the Asian American writer could not readily study the tradition. "The Hongo Store / 29 Miles Volcano / Hilo, Hawaii," a poem Garrett Kaoru Hongo wrote late in that history (I first heard him recite it in 1975), suggests how deliberate and difficult the quest for the Asian American poet's origins may be when personal experience seems the only basis for knowing, and when even that is tenuous at best.[33] A *yonsei* (fourth-generation Japanese American) poet, Hongo identifies with Hawai'i through his family's roots at Volcano, on the Big Island. "The Hongo Store" is the poet's interpretation of a small photograph showing him carried high by his father, apparently in jubilation that an earthquake inflicted only minor damage, a cracked window, on the precariously located store and gas station, while the family escaped injury. The device of using an old photo as the mute starting point for recovering a moment in family history is a common one in Asian American lyric poetry; the device itself, like the symbols in Hongo's poem, suggests how fleeting the glimpse is, and how resourceful the child must later become as an adult wishing to know his or her own personal and community histories. In Hongo's case the quest is complicated by the fact that he and his immediate family suffered having to move away from Hawai'i when he was a child. The cracked history itself is part of Hongo's sensibility, which he restlessly attempts to mend in his elaborate and self-consciously eclectic poetry and prose.

A highly structured attempt to evoke and symbolize a childhood occurs in a recent work of a nisei writer. This aspect of Patsy Saiki's fictional *Sachie: A Daughter of Hawaii* (1977) supports the reading generally applicable to Hawaii's childhood idylls that they, as Alfons Korn writes of mele, are attempts to stay the passage of time by preserving things as they are, whether they *are* in actuality or in memory.[34] Of a generation of Hawai'i writers who came of age in the post–World War II era, a period in Hawaii's recent literary history when local literature blossomed with Saiki's work in the midst of the garden, she writes in *Sachie* of a thirteen-year-old girl's life in a farm community on the island of Hawai'i sometime during the Depression.

Sachie's structure is unique, as far as I know, in the body of Hawaii's contemporary literature. Divided into twelve chapters, the book is reminiscent of the pastoral shepherd's calendar devised in the European Renaissance. Titled by the consecutive months of Sachie's thirteenth year, each chapter focuses on some aspect of the Japanese American farm family's customs, such as the observance of a festivity associated with the month. In addition, each chapter details the family's contacts with relatives in Japan or their relationships with others in their polyethnic community, all of which serve to highlight the family's and the community's salient characteristics. The calendar structure of the idyll frees Saiki to write short, anecdotal sketches (a "talk story" length and form common in local speech, and evident in some literary works such as Saiki's). These fill each month, as would entries to a journal, while the structural device simultaneously grants an overall unity to the book.

Although the book tends to seem didactic in the author's teaching of culture, as though mainly told to a teen-aged audience in school, the structural device is not merely mechanical in its effect; it also functions thematically. The calendar serves to frame the way the seasons of the year are perceived by a child growing up in a tropical clime. For Sachie, the seasons are marked by customary festivities or, say, the arrival at predictable times of certain itinerant peddlers and, of course, by the school year, rather than predominantly by seasonal changes in climate. Her treatment of seasonal time is deliberate in that she chooses to use the device of the calendar which calls attention to the seasons; yet, intuitively, Saiki's sense of time is distinctly local and Hawaiian. Writing about the Hawaiian historian Samuel M. Kamakau's education in "the Western concept of history," Malcolm Naea Chun notes that at Lahainaluna Seminary in the 1830s Kamakau was introduced to "chronology as it is known by dates rather than the typical Hawaiian means of remembering by event or person."[35] Saiki, in effect, tells time "by event or person," while the twelve-month calendar is a continual reminder of another chronology that seems mechanical and impersonal by contrast. This contrast is indeed an important element in her novel as a pastoral.

Saiki also develops something of a plot through the months, and this helps further to string the chapters together. Since her parents are very much settled in Hawai'i as Japanese immigrant laborers and farmers and are still strongly attached to their native culture, Sachie finds that she must come to terms with her "American Japanese" identity. While drawing sharp distinctions between the "Japanese" values of her rather elderly parents and the "American" values she learns in school and sees evidenced everywhere at a white friend's home, Sachie resolves to "merge the two, taking the best from each" (130–31). But though her resolution may appear to be influenced mainly by shame that her family and home are not "American" by appearances, the influence of her schooling goes a long way to nurture in her those values she considers "American," so that, recognizing she is by birth American, she need not feel shame for lacking them. On their part, too, Sachie's parents and the immigrants they may be said to represent are not simply relics of a Japan that they left behind decades earlier. *Sachie* contains sketches and characters proudly illustrating the American experiences of early Japanese immigrants and their efforts to establish families—quite aware of their pioneering contribution to Hawaii's posterity.

In a short story first published in 1951, Saiki foreshadows her later twelve-chapter work in setting and in cultural themes. "The Unwilling Bride," set on the Big Island's Hāmākua Coast, the island's northeastern, windward, agricultural brim, is doubly a reminiscence.[36] The story is narrated by Takeko, a nisei woman who has just learned of her mother's death. One way to look at the narration is to see it as Takeko's imagining what thoughts and recollections her mother must have had as she neared her life's end, with Takeko's own reveries and reflections sometimes superimposed. A good portion of the story, then, is either told by the mother as she is imagined to be speaking, or told for her by her closest and youngest, Takeko, both women reminiscing.

The mother, Namiko, was the unwilling bride to Shuji when in 1890 she was ordered to marry him and, a year later, to join him in Hawai'i, where he had returned to his work shortly after the wedding. "With the envy of the neighborhood ringing in her ears," Namiko endured the ordeal of the ocean passage but was terribly disappointed by the Big Island sugar plantation's shabby living conditions (*Talk Story Big Island Anthology*, 60). Shuji and Namiko eventually bought their own twenty-five-acre farm in Hāmākua and settled there with hard work and relative contentment. After they had children, they realized that their dream of someday returning to Japan, growing distant though still with them, would not include their Hawai'i-born children even if the dream should materialize. So that his children could see and enjoy the foliage that reminded him powerfully of Japan, the practical Shuji imported and planted persimmon and peach trees and tea bushes, "and even three pine trees which could not proudly brag about their everlasting greenness the way they did in their native land" (62).

From the implicit point of view of the daughter Takeko, the verdure of the Hāmākua farm and the evidence everywhere of the care with which her parents cultivate the land are what make possible the reposeful, humane, and natural setting that suggests an idyll of childhood. But from the explicit point of view of Shuji and Namiko, the idyll exists not so much in their Hāmākua land as in their dreamy memories of their native Japan, only mimicked in the landscape they have helped to create. Shuji, a practical man, does what he can to cultivate something Japanese in the rich Hawaiian earth, because memories and reflections alone cannot suffice without tangible signs.

Similarly, Namiko has a request of her children after they have grown and have thanked her for raising them to be on their own. Shuji, fifteen years her senior, has died without fulfilling their dream of returning to Japan. Now dying of cancer, Mother confesses her wish to Takeko: She has long wanted a formal kimono, one bearing her *montsuki* (family crest), the kind supposedly to be worn only at weddings and funerals but nevertheless worn at every opportunity by those show-off ladies at church just to inflame envy, Mother complains. And she would do so, too, she admits, if she had such a kimono. "I'd die happy if I knew I had one," Mother says; "Oh, how I wanted one . . . but I never dared tell your father." And she adds, "My crest is the three-pine-trees design" (62–63).

Namiko's grown children order the kimono, but it arrives too late. The children grieve "because they thought their last humble offering went unaccepted" (63).

Saiki refrains from explicitly directing our attention toward it, but if one were to imagine looking outward from Namiko's deathbed, where the never-worn kimono lies with its three-pine-trees montsuki, to the vicinity of the farmyard in Hāmākua, one would see growing there three pine trees, planted by her husband, Shuji, probably because they could not afford to buy a kimono bearing Namiko's crest. The formal kimono represents not only refinement and elegance but also urbanity, wealth, and even the pretensions of those "town ladies" who flaunt their silks at church. But clearly, what the issei couple have come to exemplify is a set of values that Saiki opposes to those of the "town." Namiko's and Shuji's lives embody what in Hawai'i is called *aloha 'āina* (love of the land), with *'āina* serving also as a symbol for family (*'ohana*) and community. The living crest, the three pine trees growing, alive like their very children, rooted in the Hāmākua soil, symbolizes in Saiki's story this complex of values.

Saiki's understated presentation is characteristic of some of Hawaii's childhood idylls, where the authors themselves are now seeing what they may have mainly intuited when they wrote their pieces. Some three decades after "The Unwilling Bride" was first published, literary discussion of Saiki's works began in earnest. Asked about her story and somehow surprised by my explicit connecting of the three pine trees with Namiko's family crest, Saiki commented, after giving fresh thought to her story of years past, that the living trees grow "straight and tall, unlike the artistic pine trees that are twisted and tied into what someone else wants. . . . The pine trees are symbolic of Hawaii's youth. Then there is the irony of the mother wanting the montsuki with the three pines. She did not know she had a thing of greater value," her children. Saiki's explication includes some of the assumptions that quintessentially define literary pastorals: assumptions about art versus artifice, cultivation or culture versus civilization, and about the value of nature, growth, and continuity.

Saiki is of a generation but once removed from an Asian heritage. She and her contemporaries among Hawaii's Japanese American writers —Clara Mitsuko Kubojiri Jelsma, Milton Murayama, and Philip Ige, for example—are able to speak their parents' language and so by this route, enter the Japanese culture to a considerable extent. A retired educator and active participant in Japanese American and Japanese community affairs in Hawai'i, Saiki makes use of her familiarity with Japanese customs in Hawai'i to have them play a central part in *Sachie*. In 1959 she wrote a verse drama called *The Return*—a return not of a Japanese American but of a Japanese soldier to his rural home near Hiroshima in 1946, where he finds that his wife has been scarred by the atomic bomb.[37] Cultural affinities often bring with them emotional sympathies, as must have been the case for Saiki in writing of such a tragedy, set and cast entirely in Japan. This affinity takes on greater significance when one learns that Saiki's own immediate forebears are of Hiroshima, the prefecture where the largest group of Hawaii's Japanese immigrants originated.

In writing her *Teapot Tales and Other Stories* (1981), Clara Mitsuko Kubojiri Jelsma draws directly from a vitally important source for her of Japanese lore, experience, and heritage in Hawai'i: her immigrant mother.[38] Like Saiki's "The Unwilling Bride," Jelsma's full-length work is largely her mother's story preceding emigration from Japan and, in addition, the recollected tales of settling in rural Hawai'i between Hilo and Volcano. But the *Teapot Tales* speak also of pain and struggle that complicate the work's basic nature and make it other than simple and idyllic.

Another nisei writer who has made distinctive, local use of an Asian heritage, Milton Murayama in the 1950s earned a graduate degree at Columbia University in the study of Japanese language and literature, decided against a career in teaching because of the homework it entails for a lifetime, and went on to enjoy the freedom of his nine-to-five job as a customs agent checking Asian cargo at the San Francisco airport, with his evenings free for reading and writing. Murayama also writes of issei, the immigrant or first-generation Japanese Americans, and deftly uses their language as the narrative requires, in his novel *All I Asking for Is My Body* (first published in 1975). Completed by 1977, Murayama's innovative historical drama *Yoshitsune* is a further indication of his interest in Japanese culture and history as a source of literary materials for his own works.[39]

Philip Ige's published stories present a different case. While he too is a nisei, or second generation, child of immigrants, he handles his subjects as sansei, the third generation, would. His focus is on a Hawai'i boyhood aside from any overt use of his characters' Asian heritages beyond the fact that the names of some of the characters are clearly Japanese American. We see boys at play in Ige's rural vignettes but do not hear their parents talking to them in Japanese. The conflict both explicit and implicit in Ige's stories is not the more commonly assumed yet usually deceptive generational and cultural conflict between nisei and issei, but is between the rural youngster of Hawai'i and the contrasting urban people, values, or objects that symbolize the city.

Two brothers chattering away in pidgin English at the beginning of Ige's "The Forgotten Flea Powder" fall silent when an elderly Caucasian woman in front of them in a Honolulu streetcar turns around and smiles.[40] Unused to drawing attention by their talk, except possibly in the schoolroom where they would be scolded severely for lapsing into pidgin English, the boys are embarrassed. But later, of course, back at their family's farm with their fleabitten dog Blackie and no city person to pat their heads with a bemused smile, the boys laugh, tease, and argue with each other in their own pidgin language.

In another variety of pastoral contrasting the rural and the urban, the narrator of Ige's "The New Road" remembers the many activities that the old, unpaved road supported: shooting marbles, staging mud fights, and taking solitary walks, for example.[41] The new, paved road allows none of these, and it brings increased, faster traffic on its slick and sizzling back. Worse, the manager of the plantation through which the road slices gloats over his generosity in providing the road for his "lowly" immigrant laborers. Revealing far more sophistication about detecting such paternalism than the manager would give him credit for, the narrator concludes: "To hell with the new road!"

In Ige's published works we find no trace of any notion that a Japanese American writer must use explicitly *Japanese* terms and allusions to be true to some standard. Ige writes in the local idiom, however, that itself derives partly from the cultures of Asian immigrants, among whom were his parents. He has served as an example to writers of the sansei and yonsei, the third and fourth generations of Hawaii's local writers, who are further removed than he from ancestral Asian cultures. These younger writers have taken up what Ige and others started early in their own writing careers when they belonged to certain literary societies usually associated with the University of Hawaii. Because of the GI Bill of Rights and other historical factors in the decade following World War II, Hawaii's Asian Americans seemed at last to gain their voices and their rights in education, politics, and culture. The contribution of that generation of young writers to Hawaii's literature was noticed, however modestly. When publishing "The Forgotten Flea Powder" in 1946, *Paradise of the Pacific*—the long-established, glossy magazine now called *Honolulu* —expressed the hope that a regional literature would sprout from Hawaii's grass roots.[42] With the development of a grass-roots literature comes an increasing polyethnicity and an identification with things considered "local" or treated as such and used as symbols; for instance, the old dirt road that once ran through the plantation camp.

Darrell H. Y. Lum is a master of local symbols, especially in his use of pidgin and creole vernaculars. He is also a master of the Hawai'i childhood idyll in short fiction. In "Beer Can Hat," Lum not only captures the world of Hawaii's children in the late 1970s, in a narrative delivered entirely in a child's pidgin, but he also shows that mercurial world turning into memories even as we read.[43]

"Beer Can Hat" is narrated by a newsboy who works a city intersection with Bobo, best introduced by the narrator himself:

> You know, Bobo stay lōlō in da head. Mental, you know. But good fun sell newspaper and he smart fo' go by da cars when get stop light and sell to ladies, old ladies . . . and to da mokes who tell stink kine stuff about he belong in Kaneohe Hospital la' dat but in da end day buy newspaypah and tip too! (P. 10)

Even though Bobo is mentally retarded (*lōlō*) he knows his trade: perhaps in fact only pretending to be slow, Bobo takes his time making change at the red light so that when the light turns green, the customer speeds off leaving the change in a grinning Bobo's hand. Lum says he envisions the narrator, Junior, to be nine or ten years old. Shown by the story's context to be from a working-class family, Junior is saving to buy a skateboard: "Cobra kine with heavy duty trucks, and one college edja-kay-shen. Ass what my faddah tell me" (10).

In the story's background is child abuse. When Bobo's father beats him, he also shaves Bobo's head. This humiliation of his friend is too much for the narrator, who without elaborating on the matter simply goes to his mother and asks her to make Bobo a beer can hat. This piece of apparel was quite a fad in Hawai'i one year in the mid–1970s. If nothing else, it displays the creator's resourcefulness. A beer can hat consists of several flattened beer cans, labels showing nicely, knitted together to form a simple, functional, and, above all, very distinctive hat.

Lum layers his story with characterizations that come right out of pastoral traditions. There is the child narrator, drawn as a sensitive, good boy who trusts his feelings and his parents' values; he is growing up to be thoughtful in what should be an adult's way. When the beer can hat is knit, Junior asks if he can "make 'em like one real present," and his mother understands by this that he wants to wrap the gift with "da old Christmas and birthday wrappings" (12). Here are the simple thoughtfulness and the resourcefulness (recycled beer cans and gift wrappings, of all things) highly valued in pastoral traditions. Proud of her boy, the mother hugs and praises Junior, who pretends to shrug it off but feels good. The story works in part by Lum's understatement of words and gestures. While we adult readers are assumed to be able to infer the mother's and father's good feelings about Junior, there is throughout the story the dark contrast with Bobo's abusive father skulking in the background. Furthermore, Junior himself plays two roles in the story: he is the child as swain, and yet he is also the supposedly more knowing one, in his relationship with his retarded partner. Bobo, then, is doubly the simple folk of the pastoral: he is a perpetual child (we know he is older than Junior but do not know his age); and even to a younger child, his best friend, Bobo is perpetually simple-minded, though sometimes suspiciously smart.

Out of this weave of characterizations, roles, and values comes a violent incident that tests Junior's and Bobo's relationship. Some "mokes" passing around a skinny *pakalōlō* (stupefying tobacco; i.e., marijuana) cigarette drive up in a van and ridicule Bobo in his new hat that covers his "bolo-head." One of the bullies snatches the beer can hat into the van. The narrator calls the sobbing Bobo to get away from the "no class guys." The driver orders a newspaper, and against the narrator's pleading, Bobo automatically gives one to the driver, who, instead of paying, laughs and drops his cigarette into Bobo's outstretched hand. But that itself is not the crisis. A simple misunderstanding is. Junior holds Bobo back from jumping recklessly into the street to retrieve his beer can hat, and in that moment a car runs over it. Bobo thinks that Junior holds him back on purpose to allow the hat to be crushed; and he angrily runs off to swear and cry it all out.

This conflict, this misunderstanding, is not explicitly resolved. Lum implies, however, that in a little while Bobo's simple trust in his friend will return, while Junior himself can only think that "I knew bumbye would be pau," the matter finished in due time. That is, Bobo returns to his regular self; but Junior is already moving ahead in time, looking back at the incident and putting it behind him. Implicitly, he has learned something about how even the best of his own intentions can be misunderstood. The story is not simply an affirmation of the child's simplicity. The story takes that child a step closer to adulthood and away from the presumed carefree existence of a child or a simpleton.

The narrator reflects: "Sometimes I tink, though, what going happen to Bobo. He been selling paypahs long time . . . before me and still going sell bumbye even after I quit (when I get my skateboard and my college edja-kay-shen). I hope Bobo be all right" (14). Bobo is vulnerable yet enduring, unchanging in a swiftly changing world. The beer can hat fad passes; yet Bobo is still there, wearing his battered one, somewhat like a trophy. Soon enough the narrator's skateboard, scuffed, scarred, and wobbly, will be permanently retired, while Bobo will still be pumping his aged newspaper delivery bike. Bobo is a kind of living photograph of the way things were in that "small keed time" that, although recent, already feels like a long time ago in the child narrator's reverie.

"Beer Can Hat" was originally published in *Bamboo Ridge: The Hawaii Writers' Quarterly* in 1979. In republications of the story since then, a sequel has been added in which Bobo slyly wins a carnival game by perhaps playing the fool—one can never tell for sure. He defeats a man who turns out to have been one of the bullies in the van. Bobo wins a large stuffed animal, a yellow and black tiger (for the McKinley High School Tigers, their favorite team) that he gives to the narrator's mother. The somewhat ambiguous and unresolved, wistful though happy enough conclusion of the first part is now resolved by Bobo's own triumph. The melodrama becomes a comedy, except that the end of the second part is darkly qualified by Bobo's having to return home to another problem, one which he always faces alone. At Bobo's request that they not come inside, the narrator and his father leave Bobo outside the apartment building where Bobo lives; and now Bobo must explain himself to his unsympathetic father who had forbidden him to go to the carnival in the first place and who, like a grinning skull in the paradise of Bobo's momentary triumph, will beat him again.

Among criticisms leveled against the ways pidgin has been used in Hawaii's literatures are two antithetical ones. The first is that the very success and strength of pidgin in literature should lead to the development of heroic works in pidgin; the second is that pidgin badly limits and weakens the literature's appeal to wider audiences.

Leading a round of workshops with some of Hawaii's writers in November of 1979, the fiction writer, playwright, and critic Frank Chin observed that while Darrell Lum justly deserves his reputation as the most talented published writer of Hawaii's pidgin vernacular today, Lum's fine and promising works fall short of fulfilling the ambitious goals they—and their language—imply.[44] Chin's criticism is that pidgin English in Hawaii's literature is used to characterize not heroic figures, not even mature adult ones, but children, idiots, bums, and assorted antiheroes and buffoons, categories that hardly reflect the range of people who actually speak this language of Hawai'i. That is, the language has yet to be tried and tested in a heroic work, the kind of work that Chin believes is entirely possible in pidgin, for this is the language of talking stories in Hawai'i, most often in pidgin, and certainly some of those stories and their tellers are heroic in kind. In one of Lum's dramas, *Oranges*

Are Lucky, the main character, an aged grandmother, on the occasion of her birthday recalls her immigration from China and her settling in Hawai'i. As an immigrant, she speaks a language close to a genuine pidgin. Technically, unlike the subsequent generations of creole languages, pidgin is no one's native tongue but is the language devised and learned by people crossing the gulfs between their various languages. Rather than exploiting the heroic aspects inherent in the immigrant theme, Lum plays on the relationship, generally a contrast, between the richness of the grandmother's interior monologues where she recalls her history, and the simplicity of the pidgin words she speaks to her own family, her descendants, who honor her as an ancient, simple woman. Why does she not speak with equal richness and sophistication in her two different languages, her inner and her outer, Chin asks?

What thus appears to be a narrow use of pidgin in *Oranges Are Lucky* and other works by Lum is, in fact, what Michener exploits in his novel. By putting his fabricated pidgin into the mouths of immigrants and Hawaiians to show that they are "no class" or "low class guys," as Junior puts it in Lum's story, Michener in effect ridicules the vernacular and those who speak it. Why do Hawaii's own writers also depict only characters of relatively low status as speakers of pidgin? Hawaii's own writers, after all, are trying *not* to lower them further but to ennoble them.

Chin's questions might be answered obliquely by pointing to the appeal of "Beer Can Hat" when read aloud to Hawai'i audiences. Lum's audiences recognized his achievement: he published what may very well be the first narrative, beyond a mere sketch and dialogue, delivered entirely in the vernacular as it is actually spoken. Moreover, Lum crafted his pidgin narrative without having to translate terms for the benefit of audiences initially unfamiliar with the lingo or the current slang. The unbroken pidgin narration implies that the language can be taken in its own terms—that is, Lum's story assumes that the vernacular is understandable, not gibberish, if, of course, the uninitiated reader will pay careful enough attention to the context to learn what unfamiliar terms mean as the reading proceeds. Until recently it has been rare that pidgin was used with such respect and integrity in Hawaii's writing, outside of linguistic studies. It was not only the childlike appeal of the story's language that warmed the popularity of "Beer Can Hat." On the surface, at least, there was nothing to indicate that in local audiences' eyes the story lowered the dignity or the potential of the characters, the language, or the Hawai'i audience itself.

Still, as Sheldon Hershinow points out in an article on the contemporary literature of Hawai'i, while Lum is applauded for his achievement, pidgin continues to be immersed in heated controversy, whether in school or among members of Hawaii's diverse literary community.[45] In spite of its widespread appeal in the islands, the use of pidgin in Hawaii's literature is seen as an implied declaration of independence from the standards imposed on Hawaii's polyethnic culture by a dominant one; and as can be expected, not everyone is willing to endorse such a declaration. Following many others before him, Hershinow sees not only the positive value and usefulness of pidgin in Hawaii's literature but also its danger: "Using pidgin deliberately limits the audience," he asserts. Pidgin is the literature's main evidence of "provincialism" and "parochial insularity," in the view voiced by Hershinow, whose assumptions and analyses lead him to conclude his article with the question: "Can the writers of Hawaii create a literature of wide and lasting literary merit?" ("Coming of Age?" 10). This is another version of Chin's question about going beyond the established limits to take pidgin from the pastoral into the heroic. The difference is that Chin insists it can be done; Hershinow assumes it cannot. If the answer to Hershinow were agreement that the use of pidgins and creoles does prevent the creation of a "wide and lasting" literature for reasons he gives, then *Huckleberry Finn* would have died a hundred years ago. Why in American literature should nonstandard English written by a white man be a mark of greatness while it condemns a local Hawai'i writer to obscurity?

Whether in sociological or in literary terms, the limitations associated with the use of pidgin English in Hawaii's literature are understandable, and they are functional. They are functional as, say, his child creation Lucy is to Wordsworth (whose unseen influence, by the way, is busy everywhere in Hawaii's idylls of childhood, contrary to an assumption that the local Asian American writer is influenced mainly by the East). Wordsworth affirms that a Lucy, a poetic creation, can both represent and express a valuable way of looking at life that would be otherwise poorly accessible to the adult mind and heart. Pidgin likewise brings with it a sensibility that informs these local stories and pidgin poems, and in turn pidgin is the natural medium for expressing this sensibility. Writers such as Darrell Lum seem intuitively to exploit the assumed limitations of pidgin—also, I maintain, the pastoral as a distinctive literary mode and form—in order to use the language within the context of some very broad, hardly insular, genres and modes in which the writer chooses to work.

For example, the literary use of pidgin is indeed strongly associated with childhood in Hawai'i. In other words, this association is a typical "limitation" of pidgin's use in literature. It was one's playground language, neither of the white-collar office nor of the schoolroom, where pidgin suffers and survives cycles of banishment and simply refuses to become "assimilated" into standard English. For the immigrants' pidgin continues in a living creole language alongside "standard" languages of this part of America. This assertion assumes, however, that the hypothetical reader of "Beer Can Hat" works in an office, where, again, pidgin —or in linguistic terms, creole—is not the standard but is several generations removed from the needed language of business (or "pi-ji-ness," hence "pidgin") it originally was born to be. The assumed reader is an urban adult who is also unlikely to belong to the social class of the main characters of Lum's story. The audience is that same, implicit, middle-class audience that Hershinow questionably assumes to be outside pidgin stories' reach.

All of this is to say that the implied reader of "Beer Can Hat" is such that the story is clearly identifiable as a pastoral (which is conventionally by and for educated urbanites, but is symbolically about the rural and relatively unschooled; the devices themselves are metaphors for a certain concept of what is "simple"). "Beer Can Hat" as a pastoral relates in literary ways its particulars or limitations of setting, characters, diction, structure, and so forth to presumably universal forms and workings of the human imagination. In this case Lum's pastoral is the type with the "child as swain," to use William Empson's terminology; and it is a proletarian pastoral besides.[46] Not a celebration, not a glorification, not a romanticization of the life of a proletarian child or his Wordsworthian idiot-boy of a partner, Lum's story is basically ironical in its understatement, with its naive narrator and its tension between laughing and crying. Lum simply provides an "underview" of life, from the bottom looking up, where sometimes we see more going on than we perceive from above. The childhood idyll stands poised just a step away from what Carey McWilliams, writing of Carlos Bulosan and his fictional "personal narrative" *America Is in the Heart*, calls "bitterly realistic" exposures of "deceits, self-deceptions, distortions, aspostasies."[47]

Thus, in his "Primo Doesn't Take Back Bottles Anymore" (1972), Lum's early, pioneering Hawai'i idyll, the central character Rosario Kamahele is not the antihero he would appear to be but is again actually a character out of the pastoral, this time an "unemployed laborer" as swain.[48] In his man-child way, he seems unable to live up to the complexities and changes of the modern world. But he survives, along with whatever dignity he may have. "Collector," Rosa calls himself, rejecting the label of "unemployed laborer" written in his police record. Rosa collects and recycles empty Primo beer bottles as if they were reminders of yesterday's good times, usually somebody else's but sometimes his own when his thoughts ramble into the past. His life has always been rough. His chief achievement—at one time he was the "bull" of Central Intermediate School—brought trouble as well as a superficial, if terrifying, power. It entailed having to uphold a mean reputation while he led hijackings of kids from whom he extorted lunch money; and he personally took care of challenging the bigger haole boys to fights, even though the fathers of some might be ex-marines. Virtually all Rosa has are memories of those times, not very long ago at that, although he seems aged, shuffling along now with his bags of discards. When Rosa arrives by bus at the Primo brewery with another sackload of empties only to find that the recycling operation has been stopped, robbing him of the only apparent source of his own private income and not public welfare, Rosa grabs a freshly used paintbrush and strokes his final statement on the still wet, painted-out "Receiving Bottle Empties" sign: "F-O-C-K," he writes, wet letters on the same wet field, dripping and glistening in the sun. The Hawai'i idyll—here not of childhood but of the man-child prole just short of being a bag-man, the subject of another of Lum's stories —takes on surprisingly realistic themes.

Though Chin recognizes the fact yet still calls for something else to be done with pidgin, these characters of Lum's are not trying to be heroic and failing at it. This is not to say Lum's creations are inferior to hypothetical heroic ones. In this discussion they represent others in a considerable body of pidgin stories, dramas, and poems in Hawaii's literature. As unlikely an embodiment of pastoral *values* as Rosa K. may be in "Primo Doesn't Take Back Bottles Anymore," he shuffles along the roadsides picking up rubbish so that it will not be trashed but reused. The discontinuation of the practice implies an entirely different way of viewing the island: now as a place with unlimited garbage dumps for an unlimited supply of nonreturnable containers made from unlimited resources of minerals and energy. Against this seemingly limitless view and its assumptions, Rosa the recycler has become a lowly scavenger. But Rosa's view, which can well be put in the expression, "What goes around, comes around," is an *island* view, profoundly valuing the idea that an island community cannot afford to treat either resources or disposal of wastes as if they were unlimited and infinitely possible. This *insular* value is directly antithetical to Michener's *continental* American assumptions (or assumptions as they used to be, when people treated the continent as if it were boundless) in his telling, for example, of the introduction of the pineapple industry in *Hawaii*. Beginning with Melville, and again and again thereafter, we encounter in the traditions and works discussed in this study instances where the self-sufficiency implied by Rosa's actions, which somehow have become unsavory, even antisocial, in conflict with the world of no-returns, is not merely an imagined but also a necessary self-sufficiency and interdependence among people of a global community. Along with the theme of recycling (as in the beer can hat) come various expressions of reciprocity, or at least of the need for people to care for one another. Though he is the chief bully, and perhaps because this makes him responsible for setting an example, Rosa takes care of his brother Willy, who is forever teased by the kids for being a *mahu*, a transvestite. Rosa's loyalty to his brother is his real pride; Rosa's worst, most violent anti-haole memory is tied to the time Rosa, before a big fight with a haole, insults Willy by calling him a "fucking mahu," something others may do but Rosa must never. The implication through the story is that the frightening hostility of Rosa K. originates in the crushing of him and his values by those who continually make policies and standards that rob him not only of his material support but also of his right to live in his island way in the island setting.

It is not necessarily a rewriting of the literature itself, but it is the understanding of these qualities and underlying themes that should help to give "Beer Can Hat" and other local Hawai'i idylls an enduring and more universal response. Stories like Lum's are chock full of allusions to fads, significant uses of things, places, words, and activities known only to a child growing up in the particular times and places the stories are set; and they are characterized by references to much else that appears transitory. It is precisely this transience, however, that when skillfully treated implies the idyll's truth: "small keed time" is short and runs quickly away on its bare feet. At the same time, the pidgin used in some of the idylls is a powerful symbol of the past and a lost childhood. But amazingly, like Bobo, pidgin endures. In Hawai'i still, outside the workplace, pidgin generally unites local generations and the various ethnic groups like the food heaped in generous, multicultural array on everyone's paper plate at a community potluck dinner in Hawai'i.

It may be that many cultures, including Asian and Pacific ones, have developed oral and literary traditions extolling the supposedly simple virtues of children and of the peasant and laboring classes, contrasted

with the usually well-educated, mainly bourgeois class of adults who author such pastorals and who are expected to read them. The traditional
cottage of the Japanese tea ceremony, it is said, originated as a stylized
version of a typical Japanese farmhouse admired for its rustic peasant
simplicity. There is also a venerable Western literary tradition of the pastoral which I have been discussing. Even in view of the possibilities of
making more conscious use of Asian traditions, however, with such obvious exceptions as Hawaii's writers of *haiku* and *tanka* and new immigrants
actively writing in their native tongues, scarcely any Hawaiʻi writers
today turn frequently and directly to "the traditions and languages" of
"Asia rather than to those of America and Europe" in order to work
"within their own environment" and "to tell the story of their homeland"
(Hershinow, "Coming of Age?" 7). Hershinow misleads in asserting that
local writers turn away from America, which after all *is* these writers'
homeland. Their literary creations are American by definition, just as
Hemingway's writing *For Whom the Bell Tolls* with its Spanish Civil War
setting does not diminish his or its being American. Even a dedicated
poet and editor who appears to be a special case, Richard Hamasaki,
is not to be alienated from the fold of American literature as I am defining
it. Since April 1976 the editor of *Seaweeds and Constructions*, an occasional
literary journal in which he has been assisted by the late Wayne Westlake,
Paul L. Oliveira, Dana Naone, Shinichi Takahashi, Kimie Takahashi,
and Mark Hamasaki, his interests have ranged from Asian and Asian
American, through local, to Polynesian literatures and arts, a course generally reflecting Hamasaki's focus on the native cultural roots of Hawaiʻi.[49]
Use of the native Hawaiian language, literature, and its pervasive and
fundamental traditions, as I try to suggest in this overall discussion, is
of a tradition which, since the annexation of Hawaiʻi to the United States
in 1898 has every right and (at present) no choice but to be considered
native to America, in the most profound (and to some, disturbing) sense.

The larger context for Hawaii's local writers and their works
is American, which itself does not preclude borrowing from Asian sources
(Michener and James Clavell do, whatever their manners of borrowing).
The infant United States took the idea of a civil service meritocracy from
Confucius, the quintessential noble sage, though it may appear that
extremely few scholars in America are even aware of there being such
a legacy from China.[50] To say that an influence of "Asian" heritage limits
the appeal of a work of "American" literature in a deep sense is to deny
the international intellectual foundations of the United States. Hawaii's
writers are not alien to America. But every resident of the fiftieth state

knows what it is to wince when a mainlander refers to the continent as "the states" in distinction from "the islands," just as nearly every Japanese American in Hawai'i is to some degree miffed when mistaken for being a visitor from Japan. And might not reading the ironies of the pastoral—the convention of the paradoxically wise child, for instance—be the training we need to cut through just such mistaken identities and come out laughing at them as they deserve? Conversely, might not the pastoral be a set of literary conventions perfectly well suited for examining —and not simply reminiscing nostalgically about—this aspect of Hawaii's culture with this curiously ironical and many-eyed point of view?

A number of other Hawai'i local writers have turned to the childhood idyll as the mode of expressing and examining the experience of being "local." One of the best, most complex and insightful of these is a full-length novel by the seasoned writer John Dominis Holt, a hapa haole Hawaiian with connections and a heritage both deep and lofty in Hawaii's history; but the childhood idyll seems to be favored more usually by writers in the beginning stages of planting their claim in Hawaii's cultural history. These writers have, in some respects, broken from or altered literary conventions that do not fit their sense of Hawai'i or of themselves; they are engaged in discovering something fresh and honest to say about everyday life. During the 1950s, in addition to Saiki, Jelsma (née Kubojiri), Ige, and Murayama, Seiko Ogai published narratives and sketches depicting childhood in terms distinctive to her Hawai'i, while Charles Kong, though not writing mainly or strictly about childhood, undertook the allied development of a vigorous pidgin English for use in his authentically local short stories. In Hawai'i today poets and fiction writers such as Jody Masako Manabe, Susan Nunes, Juliet Kono, Gary Tachiyama, and Vinnie Terada deal variously with childhood themes within the overall literary pastoral traditions that Darrell Lum's work exemplifies in this discussion.[51]

Earlier, when discussing Patsy Saiki's "The Unwilling Bride," I referred to a fundamental Hawaiian value much touted today, *aloha 'āina* (love of the land). I suggested that another parent of Hawaiian values is *'ohana* (family). The Hawaiian language itself, being metaphorical in form, expresses these values metaphorically, and thus holds within it the basic meaning of the Hawai'i pastoral, in the cultivation of the land, the family, and the culture. The root of the word for family is *'ohā* (taro growing from the older root). Figuratively, *'ohā* means "offspring, youngsters," or the second generation of a family line growing from its progenitor *kalo* (taro) planted in Hawaii's earth and water. The terminology of taro culture goes on to include taro shoots called *keiki* (children), a term used metaphorically in a great many contexts. Specifically, the terms identify at least one preceding generation and four successive generations descending from the *'ohā*, the seed root of the native Hawaiians' staple food as well as the word for "family" (*'ohana*). These symbols and metaphors, integral to the Hawaiian language, bind love of the land (i.e., if you love and cultivate the land, the land will return that love by feeding you), family, sustenance, and culture itself into a rich complex of values—values involving reciprocity among people and between people and nature. These values underlie the pastoral traditions of mele and of local works in English as well. In "Kaulana nā Pua," Prendergast's mele protesting the American overthrow of Queen Lili'uokalani, the central lines, "We are satisfied with the stones, / Astonishing food of the land," speak exactly and profoundly of *aloha 'āina*—the latter word, "land," containing a pun, *'ai*, for "eat" and for "food"—and its deeply related values.[52]

These Hawaiian metaphors and cultural values have shaped the experience of Asian immigrants to Hawai'i, whose original home cultures also emphasize family and the cultivation of a severely limited plot of land. Their adopted home apparently has provided a fertile and receptive cultural ground. Children of these families are born into very important roles, for each child will play a part in carrying on or planting a new line stemming from the parent and from the ancestral stock the parent represents. The children are born also into American citizenship, which until 1952 was forbidden by United States laws to Asian immigrants: historically, the Asian American children fulfilled by birth what the Asian immigrant parents could not. Furthermore, as the *kalo* / taro is the transplanted stalk that brings forth the *'ohā* when the corm of the *kalo* matures, so the immigrants in Hawai'i who called themselves *issei* bore *nisei* children. This terminology itself implies that the "first" and the "second" are culturally the *same*—as part of the developing, changing Japanese Hawaiian (i.e., American) culture—and will be followed by further generations.[53] Patsy Saiki's "The Unwilling Bride" is informed by overlapping Asian and Hawaiian values based on family and on the cultivation of a land that has become home. An emphasis on children throughout Hawaiian literature is another kind of reflection of the strength of this value. Violation of the family can have profound consequences. Indeed, this very tricky problem is posed in a work that has become a contemporary classic in Hawaii's literature: Milton Murayama's *All I Asking for Is My Body*, a complex pastoral beginning in childhood.

Hawaii's Complex Idyll

All I Asking for Is My Body and Waimea Summer

I

Two novels published within a year of each other mark the coming of age of the homegrown, complex pastoral of Hawai'i. Each one is a *Bildungsroman* plotting the development of the narrator's psyche and values. Both begin in the childhood idyll; yet both include elements of the heroic, which implicitly serves as a larger context for these mature pastorals in Hawaii's Local literary tradition. Milton Murayama's *All I Asking for Is My Body*, published as a complete novel in 1975, and John Dominis Holt's *Waimea Summer* (1976) occupy two different bands of the rainbow of Hawaii's polyethnic culture, the Japanese American and the Hawaiian.[1] The former is a proletarian novel; the latter not merely bourgeois but patrician. Though their central themes differ, these works share a way of looking at several dimensions of the past: the narrators' own youth and personal experiences, their family histories, and the histories of their peoples. They share, that is, an important element of a local sensibility, which includes the ability to note the telling details, insignificant to outsiders but vital to the child of that land.

Because each contains strikingly unexpected elements somewhere in its ostensibly pastoral text, readers are often confused by *All I Asking for Is My Body* and *Waimea Summer*, though the tone of the former is so sly and understated—and yet paradoxically blunt in obvious ways—that the casual reader may miss its point or else fail to feel its sting. Both books have been misunderstood, a fault not of these novels but of commonplace, unexamined prejudices among readers. A comparison might be made with Twain and what may have been the impossibility of his Hawai'i novel in his own time. Twain, too, made his protagonist's childhood upbringing in Hawai'i fundamental to his story, and evidently he was anxious about its possibly being misunderstood. Both *All I Asking* and *Waimea Summer* suggest that the literary conventions customary to an idyllic view of "small keed time" Hawai'i are inadequate when the writer is trying realistically to define an experience and a point of view that are not reductive. Yet the Hawai'i childhood idyll, which each local generation of twentieth-century Hawai'i has reinvented, also becomes most useful and interesting when its conventions are stretched and tested as in Murayama's and Holt's full-length works.

Their titles hint at their themes and raise simple expectations. Nevertheless, both narratives go on to work these expectations like a gardener spading the earth. "All I asking for is my body" is a declaration of independence, a statement made first by the rebellious and headstrong eldest brother of the novel's narrator, who in turn learns what it means to value, to want, and then to gain freedom from unjust obligations and servitude. But despite its title, Murayama's novel does not begin with a lesson in escaping oppression; it begins with an affirmation of authority —that is, when that authority happens to be right. Furthermore, the novel ends with a restoration of the accepted, conventional order of things, not with a rejection of it. So unexpected is the happy ending that it seems at first to be unrealistic; some readers complain that it is a *deus ex machina*.

The Waimea summer of Holt's novel is, for the main character at age fourteen, a summer *vacation*, his first visit to the ranchlands of the Big Island to stay with his father's cowboy cousin. The land and the man are legendary to the boy after years of hearing his father's stories about Waimea and their ranching kin. The memory of this summer vacation, however, begins in gloom within a decaying house. The story rises episodically to moments of pastoral calm that might conclude a more usual, less interesting gothic romance; but Holt's novel drives on to close dizzily with a vision of ancient Hawaiian warfare and bloodshed, under-scoring in stark red and black that the Waimea summer vacation the narrator expected—and the Hawaiian history he romanticizes—never were true or possible.

Both novels are set mainly in the 1930s. While Mark Hull recalls his profoundly troubling Waimea summer of that era, Kiyoshi Oyama reflects on his growing up red-dirt poor in a coastal town and then in an upcountry sugar plantation camp on Murayama's fictional version of the island of Maui. Neither of these novels is a mere exercise in nostalgia.

In these novels, the ways of seeing each narrator's personal experience, history, and the sources of one's values differ radically from anything else written about Hawai'i prior to the mid 1970s.

2

"I'll Crack Your Head *Kotsun*," a childhood idyll that became part 1 of Milton Murayama's three-part novelette, *All I Asking for Is My Body*, has the distinction of being the first and only work by a local Asian American writer to be selected for inclusion in any Hawaiian anthology edited by the long-active experts A. Grove Day and Carl Stroven. Published in 1968, nine years following statehood and the original publication of Murayama's story in the *Arizona Quarterly* (Summer 1959), *The Spell of Hawaii* contains the introductory comment that "I'll Crack Your Head *Kostun*" "gives evidence that young people of Oriental ancestry brought up in Hawaii are becoming aware of their background as a source of unique literary material."[2] Not a new observation, the remark is reminiscent of how the *Paradise of the Pacific* had heralded Philip Ige and his story of two boys and a dog back in 1946.[3] Similarly ignored, Day and Stroven's 1968 comment about Murayama's piece went unnoticed through another decade. Other events, in which Murayama and Holt both participated, meanwhile signaled an eruption of literary activity among "young people of Oriental ancestry" in Hawai'i.

Murayama's boost into his position as the author of a Local Hawai'i literary classic came neither from the help of establishment publishers nor from his distinctive inclusion in the 1968 anthology. He and his wife Dawn Pyne did it themselves. They had grown tired of being told by prospective publishers that Murayama's lean and wiry manuscript was insular in its appeal, and they laughed at well-intentioned editors who suggested that, first of all, the manuscript's title seemed to need a grammatical correction. Murayama and Pyne refused to falsify the work and its subject. To publish *All I Asking for Is My Body* they created their own publishing house at their San Francisco home and named it after their dog, Supa, as in "Super." And so in 1975 *All I Asking for Is My Body* came off the Supa Press, rippling with pidgin and mixed languages and all the local color of Murayama's style, just exactly the way the author wanted it.

The most noticeable feature distinguishing this *Bildungsroman* from any other story about growing up in any other language is Murayama's use of Hawaii's pidgin and creole lingos. Early in the story

Kiyo explains that when meaning to be understood by their parents, the children sometimes "spoke in pidgin Japanese" and as a whole "spoke four languages: good English in school, pidgin English among ourselves, good or pidgin Japanese to our parents and the other old folks" (5) In the way Murayama renders both pidgin Japanese and pidgin English for the purposes of his novel, meant for virtually any English-speaking audience, the eldest son Tosh tattles (mispronouncing Kiyo's name to tease him), "Mama, you better tell Kyo not to go outside the breakers. By-'n'-by he drown. By-'n'-by the shark eat um up" (5). Having intended by his calculated spellings and his mingling of languages to authenticate the narrative, Murayama created other stylistic effects as well. While the narration proper is so-called good English, the narrative voice overall is in pidgin—or more precisely, the literary narrative or fictive voice of a Hawai'i nisei whose native tongue is Hawaii's creole. In writing this particular work, Murayama prized the "staccato" rhythms of that voice. This can be heard in the narration and seen in the following excerpt's short words and syllable counts. The passage begins the novel:

> There was something funny about Makot. He always played
> with guys younger than he and the big guys his own age always
> made fun of him. His family was the only Japanese family
> in Filipino Camp and his father didn't seem to do anything
> but ride around in his brand-new Ford Model T. But Makot
> always had money to spend and the young kids liked him.
> (P. 1)

In this, the novel's entire first paragraph, the only word with four syllables is "Filipino," and even it sounds staccato.[4]

Murayama of course was not the first to use pidgin dialogue and related elements of narrative style in a work of Hawaii's fiction. Besides short stories published earlier by other local writers of Hawai'i, some of them among the childhood idylls discussed earlier, full-length works of fiction preceded his novel in this regard, and pidgin was reappearing in recent short fiction as *All I Asking* neared publication. But *All I Asking for Is My Body* achieves something different and something more than its most immediate forerunners. Bob Hongo's *Hey, Pineapple!* (1958), a Korean War novel about some Big Island young men trying to begin their adult lives through the war and its aftermath, comes closest to matching Murayama's novel in certain aspects of style, theme, and local Hawai'i feel.[5] It, too, is a first-person narrative; *Hey, Pineapple!*, unlike *All I Asking*, ends in melancholy and angst. Murayama's novel remains close to home, set in a Hawai'i sugar plantation camp, not in the Asian battlefield that was one of the big reasons for the immediate popularity of *Hey, Pineapple!* among Hawaii's Korean War veterans and their families.

Murayama knew, too, that he was not the only Asian American novelist from the island of Maui. Another novel involving modern Hawai'i is set mainly on Maui. Touted as coming "from the same writing school that produced *From Here to Eternity* and *Valhalla*," Jon Shirota's first novel, sarcastically titled *Lucky Come Hawaii* (1965), is a bizarre story of an immigrant pig farmer who cheers the Japanese bombing of Pearl Harbor out of bitterness over the scorn he has endured from other Japanese because he is Okinawan: another instance of the oppressed aping the oppressor when he thinks his chance has come. Followed by Shirota's own quite different *Pineapple White* (1972), where an elderly issei comes to realize that Hawai'i has become his true home, *Lucky Come Hawaii* springs indeed from a school of writing that stresses spectacular action swirling around and in the violent thoughts of the central antihero. This differs from the reflection and contemplation implied by Murayama's reminiscence of a Hawai'i childhood, no matter how vigorous Kiyo's memories are.[6] Perhaps the most memorable use of pidgin to be published just prior to Murayama's novel is in Darrell Lum's short story, "Primo Doesn't Take Back Bottles Anymore" (1972). Lum's story, discussed in the preceding chapter, invites comparison, but it offers a different version of the pastoral, with its sharply contemporary, urban setting that glares like concrete and the sun and heat off the pavement, rather than the green, rural, olden days that we usually associate with a childhood idyll.[7]

Murayama's story of immigrant plantation workers and their children in rural 1930s Hawai'i is directly relevant to the histories of as clear a majority as one might muster in a society sharply aware of its diversity, its pluralism. Though by the time of the novel most Chinese laborers had moved off the plantations, they filled private entrepreneurial and other middle-class occupations elsewhere in the colonial society, which had lacked such a class, and they had been replaced several times over by Japanese, Portuguese, Filipinos, Puerto Ricans, and Koreans imported to labor in the fields.[8] And *All I Asking* has had a literary impact beyond whatever statistics may say. Michener's *Hawaii* comes nowhere near what Murayama's book was when first published and read by delighted islanders, or what the novelette would achieve as its readership grew. With the publication of *All I Asking for Is My Body* in 1975, Hawai'i was in for a treat. Dick and Jane were not the only kids growing up in the world in our century! The novel was unprecedented, yet when I first read it in 1975, fresh from Lawrence Ferlinghetti's City Lights Bookstore in San Francisco, Murayama's story, his characters, and certainly the language were as familiar to me as if they were my own.

The narrator recalls his youth, from his childhood in the early 1930s to his enlistment in the United States Army in 1942. Set first in the fictional seacoast town of Pepelau, and then in Kahana, a remote sugar-plantation camp up the slope of a mountain, the locale clearly evokes Lahaina and the typical laborers' village of a Maui sugar plantation. As the family's second son, Kiyo is in a position to observe the conflicts that fire others in the Oyama household without himself having to take the heat. The trailblazer is his hot-headed eldest brother Tosh, who struggles to free himself from supposedly traditional filial obligations. Tosh, according to Mother and Father, inherits the duty of repaying $6,000 worth of debts originally loaded on them by an inept grandfather and increased thereafter on account of their own setbacks. Moreover, Tosh is told he must work off the family's debt, not by completing an education and working a decently paying job, but by sweating for two-bit wages in the paternalistic plantation system. His going to high school would mean the loss of his income during that time. There seems no way for Tosh to get ahead, whether for himself or for the family's long-term good, and soon Kiyo must follow Tosh's tracks in quitting school and going to work. Tosh's expression, "All I asking for is my body!" is his cry for independence from a peculiar set of injustices that even his younger brother, who tries to be sympathetic with Tosh, takes years to understand.

What appears to be the book's central conflict is deceptive, while the true issue is not so much masked or understated as it is shouted out so loudly that it deafens some readers into ignoring it. In addition, Murayama's story contains a good-sized school of red herrings (in Hawai'i, a similar phrase might be ōpelu 'ula, a fish that simply does not exist). The false issues of intercultural conflicts between generations ironically invite certain kinds of *mis*readings, as would be expected in the fun of any work of satire. But the reading of satire is usually set straight by values that readers are assumed to share. Swift assumes that readers of his "Modest Proposal" will find the eating of babies to be an abhorrent thought. *All I Asking for Is My Body*, however, rests finally on a moral truth that evidently is not commonplace when applied to the ethnic groups and their situations in this novel. The usual misreading of the novel lies in a stereotypical, shallow—and racist—assumption that the American son must triumph over his immigrant parents in a war between their respective cultures, especially when these cultures are supposedly as incompatible as the Japanese and the American, and especially when the Japanese bomb Pearl Harbor near the novel's end. This misreading is based on notions about "assimilation," whereas to the contrary the novel's local-boy protagonist Kiyo mocks those nisei who try to be "haolefied," to imitate white people. The novel's true import rests not on such generalizations about cultures and nationalities but in a radically different, humane way of viewing relationships between its issei and nisei generations and of envisioning the Japanese *American* culture they share.

All I Asking for Is My Body consists of three parts of odd lengths. Part 1, "I'll Crack Your Head *Kotsun*," originally published alone as a short story, runs eleven pages. Part 2, "The Substitute," runs thirteen. Part 3 bears the novel's title and stretches across seventy-six pages. This structure prompts many readers to wonder if the slim volume might not better be thought of as a makeshift collection of stories. But the three parts are unified by plot and theme, moving in chronological order from Kiyo's ninth to nineteenth years, and joined further by the continuous character development of Kiyo himself. The subsidiary characters— Makot, Obaban, Snooky, Mother, Father, and Tosh—appear and recede in the story as each in turn enables Kiyo to learn a lesson and thereby move onward. In this underlying allegorical use of characters, *All I Asking* resembles John Okada's *No-No Boy*.[9] But then again, the narrative does not mesh easily into a thematic whole if we insist upon reading it with certain assumptions that the novel subverts, the satire overturns.

The usual misreading of *All I Asking* takes the theme of filial piety and uses it, and the parents' insistence upon it, to exemplify what is wrong with the immigrants' hierarchical and authoritarian values, culture, and community. It assumes that, because of their American educations, the nisei children exemplify an American response to Japanese parental oppression. What this misreading evades is how greatly oppressive is the prime American institution in this novel, the Frontier Mill Plantation. The central lesson that Kiyo hears in his American schoolroom is that we should not fight among ourselves at the expense of a unified struggle against the real, big enemy. But the plantation's supreme oppressiveness and its nationality somehow slip by, taken for granted, while the "Japanese" parents are vilified in a way that neither Murayama nor his novel endorse. When the issei parents emphasize family unity by warning against individualism in time of mutual need, some readers find them oppressive. But when the American schoolteacher lectures against selfishness and preaches unity among laborers of all races, these same readers approve.

Both as a *Bildungsroman* and as a satire, *All I Asking for Is My Body* is about growing up to be aware of the blindly conventional and the hypocritical in whatever quarter of society. But one must wonder what lies behind the condemnation, solely of the "Japanese," which one reader thus states: "There is little of value in the Japanese family or community in *All I Asking for Is My Body*, except perhaps the relationship between the two nisei brothers, who complement each other and whose ideas and identities are developed during their dialogues."[10] Somewhere behind this reading lies an assumption about an intercultural conflict where what is absolutely right to the issei parents is wrong to their nisei children. But suppose that what Mother and Father in Murayama's novel claim is their children's traditional duty to them is in their own "Japanese" terms neither right nor Japanese. Suppose that it is wrong, that it is Japanese tradition turned backwards, that it is, in fact, an extension of the oppressiveness of the American plantation.

The novel, in form and function a lean comedy, is a condemnation not of "aspects" of "the Japanese family or community" but of abuses against the family and community, whether from inside or from outside the lives of the novel's three generations of Japanese Americans. Murayama himself is explicit about wanting to be evenly critical of both sources of oppression, the plantation and the communities of laborers whose lives are made miserable and thus conflict-laden by the former. He states it thus: "I will use the same yardstick of honesty for both, I will criticize the Japanese family system with the same candor I criticize the plantation system. . . . Whatever promotes freedom is good; whatever suppresses it is not good."[11] And, Elaine H. Kim quotes Murayama's paraphrasing of William Faulkner: "I want this history remembered, not lost—like it is, with love, with all the warts showing" (Kim 147). With an eloquence quite his own, Murayama thus tells us what misreadings of his novel may lack: they lack "love," and a great measure of this love, he implies here and practically insists in his novel, is the love among a great-aunt, the parents, and the children.

Because of the uncertainties of our own assumptions as readers of just such a story as Murayama's, it is not always easy to determine what promotes and what suppresses freedom in the course of this novel, but in the end the good and the bad are unambiguous. The novel's wit and fun are a challenge. In part 1, the parents' order to end the friendship and harmless summer fun among Makot, Kiyo, and their two other bud-

dies may strike the reader at first to be as unjust as the child Kiyo thinks
they are at the time the incident occurs. At one point the parents warn
Kiyo that some unnamed shame will befall him and therefore his entire
family because of his association with Makot, an older boy ridiculed by
his peers for being a *kodomo taisho*, ("general" of the kids), and because
Makot's parents are somehow unspeakably "bad." Kiyo's parents, with
older brother Tosh on their side, may sound self-righteously "Japanese"
in their unreasoning, while the community may likewise seem bigoted
in judging Makot and his parents to be somehow strange, "funny." They
are as though exiled, the only Japanese family living in Filipino Camp
(the reality of ethnic segregation in Hawai'i is thus stated in the first
paragraph of the novel). Part 1 ends with Kiyo glimpsing that his parents
are right, however, though their shared values contribute to Makot's tragedy of being an outcast trying to buy friendship.

In part 2, a great-aunt's beliefs, which Mother shares, appear
at first to be nothing but superstitions, figments and fragments of their
no longer viable Japanese culture, irrelevant and incomprehensible to the
American child Kiyo. The title of part 2, "The Substitute," refers to the
belief that when it comes to retribution (*bachi*) for a wrong, the punishment might fall not on the wrongdoer but on the substitute. Early in
part 3, Tosh blames Mother's Japanese superstitiousness for contributing
to the family's inability to climb out of their debts:

> ". . . damn wahine, she too superstitious. She think she goin'
> die, she believe in it. She talk to you about it?" "No." "Yeah,
> no can get it out of her head." "Why?" "They all like that.
> Bulaheads [Buddha-heads, or Japanese] are crazy." (P. 14)

Kiyo continues, "Mother did seem to have more superstitions than most
people," and he goes on to list some and their supposed explanations
or actual proof. Again the impression is that, to her children, Mother
is quaintly unenlightened. From what she knows and believes, Mother
puts the cultural gap this way: "It would be *zannen* [too bad] to die in
a strange place like Hawaii, *ne*?" (14). The question then is, what does
Kiyo believe in all this?

Both parts 1 and 2 conclude with Kiyo's assuming his parents'
—or at least a version of Mother's—point of view. He stops seeing Makot,
and he is relieved that a "substitute" dies in Mother's place. We would
need to set those two parts aside, then, as separate tales, to take part
3, "All I Asking for Is My Body," at face value, where in their disagreement Tosh and Father not only argue words but also throw blows. Espe-

cially here, the conflict appears to be intercultural. "Goddam old futts, they still think they in Japan!" Tosh steams (48). In the usual misreading, part 3 is seen not merely to exacerbate an intercultural conflict between two generations of the same family but also to make that conflict central to the entire book. In short, we have what must sound like a familiar but simplistic paradigm of how, in order to be "American," a child of immigrants must assimilate into the "host" culture even at the expense of his or her parents and their old-world heritage. He or she must become "Americanized," the stereotype goes, because being born American is somehow not enough but, in this case, is dependent upon race.

Fortunately, *All I Asking for Is My Body* does *not* make sense in these terms. While Tosh thunders in complaint against his parents' insistence that he support the family, his big decisions are always as his parents demand. He quits high school in order to work on the plantation. He declines a chance to turn pro boxer because it would risk what little he can do to help the family, although his steady plantation job amounts to indentured servitude (it is prior to the successful unionization of the industry). He marries and pledges more than the equivalent of his wife's entire wages to his parents for a year and promises further years of support. Tosh, as seen of course by the narrator Kiyo, is full of such contradictions. "The guy was more filial than I thought," Kiyo marvels when Tosh's usual filial actions speak louder than his rebellious words.

The issei, too, are not free from contradictions. While Mother boasts of her devotion to Japanese traditions, especially spiritual ones, she like Father is a Methodist, and her most admired elder is Great-Aunt Obaban, who was banished from Japan for breaking tradition. Father, like Grandfather before him, fails at his own business, never mind the Japanese pride that swells up in their parables for right living. Without complaint from the parents about the reversal of roles, the Oyamas twice experience the overturning of the conventional hierarchy associated with the Confucian Japanese (upheavals that would likely be felt with pain anywhere in any culture under these conditions): first, when Mother, frightfully overworked in her cottage industry as a seamstress, falls so ill for a year that her boys have to run the house and care for the younger ones; the second time, when Tosh assumes leadership of the family following Pearl Harbor and the immediate suppression of his elders, the issei, and their Japanese tongues.

Indeed, Murayama satirizes hypocrisies everywhere in the confused miscomparisons of "American" and "Japanese" ideals and realities. In the schoolroom, the pupils are implored to take great "American" ideals to heart; but the colonial Frontier Mill Plantation is their all-embracing, most immediate and powerful example of how oppressive that very "America" is. The plantation manager himself sees to it that the school-teacher is fired and blackballed for teaching brotherhood, sisterhood, and equality in the public schoolhouse on the plantation. *All I Asking for Is My Body* is not about America (and the nisei) versus Japan (and the issei). It is about justice versus injustice. Simply by its being written honestly and realistically, the novel must be satirical, for such hypocrisies—that is, such blind contradictions that make life what it is—are everywhere, needing only to be recorded for satire to result. Growing up nisei in Hawai'i means learning an awareness of such things.

Not every instance of the immigrant parents' authority over their children is unjust. In part 1, for instance, whether because of "shame" or anything else, the parents may be right in forbidding Kiyo to play with Makot. As a small boy, Kiyo cannot understand this. Only in recollection does he realize the part it has played in his growing up. Part 1 ends precisely in a Joycean epiphany. Seeing beyond what the naive narrator tells us, we find a simple reason for Mother's and Father's lack of clear explanation in forbidding the friendship; the child Kiyo himself cannot understand and so cannot recount that Makot's mother is a prostitute and Makot's "father" her gigolo. That is why they are the only Japanese family living in the predominantly wifeless Filipino Camp; that is why the Sasakis have a brand-new Model T that Makot's father drives at his leisure in the daytime when other Japanese American men and women are at work.

The fact that Makot's mother is a prostitute is never made explicit in this naive narration. Her appearance confirms the circumstantial evidence, when Kiyo catches his first sight of her dressed for work: "She was all dressed up in kimono. Mother made a lot of kimonos for other people but she never had one like hers. She had a lot of white powder on her face and two round red spots on her cheeks" (10). She laughs at the thought of a small boy addressing her, of all people, politely as Sasaki-*san* and thanking her for lunches in the honorific manner. Kiyo's parents, however, try to address the matter in terms he would understand —or at the very least, in those terms he has grown up to remember. The snacks, lunches, and movies to which Makot has treated his younger friends are bought with the earnings from his mother's nightwork, and Kiyo's parents talk about these foods as if they had been contaminated. "But can't you see, Kiyo-chan, people will laugh at you," Mother tries to coax Kiyo not to eat lunch at Makot's as he has been doing. He will look like a beggar. When Kiyo questions her, Mother says, "Nemmind! You'll catch a sickness if you go there too often," and "she made a real ugly face" (3). Even Tosh, the Oyamas' *chonan* (number-one son), reared with Father's severest slaps on the head for being impertinent, this time agrees with this parents. He warns Kiyo not to follow Makot because of the danger of doing what younger ones should not, such as swimming in the deep ocean beyond the breakers. Three years older than Kiyo, it is Tosh, Makot's classmate, who derisively calls him a *kodomo taisho*, a general of the kids, an outcast able only to find playmates among younger kids whom he bosses around and patronizes.

Kotsun is "the sound of something hard hitting your head" (4), as when Father punishes his boys. Part 1, "I'll Crack Your Head, *Kotsun*," ends darkly one night when Makot tries to shove his mother out of Kiyo's sight. Kiyo, perplexed, knows only that he would not treat his own mother that way, and that somehow Makot's mother is not like his own. He is poised at the brink of knowing, then, why his parents spoke of the Sasakis' being "bad" and of the shame in associating with them. But behind the naiveté and the surprise of this superbly understated story lies the tragedy that Makot (his name means "sincerity") has experienced repeatedly, with each new friend's discovery of what the Sasakis do for a living.[12] In a childlike reflection of a prostitute's customer, Makot buys the younger kids' friendship with foods and toys that only money can buy, but that ironically cannot buy him his mother's love. Kiyo, too young to understand such matters, backs away from his pitiable friend. And yet, along with pity *for* Makot, Kiyo gains the conflicting sense that his own parents and brother, warning *against* the friendship, knew best.

Again contrary to interpretations stressing cultural conflicts between issei parents and nisei children, part 2 of *All I Asking* shows in several ways how alike—and still individual—the characters are in their beliefs. When Kiyo lists some of the many "superstitions" Mother lives by, he at first sounds noncommittal, if not doubting:

> Mother did seem to have more superstitions than most people. She insisted that rice should always be scooped at least twice from the big bowl to the individual bowls even if the second scoop was a token one without any rice on the ladle. The double scooping protected the family from seeing a second mother, meaning your first mother would not die or run away.
>
> Mama in Japanese meant cooked rice and mother. (Pp. 14–15)

Tosh calls Mother "crazy" for believing in such things. But not all "Bulaheads" believe. Father does not. When lying ill in a hospital, Mother rubs the cleft at the end of her nose and says, "In Japan they say people with these clefts die young." Father retorts, "Don't talk like a fool, you'll outlive us all" (15). Deeply steeped in a rural Japanese up-bringing, Mother is expert in predicting and warding off bad luck, though evidently with no practical success, since the Oyamas seem espe-cially unlucky. Paradoxically, she and father are Methodists and their chil-dren are baptized. Mother converted in marrying Father, who had already become a Methodist simply because "in the old days there was nothing going on in Kahana on Sundays except at the Methodist Church" (21). But it is not only the issei who hold coexisting beliefs from supposedly conflicting sources. Kiyo does, too. Whereas his parents assumed new beliefs by conscious effort (as they adopted pidgin English for one of their languages in adulthood), Kiyo and his generation have been born into a pluralistic culture.

How naturally unified such disparate beliefs are in Kiyo's devel-oping identity is demonstrated in part 2, when Kiyo receives word that his Great-Aunt Obaban has suffered a stroke. Obaban was the first of the Oyama clan to emigrate. A wise and compassionate woman, "the only one who was kind to Mama when Mama been come from Japan," Tosh explains, Obaban had been banished from Japan because she violated the Buddhist forty-nine-day mourning period following her father's death (17–18). During that proscribed period she eloped, her first of two mar-riages, this first one ending in divorce. Though a renegade in her time, Obaban in part 2 plays a central role as Mother's confidant and spiritual counselor, when Mother's very poor health, beginning with her losing all her teeth, brings a crisis to the already strained Oyama household, which depends on the income from Mother's sewing while Father is fail-ing as a commercial fisherman. It is with Obaban that Mother talks freely about their belief in "substitutes." Kiyo explains that "*bachi* [retribution] was a punishment you got when you did something bad and got away with it. The scary part was it didn't have to happen to the wrongdoer himself, it could fall on his children or any substitute" (20). We see here that Kiyo himself leans toward the belief, though he also questions it in noting how Father "pooh-poohed the whole thing, 'If you wait long enough, some bad luck is bound to happen to everybody.'" Even Obaban herself is circumspect. "Does it really work?" Kiyo asks her about *bachi*. "Yes, if you believe it does," Obaban replies (20).

Like his issei elders Obaban and Mother, Kiyo does believe. It is not as if he has to choose to do so. First he fears that Mother herself is suffering as the substitute for someone else, a wrongdoer. Then his spontaneous and lasting response to Obaban's death not merely confirms his belief in substitutes but also allows him to console himself over the loss. The news of Obaban's stroke comes to Kiyo in the most idealistically "American" place in his daily life, the schoolroom. He at first assumes that the bad news is about Mother:

> About eleven o'clock father showed up at the doorway of my sixth grade class and my heart started pounding like a fist against my chest. He never came except on parents' visiting day when he happened to be home! "Kiyoshi," Mrs. Miki-moto, our teacher, looked suddenly very sad, "there's been a . . . some sad news, you may be excused from class . . ." "Please God, please God, please God, let her have a little breath left!" I was shaking all over and wobbling like a drunk as I walked to the head of the class where father waited. "*Baban chubu ni kakatta,*" he whispered, and suddenly I felt like jumping and shrieking like I hit a home run! "*Baban* had a stroke." "When?" "Ten this morning. They telephoned Aoki Store. I'm going ahead. She might still be alive. You get Takako, Miwa, and Toshio." "Yes." I grabbed his hand and pumped it and he looked at me like I was crazy. (P. 23)

To Kiyo there is no line dividing his pleading with the Christian god from his feeling relief that it is Obaban who is the substitute—for Mother, a nominal Methodist—in a Buddhist wheel of karma. There is no pausing over any irony that he should be thinking such "superstitious" things in the classroom, of all places. His closeness to Mother and her beliefs is now unquestionable. He goes on to see further how the present occurrence fits with other thing she has learned:

> I felt so relieved I felt kind of guilty. But *Obaban* was the logical substitute, she was old and lived a full life, Mr. Kitano [Obaban's second husband] and *Anshan* [Obaban's son] who was about thirty wouldn't miss her that much. Mrs. Kanai once told us a story in language school of a famous poet who'd been invited to a Name Day and asked to compose a poem. He wrote, "*Jiji ga shine, oya ga shine, ko ga shine*" (The grandfa-ther should die, then the father, and then the son). His host shouted, "How dare you speak of death when we're celebrating birth!" The poet said, "It celebrates happiness. It's a happy household where death happens chronologically." Things will

be looking up now that *Obaban's* put an end to the cycle of bad luck. (P. 23)

Far from pitting the nisei child against the issei parent, part 2 stresses the closeness between Kiyo and Mother, a relationship strengthened here not only in their shared beliefs but in their love for each other as well. The novel's most poignant evocation of this love is also one of the most understated moments in the entire text; and the word "love" never explicitly appears in the text except in Kiyo's pubescent fantasies about "love-making" (95). The word does not even occur when Kiyo's idealistic sixth-grade teacher asks the class to name "the queen of virtues" (36), and they do not.

The final moment of part 2, where Kiyo and Mother most directly imply their love as child and parent, is preceded by a very brief yet expressive pastoral interlude. Just after Obaban's funeral, Kiyo reminisces in her garden. It is a fine evocation of both the soft and the sharp experiences of Kiyo's local childhood:

> A light rain had fallen in the night and the trees danced in the wind. It was what I enjoyed most visiting *Obaban*, fooling around in the green-green yard early in the morning. I'd already be in the ocean with goggle and spear back in Pepelau. But here it was so cold I needed a sweatshirt. I used to climb the mango tree, pick avocados with the long bamboo pole, pick papaya, lime, soursap, starfruit and pomegranate. I picked and ate a chili pepper on my first visit and went crying to *Obaban*. These were *Obaban's* trees and she watered them, fed them manure, mumbled to them. But I wouldn't hesitate a second if it was a choice between her and mother. Children who lost a parent stuck closer together, but it was more like they were huddling closer waiting for it to strike again. They never got over that dread. (P. 26)

As part 1 ends with an epiphany, the realization that Kiyo's childhood innocence is now forever in his past, part 2 draws to an end with an elegy, a sense that with Obaban's passing, the sensations and perceptions of the child's "fooling around in the green-green yard early in the morning" will never occur again except in memory. It is not, however, a mere, sentimental memory. Kiyo's thoughts here hold together the sweet fruit and the sour, the morning chill in upcountry Kahana and the chili pepper's fire, Obaban's death and, therefore, Mother's continuing life.

What follows this is somewhat bizarre, even grotesque, in the apparent triviality with which it ends, when we might expect other words to express grief over Obaban's death. This is Murayama's understatement at its best:

> When mother and the girls showed up, I greeted them at the front gate.
> "I'm so glad you went to get *Obaban*. We must've both known, something must've told us we wouldn't see her again. It would've been too much if she too died without my seeing her. Thank you, thank you," she held my hand in both of hers and bowed and bowed. Her bony face looked fresh like the air washed by rain.
> "She was your substitute."
> "I'm such a nobody and twice I've been saved." She let go my hand and started up the slight hill to join the other women. She walked very slowly, but her steps seemed surer. She wasn't trembling. She paused and put her hand to her mouth, "I feel so ugly. It's been like losing all your old friends at once."
> "You'll have to get some false teeth," I said.
> "Yes." (P. 26)

This oddly Faulknerian bit of dialogue—with its echo of Anse Bundren yearning for false teeth in *As I Lay Dying*—includes Mother's exceptionally frank and direct thanks for Kiyo's helping her through her illness. It also includes a recognition that life must go on—with substitute teeth, as it were—and that losing one's teeth is like losing one's friends, and Obaban above all was Mother's and her family's friend. The understatement evokes the main themes of the plot and brings to a quiet close the grieving over the death of the last surviving elder to Mother and Father. The wit heard in the talk of false teeth is typical of Murayama's humor in *All I Asking for Is My Body*, though in many places the jokes are noticeably less delicate than what passes between Mother and Kiyo.

The most subtle effect of this passage, which concludes part 2, is its contrast with the ending of part 1. Instead of seeing a boy and a mother insulting and shoving each other, which Kiyo witnessed at Makot's house, we see in part 2 a different boy and his mother sharing love and respect. This wholly implicit contrast between Makot and Kiyo in and of itself tells us that *All I Asking For Is My Body* is not about a rejection of values and a cutting of ties between generations, which would make the novel a tragedy in its own terms, like Makot's tragedy.

I have repeatedly made a point that parts 1 and 2 demonstrate the bonds between the generations of the Oyama family because part

3 too often makes readers forget them. Here is where the real trouble begins. Taken along with parts 1 and 2, part 3 then should build upon Kiyo's maturing devotion to his family. In most of part 3, however, the focus is on Tosh, with Kiyo mainly observing the fights between Tosh and their parents over what they say is his filial duty to pay their accumulated $6,000 in debts. It is here that the novel seems to take a sharp turn. In their fighting, the parents and Tosh appear now to have no love and no respect for one another. While Tosh scorns his parents for being so "Japanese" in their insistence on filial piety, Mother and Father warn Tosh not to be like white Americans. "Look at the *haoles*," Tosh rails, "Obligation is to the children." "The *haoles* are inferior. They're wasteful and lazy and extravagant. They treat their parents like strangers, they steal their brothers' wives," Father strikes back (45). But in a larger context, it is not so clear that the two sides are fighting across an uncrossable cultural line. At one point Tosh accuses the parents of being *ko-fuko* (undutiful to the children), in other words negligent in Japanese terms as well as American (42). As I have earlier suggested, Tosh seen from outside the family must appear to be the very paragon of a suffering, devoted chonan. When it comes to a conflict between justice and injustice, moreover, clearly in the novel and in the author's commentary the parents are unwitting allies with the plantation in keeping the boys down. When the plantation keeps the parents in debt to the company stores, the parents cannot leave. When the parents enlist their children to help pay that debt by working on the plantation, then the children too cannot escape. The plantation thus accomplishes its own most urgent need: it retains its stoop labor force. In the actual decade in which the novel is set, the Hawai'i sugar planters made annual appeals to the increasingly educated nisei to do their supposedly *American* duty and return to labor on the plantations.[13] Injustice here respects nothing, certainly not cultural boundaries.

Its surprise ending affords the most obvious yet troublesome evidence that something other than an intercultural conflict must be central to the novel's third part. This happy resolution simply does not address intercultural conflict. When Kiyo wins enough money in a crap game to pay up the family's entire debt, the "American" nisei does not triumph over the "Japanese" issei; rather, everyone presumably wins except the other nisei soldiers who gamble against Kiyo. Either the novel is flawed —just as the conclusion of *Huckleberry Finn* may fail to resolve Huck's moral quandary over racism, though it may solve his predicament—or the central issue of Murayama's novel is really something else. And that something else is satisfied simply by the payment of the debt that has indeed triggered every fight in the Oyamas' house at the end of Pig Pen Avenue ever since Father failed at fishing and had to return to the plantation to hoe the red dirt rows. In the move from the level, seaside Pepelau of parts 1 and 2 to Kahana, where the Oyamas live near the bottom of the hill as well as the figurative social pyramid, Kiyo's "childhood was chopped off clean" (28). The tone of these words opening part 3 seems to portend something greater than the skirmishes between Tosh and his parents. The move from town to country for Kiyo is the opposite of the conventional pastoral retreat into a more idyllic way of life. With every next page, part 3 seems to lose hope for any happy ending.

It is here that another, complicating theme plays an important part. Unlike the conventional idyll, where history stands still or is screened from view, or where time's passage is seen in the moment's realization that we must seize the day for life is short, in *All I Asking for Is My Body* history itself figures directly into the novel's plot and resolution. Kiyo's winning of more than $6,000 in a crap game results from the novel's pivotal historical event, the bombing of Pearl Harbor; and his winning allows him to end cycles of debt and failure that have dogged the Oyamas for three generations of their history. The family's history of failure is at the heart of Tosh's quarrel with his parents. For himself, Tosh wants to end the cycles by refusing to assume the debt. Not only for himself but for the whole family, Tosh's "substitute" Kiyo uses his winnings to pay the entire debt and thus end the cycles of failure. He thereby restores the family to the love implicit in the childhood recalled in parts 1 and 2.

History appears in several different ways in the novel. These range from the barest suggestion, in part 1, of the continuing presence of Hawaii's original peoples and their history, to the crucial role the Japanese bombing of Pearl Harbor plays in the novel's plot and the protagonist's final development. A sense of history develops even as the narrator matures. At one point in part 1, Makot orders his three followers to pick coconuts from Pepelau's only "free" trees, "deep in the cane fields and . . . too tall and dangerous" (6). The boys' passage through the thick and cutting growth of cane is—like Rip Van Winkle's hike into his Catskill retreat, or Tommo's dangerous climb up and down into the Typee Valley—a difficult passage through dense, recent growth to something ancient and aboriginal. "We had to crawl through tall cane to get to them," Kiyo complains, "and once we climbed the trees and knocked down the coconuts we had to hunt for them in the tall cane again" (8).

Having grown up seeing such trees standing in the fields, Kiyo and his companions merely harvest their coconuts without a thought as to how these "free" trees came to grow there in the first place. From an historical point of view, however, the trees are older than the cane fields planted around them. The trees may mark the site of a dwelling or perhaps something sacred. Even before the planting of the cane fields, the spot was cultivated by Hawaiians. More recently, someone plowing the fields must have decided to keep green their memory by letting the trees stand. Furthermore, by selling the ancient trees' coconuts they gather by such hard and dangerous labor, Makot aims to buy a twenty-two rifle, a piece of machinery contrasting with the old-fashioned slingshots other boys are making out of forked guava sticks and contrasting as well with the impression of age and of history that the trees present. Makot seems to be marching the boys out of step with their peers, their ages, and their setting.

While the small detail of the tall coconut trees in the cane fields may not amount to much in itself, as Kiyo grows up, so does history's prominence in his outlook. In part 2, as a sixth grader, Kiyo hears Mother's story of her family's misfortune and her immigration as a picture bride, and also Tosh's version of Obaban's history, the history of how the Oyamas first came to settle in Hawai'i. There is a perceptible jump in tone—or, in this case, the level of Kiyo's maturity and therefore his attitudes—between parts 1 and 2. In the earlier, Kiyo marks time in terms of the summer vacation, the fourth grade he is about to enter, and the Hawaiian seasons as children perceive them—"slingshot season," "spearing-fish season," and the implied mango season (6). In contrast, part 2 begins with the novel's first mention of any specific date: "Mother had always been weak and sickly but she got so sick I thought she was going to die. It was the end of January 1934 and we all had rotten teeth but hers were the worst and she had them all pulled at Dr. Hamaguchi's and fainted and was rushed to Dr. Kawamura's" (13). Forced by the crisis to grow up, Kiyo assumes much responsibility for taking care of his younger sisters while Mother is ill, Father is away fishing for their living, and Tosh, a high school freshman, works part-time in a store. Learning history and assuming responsibility are partners in one's growing up. Telling Kiyo her history of hardships, which lead her to believe that she is suffering retribution for someone else's wrongs, Mother is so specific about dates that we might infer her to be obsessed with the exact links between the times and events that close her cycle of retribution, her "fate" (17). Mother believes that her father's death in 1915 was not so "sudden" or unexpected as it seemed:

Your youngest uncle graduated from Wakayama University in June and in August he was dead from tuberculosis. He worked his way through college and strained his health. Your grandmother doted on him and she just wasted away and died of grief in November. Then on December 14 father died of a stroke. So it was happening all the time, it's still happening, it happens in cycles of fours. It must be some retribution. What did I do? I lie here and search and search my mind. (P. 17)

In part 2 Mother's and Tosh's history lessons serve as backgrounds for the strong relationship between Mother and Obaban—and, interestingly, between Tosh and the headstrong Obaban as well. Both these histories are told to Kiyo. In part 3, however, Kiyo begins by retelling the history of the family's debt himself, starting with the most specific date he himself states so far: "On August 1, 1936, another girl was born." So Kiyo chronicles his family's hardest times, noting that "father must've been a little disappointed. He named her Tsuneko (Common Child)" (27). Caring for the new child burdens the family further, and other births follow. At one point Mother, Tosh's wife Fujie, and the Oyamas' oldest daughter Miwa are all pregnant. History here serves the novel in two ways. First, although in growing up Kiyo learns to mark time and count years in a straight-line historical fashion, the Oyamas' lives seem, to the contrary, either static or to be going in circles, just as Mother believes. Second, history nonetheless implies a continuity from one generation to the next, history, that is, as a *continuous record of change*; so in learning and reciting their family's history, first Tosh, and then Kiyo, are finding out what *ties* them to their forebears.

In Tosh's case, it is clear that he admires Obaban for her being a "black sheep," a breaker of traditions (17). At first it is not easy to see, however, how Kiyo interprets history, and yet his liberation from the injustice of the inherited debt depends upon his correctly interpreting its history. His own ideas still unformed, he adapts Mother's version of the debt's origins, calling it "a model story of filial piety, which mother told over and over" (27). But his version of Mother's story is all too straightforward and begs to be read critically, especially since Mother is terribly self-serving when it comes to interpreting matters of filial piety. How, for instance, must the following be interpreted?

When grandfather finally saved enough money to return to Japan in 1922, mother begged him to leave father and her some money. She was carrying another child [i.e., Kiyo], and they had nothing to live on for the next month. Grandfather wept and he begged mother not to ask. He needed every penny he'd saved. He had all the debts he had to pay back in Japan, he had a family of two girls and one boy he was taking back with him. There were the boat fare, winter clothing and a hundred unforeseen expenses after which he had to have enough to open a clothing store in Tokyo. Not only that, he asked father to pay the bill for his farewell party, which came to $300; he asked father to look after his two younger brothers. He cried, "I'll repay you, I'll send for you as soon as I'm successful! I can't ask for more filial children!" "That's why," mother would say to us, "our minds are at peace even if he should die tomorrow. We've done our filial duty to him." (Pp. 27–28)

At least mother is frank enough by Kiyo's account to say that she "begged" Grandfather to spare them some money, and that Grandfather "wept" and "begged" her in return. The way the story is told reveals rather than hides the probable fact that Grandfather's demands must have struck Mother and Father as outrageous and that they did what they could to fight him, though Mother, not wanting a fight from her own children over her repetition of Grandfather's demands, now denies that any fight occurred. The list of grievances and demands builds swiftly in the narrative passage above, climaxing with Grandfather's request for nothing less than a farewell party at Father's expense, and collapsing in the fatuous remarks on both sides about filiality. The battle between generations, in this novel, is about this version of the debt's history—a self-serving and romanticized version. It is not about a difference of culture.

Tosh uncovers the real crux of the issue over the family debt. Because of the role he plays, perhaps best suited to the oldest child, Tosh appears to be the hero of most of part 3, with Kiyo mainly observing until near the novel's end. Tosh sees the history of the family debt differently from his parents. Grandfather, he says, was a "thief," "a *dorobo*," and the Oyama sons are now in turn being robbed by their already victimized parents trying to recoup their loss (42). Grandfather himself acknowledged that the debt was his own, for him to repay to his children. It was not originally thought of as a matter of filial piety but as an unusual parental debt to the adult children. Things do not occur in normal chronological order in the Oyama family.

Piecing together scattered details in parts 2 and 3, indeed as

Kiyo's reflection on the first two decades of his life aims to do, we find the history to which Tosh alludes in his insult to Grandfather. The Oyamas' cycles of shortchanging and failure have lasted more than three generations. On Mother's side, they began in a sense with her parents' dying supposedly as a result of their son's fatal strain to graduate from a university. The son died before the parents, and the education never really bore fruit. Meanwhile Grandfather Oyama's education in business college stopped short at the death of his father. As chonan and with his own education incomplete, Grandfather inherited the family farm but sold it because "he wasn't any good at farming" (27). Taking a bride and her dowry, he opened a clothing store in Osaka but failed again. With Grandmother and a considerable debt, Grandfather emigrated to Kahana, where his banished oldest sister Obaban had settled (we may assume he had had much to do with her banishment), and he eventually sent for some of his children, including Father, not to share with them a good life but to put all his able-bodied children to work in the cane fields for the family—that is, for him and the plantation.

Under these circumstances, Father in turn was denied any education that might have boosted him out of the plantation. Father is educated enough in Japanese, however, to write signs in calligraphy and assist the issei community, forbidden United States naturalization, with documents pertaining to virtually the only legal citizenship America allowed them—Japanese. Like Grandfather, Father with his incomplete education is likewise a repeated failure, evidently full of ambitious dreams but, despite a taste for enterprise, with no means to fulfill them. Though he tries to escape the plantation's cycles of poverty by becoming a self-employed commercial fisherman, his approach to his trade is best revealed in his wistful comment: "The sea was so calm today. There was no current. I could practically see the papiyos [an infant Jack Crevalle, quicksilver and cobalt in coloring] in the blue water from where I worked" (43). He fails in the business and must return with his family to Kahana, resuming plantation labor after the birth of Tsuneko in 1934. No matter what his former ambitions, Father can now think only of his sons' paying the family's debts. He and Mother invent for this purpose a singular illogic, a conundrum by which they fool themselves and everybody but Tosh: we paid our filial debt to Grandfather, they say; and likewise, you the child must repay us the parents the amount of our consequent debt. What nobody but Tosh sees is that if he were to pay his parents the $6,000, which he would do if he could, then *they* would end up having "paid" nothing to anyone, their professed payment to Grandfather entirely made up to them by someone else, Tosh. So how can they boast of having done their filial duty?

It needs to be made clear that while the reciprocal parental obligation, on the one side, and filial piety, on the other, are not exactly intergenerational business deals in the Confucian system, the idea that children owe something to their parents is itself based on the commonplace observation that since parents raise the children eventually to be on their own, therefore, when the parents can no longer take care of themselves in old age, the children should reciprocate the care they earlier received from their parents. This reciprocity extends throughout life and indeed a family's lineage, and it may also be thought of as mutual respect, reverence, piety, and love. The obligation of the parents to their young children, in the context of *All I Asking for Is My Body*, ought to consist of child-rearing and the education to enable the child to contribute to the welfare of the family and society as an adult. But both Tosh and Kiyo, and in their own times Father and Grandfather, are denied their educations, and, contrary to the usual order of things, Tosh and Kiyo as rather young children have to begin to support their parents' family. What then is it that Tosh, a teen-ager, is supposed to be *re*paying, and how? What besides his "body" has he received? And, in truth, he has not received even that.

Despite his fighting for a high school education and a chance for a decent career outside the plantation, Tosh quits school on his parents' orders. Except for Kiyo, the second child, it is the younger ones who are able to continue in school thanks to Tosh's income. Kiyo, too, has to drop out of school. The situation is incredible when compared with the glowing stereotypes often painted about Japanese Americans valuing education and number-one sons (i.e., a hierarchical ordering of family members by age and gender) above all. But the fictional Oyamas are not a rare exception. Murayama's depiction of the family is highly realistic not only in showing the chokehold that the plantation's wages, the plantation's stores, and other deductions inflict on the family's survival and values but also in characterizing the chonan and his expected duties in a far-less-than-ideal family. And what laboring family on the plantation in the 1930s enjoyed ideal economic circumstances? In many families the hierarchy of age meant not that the older ones benefited most, but that they sacrificed their own educations for their juniors. And furthermore, what individual benefit, if any, is it that the eldest son and daughter are supposed to inherit?

Grandfather dropped out of school and failed. Father lacks an education that might have taken him somewhere better, permanently. Tosh and Kiyo drop out of school. Tosh fears that even his own children (the first one only three months younger than Mother's last born), nieces, and nephews will be forced to ride these cycles of poverty. Yet in the world outside Kahana, time and history seem to accelerate while Tosh and Kiyo are stagnating. History intrudes, however, with increasing consequence. Tosh loudly criticizes Japan for invading Manchuria, and, like most of his nisei peers in the 1920s and 1930s, he gets Father to cancel the children's Japanese dual citizenships, which used to be conferred when community secretaries such as Father reported the individual births of nisei to the Japanese Consulate. For several years, Tosh and Kiyo pass the time in amateur boxing, so that they pace themselves through these years of their physical maturing by seasons of training. Tosh fights in the Territorial championships but, to Kiyo's surprise, refuses an offer to turn professional, because, Tosh replies, of "family obligations" (70). Though he thus chooses to remain confined with his family on the plantation, Tosh by his words and example expands Kiyo's sphere of vision to include: the plantation seen as a feudal, colonial oppressor; Manchuria and Japanese warmongering; U. S. citizenship as a political tool, a birthright, and a responsibility; wild opportunities in the poor man's sport of boxing; the meaning of history in their lives; the many faces of injustice, sometimes indeed their parents' own.

It is one of the odd twists in Hawaii's Japanese American history that the Japanese raid on Pearl Harbor opened the way to the Hawai'i nisei's eventual education and new life off the plantation. The event traumatizes Kiyo. It forces him to think very seriously about Tosh's comments on Japan's invasions of Manchuria, about Father's cancellation of the dual citizenship, and about all the Japanese ideals his parents and the Japanese language-school teacher have preached, now betrayed by this treacherous act of the Japanese Imperial Navy. On a personal level, Kiyo's deliverance from the plantation and from the family's debt and seemingly self-perpetuating cycles of failure and unjust obligation comes from a double realization and the act, the risk, which that realization requires Kiyo to go on to try.

First, Japan's treachery shows Kiyo that the nation idealized by some issei can be not merely mistaken but horribly wrong. Analogously, this makes possible what Tosh has been saying about Mother, Father, and Grandfather: in the issue of filial piety and the family debt, they have been wrong, surely something very difficult for any child to judge and admit. With no elder to check them since Obaban's death, Mother and Father have been dictating their own misinterpretations of "filial piety." This is the advantage to being an immigrant: one can establish as "tradition" a practice only imperfectly remembered and understood, by one who left Japan while relatively young, with no elders around to make corrections. It is his issei, first-generation parents who have been untrue to the concept and value called "filial piety," not Tosh. Just as earlier in the novel Tosh consults Mr. Takemoto, the Japanese language teacher, about the meaning of filial piety, so, after Pearl Harbor, Kiyo seeks out the teacher who, sickened by the Japanese attack, admits that sometimes the Japanese suffer from *shimakuni konjo* (the narrowness of an island nation) (82). By his own feelings—which confirm his local identity, evident since the very first paragraph of the novel—Kiyo knows that there is no question about his difference from the enemy: he is not a Japanese. He is a nisei, a second-generation Japanese American. Father, too, of the first generation of Kiyo's culture, shows by his actions following the air attack that he must show his distance from the enemy. Kiyo grows able to admit the possibility and the reality of his own parents' having been wrong about some ideals they have preached. No longer feeling *obligated* to pay the family debt and to comply with what his parents have been claiming to be "Japanese tradition," Kiyo shortly *decides* on his own, at age nineteen, to enlist in the U.S. Army when the call for volunteers reaches Kahana.

The second part of his double realization is that Kiyo thus grasps for the first time what *freedom* is. Tosh charges that their parents cannot see beyond their own noses in their being in debt and still having more children. Tosh, too, however, in part because he is so filial beneath it all, strikes Kiyo as fighting within and against only his most immediate circumstances. As Murayama puts it, Tosh "is not arguing for the liberation of the masses. He's fighting for his own specific skin."[14] While the same applies to Kiyo, at the climax of his growth in the novel he recalls his sixth grade teacher Snooky, the 1930s radical idealist who speaks of freedom as a universal value while everyone else speaks of duty and obligation.[15] Kiyo may just as well acknowledge at least two other figures: Obaban, for somehow having remained true to her principles, and Tosh himself. He has learned from all three. Kiyo defines his freedom in an even earthier way than Tosh. In Kiyo's own declaration, "shit" means injustice, whether the plantation's or his parents':

> Snooky gave me a glimpse of what it could be. I would have
> to get out and be on my own even if the old man was successful

and he was doing me the favors, even if the plantation made
me its highest *luna*. Freedom was freedom from other people's
shit, and shit was shit no matter how lovingly it was dished,
how high or low it came from. Shit was the glue which held
a group together, and I was going to have no part of any shit
or any group. (P. 96)

To follow his new realization of the meaning of freedom, Kiyo
acts. He joins the Army. This sounds like an awfully comical self-
contradiction: join the Army at war in order not to be part of any group.
But, secure in his Japanese American identity and free from confusion
about being "Japanese" or being obligated to false "traditions," Kiyo not
once says anything about enlisting in order to prove his loyalty to America, a loyalty that after all is assumed of Americans, needing no "proof,"
but in wartime needing to be marshaled and acted upon. Free of any
superficial patriotic jargon, Kiyo states his reason for enlisting in a pun-
gently individualistic way, asserting that "everybody in Kahana was
dying to get out of this icky shit hole, and here was his chance delivered
on a silver platter" (98).

In short, Kiyo has grown up. In his way of understanding their
lives, he at least catches up with Tosh. Up to here, it bears repeating,
Kiyo has been a naive narrator, one whose words cannot be entirely
trusted, especially since he has never before questioned his parents' infalli-
bility in defining filial piety and the debt. But now, realistically and with
understanding, he makes explicit in his own way a kind of class consciousness:

> The camp, I realized then, was planned and built around its
> sewage system. The half dozen rows of underground concrete
> ditches, two feet wide and three feet deep, ran from the higher
> slope of camp into the concrete irrigation ditch on the lower
> perimeter of camp. An outhouse built over the sewage ditch
> had two pairs of back-to-back toilets and serviced four houses.
> Shit too was organized according to the plantation pyramid.
> Mr. Nelson was top shit on the highest slope, then there were
> the Portuguese, Spanish, and *nisei lunas* with their indoor toi-
> lets which flushed into those same ditches, then Japanese
> Camp, and Filipino Camp. (P. 96)

While it seems Kiyo can escape from the plantation thanks entirely to
the war, he must actively choose that route by recognizing and rejecting
the flip side of the system, the kind of security in confinement the planta-

tion offers, where "everything was overorganized" in "the scheme to keep you contented" (96). The one problem that remains is the family's debt. The other moral issues have already been settled, choices made, in Kiyo's comprehension or made irrelevant to his life for now.

Because those moral issues have been settled, the novel's ending is not a *deus ex machina*, and it achieves several interesting effects. As Kiyo puts it, his victory in a game of craps is a combination of "manufactured" luck—in that he gets to the big cash pot by learning how to "padroll," to cheat—and of luck itself, for the gamblers prevent the possibility of his padrolling in his final toss of the dice. He has taken the entire matter as far as possible into his own hands and wits—he invents a padroll system on his own—yet one of his persistent characteristics (temperamentally unlike Tosh) comes into play; namely, his ability to accept whatever the outcome. With regard to the novel's plot, the dice game underscores Kiyo's sudden entrance into a world where relatively large sums of money continually change hands, compared with the closed, stagnant economic life in the plantation community. This new world of the army barracks is no less realistic, certainly, than the plantation. But whereas Kiyo's winning the money in such a sudden development might be expected to come as a given at a story's Aristotelian beginning, here it comes at the end. We are left wondering, then, of the win's consequences, especially for Kiyo.

But the new story he is now implicitly beginning, with such an ending to *All I Asking for Is My Body*, is no idyll at all. Childhood and growing up in a rural world that the plantation has kept retarded are finished. The untold story ahead is a heroic one, of Kiyo's fighting in World War II, a story that has no place even in the complex pastoral design of *All I Asking for Is My Body*. "I manufactured some of the luck," Kiyo writes Tosh when sending his winnings home for the older brother to turn over in payment of the family's debt; "but I think the Oyama luck has finally turned around. Take care the body" (103). The final sense is that, although Kiyo is going his way, the family is now made whole again. And further, his final words are: "See you after the War." To Murayama, this implies that Kiyo's final, lucky roll of the dice is a good omen for his survival.[16] Kiyo and Tosh do not depart from "tradition" in such belief and in the greater matters of family and community values. To the contrary, they fulfill tradition by actually accomplishing what each of them can to take care of their family responsibilities and not pass their debts on to others. Kiyo's payment of the debt—Grandfather's debt, not his and Tosh's—plus the G.I. Bill of Rights that is later to grant educations to the war veterans will one day make it possible for Kiyo to complete the schooling which Obaban, Grandfather, Father, Mother, and Tosh all have been denied. In this and related senses, Kiyo resolves a set of problems three generations old. The result is the affirmation of community values—and yes, of love—that is the motive of comedy.

3

While Murayama's novel resolves conflicts and affirms the community's history and values as these should have been, John Dominis Holt's *Waimea Summer* guides us through a powerful and troubling exploration of a profound "dark side" to the Hawai'i idyll. It is not that the novel questions a venerable history and ancient values. Rather, Holt questions *how* one may safely approach that past. Whereas the childhood idylls of Hawai'i, including the most complex ones discussed earlier in these chapters, may be said to be related to the Hawaiian *mele hula* and its moods, Holt's novel is akin also to *oli*, a category of oral poetry that includes chants devoted to serious and somber themes, here framed within the nearly inadequate confines of a complex pastoral romance of Hawai'i.

The title of Holt's *Waimea Summer* ought to suggest a stock situation for a pastoral romance. It is after all a Honolulu (i.e., big city) boy's summer vacation in the country, narrated by Mark Hull as an adult reflecting on the events of his youth, his fourteenth summer. The story has the makings of a conventional childhood idyll.

But *Waimea Summer* resists such simple categories. The narrator from urban Honolulu steps into the seemingly backward rural landscape only to find the setting and its people profoundly disturbing, perhaps even more so in retrospect than when, at fourteen, he lived the adventure he tells. In that Waimea summer, people both initiate and suffer the consequences of an ancient Hawaiian spiritualism which is imperfectly understood, incompletely remembered from the old days of Hawaii's monarchy and earlier—like the crumbling histories, family, local, and Hawaiian, that the boy Mark avidly seeks to repair. The novel is pervaded by melancholy played in an elegiac key. Yet, even while lamenting its passing, while warning that the past is not entirely safe ground, Holt probes restlessly: How far back into the past or how recently, in how much and what kind of detail, in what spirit and for what reasons is it wise or even safe to go in matters that invoke both the sacred and the evil still casting shadows on people's faint memory and living fears?

Contrary to expectations suggested by the novel's title, the tale begins on the dark side of life in Waimea for young Mark Hull:

> At four in the morning, three days after I arrived on the Big Island to pay my first visit to Waimea, I awoke and was gripped by a sense of doom and apprehension, even before I could shake off the lingering remnants of sleep. All the things I'd heard said about Waimea being a place ridden with ghosts and black magic seemed now to be true. Before this, the excitement of being at last in this place my father had so endlessly extolled, my explorations around the once handsome house and garden, and exhaustion had successfully kept back the age-old sensitivity Hawaiians have to the world of spirits. But this morning, in my darkened room, a chilling sense of portent and unseen things being everywhere had complete hold of me. The fourposter in which I'd felt quite comfortable for three nights now seemed forbidding. The handsome quilt of the breadfruit design, which had been specially granted, felt now like a shroud. (P. 1)

And like a shroud, too, the past—the history of the family and the place—envelopes Waimea.[17] Mark has come to visit his middle-aged cousin on his father's side, the self-styled "glorified cowboy foreman" Fred Andrews, and also Fred's children, the youngest of whom are Henry, Leihulu, and the four-year-old Puna, a boy who, despite everyone's love for him, becomes the scapegoat to propitiate the conflicting parties and forces in the novel. A loud, proud, hard-riding man who has spent years on the Waimea range and in mischief with the *paniolo*—the Hawaiian cowboys—Fred has watched the once-stately house of his gentry-class parents, the breeders of Hawaii's finest horses, moulder away with him as its master. Yet Fred himself is unsinkable. He has already survived three wives, each of whom in her time could not sweep away the decay of the house.

Fred himself symbolizes a romantic and heroic history. First cousins, Fred Andrews and Mark's father, Mark Hull III, "had been good friends since Fred's visit to Honolulu way back in the waning years of the Hawaiian monarchy" (2). At nearly the age of sixty, Fred already has the kind of venerability and heroic stature that young Mark worships: "From the moment we met, I viewed him as an historic relic: something to be treasured and admired" (7).

While Mark pulls on his boots that first morning, full of foreboding, he is startled by the apparition of a "lithe young Hawaiian with a thin, bony face" who appears "as suddenly as if from the spirit world, at the opposite entrance to my room. In the light of the kerosene lamp held close to his chest, he stood silent, his coppery skin, ebony eyes, and black beard all glistening in the flickering light." Fred shouts from the kitchen to the young Hawaiian, "as though he had used clairvoyance to determine the presence of the silent man in my room"; Fred roughly orders the man to saddle his horse. Mark sits shivering, "caught in the crosscurrent of Fred's loud, telepathic command and my visitor's silence." The Hawaiian, moving "with seeming stealth," lights the bedside lamp and introduces himself "in a voice weighted with sonority": "'I Julian Lono, . . . I'm da brudda-in-law of dat white peeg insigh da kitchen.' He gripped one of my hands and shook it" (3).

This Hawaiian is not Mark's but Fred's antagonist. The novel's conflicts at first seem focused on the rivalry between Fred and Julian, the brother of Fred's most recent wife, Miriam Lono of the famed Waipiʻo Valley, which comes to play an explicit part later in the story. Julian calls Fred a "white peeg." Fred calls Julian a "Goddamned hoopau-ai," a "particularly defaming Hawaiian term for laziness" which means to "waste food," "one not worth his food" (4). Julian, not much of a horseman since he was reared in a taro-growing and fishing community, has been living at Fred's for about five years, beginning when his late sister Miriam was mistress of the house. But we learn in the novel's course that the source of their conflicts is not so much Julian's dependence on Fred as it is their jealousies over the youngest child, Puna, and the dark accusations the adversaries scream and rumor about yet refuse to discuss; namely, that the other prays evil upon hapless victims. Fred, Julian suspects, has caused the deaths of Miriam and of Fred's two previous wives by enlisting the services of evil sorcerers, *kāhuna* of an especially feared type. This wild suspicion is matched by Fred's: when his youngest, Puna, becomes unaccountably ill and listless sometime after Fred has banished Julian from the house, Fred fears that someone may be placing *hoʻomana* on Puna, praying the small boy to harm or to death. He suspects Julian somehow to have been a curse within his home, while Julian feels the house cursed by Fred. The ailing Puna is Julian's special nephew, his *punahele* (child especially cherished). Meanwhile, in his worry over the boy's health and by his actions to have Puna well cared for, the seemingly unsentimental Fred shows himself to be a man of deep, loving sentiment for this youngest of his motley brood. Fred and Julian are thus rivals for Puna's affections.

The larger, thematically more encompassing conflict takes place within the fourteen-year-old Mark Hull. He begins as a hero-worshipper, befitting a boy his age, of a hapa haole—that is, half-white, half-Hawaiian—family that was once highly prominent but lost its estates through two generations of decline. He has an already deep and sensitive love for history, a love immediately recognized and indulged by his elders time and again in the novel. These elders—including Fred himself; the matriarch Aunt Nita Warrington of the vast Stevenson Ranch of Waimea; Uncle Albert Baxter, the ranch's manager; and the sagacious, wizened Abraham Hanohano of Waipi'o—teach Mark the history of their families and his and of the parts they played in the days of the monarchy. All but Hanohano, however, stop the reminiscences they enjoy with the boy by saying that these things they speak of are of the past, *pau*, finished, with sharp warnings sounding in their voices.

The elders' warnings come predictably whenever Mark inquires about Hawaiian spiritualism. For Mark Hull, the issue is not the truth or falseness of the ancient and evidently still effective arts of the *kahuna*. Rather he seeks to know if he must choose between ancient and modern faiths or if he can resolve their differences: that is, the way of modern Honolulu, or the way of "primitive" Waipi'o and the Puu Kohala (in actuality, Pu'u-koholā) *heiau*, or temple. To the sensitive Mark, though not necessarily to others, the two ways of faith represented by these places are in conflict because, while they are of two different historical times, both are concurrently present in his experience. He thinks he can see in Waimea how the clash, the grip, and the twisting of two stubbornly persistent faiths have been a malady.

By "two stubbornly persistent faiths," one of which entails belief in ancient Hawaiian spiritualism, the other faith need not be the Christianity of, say, Twain's projected Hawai'i novel. To begin with, most of the characters in Holt's novel are of mixed races, and most to some degree believe (or want to believe) in the myths and values of both ancient Hawai'i and European America.[18] Opposite Hawaiian spiritual values, however, is a belief in the high status, conferred by past glory and coupled with confidence in further upward progress, of great, wealthy families of Hawai'i, their haole descent often mixed with patrician Hawaiian blood. *Kama'āina* (settled in this Hawaiian land), these are propertied families whose fortunes were established by heroic individuals during the nineteenth century. The Waimea setting on the Big Island must have suited their dreams grandly, as the spread of land there comes as close as anyplace in Hawai'i to giving the impression of unlimited horizons reminiscent of the American West. Mark Hull's admired heroes seem nothing short of Byronic in his imagination. Through their exploits, the old way obviously gave way to the progress of the new; and in time Mark's own family too, once powerful among the new landowners, lost status. Yet precisely because in life it seems the Hulls' former height is gone forever, Mark wants to regain both ways, the one literally pastoral, ancient and thus timeless in that setting; the other Promethean, heroic, and marked by great changes, these two antithetical ways of seeing seemingly unified by the youth's romantic imagination.

The most revered hero celebrated in *Waimea Summer* is the long-dead Uncle Tony Stevenson, founder of the immense Stevenson Ranch which, if the book were fact instead of fiction, would be the Parker Ranch of Samuel (Kamuela) Parker, the actual Waimea ranch famous as the largest individually (not corporately) owned cattle ranch in the world. So thoroughly intermarried that Mark Hull is naturally a member of most of them, these families have tremendous faith in individual progress, social and economic heroics, and the superior civility of European aristocracy with whom these families boast of ties whether by blood, breeding, or influence. Indeed, their faith is such that their misfortunes assume tragic, even mythical size, for misfortunes seem utterly unaccountable in a world supposedly under the patriarchs' control. The deaths of Uncle Tony Stevenson and certain of his heirs strike the inquisitive, historically bent Mark in just this way. He glimpses a conflict between the heroic control over a manifest destiny Uncle Tony wielded in life, versus the ill-understood, poorly controllable, yet seemingly powerful, pervasive, and too easily aroused spiritual forces far more deeply seated in the ages of the land. Yet these Hawaiian forces in a sense give the gentry of Waimea a final grip on things, the final explanation for the events in their histories and their lives. Thus appropriated by the gentry, Hawaiian spiritualism, whether in its belief or its effects, is not confined to native Hawaiians.

Holt gives his *Waimea Summer* some stylistic features that themselves suggest the nature of Mark's experience during this summer of his coming of age. The novel's chapters—if that is what they are—are unnumbered. The headings and, occasionally, the margins are graced by line drawings corresponding to that place in the narrative. The lack of chapter numbers suggests that they constitute something other than a conventional sequence. And indeed the plot unfolds not to a single climax but in a series of three rather distinct episodes, each with its own logic, and yet each taking part in the overall, chronological narrative, which too has its overall beginning, middle, and end. This structuring of the novel may well suggest Holt's strength: he is an oral storyteller *par excel-*

lence, and it is as if *Waimea Summer*, with its three implicit episodes, would thus satisfy listeners hearing the entire work in several sittings. But more than that, the three episodes successively cut deeper and deeper into Mark Hull's psyche; and here reside both the plot and the theme of the novel.

The first of what I am calling "episodes" extends to page 141 of the novel. However strongly Mark feels the ghostly influences of Hawaiian spirits, as in the novel's opening paragraph above, the theme of the first episode is not belief but superstition. That is, these pages are about Mark's coming just close enough to belief in Hawaiian spiritualism that he is frightened and distressed by what he sees. The central object or sign of his fears is a natural phenomenon and an omen, a phosphorescent fireball he sees one night:

> The wind was blowing, wild again, swaying perilously the great trees. The "thing" appeared first a small flame and then, as it approached, an orb. I had heard it described so many times by Hawaiians: the *akualele*, the flying god, an evil spirit sent out to find victims. It circled the Punohu house, then Fred's, and then streaked off, leaving a long coruscant trail behind. I stood frozen in my path, shaking. (P. 43)

He immediately denies having seen anything, and only much later Mark talks about it with a Japanese American physician who says he is not bothered by such things. This, the novel's longest episode by far, ends with Mark being overwhelmed by his seeing signs in nature as he feels a Hawaiian continually does.

The second episode, pages 143–64, ostensibly concerns preparations for the great chauvinist Fred's fourth wedding. While his bride-to-be Lepeka (Rebecca) moves permanently into the Andrews house, Fred takes Mark and two jolly paniolos up towards the Mahike Forest to do some needed work and to gather ferns and other decorative foliage for the wedding. This episode is thus peripherally about romance in the most public, communal sense: the wedding. After the distress that Mark's superstitiousness earlier brings him, the overnight outing by horseback seems a fresh start. Paralleling the wedding of Fred and Lepeka, however, is Mark's sexual initiation, which occurs up the mountain, in an irrigation-worker's cottage when everyone is dead drunk but Mark and the ditchman's young wife from Japan, who seduces him. This clearly becomes the central event in the second episode. It both troubles and elates Mark at the same time. Like the first episode, the next day this one ends with a note of anxiety and even of alarm.

The third episode, pages 165–95, involves Mark's stay in Waipiʻo Valley, where he and Fred's grown son Ben seek a kahuna to undo the harm they believe they prayed upon the youngest child, Puna. Again we begin with a journey, not this time on horseback but by car and, to descend the steep valley walls, by donkey. In Waipiʻo, Mark is welcomed by Abraham Hanohano, a hearty and learned Hawaiian who becomes for the moment his mentor, questioning Mark about Hawaiian history. Though Mark still senses fearful signs all about him in the night, Hanohano and the valley seem benign enough, until the next morning Mark experiences and witnesses a shocking display of the actual practice of power—that is, politics—among rival kāhunas following news of Puna's death. There is then the funeral, where the spontaneous *kanikau* (dirges), including Julian's, wail everywhere.

Mark believes the death and mourning have brought the summer to an end, all romance and all tragedy played out. But at Kawaihae Harbor, where he awaits the boarding of the boat to Honolulu, Mark enters the Puu Kohala heiau (temple) and there has a stunning vision of chiefs, warriors, and priests of the war god Kūkaʻilimoku, all standing for a past reality and final warning not to romanticize history, not to forget that Hawaiian history also means bloodshed, and that, while one may study history, the reliving of history would be a fearsome and terrible thing. The third episode and the novel end with Mark running away from the grasp of the old keeper of the temple, down the hillside, toward the waiting boat to Honolulu. It is a strange summer vacation.

Each episode begins in the morning, with people waking up to get something done. A topographical symbolism seems also to be at work. Whereas Fred's house in Waimea is a third or so of the long incline up the side of Mauna Kea, Mark's greatest, burning, confusing elation comes higher up the mountain, at a great forest's edge, in the embrace of Kimiko Moriyama. And the descent to sea level, the floor of Waipiʻo Valley, is reminiscent of an epic's journey to the underworld—there Mark is forced into deepest struggle with his fundamental beliefs, his assumptions, his values, and his morals.

Such a spare account of the novel's three episodes notwithstanding, *Waimea Summer* also evokes what is most beautiful about the natural setting and the culture it nurtures. There is the Waimea landscape itself, where the sun is bright yet not parching and where the notoriously chilly winds and sudden rainstorms—or the *Kīpu'upu'u* "chicken skin" rain special to Waimea—sweep the northwestern slope of Mauna Kea. To the Hawaiian, a portion of the Waimea pastoral landscape is associated with the hula, while Mauna Kea's lofty, solitary peak inspires a contrasting awe in the spirit of the heroic. This is how Mark sees the countryside on the morning that begins his story:

> Above the eucalyptus trees across the road upon which the house faced, the mauve mist-surrounded peak of Mauna Kea rose to the height of nearly fourteen thousand feet, a powerful and awesome physical presence. Behind us, in contrast to the lonely magnificence of Mauna Kea, the rounded, grassy Kohala Mountains protected Waimea from northern winds. These were friendly mountains near at hand, and as comforting as the engulfing arms of a lover's in embrace. In such a setting, the friendly spirit of Laka, patron of the hula, could very well be alive and thriving in the forests of lehua and koa. Mauna Kea and its forested peak were the territory of the remote icy spirit of the goddess Poliahu.[19]

> Growth of tree, shrub, and other plants was most fiercely luxuriant. I had the sense that the gods had blessed Waimea as once the God of the Old Testament had bestowed magical, extravagant beauty upon Eden. (P. 11)

The "sense" of such an Edenic setting, of course, takes the panorama out of time. In the novel, however, the inhabitants are sometimes acutely aware of historical change and the personal losses time brings. Waimea to these people cannot represent escape from history but is itself the locus of history, concentrated here in remnants of the past such as Fred Andrews's house, as if history, time, and change were bound in Waimea to crawl their slow course.

Like "Ipo Lei Manu," the love song Kapi'olani wrote for her Kalākaua, Hawaiian mele in *Waimea Summer* originally composed as songs of sweet joy have come to be elegies, reminding the Waimea gentry of things and people of an earlier, somehow brighter day. At a Fourth of July dance attended by all of Waimea and "a host of . . . dates, guests, or relatives," the look of pleasure in the smile of Anita Warrington, the *grande dame* of the Stevenson Ranch, is infused with melancholy as she listens to a song composed by one of the earliest Stevenson women. "What memories had the song brought back to her?" Mark wonders. "Always these shreds of the past enter our lives in Hawaii to sting, to prick, to hurt" (90). Even the rugged Fred "seemed under a spell, thrust briefly out of his world of hardtack, dawn risings to check pasturelands, and long horseback rides, high above the swaying mist-grey lehua, in lonely contemplation of the beauties and wonders of Waimea." Indeed, listening to the mele, Fred seems lost in solitude as though upon his horse in that idyllic landscape. Others "drifted in the same motionless veneration. Hawaiian songs too often were a harkening to the past, to your people, reminding you of breakdown and defeat," Mark observes, perhaps characterizing his own reaction, his own family having lost the opportunity years ago to inherit the Stevenson Ranch (90).

Outside the lyrically static, melancholy world of mele as Mark hears them is history—history as Mark views it. In his narration, every moment can instill a history lesson, even when the precocious fourteen-year-old encounters a grove of oranges, early in the novel while Julian leads the children on horseback:

> High above the stream we reached a plateau that extended some distance at the base of a small mountain.
> "Heah! Heah! Look! You see da oranch?"
> "What big trees they are!"
> "Ole buggahs, dass why!"
> "I wonder who planted them." They could have been survivors of the original seedlings left here by Vancouver's botanist.
> "O Kekua Nalani paha! Our Lord in Heaven, perhaps," Julian answered. (P. 19)

The Hawaiian songs, the old photos of the Andrews household in its heyday, the house itself as a relic, and even Vancouver's oranges stir Mark to recover the past in his thoughts, there to digest it in his hungry understanding. It is not the delving into the past, but Mark's many remaining uncertainties and lack of knowledge about it—and his romantic way of seeing the past as something that can only be preserved, like Keats's "cold pastoral" on the Grecian urn, ever discontinuous from life in the present—that cause the melancholic air, the "Waimea sadness," Mark calls it (130). His melancholia is perhaps as different from his elders' as is his sexually inexperienced understanding of Hawaiian love songs.

Several important passages in the novel are devoted to Mark's genealogy, a part of his historical education. These are contemporary, informal versions of the Hawaiian genealogical chant, as it were. The passages provide a retreat into the weave of history in order that Mark may reemerge with a better knowledge not only of the past but also of his relatedness to that past. Here again would be the pattern of conventional, pastoral retreat and return, except that as in the conclusion of Melville's *Typee*, the knowledge the narrator gains is problematic still. He ends up knowing less than expected from the facts he learns of his history, for the facts do not answer the question at the heart of his deeply subjective interest.

The first lesson in genealogy occurs on one of Mark's rides with Fred across the ranchlands. Fred lets Mark talk freely about what he knows of their family history, and the boy proves that he knows a great deal indeed. At the crux of the history and Mark's question about it, he knows that Tony Stevenson, founder of the great ranch, was to have married Mark's great-aunt Sybil Hull; but Tony Stevenson was killed, thrown by his horse, before the marriage could take place. Mark traces the genealogy and inheritance of the Stevenson Ranch from there to his contemporaries, the Dinwiddie twins, Eben and Lemuel Gaylord, the wards of their grandmother, Anita Warrington. So intimate is Mark's knowledge of his and the Dinwiddies' genealogies and families that Fred, who thus far has been encouraging Mark's talk, exclaims, "You'll be living in the past the rest of your life, if you don't watch out!" (72).

Along their ride, Fred brings Mark to the empty site of the old Stevenson mansion, which once welcomed Jack London, the Prince of Wales, and Alice Roosevelt, who still are less impressive to Fred than all those he remembers to have been "'everybody that was anybody in the islands'" who came to Puu-malu (74). Fred goes on to teach Mark how, while the Stevenson Ranch prospered beyond Tony Stevenson's death, the Hull fortunes swerved and dropped. Had Uncle Tony lived and married Mark's great-aunt Sybil Hull, his own cousins would be the ranch's heirs, and he would be riding alongside them. But Fred adds to this history and speculation. According to Fred, the decline of the Hulls was caused by a failure of human judgment. At a critical time in the histories of both the Stevenson and the Hull ranches, the Hulls were negotiating to hire Albert Baxter, a rancher, to manage their lands at Manulani (73), on Oʻahu.[20] But they made other plans instead, and their land managers converted the Hull ranchlands into sugar and pineapple fields, as Mark ruefully remembers. Albert Baxter, meanwhile, became the manager of the Stevenson Ranch, and under his stewardship it prospered vastly.

Every relevant genealogical, historical fact emerges and finds its place in the discussion between Mark and Fred. It is here that Mark tries out the kind of question that really concerns him because he does not know what its answer is or how to answer it: "'Is it true Lemuel Stevenson [inheritor of the Stevenson Ranch after his elder brother Tony's accidental death] was prayed to death?'" (76). He asks it as if without motive. But Fred's retort is quick and reproachful:

> "Nothing but bullshit! I want to tell you something, boy, for your own good! These matters should not be talked about. They belong to the old days, and only to the people concerned! Hawaiians are deeply respectful people. Unless a person is sure of something, they don't like to hear him talk about it. They call it waha kani, or waha he'e! Remember this, boy." Fred looked at me sternly, "And don't you ever forget it." (P. 76)

Mark has heard Fred lock himself in a room and chant to stones he has collected in the forest; nonetheless, Fred cuts off Mark's inquiry into the dark side of Hawaiian spiritualism. Perhaps this is because Fred knows something about it. Some forty-five years separate Mark from Fred. Two other instances where Mark, in conversation, touches the subject of Hawaiian spiritualism also occur in the presence of elders like Fred, people old enough to have experienced the history of the Hawaiian queen's and thus the monarchy's overthrow. Albert Baxter himself, the manager of the Stevenson Ranch, recalls the Hull brothers, Edward and Willson, when Mark asks about these men, his own blood ancestors. These are the two who considered hiring Baxter to manage their Manulani estate, but failed to do so. It was in 1896, Baxter recalls, "just after the Queen's supporters attempted to overthrow the provisional government" (119). Baxter tells Mark that Edward Hull wanted him hired, but brother Willson Hull disagreed. The cause of the disagreement: "They hated one another! I heard that Edward had caused the death of Willson's finest breeding stallion in some careless mixup, and *that* was really the cause," Baxter recalls. Mark immediately recognizes the horse in Baxter's story: "I've heard about that damned stallion all my life! His name was Kepalo! Devil!" (120). And so the youth finds in Baxter's story confirmation of how the accidental death of a horse—an aptly named one—may have altered his family's fortune for the worse and forever.

At just such junctures, when his inquiries and discussions with his elders have led Mark back to the accidents and the unexpected deaths which, though beyond human control, have had great consequences in these families' histories, Mark surprises his elder with a question of Hawaiian spiritualism. "They say Uncle Edward was prayed to death by a kahuna," Mark says, casually and as if out of their discussion's context;

"He'd cut the lip of a paniolo's son who had thrown a rock at my cousin Columbus Hull that made a big gash on the side of his face" (120). Immediately upon saying this, Mark is sickened with the feeling that he "had said too much."

Baxter, like Fred, rebukes him: "I hope, my boy, you don't believe that nonsense! Edward Hull was as white as the rest of us! As white as you are! Don't let yourself be taken in by that nonsense! It's destructive! And, if I were you, my boy, I wouldn't repeat that story. Why, if I'm not mistaken, your family is Episcopalian, among Bishop Staley's first parishioners!" (120). There is a note in Baxter's voice, as there was earlier in Fred's, suggesting that these are warnings, not scoldings, deriving not from the elders' disbelief in spiritualism, but from their firsthand knowledge of its power.

Mark need not persist in his inquiry into the dark side from here. It pursues him; everywhere he looks, it informs his point of view. In his third discussion with a senior member of the gentry, it is Aunt Nita Warrington herself who opens the subject. "All this primitive nonsense can be harmful," she states, explaining why she keeps the Dinwiddie twins away from Waimea for most of the year; "We don't know enough about it to make it meaningful anymore" (131). Yet by her very words, she believes in it. She advises Mark to go home to Honolulu if he is sensitive to the spirits of Fred's home. Her words underscore her simultaneous belief in and denial of the powers of the kāhuna:

> Every time one of the Stevensons died, the Hawaiians would say kāhunas were at work. My husband [Lemuel], my daughter [Kiliwehi, late mother of the Dinwiddie twins], Tony. I want my grandsons to be free of this kind of nonsense. Too many have suffered. Don't bother, Mark! Get a good education and free yourself! (Pp. 131–32)

There would be nothing to free oneself from if it were not assumed to exist in the first place. And because they still know and fear the old spiritual power, Mark's elders implicitly acknowledge it. Whenever he asks whether kāhuna caused this death or that accident, never do they answer him with a firm, outright, assuring "No!"

At Mark's every allusion to those *kāhuna* capable of praying a victim's death by their *pule 'anā'anā*, his elders' own fears or respect for the art seem to spring to their faces and from their tongues. In a chilling moment at the conclusion of Mark's final interview with Aunt Anita Warrington, she remarks about how badly the boy Puna looks. "You tell

Palani to keep an eye on him," she refers to Fred by one of his Hawaiian names. "I have a feeling he's suffering inwardly! He's practically under a spell!" (133). Then it happens:

> I looked at the lightly powdered, slightly rouged, and heavily perfumed dowager. Her face was shaped suddenly into a grimace of evil. "He's *not* under a spell!" I choked, cleared my throat. "But he's very unhappy."
>
> "Hawaiians are funny about children." Her voice was flat, almost without timbre. She broke off. "Sometimes children suffer dreadfully because their elders are poopaakiki. Do you know what I said, Mark?"
>
> "Stubborn."
>
> "More than that—foolishly stubborn! Foolhardy!" (P. 133)

The look that Mark has seen on Aunt Nita's face, that "grimace of evil," like clouds fleeing across the moon and stars, throws Mark into confusion. She has given him a singular gift in recognition of his love of history: Uncle Tony Stevenson's spurs. Now these become the focus of Mark's uncontrollable fears. Teased by his younger cousins about possessing "*make* man" spurs (a dead man's spurs), Mark withdraws "to the place where the goats were tethered to the watercress patch on the stream," a place where the shaken youth, like one under *ho'omana* (a spell) retreats when he needs a look at himself:

> A night heron flew overhead. I was instinctively fearful. They were night birds and brought bad luck to those who saw them by day. I cursed myself for being afraid. Hawaiians see omens in everything. I cursed myself for being Hawaiian. Look at me, I thought, sitting here imagining I'm surrounded by spirits, that they will reveal things to me in the shape clouds take, in the particular rustle of trees when a breeze passes through their foliage, or in the pattern of the water as it passes over rocks. And I was helpless for I could not sort out the good from the evil portents. (P. 136)

Mark is an anachronism, too late to live in the time of the Hawaiians he imagines. His modern culture no longer supports the way of seeing and interpreting signs he describes here, and he fails alternately to see Hawaiian culture as still living and changing today.

Shortly afterward Mark Hull, intruding for the only time in the novel as the adult narrator, quietly admits that the history, the intricate, subtle relationships among people and events he wove as an adolescent, "was an aesthetic one," not truly factual (140). The connections were his own creations, in that—like Faulkner's Gail Hightower—he infused them with his sensibilities and perceptions of truth and beauty and with his need to relate himself, a child of a family who has become middle class, to something of great and lasting dignity.

The gap between aesthetic and realistic truth widens in the second episode when Mark makes love with the woman who lives at the forest's edge. She insists that they both wear masks in a strange, unexplained, and private ritual perhaps meant to imply the secrecy and the intimacy of their act, their protection from exposure. Mark recalls accepting his mask "with misgivings, but they were not about what mana [spiritual power] or signs it contained" (156). "My previous knowledge of sex," Mark thinks the next day, "came from obscure, most often humorous allusions and metaphors in Hawaiian songs and conversations. I could not make them jibe with my experience in the night" (157). The affable paniolo Kapua Gomes is unaware of Mark's seduction. The next day, in an unwitting parody of the night's lovemaking, he drapes leis of maile vines around Mark's hat and shoulders and laughs, "'Eef you was one wahine, Markie, I geev you one keez now! . . . Wat da hell, why not!'" and "planted a hairy kiss on my cheek" (159).

Mark's disorientation the day after his sexual initiation is heightened rather than soothed by the mixed Hawaiian and pidgin banter among the cowboys Kapua Gomes, Ernest Moluhi, and himself. One of Mark's characteristics is his revulsion at the sight of blood. Fred leads the ranch hands in the capture and slaughter of a wild longhorn bull they discover with its mate; the throwback breed has been polluting the modern herds. In this second episode, a theme is thus concentrated. Though it is never stated explicitly, never expounded upon or resolved, its import is clear. The episode brings together Fred's and Lepeka's wedding plans, Mark's first lovemaking, the paniolos' mock romantic banter, and the animal mating or breeding of cattle of two different races, as it were, one of them thought to be primitive and inferior. The haunches of raw beef the party packs home; the heady, spicy fragrance of the maile and fern collected for decorating the wedding; and the confluence of these swirling thoughts opened by his first sexual experience make Mark want to retch. His mount, Black Beauty, gallops dangerously when the confused and sickened Mark fails to rein him in. Mark and Fred ride hard into a great commotion at home. Puna is inexplicably and seriously ill once more. The romantic, sexual, and procreative theme is brought up short with a continuing threat to a Hawaiian child's life.

Now concluded, the novel's second episode thus traces a pattern Holt has drawn, in larger compass, in the first. The initial expectation of a vacation, a retreat, swings around to become a painful exploration of Mark's beliefs, values, and way of seeing history and his present environment. In the first episode, the experience is with spiritualism, or, more pertinently, with Mark's wanting oxymoronically to *believe* in *superstition*. In the second, the experience is with sex, and a question both implicit and explicit for Mark is how sex, no matter how refined Kimiko Moriyama and he may have been in her ritual of the masks, is related to human expressions of love and romance, on the one side, and the rutting of animals on the other. Each episode ends for the moment with turbulent thoughts and unresolved feelings for Mark, yet with a contrary sense that this part of the story has run its course. This latter impression is set especially by the changes of scene and mood immediately following an episode. Just as Fred's plans to take Mark on an overnight ride to Mahike Forest signal a pastoral retreat—which, as I have been saying, becomes more complicated rather than more simple—their return home only to learn of Puna's relapse is followed immediately by Fred's arranging for Mark to accompany Ben Andrews on a trip to the still deeply Hawaiian, reputedly idyllic Waipi'o Valley in search of a kahuna to undo Puna's harm. Soon the mood and expectation again are of a pastoral retreat.

Using a term introduced earlier in our discussion of mele, Hawaiian poetry, we might say that in *Waimea Summer*, what would ordinarily be the *kaona*, the inner or underlying meaning or subtext, indeed comes to the surface so insistently and repeatedly that it becomes the main plot itself. It seems, too, that Holt's lifting of the kaona to consciousness empties more space underneath, allowing still deeper kaona to flow within and move upward. Thus, in the first episode Holt brings the spiritual kaona to the surface, there to stay for the remainder of the novel, while in the novel's subtext spiritual themes continue further to develop. In the second, he raises the romantic and the sexual, and this, too, is to reappear in a still more deeply cutting way shortly afterward in the novel. The kaona seems continually to be replenished; the novel thus gains a peculiar depth as the successive episodes cut deeper into it. Narrated from the point of view of an adolescent often desperately eager to interpret, to abstract, and to "see omens in everything," the story is bound to have this characteristic, if the writer is to be true to his narrative's fact of its being told by a man reflecting on his youth when his own intuitive depths were tested for the first time.

In this characterization and, of course, consequent narrative style and structure, *Waimea Summer* is very nearly the opposite of the understated *All I Asking for Is My Body*, where the narrator's inner growth or struggle is rarely discussed but is implicitly paralleled by the open battles between Tosh and their parents. If one were to examine the style of *Waimea Summer* more closely, one might well find that Mark's own part in dialogues is small compared with the vigorous pidgin chatter that surrounds him. The great volume of his narration instead is reflective and is told in Holt's distinctive Latinate diction and elegant locutions, a manner of speech that sometimes clashes with pidgin when in dialogue Mark switches from one to the other. We may be reminded of a difference between Henry James and Ernest Hemingway: Holt, with hypotactic complexities faintly echoing James's, wields like James a style especially useful for articulating the psyche of the protagonist; meanwhile Murayama, with his deliberate parataxis, delivers external actions, or thoughts in terms of straightforward mental actions or steps, and leaves to implication and inference a great deal of his protagonist's inner plot.

Having twice peaked and continued on, the plot and repeated suggestions of a pastoral mode lead us to expect that surely the trip down into Waipi'o Valley must be the hero's true pastoral interlude at last, already twice frustrated. Here Mark meets Abraham Hanohano, a fisherman who invites Mark to stay with him and his family. Hanohano's "disarmingly cultivated" English stems from his more than fifteen years of schooling long ago at Lahainaluna, on Maui, Hawaii's first Western-style high school (the one Tosh Oyama was to have attended at about the same year as Mark Hull's Waimea summer occurs). Modeling himself after the nineteenth-century Hawaiian historians he most respects, Hanohano taught in Kohala, neighboring Waimea, for four years while living with missionaries. He then headed the valley's school upon his return to Waipi'o. Unlike Fred Andrews, Albert Baxter, and Anita Warrington, Mark's elders among the gentry, Hanohano amiably answers Mark's question about why everybody on the island believes in "spooks": "People don't *believe* in spirits here, Sonny. They *live* with them. They're a part of life!" (172). The man betrays no fear of the subject. As is his nightly rite, Hanohano offers the family's evening prayer before their meal. One does not know whether to expect a Hawaiian or a Christian prayer. Hanohano proceeds to chant in Hawaiian, offering a long prayer that seems to transport Mark's spirit "back hundreds of years" (172).

At Fred's, Mark does the cooking—an astonishing gourmet at age fourteen. At Hanohano's, the meal is simply poi, made from taro grown in that valley, shrimp from the local stream, made with *kukui* (candlenut) and shoots of fern, and assorted "bowls of fish, beef stew, and salted beef cooked with taro leaves" to feed the large family (172). "Tasty, indeed, is the food of the land!" Hanohano and the family chorus in agreement (173). Mark could well be transported back a little less than one hundred years at this moment; for his experience of the self-sufficient simplicity of the setting and Hanohano's hospitality reawakens a myth that Melville exploited in *Typee*. Earlier in Holt's novel, Moriyama the ditchman is admired for having created a Japanese-style house and garden at the forest's edge by importing some of the materials and all the ideas from another culture. In Waipi'o Valley, by contrast, the Hawaiians conform entirely to what appear to be or to have become native and local.

Mark's sleep that night, however, is troubled by nightmares, a confusion of the Biblical story he fell asleep reading of Moses and Pharaoh, frogs croaking and dogs barking outside, and a night heron, the Auku'u, the ominous bird that appears at such spiritually dark moments in the novel "like Pharaoh's sacred Ibis" (173). Reminded by the Hanohano family of his parents in Honolulu, Mark becomes homesick, and the image of Puna comes to him insistently. Hanohano finds Mark thus distressed and nearly fainting. Again Mark has company for the night.

The two of them spend hours in a kind of catechism, where Hanohano's questions and answers about Hawaiian secular history, too, are vested with spiritual force. Knowledge itself is powerful. Power is *mana*. *Mana* is spirit. Hanohano implies that Puna's illness is caused by the bad mana of Fred Andrews's house. It is an unclean place. Hanohano explains: "Mana is spirit. It's the life force—unseen and without form. Mana is in people, in things. It's the essence of the universe." People who learn skills well can win good mana. The ancient kāhuna, taught correctly in their arts, had mana. "Not like the charlatans around today who only know how to scare people" (176). The old man speaks expertly of Hawaiian history and culture. Referring to the books of Hawaiian history, by Hawaiians, on a shelf, Hanohano calls it "our people, our history"; and Mark listens (as Fred had warned him not to speak first about things he does not know) while the elder speaks of "dead chiefs, dead kings and queens, their triumphs and tribulations, as though all the complex welter of their times, their acts and beliefs were current events" (177), a manner of historical storytelling in which Holt himself has mana. Had Mark visited Puu Kohala at the Kawaihae harbor where the cattle boat calls? Hanohano asks, then commences an animated lament that not enough has been written about Hawaiians by Hawaiians beyond the beginning provided by David Malo and Samuel Kamakau in the nineteenth century. Do you understand my point? His look questions Mark, and it implies a request that Mark write the needed history. But the entire night's lesson ends in Mark's anger when Hanohano intones that Puna will die, and Mark accuses Hanohano himself of being a "goddamned kahuna" (177).

In sum, in the night the still-smouldering anxieties of the first episode are rekindled. Added to them, however, is a different view of history Hanohano offers: not superstition but knowledge, not belief in spirits but living with spirits. The trouble with Mark is that he has been romanticizing history, preserving it as a series of discrete and discontinuous events serving as casually related stepping stones, one to the next. The idea of a living history, like the idea of living with spirits, suggests that, as in the manner of Hanohano's storytelling, history and the past are still alive right now. History is the flow itself, not the stones leading across it. There is no need to step backwards into the past, for history, a flux and an immanence, is forever catching up and caught up to us, always renewed, informing our ever-changing lives. Perhaps one of the handiest contemporary works to compare with *Waimea Summer* in this regard is Leslie Silko's *Ceremony*, where the Thought Woman is conceived to be at work not only in some mythological Laguna Pueblo past but also in the very process of the author's writing the novel's words; by the novel's style and theme, Tayo *is* a mythical figure alive in the present and renewing his identity.[21] Mark's attempts to capture the past already bias his view in favor of the heroic and the glorious of the past or what he dreams these concepts to be, for who would want to preserve memories of the small and the overshadowed? The dark side of Hawaiian spiritualism for him as yet raises a shallow question merely of superstition versus belief, neither of which Hanohano sees to be that dark side's reality.

That morning Mark witnesses Hanohano's reality of a living Hawaiian culture and the living practice of kāhuna. First, Hanohano takes Mark to the beach, so they may cleanse themselves in the sea and the breaking dawn. "We will pray to Lono," he gently instructs Mark. The old man's chanting disturbs Mark by reminding him of Hanohano's unwelcome prediction of Puna's death. But then with exuberant shouts Hanohano runs naked "into the green wall of an oncoming wave," bobs like "some sea-borne turtle" in the foamy waters of the wave's wake; and with the yell of a savage Mark plunges naked after him into the surf. Hanohano teaches the formal and decorous youth a lesson in how to let the drawstring loose: crash naked and yelling into the surf that curls in the dawn! This and what more they do there are part of a living Hawaiian culture, as Hanohano demonstrates.

Second, there is the living reality of the kahuna. The report now reaches the valley that Puna has been killed by a goat meant to be fed to Fred's dogs. Apparently taking the news calmly, Mark prepares to leave, first of all by informing Ben Andrews of the tragedy. What next happens at the house of Puali, the kahuna Ben has been consulting, where Ben has been lolling in the company of Puali's granddaughter is an astonishingly vile barrage of insults and epithets Puali spews at Hanohano. When Puali's curses plunge to their deepest, lewdest viciousness, Hanohano suddenly urinates into his own hand, rubs the liquid on himself and Mark, and flicks the remnant into the surrounding air to ward off Puali's evil.

Mark and the Hawaiian farmhand who has come with the news of Puna's death are shocked by the battle they witness between these rivals, apparently for the control of the valley. The Waipi'o social fabric suddenly appears torn, its culture bitterly political in whatever may be the kāhunas' own terms. Hanohano pulls Mark aside and apologizes for the vulgarity of what, he explains, had to be said and done. What Mark has witnessed, then, is also a part of the reality of the kahuna, the living with spirits, whether in harmony or in acrimony. What concerns Puali is "rubbish," Hanohano insists; "The real things, the strong things, are the ones we talked about last night" (181). "I'm not afraid of anything!" Mark growls, grim and hardened by the morning's shocks, and he seeks strength in Hanohano's comforting embrace. Puali has insulted the old man by insinuating that Hanohano has seduced Mark. Mark's reference then to "the early morning intimacy on the beach" hints also at a homosexual union having occurred, and remembering it, Mark pulls away from Hanohano's protective arms and walks from the scene alone.

As if his being seduced by Moriyama's wife were not enlightening and troubling enough, Mark thus is introduced to another aspect of sexuality, in a Hawaiian context. The entire novel hints at such a force behind certain conflicts, as when Fred blurts out his suspicion that Julian, whom Fred considers a kahuna from Waipio, is also to Fred "a God-damned mahu" (homosexual), who has been advancing on Mark since the morning on which the novel begins (68). If this is so—or even if not so, the importance resting in Fred's perception of such a thing—then this sexuality seen from a point of view different from Mark's naive one has been alive all around him through much of his stay in Waimea and, after Fred kicks Julian out of his home, through Julian's letters to Mark. Even in what he thought were his most anxious, disillusioned, and therefore most realistic moments, Mark did not know this in the conflict between Fred and Julian. As for the darker of the kahuna's arts, Mark witnesses in Waipio at least one instance where they consist far less in secret signs and mysterious curses than they do in obscenities whose meanings are bluntly heard or easily guessed.

In a sense forming a concluding episode of its own, the novel's final beat occurs down at Kawaihae, the harbor where the interisland ship *Kamoi* is loading Waimea cattle in the region's unique way: by having the cattle swim to the boat, there to be hoisted aboard one by one. It is after Puna's funeral, where Julian returned in lamentation and Mark, emotionally more free thanks to the summer, has grieved so exhaustively that once more the story seems completely over, indeed resolved. Mark is waiting for the departure of the boat for Honolulu; but it is delayed by the arrival of sharks which threaten the swimming steers. Mark takes this opportunity to inspect Puu Kohala, the nearby heiau that Kameha-meha the Great ordered built and dedicated to his war god, Kūkaʻilimoku, the island-snatching one. Hanohano had asked Mark if he had visited this very temple.

Inside Puu Kohala, Mark hears "the sound of an old person chant-ing," and from the hillside vantage of the heiau he sees sharks circling a canoe whose occupants and one foolhardy man in the water appear unable to scare or to lure the sharks from the cattle. As is characteristic of him, Mark turns away from the sight when he sees the water, sliced now by many fins, suddenly redden with blood. At that moment an old man in torn dungarees appears to warn Mark not to sit on the stones, for they are reserved "for those of Keawe," the legendary chiefly lineage of the island (192). He is the *kahu* (the keeper) of the heiau. Mark replies in Hawaiian that he himself indeed comes from the chiefs and impresses the startled and embarrassed kahu with a recital of genealogy (as is cus-tomary, the male's version consisting of the names of his grandmothers), with full names "each fifteen to twenty-five letters long." Out of the rag and bone shop of his memory, the kahu honors Mark with a chant of "your family genealogy—one branch" (192).

It sounds at first like a parody, a comic relief from a most momen-tous and emotionally taxing summer for Mark. This kahu seems to be Melville's old Typee sage, the one who, though tottering about, nonethe-less pounds and pummels Tommo's bruises and wounds in the name of healing. Imagine Wordsworth's Leech Gatherer actually answering the speaker's loaded questions about life in the profundities of the bogs.

But the kahu of Puu Kohala proves to be indeed earnest about the history he knows from the point of view of the ancient Hawaiians, a point of view existing in the same space as the present, as though defining an entirely different dimension in space and time. Aware both of his own and of Mark's ways of seeing, the kahu is impervious to the youth's testiness. They see a steer ripped by the sharks, and the kahu sees the animal as "a small sacrifice from such a rich source!" (193). He tells Mark of how Kamehameha, charging into the water from this very temple, fought a shark that bore the name of Kamehameha's hated enemy, his cousin Keoua Kuahuʻula. Kamehameha pounded the shark senseless and tore apart its jaws. The ancient man, rapt in the story he tells, chants the final lines: "What a thing to have been privileged to see! Only the gods can grant the strength given to the Lonely One. My grandfathers witnessed the strength of the Great Kamehameha!" (194). That strength, that Lonely One, also slaughtered and sacrificed the chief Keoua Kuahuʻula and his retinue on these very stones of Kawaihae and Puu Kohala, Mark reminds the kahu, who smiles and says that the gods craved human blood in the old days, not in his time when Puu Kohala stood already in ruins, but when his grandfathers lived.[22]

In an even more intense way than Hanohano's, the old man presses a living Hawaiian history upon Mark. It is ironic that the boy whose love for history has been prodigious pulls back. The man hints that Mark must stay to become the temple's next kahu. Made increasingly real to him in Waipi'o and atop Puu Kohala, history is no longer an abstraction or a mere enthusiasm. The old man makes demands of Mark, and he promises power in return. History requires responsibilities and dictates values; history is political in its involvement with power—history, that is, as Hanohano and the kahu live it in their respective spheres of Hawaiian culture. The boat is finally loaded and leaving. One final, dizzying vision leaps into Mark's eyes, tempting and repelling him like whatever it was that Christ saw in his last long moment alive on the cross:

> As I back away from the old man, chiefs are gathering in the
> brilliant noonday sun. Attendants carry kahili, tabu sticks, and
> images held aloft on long poles. The walls of the heiau teem
> with wooden sculptures of angry, protective deities. The oracle

tower, covered with white tapa, rises fifty feet from the lower platform. Under the tower, kahunas in white tapa, stand chanting prayers.

The chiefs take their seats on the row of stones along the edge of the higher platform. They wear crested feather helmets and large-patterned cloaks of red and yellow feathers. The Great One arrives. His helmet and cloak are a purity of rarest yellow feathers. He sits. Drums beat. A chant is intoned—vibrant, vehement. The chiefs sit immobile, and the scene dissolves into its own eternity. The old man and I are alone. Someone is calling my name. (Pp. 194–95)

So the story ends: "'Stay, child! Stay! You belong to us!' The old man whines, pawing me, holding my sleeve. With a seizure of strength, I pull away and run pell-mell down the hillside" to the waiting steamer *Kamoi*, which means "the king" (195).

Stylistically, nothing in the novel quite prepares us for this final scene, this noonday bright and fearsome vision of Kamehameha's war court assembled at the heiau. Yet it results from Mark's entire summer's experience, mentally, bodily, and spiritually. Up to now, Mark Hull's questions, his confusions, fears, and anxieties, like his little cousin Puna's depression, took shape not in visions and hallucinations but simply in his and others' interpretations of ordinary natural phenomena and some-times bizarre human ones. Readers of Holt's novel usually are baffled by the urgent, visionary or perhaps even supernatural, present-tense ele-ments of the final scene. But considered closely, it appears that for Mark Hull, this vision of the Lonely One (the meaning of "Ka-mehameha") seen in a nauseating proximity of blood—the sharks' slaughter of the cattle, the history of Keoua Kuahu'ula's massacre, the bloody warfare, launched from this very temple, by which Kamehameha united the islands into a kingdom—brings Mark to the teeth of what it would mean for him to live further in the past should his romantic attraction to it persist. Hanohano's living history does not mean *re*living history. Like the terri-fying cannibalism Tommo finally cannot romanticize away, Mark's final vision of the past he thinks he has been trying eagerly to seize drives him running down the hillside, a frightened and wiser young man.

It should be clear that there is nothing sentimental about *Waimea Summer*, with its pervasive elegiac tone in remembrance of past things and people. Artistically, the book is an example of Hawaii's contemporary literature at its best. One element in particular of Holt's style deserves mention, and that is his superb handling of language, Latinate locutions and all. The English of the narration ranges from the British of Mrs. Warrington, through the cowboy lingo of Fred Andrews, to the cultivated diction of Abraham Hanohano. Holt's range extends to an impressive variety of pidgins and creoles. These include no less than older and younger Hawaiian, Japanese American (again of two generations), and a Portuguese pidgin or creole English or Hawaiian, the last of these being the broad language and accents of the gregarious Kapua Gomes. When Holt uses Hawaiian—words, phrases, whole sentences—he does not break the flow of his narrative prose to translate. The context he creates invariably accomplishes that for the general reader, who may not know any Hawaiian other than what this book will pleasurably teach along the way. What this integrity in Holt's use of language exemplifies, too, is the novelist's fine sense of how the elements of his technique together contribute to *Waimea Summer* as a whole and highly polished novel. This stylistic and structural polish makes possible the development and expression of the novel's rich and continually upwelling kaona.

Both *Waimea Summer* and *All I Asking for Is My Body* contain a theme of spiritualism, though in very different ways and of differing cultures. The theme is embodied in the kāhunas of *Waimea Summer* and in Obaban and Mother of *All I Asking*. In Holt's novel especially, the apparent survival of spiritualism overtakes and fuses with Mark's desire to recapture the historical past he at first glorifies. As there must be right and wrong ways to approach spiritual matters, the narrative shows, so must there be right and wrong ways to study Hawaiian historical materials without being harmed by one's own fears or misgivings about one's ignorance or about reopening subjects long ago buried, but buried still alive.

As it is for the fictional Mark Hull, so it is for many who, in what is now termed a Hawaiian Renaissance, delve deeply and fervently into Hawaii's past: elders at some point warn against probing further into matters considered dead or into matters considered spiritually dangerous to touch. In this sense, *Waimea Summer* reflects directly what is still a social, cultural reality. The first time I personally had the honor of meeting with a group of *kumu hula* (teachers or masters of hula) to discuss their art, I was impressed by the strength of the felt need for restraints placed on the depth and nature of the spiritual aspects of the study and practice of hula. The deference shown to the ancient worship was offered by the "traditionalists" or "purists" and the "moderns" or innovators alike, in our meeting. The kumu hula Wayne Change noted that almost no one deals anymore with the worship of Laka, the friendly patron deity of the hula. It is too deep a thing to recover, he said—and too dangerous. I was to see in hindsight that I was being told what Mark is told by his elders in Holt's novel: about the spiritual aspects of Laka in modern times, Chang stressed that we understand so little of the religion today that it would be dangerous to tamper with it. Perhaps some do know enough to tap its powers, but certainly not enough to control them. Chang and the other teachers gathered there in the home of kumu hula Kaha'i Topolinski that evening went on to illustrate Chang's cautions with anecdotes, "talking stories" of the powers of the worship of Laka and finding out that together they knew a bit about the worship of Laka after all. But Chang respectfully concluded the talk by stating that the hula, mele, and oli of today are for art and entertainment, not for worship.

It is perhaps because the hula, the mele, and the complex pastoral of Hawai'i are felt to be part of a larger heroic context that they still provide us with literary contexts for contemplation, aside from the novel's necessary strong thematic conflicts. Compared with fighting in Europe in World War II, Kiyo's childhood in the 1930s must be relatively peaceful, whatever Tosh's thunder and Mother's stubbornness. Compared with the warfare Kamehameha waged, or with the overthrow of Queen Lili'uokalani, Mark's spiritual, sexual, and epistemological crises are not merely normal and peaceful but are indeed the subjects of the narrator's contemplation, not his struggle, when he looks back upon them as an adult.

The importance of historical contexts to the creation and the reading of these works should not be underestimated. In writing *Typee*—and, for that matter, *Moby Dick*—Melville insistently (and by order of the publishers of his first book) discoursed on Nukuhiva and on whaling, respectively. Without using Melville's expository approach, Holt and Murayama also write history into their stories, for without history, their stories make no sense or make the wrong sense. In the case of Holt's complex pastoral romance, the historical context is everywhere in the text, and the true understanding of this context is itself the text's plot, Mark's aim. This understanding is considered vital to restoring and sustaining a living Hawaiian culture.

Authentic native history is central to the current Hawaiian Renaissance, which itself has a history reaching back more than a century, and John Dominis Holt is one of those most credited with its renewal. His novel cautions that the Hawaiian culture being renewed, especially since the 1960s, should not be a negative political force, should not be confused with the evil resulting from the manipulation of fear by those whom Hanohano calls "charlatans." Fear stems from ignorance; and this ignorance is born in part from the dominance given to interpretations of the historical changes wrought by the Cooks and the Vancouvers and all they represent in Hawaiian history. It is a general ignorance of the history the Hawaiians themselves made, as certainly Kamehameha and his successors did. Kamehameha's unification of the island chiefdoms to create a kingdom established as strong a sovereignty as could be prayed to withstand, however briefly, Western incursions in the nineteenth century. Queen Ka'ahumanu's and her son Kamehameha II's abolition of the tabu system in late 1819, just prior to the Protestant missionaries' arrival, served among many purposes to enfranchise women in a population which, already withered by foreign diseases, could ill afford politics to be limited solely to its male portion. But this history is buried under a European version which makes Captain James Cook, whether for good or evil, the greatest agent of change at the beginning of Hawaii's written historical period—and not Kamehameha and Ka'ahumanu. The abolishment of the tabus and the adoption of Christianity get credited loosely to the missionaries, and the missionaries and other empowered colonials in Hawai'i appropriate whatever native achievements in history and culture they may choose while at the same time they literally impose their own cultural sanctions on all aspects of Hawaiian life. This sweeping change, too, is part of a living Hawaiian history.

But again it is a history, Holt shows us, where native Hawaiians act and are not simply acted upon. A creator of the renaissance from which the current rebirth continues to grow in Hawai'i, King David Kalākaua actively revived ancient Hawaiian culture he already felt to be dying by the time of his reign from 1883 to 1891. For his own coronation Kalākaua created a program that included an afternoon and night of hula and mele, among which were *mele ma'i,* genital chants celebrating the sexual parts of royal personages, a traditional mele type and theme. The white populace of some quarters was mortified by the resurgence of this most authentic and, to the haole, lascivious display of native culture. Undaunted, Kalākaua pushed forward his Hawaiian renaissance throughout his reign. He organized a secret society of men of Hawaiian blood, the Hale Naua, whose object was "the revival of Ancient Sciences in Hawaii in combination with the promotion and advancement of Modern Sciences, Art, Literature, and Philanthropy."[23] Beyond his death Kalākaua incurred the wrath mingled with wild fear among those who wished Hawaiian culture buried dead or alive for good, when the Hale Naua marched openly in their king's funeral procession looking very, very ferocious.

Two years after Kalākua's sister and successor, Queen Liliʻuokalani, one of history's most gifted composers of mele, was deposed by Americans led with supposed reluctance by Sanford Dole and seeking forever to have Hawaiian sugar be favored by the United States as a domestic product rather than taxed as foreign, by forcing Hawaiʻi to become part of the Union. To the Hawaiians, to say that it was not a popular uprising and overthrow of the throne is a droll understatement. We see in Holt's novel how Hawaiians tried unsuccessfully to rally to the aid of their queen. Laka the sometimes female, sometimes male deity of the hula, Kamehameha, Kaʻahumanu, Kalākaua, Liliʻuokalani, each heroic, none of them mere victims or pawns of omnipotent powers: these are but part of the Hawaiian mythology and the Hawaiian history—what the character Hanohano calls "our people, our history"—to which Holt alludes in his very complex pastoral novel, whose heroic context is this entire history.

In 1971, commissioned by the University of Hawaii Department of Drama to write a play with Liliʻuokalani as heroine, Holt wrote and produced *Kaulana Na pua, Famous Are the Flowers: Queen Liliuokalani and the Throne of Hawaii*, a play in three acts.[24] Such a drama in the Hawaiian heroic literary tradition complements Holt's complex, pastorally inclined, often dark short stories. These stories appear in *Princess of the Night Rides and Other Tales*, which contains pieces that could be shavings from the fine-grained work Holt sculpted to create *Waimea Summer*.[25] Together such works show the range of Holt's work as a writer and his view of Hawaiʻi, especially if we add to them his nonfictional studies of the monarchy and other topics in Hawaiian history. His collection of essays, delivered as a series of lectures in 1964 at the Kamehameha Schools for native Hawaiians, *On Being Hawaiian* awakened the nearly century-old Hawaiian Renaissance by addressing questions that continue today to focus passions and intellects on Hawaiian cultural strength and Hawaiian political issues: Who is a "Hawaiian," and what does it mean to be one, in our time and in this place?[26] Those further acquainted with Holt and his work no doubt see more of his persona in his fiction than can I. But Holt, the namesake of Queen Liliʻuokalani's husband Governor John Dominis, is modest in his works about his own place in history. The fact that his writing is about his own, actual forebears is inevitable. After all, simply to write about the Hawaiian and haole aristocrats, the gentry, and their families, he must be writing about his own kin. Indeed he speaks of nineteenth-century royal figures in exactly the voice and detail of one's talking about a favorite aunt who lives in the next valley over. This man's actual life and history—which in Holt's case cannot be merely a personal history—also make Mark Hull's story seem by comparison an idyllic though momentous Waimea summer vacation.

In the summer of 1979, in the city of Hilo on the Big Island of Hawai'i, Holt was a featured participant in a discussion of the pastoral in Hawaii's literature, at the Talk Story Big Island Writers' Conference.[27] He spoke elegantly of the island's beauty. He and others spoke too about the sense of creative power the island's Kīlauea Volcano engenders in the viewer's very guts. The Big Island is uniquely inspirational. Holt illustrated this in his notable talk-story manner. The discussion dwelled on the sunny, idyllic side of the island's features and on the oral and written literature that expresses and evokes it. Asked about the dark side, Holt told a startling, archetypal tale of a wild pig crossing a Big Island road. Halfway across the asphalt, the boar was smashed by a car that caromed down the road and betrayed every green, pastoral memory of what the island may once have been, unspoiled by roads and autos. But the machine invading the garden is one thing. For another, there is the boar itself, whose ancient progenitors were imported from Tahiti by civilization-building Polynesians. Even the boar with its curving, knife-edged tusks represents danger to the hunter, his dogs, and his horse. The dark forests of the Big Island hide secret fears in their thick underbrush, and their green gloom and scent. The sense of the meeting was this: it all depends on what we choose to make of this obviously highly complex setting, this Hawai'i, its history, and the people who live in it.

Hawaii's Heroic Literature

"Our People, Our History"

I

When one evening in the early 1950s, O. A. Bushnell saw a stage drama about Captain James Cook, he muttered, "I can write one more better one." To prove it, he resumed a serious hobby of writing that has resulted not only in *The Return of Lono: A Novel of Captain Cook's Last Voyage* (1956) but four subsequent historical novels of Hawai'i as well.[1] Once a student writer and president of the University of Hawaii's young and active Hawaii Quill Society in the early 1930s, Bushnell indeed responded to the unsatisfactory drama about Cook by writing his own. The result was "junk," Bushnell admits. But he went further: he transformed the drama into a novel that now, thirty years after its writing, remains fresh through several reprintings, including a number abroad, as a living fictional testament to the heroism and tragedy of Cook. It is, too, an interpretation of Hawai'i and its people at the moment of their entrance into the West's recorded history. Like *Typee*, its plot turns upon the occurrence of death in paradise, a theme complicated once more by ethnocentric misunderstandings, this time explored by a native of Hawai'i using his superb creation of a first-person narrator among Captain Cook's shipmates.

Bushnell was eminently suited for writing the work. *The Return of Lono* is well tailored to fit Bushnell's own attributes and is naturally shaped by those same attributes, including his limitations and biases. Hawai'i-born, third-generation descendant of a mix of European immigrants to Hawai'i including Portuguese and Norwegians, Bushnell grew up learning to read the pulse of the land and its people. He is a *keiki o ka 'āina*, child of the land, and this fact bears importantly not only on the authenticity of his writing but also on his credibility to Hawai'i audiences—and to himself—as a writer of Hawaii's historical fiction.

As a boy, Bushnell accompanied his father to gatherings of the Hawai'i Portuguese community's Camoëns Society, a cultural group named after the creator of the sixteenth-century Portuguese epic, *The Lusiads*, about the real-life heroism of Vasco da Gama and his Lusitanian stalwarts. Camoëns asserts in his epic that he is recording history and is bearing witness. He insists that da Gama's adventure of global exploration actually took place and was not the distant, imagined, mythical event created by his epic-poet predecessors. Furthermore, Camoëns fervently states that unless he were to write of it, the very notion of Portuguese heroism itself would be lost, and consequently there could be no more Portuguese heroes in real life, nor any poets.[2] Bushnell himself, in undertaking *The Return of Lono*, went on to create a historical fiction in which the actual and the imaginary interact in such a way that we witness the birth of modern historical, heroic myths spawned by Cook's "discovery" of Hawai'i, by the tragedy of his death, by various sorts of condemnations of him, and by these first known Western visitors' own acts. The narrator's point of view is limited to these visitors' acts, but Bushnell allows us also to glimpse what the Hawaiians are up to and the visitors are blind to—that is, to overhear and to infer the view from the shore.

Aside from the love for literature that has sparked Bushnell's lifelong interests, he chose a career in science. In the 1930s he earned his graduate degrees in biological sciences and returned to Hawai'i to work for the Territorial Board of Health. He has achieved a highly respected place among scientists for his research in microbiology and has become widely known through his scientific publications—somewhat the way Cook and Hawai'i became known to the West because the *word* of the expedition, both written and oral, reached the world outside Hawai'i. A recognized expert on Pacific island diseases, Bushnell since 1970 has been emeritus professor of medical microbiology and medical history at the University of Hawaii. He is still writing historical novels of Hawai'i because, as he sometimes says, echoing Camoëns perhaps, no one else of Hawai'i is doing in Hawaii's literature today what he feels must be done with historical topics, characters, and events.

When I compare Bushnell and Cook as writers, insofar as their reputations alike depend upon their published words of historic deeds, I think, too, of their similarities as scientists. Bushnell's scientific background is highly pertinent to his literary work on Cook. As is clear in *The Return of Lono*, Captain James Cook was a scientist, a man of reason, a man of the European Enlightenment. Bushnell's story of Cook the man, thought to be Lono the god, is an enactment of a war between reason and faith, between Cook and two Calvinists aboard his H. M. S. *Resolution*: William Bligh, ship's master (later of H. M. S. *Bounty* infamy), and John Ledyard, a Yankee, corporal of the Marines. This archetypal conflict is also internalized, raging most tragically within Cook himself.

Certainly, conflicts and other interactions between the Hawaiians and the foreign voyagers also play important but subsidiary parts in the narrative. To the author's credit, however, these too predictable conflicts are not as central to *The Return of Lono* as one might expect, given the conventional formula—perhaps even in the drama Bushnell had disliked —in which unquestioned British reason is pitted against native superstition while, grinding away in the wings, is all the racist machinery of the noble savage as satirized by Melville and Twain. Rather than playing out a mainly intercultural, interracial conflict, Bushnell parallels the conflict between reason and faith among Cook and his people with a like conflict among the Hawaiians ashore, where the rival parties are the reasonable priests of Lono and the cruel priests of the war god Kū, who demand and exact total faith and obedience. Quite unaware of them, when on shore the visitors are caught in the middle of this and related struggles. Bushnell's choice of parallel conflicts within two different cultures implies that if it is human for Cook and Ledyard to argue thus in one culture, then it is human likewise—not subhumanly primitive —for Kailiki the younger priest of Lono to argue against the priests of Kū. Bushnell plots his novel in a way that implies his egalitarian view of the two races.

The novel's structure, settings, and other elements support this observation about parallel conflicts. Probably because of its original form, Bushnell's novel itself is structured like a drama in three acts, with the *Resolution*'s quarterdeck serving as the main stage. On the quarterdeck Cook delivers his orders, receives reports from shore parties, deliberates courses of action, and receives the visits of Hawaiian chiefs and priests and of officers of the sister ship, *Discovery*, led by his comrade Captain Charles Clerke, whose suffering from tuberculosis draws great sympathy from Cook. And it is on the quarterdeck that Cook and the subordinates who malign him stage their final debate. The quarterdeck's confines within the ship's rails and the ocean's embrace hardly allow physical action. The emphasis on the quarterdeck stage is on words, words by which men attempt to reach understandings with other men. On a more light-hearted note, too, the quarterdeck is the setting for displays of verbal wit in which the jovial wag James King and the dandy James Burney excel. The quarterdeck moreover is a symbol of the upper class aboard the ship, and of the differences in class separating the privileged from the crew living and laboring amidships and below.

While the tiny quarterdeck is an auditorium for words, the novel's other setting, various points along the Kealakekua shore, is an arena for physical action. Here the largest single mass of Hawaiians Cook and his men have ever seen prostrate themselves at the command of Puʻou, the high priest of Lono, when Cook first approaches Hikiau, the heiau sacred to Lono. In the temple, Puʻou offers Cook the putrid remains of a sacrificed pig, dead too long, or not long enough; it splatters on the paving stones at Cook's shoes when he declines taking the gift from Puʻou's arms into his own. They stand in the sacrosanct confines, a sanctum forbidden to all but the priests, the chiefs, and those among the visitors judged to be the god Lono and his sons. There Puʻou and his noble son, the priest Kailiki, offer their words, the *Kumulipo*, the Hawaiian creation chant involving and binding the entire Hawaiian cosmos together in a primeval genealogy.[3] They direct the chant toward Lono, the benevolent god associated with the land's fruitfulness, with the blessing of rain, with the new year, the observance of which coincides, as happened a year earlier on Kauaʻi, with Cook's arrival. *Lono i ka Makahiki*, Lono of the New Year, he is called—ever changing, symbolized by the many-shaped cloud above, the sacred kukui tree shimmering light-green in the forests below. It is on Kealakekua's shore that the novel's narrator, an eighteen-year-old midshipman devoted wholeheartedly to his captain, finds his island love, Kailiki's daughter Hinahina. In this setting, too, across the bay, at the jagged rocks that reef the village of Kaʻawaloa, Cook is killed by an angry host of natives.

The two settings are stages for two different yet concentric spheres of events. On the shore, we witness actions; on the quarterdeck, we hear actions set into motion and reflected upon or argued about with words. If one were to visualize a connection between the novel's two settings, the dominant image would be the ponderous, awesome mountain slope descending like a colossal pathway, a ramp from distant heights into the sea at Kealakekua, which thus means "The Way of the God," the god Lono. Here, at the joining of land and sea, Cook arrives; here, Lono is believed long ago to have left Hawaiʻi, promising someday to return with his bounty. At this juncture, fact and myth are the same.

Apart from the Hawaiian legend of Lono, Cook's arrival at Kealakekua in 1779 was in fact a return for him to the islands. On Monday, 2 February 1778, Cook's *Resolution*, and under him, Clerke's *Discovery* left their explorations and refreshment of stores at Kaua'i and Ni'ihau for Alaska in search of the Northwest Passage, which if discovered would fetch the finder a prize of 20,000 pounds in England. The expedition coasted the American Northwest, collecting observations of the natural features and the peoples encountered but failing to find the fabled passage. On Thursday, 26 November, of that same year, sailing out of a tropical storm and searching for a warm southern haven to await another season before resuming his northern search, Cook once more sighted high land, this time the island of Maui.[4] But nearly two restless months passed before the expedition landed, though native canoes, splendidly loaded and sometimes numerous, time and again reached them to trade food for bits of iron. During the white men's absence of ten months, word of them apparently had spread southeast from Kaua'i to the "leeward islands"—O'ahu, Moloka'i, Lāna'i, Maui, and now Hawai'i. Cook worried deeply that his crew might also have sown venereal disease at Kaua'i and especially at Ni'ihau, where a shore party was once stranded overnight by high seas. This accident gave the sailors their one chance to break Cook's tabu against sleeping with the Hawaiian women. His return to Hawaiian shores was thus fraught with expectations of danger.

In *The Return of Lono*, it is now 1779. On Sunday, 17 January, the ships at last drop their anchors in a hospitable bay. All of part 1, "Paradise Gained," takes place on that day. As he is spare with his settings, likewise Bushnell with his dramatic technique observes an almost Aristotelian unity of time, confining each part to the space of a single day, with one important exception. Part 2, "Idols and False Notions," takes place on Wednesday, 3 February 1779, the eve of still another departure from Hawai'i with the intent of resuming the northern search for the passage. Part 3, inevitably titled "Paradise Lost," is set like the others in Kealakekua, the bay and the shore, but on two days: Thursday, 11 February, and Sunday, 14 February 1779. The earlier is the day of the expedition's miserable, tattered return yet once more to the bay, the *Resolution*'s foremast sprung and all the sails, rotting since the poorly funded expedition's start, ripped by a gale; and the later, 14 February, is the day of Cook's death.

In Bushnell's version of the tragedy, the visitors are at first unaware that Cook is regarded as a god. Bushnell's main narrative device allows us to "learn" of this identification, however, as it must have dawned one by one upon those aboard the *Resolution* and the *Discovery*. This principal narrative device is the first-person narrator, who is more complex than the prototypical narrator in *Typee*. Melville's Tommo tells his tale fresh from his recent adventure—he still sounds breathless— and it is an adventure in which Tommo himself is the main character, the hero. In contrast, Bushnell's narrator John Forrest looks back across fifty years to recall the adventure he lived and witnessed when he was eighteen. Clearly, his ostensible subject is not so much himself as Cook, whom he adored, and others who have become fixed in his thoughts. But the retrospective allows us also to read and to infer how Cook's tragedy has affected the narrator over his troubled life since then, to judge what he has learned and what he still has not. It is this subtext that ultimately animates the expressed conflicts between reason and faith, for in this subtext we find that Forrest himself is conflicted without knowing it.

Forrest at age sixty-eight is a self-described recluse, considered eccentric if not misanthropic by his neighbors. While in his utter loyalty to Cook, he sides with the powers of reason, scorning Bligh's and Ledyard's blind faith, Forrest fifty years later still invokes in memory the never-aging face and figure of his beloved Hawaiian "bride" Hinahina. He knows firsthand that the Hawaiians do not necessarily think Cook a god, for he hears that some Hawaiians see Cook to be a politically and militarily useful *man*; but Forrest does not relinquish the idea of Hawaiians as being blessed or cursed with primitive faith and gullibility. In contrast to the condescension implicit in his romance for the islanders, Forrest gravely, profoundly struggles still, fifty years later, with the questions that tormented Captain Cook to the very hour of death: does God exist? What reasonable proof do we have? Is reason enough? This is not to suggest, however, that the novel climaxes in a storm of such abstractions, or that the theological, philosophical contest takes place exclusively in such terms. Cook and, through him, the devoted Forrest are driven to these questions by the stunning realization that the Westerners' visit has changed Hawai'i irrevocably, in some horrid ways for the worse. In effecting these changes, Cook holds himself responsible and is deeply disturbed by the thought that he may be causing what only God should cause to happen to a people. Or Cook may be tampering with what cannot be changed, the course of history, in his great concern that these innocent natives not be contaminated by disease. What if such contamination were somehow foreordained by historical processes that cannot be altered by a puny man? Recalling both the joys and the gravity of his Hawai'i experience, the old John Forrest is kin to T. S. Eliot's Magus pondering how the world changed with the Birth (or was it Death?) he witnessed in faraway Bethlehem years ago.

Throughout the telling of the tale, the older John Forrest's explicit, reflective, mature interpretations of what happened at Kealakekua in his youth, the foreshadowings of events to come thus built into the narration, all contribute to the sense that the story's tragic ending is foretold. "Paradise Gained," the title of part 1, coming as it does at the entire narrative's head, implies that the story will devolve surely into a "Paradise Lost." The first words of the novel echo Macbeth's first words in the tragedy bearing his name: "*So fair a day* we had not seen since we'd come into those tropic waters" (emphasis added, *Lono*, 4). Regarding his exuberance on the day Cook's expedition anchors in Kealakekua Bay —the day on which part 1 of the novel is set—Forrest says in hindsight:

> My senses were so sharpened that day that I cannot forget,
> even to this day, all that they embraced. But if I accepted all
> perceptions then, why did I not comprehend then what seems
> so obvious now? Why did I not see the dangers to our situation,
> underlying our every act and thought as the jagged rocks and
> the encroaching reefs underlay the waters of the bay into which
> we were passing?
>
> The truth is that I saw, but I did not see all. I heard, but
> I did not hear all. I saw only what I wanted to see, I heard
> only what I wanted to hear. I saw the green hills beyond, be-
> cause I was hungry for the sight of green; but I did not see
> the rocks along the shore, or the reefs beneath them. And,
> even though it was the largest object to my vision, my eye
> slid easily over the black arch of Kealakekua and I did not
> see it there, soaring above us, like a cruel wave of rock poised
> to crash upon the tiny bay at its foot. . . .
>
> My only comfort now is that I had much company in my
> Paradise of Fools, for few among our joyful group that day
> saw the signs which denoted that with us the Serpent was
> also come into Eden. (Pp. 8–9)

To the old Forrest, the tragedy reenacts the ancient story of Eden and the Fall—that is, in spite of his doubting of faith, his own view is conventionally Christian. Even the old narrator evidently does not see this about himself whether as a youth or as he is now. His words indeed imply without circumspection that the awareness he should have had is Bligh's and Ledyard's of how the visitors to this Eden bore with them

the Serpent or were themselves the evil. There is, however, a major difference between Forrest's and Bligh's assumptions about the archetype re-
played: Forrest considers the natives to have been innocent before the
ship's arrival; Bligh most certainly does not.

By either assumption, however, the basic version they share of
the history of Cook's last days ascribes all power and responsibility to
the visitors. They are the agents of change; they act upon the defenseless
natives, who then are left fallen and guilty, hurt beyond measure by new
evils the outsiders bring upon them. With this assumption of the visitors'
omnipotence, Forrest cannot perceive, much less fathom, the Hawaiians'
struggles for power which occur all around him on the shore. Bushnell
shares with earlier writers such as Melville and Twain an ability to criticize this narrow outlook which informed the very age when Europeans
made their greatest "discoveries" and imperial claims in the Pacific. What
develops into Forrest's dialectic of the paradise and the hell of Hawai'i
is exclusively classical (neo-classical) and Christian in more ways than
one. While his viewing paradise and its spoliation in Biblical terms is
explicit from the very opening pages of the novel, more subtle effects
of Forrest's ethnocentrism include the sights he happens to notice, in
the way he depicts them.

For instance, there is his description of their approach to Hikiau,
the temple of Lono, the priests of Lono leading them. The moment epitomizes Forrest's view of the undifferentiated mass of Hawaiian people as
being powerless in their own realm, wholly and literally under the sway
of the priest's arm:

> As the High Priest came before their great canoe, drawn up
> on the beach, he turned to the surrounding throngs of Indians.
> Throwing up his arms in command, he shouted in their
> tongue: "Make way for Lono! Lono comes! For Lono the pros-
> trating *kapu!*" Then he turned around to Captain Cook and,
> leading the way for his people, threw himself full length upon
> the stony sand.
>
> With a great sigh, with a wavelike collapse as of the wind
> blowing across a wide field of ripened grain, the brown bodies
> fell down upon the ground and lay there. Shoulder to shoulder,
> flank to flank, they covered the beach before us; and, as we
> watched, the ripple widened its circle round both sides of the
> bay, and we saw the people dropping in obeisance until in
> the distance we could no longer distinguish them from the earth
> to which they fell. (P. 81)

Some of us cannot help but be reminded here of a big Hollywood picture, perhaps *The Bounty* and the hundreds of natives crowding the shore to welcome the ship with exotic, primordial pomp and unison. Up through this place in the novel, Forrest has been narrating their arrival and the greetings of Hawaiians aboard the ship, *Resolution*. The passage just quoted narrates Forrest's first moment ashore. The feelings are heightened by his consciousness of this, and thus the moment is a revealing one. It is important to note that even the high priest prostrates himself and does so ahead of the other natives. The visitors, thus, are clearly the most powerful central figures in the scene, or the visibly topmost link in a chain of being. This view of the strict and simple ranks of power—the Hawaiians with theirs, but Forrest with his implicit belief in a great chain of being as well—persists for Forrest thereafter. But, as becomes problematic in the novel's themes though not in Forrest's thoughts, his disturbance over the common natives' oppression by the priests is contradicted by his simultaneous belief in the Hawaiians' universal, prelapsarian goodness.

For all the bitter and sour intrusions of the old Forrest in his storytelling, the tale is still mainly the young man's, seen as his senses, desires, and folly dictate to his powers of memory, still more green with promise than darkened with foreknowledge. The youthful Forrest recalled in age serves as a kind of naive narrator, at home in the Hawai'i pastoral yet faced, like John Dominis Holt's Mark Hull, with the world of the heroic. As with Melville's Tommo at the start of his adventure, Forrest tells of his paradise dream—and its seeming fulfillment—on the warm, inviting, green and sunny isle, on "that glorious day, all blue and golden in the sparkle of the sun," when "we made entry into a land that looked to us like Paradise" the morning after an "orgy of licentiousness" which the sailors try, like Adam and Eve, to hide from Cook (*Lono*, 6).

What the narrator admits to us with his mature, ironical, urbane tone and manner is that as a youth all he knew was how perfectly these islands and their noble savages fit into his dreamy preconceptions that blind him from reality. In his guileless way, the young one confuses this with *being* a native. When Captain Cook asks the young midshipman whether he has spoken with these "Indians" of the island of Hawai'i, Forrest remembers with chagrin his burning desire "to be as they were, and—some wonderful day—to live among them" (53). Talented in learning languages, he had most certainly spoken with these people and had taken every opportunity to do so in the expedition's prior "transactions" with them. On the quarterdeck, the captain and his officers preparing to welcome the first canoes bearing chiefs and priests from Kealakekua, Cook reminds the youth of his folly: "Do not let your fondness for the native life lead you into the bush here as it did in Ulietea. . . . An Englishman's place is on England's ships—and not in some native haystack" (55). In Ulietea, Forrest had tried to desert the ship with a companion, rather like Tommo and Toby lighting off for their plot of green on Nukuhiva. Ashamed and repentant, Forrest inwardly swears henceforth unswerving loyalty and devotion to this captain. Now the older narrator asks in hindsight, as if he learned forever by that mistake, "How could I explain to him that that foolish flight into the bush had been a romantic youth's first unthinking response to the license and beauty of Polynesia after the cold dreariness of the Antipodes? How could I tell him that I regretted the misadventure almost as soon as it began . . .?" (55). Nonetheless, he was to repeat the misadventure at Kealakekua.

Forrest proceeds headlong from the long welcoming ceremony at Hikiau, with all its expressly, heavily historical and mythological import, to resume fashioning his paradise while thinking it already done. The first allurement he seeks is sex, no matter that Cook has only that same morning warned him not to. Forrest follows the lure of the drums signaling the sensual hula like the throbs of a lover's heart. He heeds wild shouts of the sailors left outside on the beach because, much to their happiness at the moment, the priest has excluded them from the temple's sacred precincts on account of their being men, not gods. The reception Forrest receives outside the temple overwhelms him. Whatever his sexual fantasies, the reality of his situation is unbelievable. A hundred women, it seems, surround him to win his favor. In the wild crush Forrest desperately chooses one but soon abandons her in the bush; the ordeal of being smothered by women in every conceivable shape, all offering themselves to him, has unmanned him.

Fleeing, Forrest literally stumbles into the arms of love: in his path, working at a household task, is Hinahina, beautiful daughter of Kailiki, the younger priest of Lono. Like Tommo's Fayaway with her blue eyes, Hinahina is an exception, if the earlier mob of supplicating, inviting women were the norm. She is slender, her cheeks dimpled, her teeth "most perfect":

> She stood revealed in all her beauty, a goddess there before
> me. Unlike so many of her people, she wore no tattoos to
> stain her skin, and no excesses of pretended grief over the death
> of a chief had led her to scratch and mar that smooth surface

or to knock out a tooth from that perfect mouth. Even her
hairdress was different from the short and towsled mop of stuff
that most of her sex affected. She was different from any of
them I had yet seen, and in daring to be different she achieved
a beauty that I never saw equalled, in my sight, in any land.
(P. 113)

It might well be said that fifty years after this moment in Forrest's
life, the reason why Hinahina alone has not aged in his memory is because
she is so thoroughly a myth—like the Fayaway whom certain fans of
Typee journeyed to Nukuhiva to find—that she stands forever outside
of time itself. She exists nowhere except in books, which we of course
conventionally think and write about in the ever-present tense of literary
criticism. It is obvious in reading Bushnell, here and elsewhere, that the
author himself is a cultivated reader, and in Forrest's first sight of Hinahina
we have the most overtly playful sign so far that the narration not merely
echoes Shakespeare or the Bible but may also verge on parody. And yet
at the same time Forrest asks us, by his tone, most wondrously to take
him seriously. Bushnell's fun with the Eurocentric description is not so
broad as Melville's giving Fayaway blue eyes, but it is close.

In all noteworthy respects but one, Bushnell's Hinahina is the
same, astonishing, mythical creation as Fayaway. But Hinahina is expressly endowed with a grasp of reason and the ability to see quickly
the value of literacy, qualities Melville's Tommo takes no note of, whether
in Fayaway or the rest of the Typee. Like her noble father Kailiki in her
thinking, Hinahina suspects that Forrest, Cook, and the rest are men,
not gods. On the one hand, Forrest delights that they have reasoned this
truth out for themselves. On the other hand, he does not perceive a danger
clearly undercurrent in Kailiki's talk: the knowledge that the visitors are
haole—foreign people, not gods—is not to be talked about. Forrest barely
hears his warning and fails to grasp it. Its political significance is irrelevant
to Forrest's deaf "nocturne," his moonlit idyll rising above any everyday
Hawaiian way of life. The three have in effect formed a conspiracy, and
yet Forrest fails to question the roles each plays. What if Hinahina and
Kailiki, soon to be joined by Pu'ou his father and the high priest of
Lono, themselves thus entertain Forrest simply for the purpose of extract-
ing information, something of tremendous value to the Hawaiians at this
historical moment when rival chiefs are waging battles for control of entire
islands and the whole chain? What if Forrest on his part were to do likewise: that is, were to seize the opportunity not only to learn about a

timeless Hawaiian mythology but also to spy out the current affairs of the Hawaiians (not to interfere further in their destinies but to learn who these people are as his contemporaries)? What is it about his philosophy which retards him from seeing (as Cook does) the Hawaiians within an historical process rather than as standing outside the passage of time? Kailiki asserts that the Hawaiian people are changing, and he sees Cook's arrival as a timely occurrence. It is the right historical moment: "Once long ago Lono tried to make light the burden of all men," Kailiki says; "Now he has returned, as he promised—and this time he will not fail." By tone and context, Kailiki implies that it is up to the priests and follow-ers of Lono the god to *make* Cook the man into a great symbol. By what may be hinted and by what is wholly unsaid or uninterpreted, be-cause it lies outside John Forrest's preconceptions, Bushnell requires us to ask just such questions, unless our own idea is to be a John Forrest, ultimately a tragic figure unable to come to terms with his experience.

Bushnell proceeds to reveal the undercurrents of Hawaiian politi-cal intrigue which Forrest witnesses but does not understand. After the first night when, too, Kailiki "marries" him to Hinahina, there appears for the only time in the novel a quartet of Hawaiians, commoners some-what resembling the chorus in a Greek tragedy. Forrest chances to over-hear these folk, who are conversing in private about the visitors at the risk of being executed for speaking as they do. Waking from a morning nap and hidden between beached canoes, Forrest hears voices nearby. By the manner of each, he names them the "Questioner," the "Melancholy Poet," the "Worrier," and the "Spectator."

In his sardonic, cutting voice the Questioner asks in what abased way the commoner is to act when the god Lono walks by him. If, as the Poet softly tells the Questioner, the commoner is to prostrate himself in the *kapu moe*, "the prostrating *kapu*, the burning, the abasing *kapu*," then, the Questioner asks, is the god's approach "no different from the coming of a high chief?" "Only as the parent fish differs from the finger-ling; only as the great wave on the reef exceeds the foam on the shore," the Poet answers. "Then why do we rejoice?" the Questioner presses; "The burden is not lightened from us" (125).

Forrest thus learns how onerous is the tax the visiting ships re-quire of the people for food and nearly every sort of offering, not only to replenish the ships' stores and daily provisions but also to supply the materials for increasingly great observances of Lono's return. A new voice breaks in, the Worrier's: "This is a hungry god, a devouring god, a god with a big belly. What will be left in the land for the people?" (125).

The Spectator adds: "The lesser gods who come with Lono hunger not only in their bellies. Not since the forested canoes moved past Hookena has many a man seen his mate" (126). The quartet ask one another who has seen and what is known about the god Lono. The manner of Lono, answers the Worrier, is "as of an old man, a man older than Pu'ou, . . . a man so old he is white all over, as if from drinking too much of the awa" (126–27). The Spectator finds the assertion incredible, for who can drink more awa than Pu'ou, notoriously fond of the ceremonial soporific, which over time turns the skin into the white scales and flakes that cover the old high priest's body? The Worrier warns his companions to be silent. They can be turned into "long pigs"—human sacrifices—in the temple for talking so. The Questioner nevertheless persists, "But how do the priests know this is Lono who comes? What is the sign of Lono? How is it known that this is not an old man, come to visit Kealakekua?" The Worrier moans in reply, "If they tell us this is Lono, then this is Lono!" And Forrest observes, "There was the cry of orthodoxy, the voice of submission" (127).

This small gathering—a fisherman, a taro farmer, a friend, and perhaps a kinsman from an outlying village—argues over the matter for a moment longer; but the remainder of the conversation reveals to the listening Forrest their heavy burden of fear. Their fears are enforced by every command of the priests, every restriction imposed on them by kapus, some of these requiring utter silence for up to three days at a time. After one of them has spied the *Resolution*'s boat heading towards their shores, the apprehensive commoners "moved off in silence, too proud to grovel, too uncertain of themselves to stay" (129).

Even as he had disregarded his captain's words against sex, Forrest now fails to apply the words of the quartet to his relationship with Hinahina and Kailiki. Kailiki after all is a priest of Lono, and Pu'ou, Kailiki's father, is the high priest of Lono. These are among the very priests the quartet on the beach has spoken of with whispered fear and resentment. But rather than pursue any doubts about the priests, Forrest assumes the role of an innocent in an alien paradise. He answers the priests' questions and teaches them about his home and about reading and writing, with which the noble Hawaiians are most impressed. He learns tolerance of what to him is a repulsive consequence of a cultural practice: that is, he learns not to recoil from the touch of the scurf-covered awa addict, Pu'ou, so that in peace of mind Forrest can learn more of the culture and listen even to Kailiki's discourses on his people's fears and burdens.

Here Bushnell takes the opportunity to fill out the story of Lono. Lono, explains the younger priest, long ago came to Hawai'i "from a distant land," "a great visitor, who did mighty things" among Hawaiians, who called him *Lono*, "which is to say, the new tidings, the new knowledge":

> He taught them the cultivation of the sweet potato, a vegetable new to them with his coming; he gave them some of their rude art, and some ceremonies in their religion, most notable of which was a feast of games and rites, which they called the Makahiki, that came in the month of the new year, at the time of the rising of the Pleiades over the rim of the eastern sea. Living among them, he took a wife of their people. From their union issued the noble house of 'I, first in the land, the house of the High Chief Kalaniopuu. (P. 135)

But "because of Lono's helpfulness to men," Kailiki says, "'the gods grew jealous.'" Afflicted with some madness no longer remembered, Lono was driven out of Hawai'i by way of Kealakekua, where he descended the long slope thus called The Way of the God. First a legend, then, as generations passed, a god, Lono was still awaited, for in departing for Kahiki he had promised to return. The god Lono was a kindly god, demanding no human sacrifice, in contrast to "the ferocious and bloody god of war, Ku," and "unlike the remote progenitor god, Kane." Lono is the god of what is good, close at hand: he is the god "of all growing things" (135). Kailiki's discourse on Lono explains to Forrest much about how the visitors have been received—by a people whose waiting has now ended. And yet despite the explicitly political nature of Kailiki's words, his lesson confirms more than explains, for Forrest hears in the tale what he already wants to hear. He hears words of welcome for the "gods," and he forgets that the quartet of Hawaiians on the beach did not rejoice in Lono's return.

From these sunset conversations with the three noble Hawaiians, Forrest achieves what might be called a duality of vision. Looking back fifty years, on the one hand he realizes that the chiefs and priests have since antiquity enforced absolute control over the commoners (though he does not appreciate a need for such control to maintain the islands' self-sufficiency, the population's sheer survival). On the other hand, he revels in his private dream of a romantic Hawaiian paradise:

> They were governed by a code of civil laws issued at the whim of the Chiefs or inherited from antiquity, and by a veritable

network of interdictions imposed by the priests who served their many gods. The result was an autocracy of cruelty, symbolized by their malign deities.

It is of these aspects of Hawaii that I think when gushing females and sybaritic youths entreat me to tell them of "the romantic South Sea Isles," expecting me to titillate them with accounts of endless feasting and languorous seductions and idylls under the palms. Naturally I tell them instead of the cruel gods and the crueler chiefs, of the discomforts of grass huts and the itch that comes from the salt of the sea, of the monotony of the diet and the serfdom of the commonality. (And yet, and yet—it is not of these things that I myself think when I am alone with my memories: I think of Hinahina, of that great full moon rising over the mountain, and of swimming with her by moonlight, naked in that phosphorescent sea; I think of the graceful dancing people, of laughter in the shadows, of idylls under the leaning palms. . . .). (P. 133)

From Forrest's point of view, Hawai'i and its natives are a heaven and a hell. The dialectic seems inescapable, and it fills Forrest's thinking.[5] In *The Return of Lono*, a work by a native-born author creating a narrative told not in a local but in a kind of tourist-heroic tradition, there are at least two different expressed or implied ways of envisioning that dialectic.

First, expressly and implicitly, Forrest's way, fitting his self-image as a man of the European Enlightenment, is based upon neoclassical and Christian assumptions, as I have already suggested both in his case and in discussing other characters in Hawaii's literature, for instance, Mark Hull of *Waimea Summer*.

A second way of seeing the duality of vision, however, is not as a doubling or expansion of vision but as a further indication of its limitations. This is exactly what we see happening when Forrest, breathless with what he has learned, tells all ears aboard ship how the Hawaiians have cast them in timeless mythological terms. Forrest's story explains to Cook and his subordinates why they have been welcomed as they have, with high ceremony and by presumed ranking of god, lesser gods, and men among them, all Hawaiians ranked below: again, dependent links of a great chain of being. When Cook and Forrest see beyond this, however, Forrest's vision is fixed still in timeless mythologies, as the two of them note a similarity between Lono and Prometheus, which supports the title and theme of chapter 2 of the novel, "Prometheus to the Pacific." This identification, like the notion of the noble savage, seems for the moment to provide the visitors a satisfying understanding of themselves and the "Indians" in their situation together. But in reality, all these identifications are just that—momentary, snatched out of the flow of time—entirely without any current (running, ongoing, continually changing) or historical and political context except for the fact of their own arrival in Hawai'i, as though it were forever the one and greatest event to occur there.

By the analogy between Lono and Prometheus, Forrest expresses his intellectual comfort within a certain kind of notion about human universality: it assumes that if one were to dress in the costume of another culture, like the Tahitian Omai in a British gentleman's outfit, one could fool a Dr. Johnson. Or, to put it another way, the human form stripped of ethnic costumes—and racial coloring—is universal, like nude statues in white marble. In Forrest's view, Cook and Lono and Prometheus appear to be, so to speak, all of the same color.

It is a rare tourist who reads the local newspaper to find out what is going on in city hall. Forrest can hardly be singled out for how he views the Hawaiians. But it is not that he is simply too young or naive to know better. For his view of his own shipmates and captain is thick with the same issues and arguments he fails to take seriously on the shore. Part 2, "Idols and False Notions," uses the quarterdeck of the *Resolution* as a main stage. By his orders Captain Cook is completing one task, the astronomical observations that are part of their mission, and hastening to complete another, the provisioning of the two ships for the voyage northward, again to search for the Northwest Passage. Whereas any conflict between reason and faith among the Hawaiians at best lies dormant in Forrest's thoughts, here among the voyagers the conflict rears up and tramples the expedition into disorder.

Bushnell uses a rather intricate interplay of characters and circumstances to develop this major part of the novel's overt plot and conflict, for here the actions are few, the words among characters many. Part 2 occurs on Wednesday, 3 February 1779, the burial day of William Watman, body servant to Captain Cook. It is also the day before the planned departure for the north. Watman, an elderly man, has died of a stroke. But the lumpish, mean William Bligh and his religious partner John Ledyard, the corporal of the Marines and American colonist whom Forrest calls "an avenging angel, in a nimbus of light, speaking out of a fanatical purity" from which some shipmates recoil, have begun to preach their own version of what is happening to the visiting crews. To them, old Watman is the first witnessed death provoked by James Cook's blasphemy, his presumption of being—his very pretense of being—a god, a heathen god, and deceiving the native peoples besides. The fundamentalist pair and their rather numerous followers fear and yet exult that the expedition is doomed. They rejoice in misfortune, the proof of their divinely gifted seeing.

To his own mortification, the sharply witty First Lieutenant James King, whom the Hawaiians have nicknamed "Lono's son," discovers when arguing with Bligh and Ledyard over religious issues at Watman's burial that several sailors have been converted to the faith. These sailors have come down from walking along the great slope of Kealakekua; instead of "The Way of the God," they call it "The Way of God." Not present on the scene but overhearing King report it to Cook, Forrest notes how "even then . . . they had dispossessed the heathen god of his cliff and have given it over to their Jehovah" (153).

Still another difficulty grows from religious issues. Ship's Surgeon John Law insinuates cryptically to Cook that Watman's death has shown the natives that their visitors are mortal. The presumption of their godhood can no longer reliably protect the men from harm by the natives, who meanwhile have become much more aggressive in taking anything of metal. The issue concerns both the visitors' beliefs and the natives' presumed beliefs in them. Just when the foreigners' supposed spell over the Hawaiians is thought to be broken by Watman's death, their own ranks of the faithful rise sharply. And though it is not a class struggle, there is a vague and somewhat menacing sense, from Forrest's point of view, that Bligh's fanatically religious rebellion against Cook has many followers among the common seamen. It seems a popular rebellion, the lower main and foredecks against the privileged quarterdeck. Likewise on the shore, the priests of Lono, whom Forrest through their special friendship considers reasonable, are trying not only to stem swelling discontent or loss of faith of the masses regarding their hungry visitors but also to quell popular sentiments for war against rival districts. Meanwhile, whereas the natives appear less and less to believe in Cook as Lono, the haole increasingly believe in their own mythical conception of Hawai'i as a paradise now about to be lost.

Indeed, Forrest's own assumptions about the Hawaiians grow more Christian than ever, even while to the contrary he champions Cook as the Man of Reason, Cook the Scientist. Fifty years later, in his afterthoughts, he is still a believer in the paradise myth: "But it was easy to take things among the gentle people, and in those weeks of our lying-over we took all that we could from them. Not only food, and gifts,

and women did we take, not only the labor of their hands and the proven-
der of their lovely island. We also took from them their innocence." Forrest tries to confess. "Kailiki's words to me were upheld: the great change
among them was begun" (143–44).

The conflict between reason and faith is for a moment quelled
by Cook's setting right a false charge against him. As John Law archly
puts it, "Even the members of your foolish crew would find this strange
logic coming from you, sir," when Cook condemns any of his officers
who have violated his rule against sex with the natives (173). At first
puzzled, Cook thunders a command that Law explain his insinuation.
The ragged story tumbles out of Law. A year earlier, the "Princess of
Kauai" boarded the *Resolution* under the cover of night and draped in
a dark kapa mantle intended to hide her from sight. Ushered swiftly
into the captain's cabin, the princess spent the night there. Everyone else
aboard assumed that the mysterious tryst must naturally have involved
lovemaking. This strange Kaua'i incident and the rumor it set loose constitute one of the main sources of restlessness among followers of Bligh
and Ledyard. Can the men be blamed for breaking Cook's rule forbidding
sex, when their captain himself showed them how to do it?

Cook, struck by what he knows to be the absurdity of the charge
that Law has repeated, laughs "not the hysterical laughter of relief that
others might have called upon; but the quiet rueful laughter of a sad
and tired man. It was not much better than crying, . . . he laughed
so tragically" (176). At that moment the ailing Captain Clerke arrives,
painfully ascends the companionway, and stands beside his friend with
a cheering smile. Despite Clerke's attempts to "shrug the whole matter
off" as merely another instance of a crew wanting to belittle their captain,
what appears to be a great bitterness wells up in Cook:

> With a pained smile he looked up at Clerke standing thin and
> stooped beside him. "I am the one who is different here—
> I am the greater fool, for having thought I could compel His-
> tory."
> Then he looked down, deep down into himself, and for a
> long moment he sat there, his head upon his hand. Among
> us who watched his travail there was silence as he tasted the
> bitterness of his loneliness. (P. 177)

The festering rumors spread by malcontents have infected the crew and
have already caused the loss of the paradise the crewmen thought they
had gained in Hawai'i. Since only Cook, Clerke, Law, the Third Lieuten-

ant John Williamson, and Forrest are on the scene, Clerke urges Cook
to tell the others about the Princess of Kaua'i, it now being others' turn
to wonder what Cook means by his sorrowing laughter, his rueful words.
"But what good would it do now, Charles, save to add another tale to
the collection of this voyage? How can I convince them," Cook pleads,
"that my visitor was no fawnlike princess, slender and soft-eyed, of the
kind their fancies urge upon me? How can I tell them she was a mountain-
ous villainess of a woman, come to solicit not love but weapons for
a rebellion on her quarrelsome island? They'd think me a liar, and rightly
so" (178–79).

Cook differs in two ways from Forrest in their thinking. He
does not assume Hawai'i to be or to have been a paradise in the Christian
sense, but merely free from certain diseases. The Hawaiians are not an
"innocent" people in the way Forrest conceives. They scheme politics
and they make war. And, second, Cook seems to think of history as
a process larger than his individual self (his own comparison of Lono
with Prometheus notwithstanding, since Cook does not believe himself
to be Lono) and larger even than the culture his ships represent. This
contrasts with Forrest's notion that "the great change" among the Hawaiians was "begun" by Cook himself and, following him, advanced by the
haole.

As for the next charge, that Cook has imperiled the expedition
by his blasphemy of allowing himself to be called a god, Cook replies
by considering what would happen were he to "admit to the justice of
their charge, and let the matter lie":

> To bring the question home: do I not play God for all of us
> each time I set the course of this ship, sailing her into unknown
> seas, to confront unknown dangers that might bring unknown
> fates to all of us aboard? . . . Did I not choose to winter here
> in the Sandwich Islands, instead of in some cove along the shore
> of New Albion? Did I not decide, little more than a fortnight
> past, that we should put into this bay to refresh ourselves?
> Did I not, by those actions, decree that death should come
> to Watman here, and disease to the Indians, and new perils
> and new joys should overtake us in a place we should never
> have seen had it not been my decision that set us down here?
> Can you deny, then, that I am as a god, master of this ship
> and of its sister ship, lord of its crews, and arbiter of all their
> destinies? (Pp. 190–91)

Standing by in the scene, Law accuses the captain of blasphemy in speaking. When you have before you a man who has lost faith in God, Cook asks, would you rob him of his self-reliance, his power to decide, and his mind as well? Here on the quarterdeck, the battle lines of reason and faith are drawn as they were at Watman's grave ashore.

In the final chapter of part 2, following immediately after Cook's exchange with Law, King returns to the *Resolution* with a grotesque trophy: the gigantic, hideous, grinning idol representing Kūkaʻilimoku, the war god. Staring balefully above the ship's rail on its approach, the image of Kū startles the disputants on the quarterdeck. With considerable relief, Burney peers over the rail to find that the idol is conveyed by King in the pinnace circling the ship below. Nervously Williamson remarks that, by its approach, "it reminds me of Birnam Wood." Cook can no longer restrain a savage rage: "Am I a Macbeth, then, that I should fear the transplantation of an image graven in wood?" he snarls at them all; "Have I killed a king, have I stolen a kingdom, have I usurped a throne? Why, then, do you tremble?" (196). He begs to be left in peace, just as he leaves his crew to take care of their own minds and souls.

Afterward, alone with Captain Clerke, though Forrest still listens at his writing table, Captain Cook articulates the questions that increasingly disturb him in the face of the changes he has wrought or has been responsible for in the places he has discovered: "Is reason alone enough?" Cook asks. "The agony of the reasoning man is this," he tells Clerke: "he is unable to believe in God, the while his heart cries out to him that without God his life is meaningless" (199).

Forrest, hearing this, now sees and smells and perceives what, enraptured in paradise, he could not perceive before. "The smell of rotting seaweed came off to us from the land, the stink of death and decay." He tells of the "evil encroaching suffocating silence" in the wake of the captain's question, "and in that soundless timelessness we were as corpses sunk in some deep level of the sea, making rendezvous for unscheduled journey to some uncharted destination" (199–200). At the wearisome day's end, Forrest sees the full force of the setting sun catch the wall of Kealakekua, "transmuted by it into a thing threatening and evil":

> Every rock, every stunted bush and clump of dry grass upon
> that escarpment was lighted up, and I was startled to see, as
> I looked upon it, that its bulk was not pure black as I had
> thought it was since first I'd seen it in the morning's upright
> sun: now it was red, the color of spilled and clotted blood.

And on our ship there was no escape from that dreadful au-
gury: the lurid sunset cast that same bloody hue upon the masts
and spars, upon the furled sails, upon the ropes and stays, upon
the image of the god towering above the deck upon which
my Captain sat, oblivious to its presence. (P. 204)

With references once again to Macbeth and to Forrest's smelling
the stench blown from the shore, we recall the novel's beginning and
its foreshadowings of this very moment. We realize that at this moment
Forrest understands his failure to perceive Kealakekua's reality, the failure
for which he criticizes himself at the novel's opening; and now, he himself
hears the echo of Macbeth. The moment also recalls the episodes in *Typee*
when Tommo sees a preserved human head and after the Typees' victory
feast, the bones. The haole are now seen by the Hawaiians to be just
that—foreign people, not gods. Furthermore, in the towering, blood-red
image of the war god Kū, Forrest sees that death, too, is speaking. *Et
in Arcadia ego*: "I, too, am in Arcadia," says death in the simple pastoral
Forrest dreamt while, without wanting to be aware of it, he and all the
others, foreign and Hawaiian together, have been actors in a heroic tragedy. And like Tommo, Forrest, too, is nonplused by the overturning
of his assumptions about himself, his race, and about the Hawaiians, who
at the moment appear to him to be as profoundly flawed as any other
human beings. Cook, the Hawaiians, their gods, their land are uniformly
colored with blood, with mortality itself, in Forrest's realization.

In this apprehensive mood Forrest narrates the two ships' departure from Kealakekua on 4 February. Part 3 of *The Return of Lono*, "Paradise Lost," opens a week later, on Thursday, 11 February 1779, back
again in Kealakekua Bay where the ships must undergo repairs for the
storm damage suffered in their aborted northward passage.

The conflict between reason and faith darkens Cook's quarterdeck in the novel's final part. But ashore, an ominous change has occurred
which baffles Forrest. Instead of welcoming the sodden ships' return with
ceremony or even with hospitality, the Hawaiians huddle fearfully and
wordlessly under the kapu cast by the priests of Kū. What is happening
among the Hawaiians is roughly analogous to what is taking place aboard
Cook's ship. Like Bligh and Ledyard and their God, the priests of the
war god Kū, demanding harsh sacrifices and unflinching obedience, com-
pete against Pu'ou, Kailiki, and the other priests of Lono for power. When
King, Forrest, and a small party land that day in the village of their
recent joys, they are met with a deathly silence: the silence of the kapu.

It is evident in Forrest's point of view that this recently paradisiacal shore is now lost. To him, it is a fallen, mortal world. A Hawaiian friend is killed instantly with a stone slung at his head the moment he offers Forrest and King an extended hand and a wide smile of welcome. The secret police of the priests of Kū capture the shore party, as if the haole now were trespassers. The enforcers of the kapu look like huge insects as they silently move, naked and gigantic, toward and about their captives; on their heads they wear large polished gourds whose inner darkness conceals the wearers' features, except for eyes that gleam behind the visor openings. Forrest and King are fortunately rescued by Kailiki, who sends the police on their way. His voice of reason wins this skirmish.

In history, the cause for this change in life on the shore is chilling, when one reflects upon the part it played in the tragedy of James Cook. Forrest never mentions this cause; and whether or not Bushnell deliberately withheld it, it is reasonable to assume that a John Forrest would simply never have learned enough during his visit to report it. When on 4 February 1779 the two ships under Cook's command left Hawai'i for the north, it was the ending of the Makahiki season of Lono, the good god, during which season warfare was forbidden and Lono's priests naturally presided over the games and competitions that took the place of bloodshed. By the time Cook's expedition was forced by bad weather to return to Kealakekua on 11 February, the season had turned: it was now the season of Kūka'ilimoku, "the eater of men," literally the "island-snatching war god" of Kamehameha himself. Because they had already overstayed their recent visit, and because the season for celebrating Lono's return had passed, Cook and his men returned instead to an unexpected truculence and hostility. Cook's expedition may thus have blundered into trouble literally for not heeding or probably not even knowing the Hawaiian seasons. And even if they had known, one wonders what they could have done about it. In this context, the largest figures in Forrest's sight in the novel—and these figures are his fellow voyagers and himself—suddenly shrink. It is they who are victims of fate, circumstance, ignorance, coincidence, history—all of these so beyond their control that even now Forrest cannot quite conceive of them. Forrest's narrative point of view descends, so to speak, from romance to realism, and now to a kind of naturalism. The resemblance of the secret police of Kū to giant insects who execute control illustrates this turn.

Just as Forrest suggests at the novel's beginning that he underestimated the size of Kealakekua, we can see how, outside the voyager's point of view, a larger context diminishes these characters and their story.

Curiously, whereas the sketches and prints of John Webber, the expedition's artist, show the ships standing tall against the slope of Kealakekua in the near background, the naked eye sees from the highlands, from the air, and from the shore a massive mountain slope, against which yachts the size of the *Resolution* appear as mere as fingernail clippings in the broad blue bay.

As Forrest's subjects shrink in his view, others, such as Bligh, see theirs swell in proportion. Bligh's view, of course, is Biblical, allegorical, and sweeping in its condemnation of human failures. On the quarterdeck of the *Resolution*, Captain Cook confronts Bligh and questions him about the charges he has made. Bligh bluntly asserts his conviction that the storm that has driven them back to Kealakekua is another sign of God's wrath. All are being punished for Cook's wrongs.

Sunday, 14 February, three days later, seems barely to break into daylight. It begins wet, cold, gloomy, and joyless. Forrest emerges from breakfast below to stumble into what, in his dark mood, he can hardly stomach. A prayer meeting is in session amidships. He tries dodging it by pushing his way past, but for a moment, thinking it may be a burial services, he pauses to listen. With no surprise at all, Forrest hears the resonant voice, the New England accent of Ledyard, who, elated with his own certitude and righteousness, preaches hellfire and brimstone to this troubled flock. Forrest mounts the quarterdeck in search of his captain and stops in shock upon seeing what stands beside Cook: the idol of Kū has been moved and secured in such a way that "it looked as if it had been crucified" on the mizzenmast, fastened there with a "hint of triumph" now on its face; and the idol dwarfs the man who stands there grimly beside it (235).

Despite the fierceness of the quarterdeck setting with its powerful visual suggestion allying Cook with Kū, the real fire of hellish religious fanaticism is raging below on the maindeck where Ledyard condemns those he has judged guilty of transgression and calls loudly for God's succor in this dangerous time. Apparently an otherwise perceptive man, Ledyard "in religion . . . became orthodox, and in prayer . . . became proud, falling with ease into the traditions of his kind who thought themselves the Chosen People and commanders of the God who had created them and chosen them"—"commanders" because of the way Ledyard addresses his God by imperatives in his supplications (237).

The deism of the Enlightenment evidently having itself failed to support the faith he craves in both God and reason, Cook isolates himself in self-doubt and begins to turn against his sympathizers. Of three charges Ledyard and Bligh shortly afterward bring directly against Cook—that he set a sinful example by spending the night with the Princess of Kaua'i, that he has permitted his sailors' debauchery, and that he commits sacrilege in presuming godhood—the first is the easiest and the most dramatic to refute. Cook discloses to his accusers, for all to hear, that while alone with the shadowy Princess of Kaua'i, he was "in the presence of a woman as tall as I, as old as I—and three times my weight" (256). Those who have been loyal and sympathetic to Cook are aghast at the disclosure; for they, too, have assumed that Cook had violated his own rules, and, just as mistaken as Cook's accusers, in their hearts and minds Cook's allies allowed him the liberty to do so. Now hearing the facts, Cook's stalwart First Lieutenant John Gore, representative of his staunchest supporters, gapes at the realization that a "monstrous growth of misunderstanding has risen." It has risen "out of innocence, . . . particularly an innocence of the facts," offers Cook sarcastically (257).

The fable and the truth of the matter, though relatively simple to correct with Cook's facts, raise some points that further complicate the story and layer the novel's themes with still more conflicts. For one, in Bushnell's tale, all become aware soon after Cook's describing the princess that he has been betrayed by Williamson and Law. Both men, on the eve of their ill-fated departure to Alaska, had heard Cook tell the plain truth of the incident. Obviously neither of them had informed the others amidship and below, once they left the quarterdeck, that the lurid rumors were false. They had allowed the falsehood to continue on its tragic course, and now their perfidy is exposed in the pall of that Sunday noon. Nothing, however, is made of the fact that Forrest and Captain Clerke, too, had heard what Cook said to Law about the Princess of Kaua'i. Why did they not correct the untrue rumor?

Secondly, the Hawaiians' military motive behind their hospitality surfaces again in the falsehood now corrected. Besides the maneuvering of the Princess of Kaua'i, evidence that Lono's return is being used by rival Hawaiian parties to gain political ascendancy now and then appears throughout Forrest's narration. One such rivalry exists between the priests of Kūka'ilimoku and those of Lono. Another evidence of political strife is far more momentous in its overall import, yet by virtue of its complexity and magnitude it is far less comprehensible to Forrest in his recent days and nights as the enchanted visitor. While Forrest and the others have seen their stay at Kealakekua as the most important concern of the Hawaiians there at that time, the venerable High Chief Kalaniopu'u and his young chiefs, mainly the scowling giant, Kamehameha, who was in the first party to board the *Resolution* at Kealakekua, are plotting war against rival districts of the island of Hawai'i, against the chiefs on Maui, and eventually the entire archipelago. They have been assembling at Kealakekua not to welcome Cook, but to hold war councils during the final weeks of the peaceful Makahiki while awaiting the coming season of Kū.

James Cook's death occurs out of Forrest's sight, offstage, *ob scena* as is it would happen in a Sophoclean tragedy. Cook is killed at the village of Ka'awaloa on the bay while Forrest remains behind on the quarterdeck. Captain Clerke has reported with alarm that his ship's cutter has been stolen by natives. Cook, terribly agitated by the insolence of Ledyard and his followers and distressed by his own doubts, tries decisively and with foolish treachery to set out to recover the boat. His plan is to lure Kalaniopu'u to the *Resolution* and away from Ka'awaloa, where the high chief at the moment is resting from the war councils. Kalaniopu'u is to be held hostage aboard the ship until the cutter is returned. Cook orders the trustworthy Lieutenant Molesworth Phillips to command the boat that will take him ashore and guard his safety. But to nearly everyone's astonishment and dismay, Cook puts the singularly untrustworthy John Williamson in charge of a second boat intended to provide further protection. Williamson himself is clearly shaken, terrified of what may happen in such an assignment. Against all better judgment and advice of those still loyal to him, Cook insists on appointing Williamson—in order, he says, to give the young man a chance to gain some experience and perhaps to redeem himself from his proven cowardice in earlier transactions. It was Williamson who in a panic had shot a Hawaiian extending a helping hand when the very first of their shore parties was landing at Waimea, Kaua'i, in 1778.

As Forrest composes the story from others' various accounts, events on shore soon go badly for Cook and the small group that lands. Though Kalaniopu'u is at first compliant, he is nevertheless prevented by his alarmed people from going with Cook to the *Resolution*. As Cook tries to escape from a surly mob on the beach, hostilities break open. Both sides suffer casualties. Cook is struck, his moans signaling his mortality to any Hawaiian who may yet have thought him a god. Raging from weeks and indeed lifetimes of having to feed the hungry gods in fearful obedience to their priests and chiefs, the mob seizes Cook, hits him, stabs him, drowns him until he is dead, and smashes his corpse against the rocks dividing the water and the shore.

And so Cook is killed while, nearby, Williamson and his squad float in deadly silence—perhaps thinking that the last, desperate wave of Cook's arm to summon their help was meant instead to ward off the guardian boats. Williamson's crew does not fire a single shot to defend their captain. In the three days that follow Cook's murder, the Englishmen, full of vengeance, launch fitful reprisals against the Hawaiians and ostracize Williamson with great loathing. Some crewmen beat Ledyard soundly for his righteous humbug that the furious sailors are now convinced had something to do with the death of their captain. Ledyard and his followers beatifically suffer this attack like martyrs.

With Kailiki serving as mediator, a few scant, grisly remains of Captain Cook are returned to his men as Hawaiian custom prescribes; these are buried at sea. A truce is fashioned; the ships are made ready to sail. Somehow a semblance of friendship between the alien parties is restored, so that when they leave the Bay of Kealakekua, this again is what Forrest and his shipmates see:

> The natives were collected on the shore in great numbers, or
> gathered around us in their canoes or swimming in the sea,
> as on the day of our arrival; and as our ships passed among
> them they offered their farewells with every mark of affection
> and good will. (P. 290)

It is difficult to judge the tone of this final farewell where, in spite of the tragedy that has come to pass, the end repeats the aloha of the beginning. The words here intimate Forrest's wry thought that, for the natives, life simply and falsely resumes as usual. But Bushnell also seems to be suggesting that it is Forrest, with his ethnocentricity, who is himself not truly changed by the experience, so innocent and reduced from human stature do the Hawaiians once more appear when captured in Forrest's memory of that final moment of aloha.

Bushnell's *The Return of Lono* may claim the distinction, in certain of its aspects, of being the first work of the heroic in Hawaii's modern historical literature, outside of Hawaii's quite large numbers of immigrant sagas. To be sure, long before Bushnell wrote the narrative in the mid-1950s, many of the elements that coalesced in his treatment of Cook were already evident in nonfictional primary sources and histories, and in romances such as Jarves's *Kiana* and Twain's never-published novel of Hawai'i. The sharpest and most meaningful of these elements I speak of is Bushnell's circumspection—his not taking for granted, for instance, Cook's achievement of "discovering" the Hawaiian Islands, the Hawai-

ians' view of Cook as man or as god, and the condemnation heaped
on Cook by his opponents on the voyage and by the followers these
opponents afterward gained at home. The author's thorough study of the
voyagers'—and the Hawaiians'—widely varying narratives of the Hawai'i
"transaction," as well as his examination of the proceedings and inquests
of various sorts following the return of Cook's ships to their home without
him, enabled Bushnell to state in his prefatory note what was and still
is provocative for various reasons:

> One of the greatest ironies in Hawaii's history lies in the fact
> that the greatest man to visit her shores is today the least known
> and most despised. I hope this story will help to comfort, how-
> ever belatedly, the patient shade of Captain Cook.

That Cook should be the hero of our first modern historical novel
of Hawai'i is rather fitting, for the published writing of Hawaii's history
literally began with his arrival. But conversely, the fact that the hero
is not a Hawaiian but "the greatest man to *visit*" Hawai'i admittedly per-
plexes some (emphasis added). What then of the preeminent Hawaiian
historical hero, King Kamehameha, who plays only a cameo role in
Bushnell's novel?

However provocative Cook's name, it may be that after nearly
one hundred and eighty years had passed between Cook's death and
Bushnell's novel, the known facts of the historical event had lost their
ability to hurt any interested parties, so that Bushnell could expect a
sufficiently open reading to make writing the story worthwhile. It may
be, too, as I have suggested earlier, that because of a combination of
apparently insufficient information and hesitation to deal with a historical
figure whose story is probably far more complex than Cook's in Hawai'i,
no one yet has written an adequate novel about the hero Kamehameha,
though he figures in many Hawai'i works as a chief standing to the side
of the main figures. Like a monument or an idol representing military
conquest and a political greatness too great to be faced directly, Kamehameha stands scowling and silent.

Charles M. Newell's 1885 novel, *Kamehameha, The Conquering
King*, does not attempt to fathom the heroic depths of the Lonely One
and his achievements.[6] Newell's romance makes no pretense of being
"modern" like Bushnell's where the hero's psyche is an important battle-
ground as it is for Melville's Ahab. Indeed, Newell's and other such relics
of the later nineteenth-century Western fiction of Hawai'i make conspicuous use of the threadbare conventions and clichés of Europe and America,

perhaps in their authors' attempts to instill a sense of enchantment and exoticism through incongruous descriptions and improbable events, while still dealing in familiar allusions. Far removed from actual encounters such as Melville experienced with the Polynesians, Newell writes of a Hawaiian princess bounding "like a fawn" down a slope to meet her love; but there were then no fawns in Hawai'i. Newell is also fond of mermaids, European in appearance though perhaps inspired by tales of *mo'o*, guardian spirits of waters—in one of his romances, a princess lures a shy mermaid to shore for a meeting. Kamehameha is time and again described as being a Hercules, and allusions to Greek epics are everywhere evident in such highly romanticized versions of the heroic in Hawaii's literature. Today a Hellenic Hawai'i would seem an unlikely site for Kamehameha to build his kingdom in a heroic work yet to be written about him. But the native Hawaiian heroic novel—as Bushnell fervently urges —has yet to be written for Hawaii's people and culture, and by a native Hawaiian.

The fact is that not only have native Hawaiian heroes been scarce in Hawaii's literature but so have any literary heroes from among the non-Caucasian peoples who have settled in Hawai'i for well over a century now. Surely aware of this as he continued his novel-writing beyond *The Return of Lono*, Bushnell in 1963 published *Molokai*, a tale containing moments of great joy and pathos but pervaded with anguish; it is about three Hawaiian or part-Hawaiian exiles at the Kalaupapa Leper Settlement on Moloka'i and about a German doctor's experiments there to see if a healthy man can be infected by leprous tissue grafted under his skin.[7] A native Hawaiian convict serves as the doctor's experimental "animal." This is no mere diabolical fiction; Bushnell, the medical historian, bases *Molokai* solidly on fact. In 1884, the novel's setting, a scientist working at the colony actually performed the experiment. But more important, *Molokai* is, like *Lono*, an intense examination of moral issues inherent in the characters, the plot, and the setting. Father Damien himself is not central to the story, though he appears occasionally and is everywhere evident in whatever humane elements abide on the bleak peninsula. Of special interest in the context of the present study, however, is the character Caleb Forrest, a descendant of John Forrest and Hinahina. A Honolulu attorney with more than hopeful prospects of a brilliant career and an equally dazzling life in Honolulu's high society, Caleb discovers that he has leprosy. The character and his story echo precisely what Mark Twain describes in his lost story of Bill Ragsdale, the half-white court interpreter who eventually dies of leprosy. Without knowing of Twain's unpublished novel, Bushnell bases his Caleb Forrest on the same Bill Ragsdale because of the intrinsic fascination of that historic figure.[8]

In *Molokai*, Bushnell further develops the device of the first-person narrator he used with considerable success in *Lono*. Molokai is narrated by three characters in turn: Newman the scientist, telling of himself and his specimen, the magnificently handsome convict Keanu; Malie, an extremely beautiful court lady whose flawless face belies the disease her body bears; and Caleb, bitter and misanthropic over his horrid fate. Through each of these narrators' limited points of view, we are permitted to see things filtered in a way made acceptable to us, because the author is thus inviting us to examine *critically* those prejudices, beliefs, and perspectives of the individual narrators. Bushnell, of course, was not the first to use such a narrative device in modern American literature. But it comes as a surprise to hear from him that he has never been able, for some reason, to read Faulkner. Still, somewhere in his long literary experience he might have heard that his narrative technique would be immediately recognized as resembling Faulkner's in *The Sound and the Fury, Light in August*, and many other works. Bushnell might well say that such a technique comes naturally to a writer raised in a society characterized by the coexistence of different cultures and points of view, where, too, one is aware (as Twain and Faulkner knew) that what the outside world thinks of this locale is at odds with what the local people know.

Bushnell's third novel, *Ka'a'awa*, is set in a slightly earlier historical time, in the 1850s.[9] Here again are first-person narrators: Hiram Nihoa, the kind of inquisitive person Hawaiians call *nīele* (nosy), who circles O'ahu by horseback on a mission ordered by King Kamahameha III; and Saul Bristol, a brooding, suicidal New England recluse on his ranch at Ka'a'awa, on Oahu's windward shore. The elderly and lively Nihoa, sent by the king to sniff out the source of rumors of international intrigue on the windward side, confronts the enmity that still rankles between the defeated family of Kalanikūpule, O'ahu's last king, and the powerful Kamehameha family, who alone have ruled all Hawai'i since their victory at Nu'uanu in 1795. With the help of Nihoa, his wit, and his humor, Bristol gradually regains faith in himself and trust in his fellow humans. Bristol's story becomes one of achievement: he learns from the Hawaiians, and he climbs to the very source of the spiritual power that pervades Ka'a'awa from the lofty sacred mountain behind his ranch. Of all Bushnell's novels, *Ka'a'awa* is richest in Hawaiian legend and lore. Of all the characters peopling his novels, Bushnell best likes the *nīele* Hiram Nihoa.

In his fiction, Bushnell has most recently completed a set of works which, if it were not for their magnitude, we might call a long-time pet project. In *The Stone of Kannon* and its sequel, *The Water of Kane*, two full-length novels, Bushnell presents the story of the "Gannen Mono," the First-Year Men, the first Japanese to arrive in Hawai'i to work on the sugar plantations.[10] The Gannen Mono arrived in 1868, the First Year of the Emperor Meiji, and their name for themselves refers to this Japanese event. Bushnell uses the historic immigration of 154 Gannen Mono, both men and women, creating several fictional characters to show, in the span of the two novels, the Japanese as they adapt their new surroundings to themselves—and vice versa. With Ishi and the other immigrants, Bushnell mixes in the now-invigorated Saul Bristol, who has moved from Ka'a'awa to Maui, as well as historical figures and events of the time.

Unlike his earlier novels, Bushnell's sagas of the Gannen Mono are narrated in the third person, and this narrative voice causes some problems. Some readers find the voice awkward, like someone trying to imitate a Japanese speaking fluent but unidiomatic English, just as, say, the English presumably translated from Hiram Nihoa's Hawaiian report to the king in *Ka'a'awa* is in a syntax, diction, and idiom imagined to resemble the Hawaiian tongue. The narrative of John Forrest, by contrast, moved writer John Dominis Holt to say that Bushnell must have been born in eighteenth-century England. But clearly, in creating Forrest's narrative voice, models abound—both for modern novelists like Bushnell to affect in their writing, and for readers today to recognize, for such voices beckon us into a familiar literary world of "Enlightenment English." Voices of the Hawaiian native or the Japanese immigrant, however, when "translated" into English, as yet have no established literary character except in demeaning stereotypes. Lacking literary models, readers familiar with these peoples' voices from real life will of course judge them by the way people actually speak—which Bushnell's unprecedented novels of the Gannen Mono presume neither to represent nor to mimic.

Indeed, in spite of the years of study and research he has lovingly and painstakingly devoted to the novels' subjects, Bushnell will not pretend to write in the first-person voice of an imagined Japanese narrator. In his Preface to *The Stone of Kannon* he offers an apology of sorts— published in 1978 while he was helping to plan the polyethnic Talk Story Conference. Bushnell states why he of all people wrote the Japanese immigrant story of Hawai'i:

If you are wondering why a writer who cannot claim a Japanese ancestor is telling this story, the answer is both simple and saddening: no novelist of Japanese ancestry has yet done so. Accordingly, for lack of such a writer, I have decided to tell it myself. Not incidentally, I have written this story as much for nisei, sansei, yonsei, and gosei, as for all those other haoles of any ethnic group who don't know anything about either the Gannen Mono or Hawaii in 1868. (vii)

Bushnell recognizes that the appropriation of voices foreign to one's own ethnic group can sometimes draw resentment, especially from those the author most seeks to favor with the gift of his or her work. But he echoes the note struck by Camöens and, closer to home, by Holt. Bushnell tells of "our people, our history" in order to save a shared Hawai'i heritage and culture from degenerating into a brittle fulfillment of someone else's dream, someone else's story. In early 1978, when Bushnell and others of us were working to bring knowledge of Hawaii's grassroots literature to light, we did not yet know the extent and significance of earlier fictional works by Japanese Americans about Hawaii's Japanese immigrant pioneers. Nonetheless, only Bushnell's novels are about the Gannen Mono, who, like Cook, were at the vanguard—and were heroic. Today, the actual men and women of the Gannen Mono remain largely nameless except to their many generations of Hawaiian descendants.

2

The historical figure as hero predominates in the dramas of Aldyth Morris, whose professional debut dates to "about 1956," when her three-act adaptation of Fook-Tan Ching's *The Fourth Son* was performed at the Phoenix Theater in New York City.[11] The play, set in imperial China, "was written at the request of the Dramatic Chapter of the Hawaii Chinese Civic Association" in 1954.[12] *The Fourth Son* was followed in 1959 by another China drama, *The Secret Concubine*, performed at New York's Carnegie Theater in 1960.[13] These dramas have been eclipsed by Morris's more recent "monodramas"—one-character plays—bringing to life Captain Cook, Robert Louis Stevenson, and Father Damien for each one's fascinating hour or two on the stage. Her *Damien* (1980) has received deserved attention, thanks in part to a PBS broadcast performance. Recently Morris has been "at work on a one-woman script on Lili'uokalani."[14]

In Morris's playwriting career, we can see something of the pattern of Bushnell's fiction writing. Both have undertaken increasingly challenging tasks in the development of a Hawai'i heroic literary tradition. They have moved, first of all, from the distant Chinese, in Morris's case, to the local Hawaiian setting, then from the historic figure who is already a literary hero, to ones not yet fully born out of massed facts into the world of imaginative literature. Such are the Gannen Mono and Lili'uokalani.

Another feature shared by Bushnell's, Morris's, and other works of the heroic in Hawaii's literature is the high value placed on the common person and on common humanity. This emphasis, of course, characterizes American literature in general and the novel as a genre of the middle classes. But Hawaii's case is exceptional. Hawai'i is the only one of the United States to have been a monarchy in recent history, the only one with a royal palace recently restored and symbolizing a revered though not commonly interpreted past. As in *The Return of Lono*, the Hawaiian ruling class may represent a power that is at once oppressive and humane, but its quality tends to be measured today by the degree of suffering of the common Hawaiian under the rule of chiefs and priests. A stress on the leader's sympathy for the commoner may be seen in both Bushnell's and Morris's works on Captain Cook, where the hero is distinguished as much by his deep concern for the health and well-being of his crew and for the peoples they visit as by his profoundly solitary nature. In Bushnell's novel, moreover, the hero Cook has a mediator in a common man, the narrator John Forrest—an Ishmael to his captain.

Complicating matters in more recent times—that is, in the final years of the monarchy, the era of Kalākaua and Lili'uokalani—is the oppression of the native monarchy itself by strong American political, cultural, religious, and economic influences. The Hawaiian monarchy becomes identified with the ruled rather than as the ruler, within an imperialistic Western sphere. Working against the vocal censure by American community spokesmen such as William D. Alexander, son of a missionary, the popularly elected King David Kalākaua created his Hale Naua secret society for the restoration of Hawaiian culture and openly revived the traditional Hawaiian hula.[15] Kalākaua thus became a champion of the native people and culture, a serious role underlying his cavalier epithet, "the Merry Monarch." Even Kalākaua's popularity, however, was dependent upon how his people saw him in relationship to American powers, by whether and how he was dominated by them in his reign. As for his sister and successor Queen Lili'uokalani, the song title repeated in John Dominis Holt's drama about Hawaii's last reigning monarch,

Kaulana Na Pua, Famous Are the Flowers, attests to the bond connecting Lili'u with all her loyal subjects, the "flowers" of Hawai'i. Her story, too, tells of domination by foreign powers over the Hawaiian monarchy and the commoners of the realm.

Morris's recent monodramas, both in substance and technique, bear out this reading of the hero as an otherwise uncommon individual whose esteem lives in his or her sympathies with the common people. At the climax of Bushnell's novel, Cook insists in an irrational outburst that he has mastered self-reliance. This as much as anything else in the novel expresses the character's tragic flaw. In Morris's *Captain Cook*, the hero addresses his monologue to an imagined audience of Hawaiians who already know the story of his death.[16] It is as if Cook were reporting to this audience at Kealakekua because he holds himself somehow accountable to them—as if his resting place, Hawai'i, has become his home forever on earth, though he may ever yearn for the England of his birth. Meanwhile, not as the drama's figure of highest authority and thus above the class of common humankind, Morris's Cook plays his roles as a subordinate to the British Admiralty and King George III. He is at their service and is at odds with his superiors in a way that sympathetically allies him with his shipmates and the Pacific islanders. This sympathetic and humane outlook become the basis, then, for Cook's address—faintly an apology—to the Hawaiians.

Details of Morris's *Captain Cook* underscore the hero's commonality with his fellow voyagers, even following his elevation to the rank of commander by King George III himself. So that Cook can tell the story of his own life and death, Morris has him speak from beyond the grave. At times he directly addresses the imagined Hawaiian audience, who otherwise overhear Cook reenacting his conversations with memorable individuals. At times he addresses his wife Elizabeth, whose presence throughout the drama is felt though never seen. Cook spins vignettes from his memories of individuals who mark significant moments in his life. These are the people whose faces appeared to him as he was drowning in Kealakekua Bay; these faces form a montage of Cook's life at the moment of his death.

We meet John Walker, the man at the Whitby shipyards who hires young Cook as an apprentice on a coal boat when the lad is eighteen, the son of a farmer, and aching unaccountably with a desire to go to sea; and a Mr. Holland, the nearly anonymous man who taught Cook the principles and application of parallax to navigation when Cook, now a ship's master of the Royal Navy, took part in the defeat of the French at Quebec, 1759. We meet the nameless ones who reappear to him in his last living moment: a deserter hung from the yardarm, a sight that moves Master Cook to vow never to order so inhumane a punishment should he himself be a captain some day. Sympathizing with the would-be deserter, he says "God knows, I understand the urge . . ." (9). And the nameless old Tongan woman, generously but fruitlessly offering Cook the favors of "a personable young girl" in return for the earlier kindness Captain Cook showed the old one on the first of his three Pacific voyages. And one of his men, grimacing under the lash for refusing the fresh food Cook orders all hands to eat to prevent scurvy. Each person appears and is fixed like a photograph in Cook's final memory of the three Pacific voyages: his botanist, Mr. Banks, who on their first voyage rescues the indispensable quadrant some Tahitians stole; King George III, receiving and congratulating the greatest naval officer of his kingdom, as Cook is promoted from captain to commander—then to post captain, which, to his dismay, designates him a retiree before he is even fifty.

On his second Pacific voyage Cook fails in three years of exploration to find the fabled southern continent. Or he succeeds—determining that it does not exist in the shape people have dreamt of it. He and his men suffer the intense cold of their repeated forays into the Antarctic Circle, never before penetrated by seamen, where they find not the fabulous continent looming rich in centuries of dreams, but a land so frozen that upon its watery approaches the entire farrow of the ship's breeding sow freeze to death within scant hours of their birth. It is a difficult thing to be disillusioned of such a dream as was the southern continent. When Cook reports to the Admiralty his conclusion that the continent is not elusive but nonexistent, the disappointed and crestfallen lords cheer up when one pipes: "There's still the Northwest Passage to be found" (43). Soon—too soon for Cook's patient Elizabeth—Cook sails again, this time in search of the Northwest Passage.

He does not say much about what happened in Hawai'i, in Morris's monodrama, for the stated assumption is that the Hawaiian audience Cook addresses knows the story already. The main details and events are sketched; and the climax, the moment of Cook's death, itself forms the drama's framework. Morris's Captain Cook does not say anything about Bligh or Ledyard. Perhaps it is because their parts in the drama are already known infamously enough—or because, to Morris, something concerned Cook more than did these two accusers.

And Morris's Cook is, at any rate, not the same tragic figure as Bushnell's. Morris's speaks from the afterlife, all passion spent. Moreover, the main conflict he recalls is with powers outside himself, not at first his own self-doubts. Two weeks out of England on that last voyage, we learn in Morris's play, all board the *Resolution* find that the ship leaks as if it were not even caulked. A rainstorm runs through the maindeck to the crew's quarters below as if there were no roof over their heads at all. They find that the caulking has been "scamped," the whole ship inadequately outfitted—because, conclude these men whose lives depend on the ship, at the time they set sail in 1776 the Admiralty was funneling all resources toward the crushing of the American colonists' rebellion. A fleet of Hessian mercenaries was outfitted well and sent fully equipped to America, but not two converted Whitby colliers, the *Resolution* and *Discovery*, bound on a mission neither of "imperialism," "exploitation," nor "oppression," but of "the discovery and delineation of the habitable areas of the world"—a mission that is Cook's "whole passion" (46). So commences what Cook calls "the conflict in my soul." He scrutinizes the good and evil caused by his own actions and by his own voyages: "My passion to discover the Northwest Passage is as strong as ever, but I feel betrayed, and have begun to question everything—even the voyages themselves. I have begun to sense my doom" (47). His questions are about politics, power, and imperialism, not about reason, faith, and belief. In this frame of mind Cook happens upon Hawai'i. As for the rest, as Cook sums it: "You know the story of our return in November . . ." of 1778, which culminates in Cook's death in February of 1779 (47).

The hero as a common man with deeply and vigorously rooted sympathies for his fellows emerges even more clearly in Morris's *Damien*.[17] Father Joseph Damien de Veuster was the Belgian priest who, from 1873 to his death in 1889, served the lepers exiled to an inhospitable, wet and windy "sour tongue of land." Kalaupapa, Molokai'i, was the leper settlement where the Board of Health regularly dumped boatloads of people afflicted with the abhorrent *ma'i Pākē,* the leprosy for which Chinese were blamed and against which Hawaiians in particular had no immunities when it appeared in Hawai'i in the mid-1800s. In *Damien* we hear from the hero, rough-hewn out of Flemish peasant stock, how the Board of Health and sometimes his own Church superiors in Honolulu deny the means to make Kalaupapa anything more humane than a living cemetery where wild pigs feast in the shallow graves; and we hear, too, about the efforts of Damien's superiors to confine his movements and take control of contributions people donate from afar owing to his growing fame as a living saint. Damien, in fact, commands Robert Louis

Stevenson's attention in Morris's play about the famous writer, who himself became embroiled in controversy over Honolulu's treatment of the
leper settlement and its Catholic priest.[18]

Like Cook, Morris's Damien also speaks from the afterlife. The
occasion is the reinterment of his body, leprous sores miraculously healed
in the grave. In 1936, Damien's body is moved from Moloka'i to Louvain,
Belgium, where he now receives a hero's welcome. Yet when he remembers how his early life led first to his hearing the call to the priesthood,
then the "call within the call" with which he was blessed, Damien reas-
serts and reclaims his own earthy character, his own lowly origins. "As
for the rudeness of manner and appearance," he refers to criticisms by
which he was denied admission into the American College of Louvain,

> I told them then, I tell them now: I come of peasant stock.
> We peasants aren't given to delicate language and fancy man-
> ners. We distrust formality. We say what we have to say, do
> what we have to do. We are what we are. It is our nature
> and we will face death rather than go against it, because we
> believe our nature comes from God. (P. 32)

We find in Morris's monodrama a hot-tempered, strong-willed, yet self-
effacing and prodigiously compassionate "man, a priest, a saint" contending with political authorities against whom it is next to useless to contend,
but above whom the heroic individual, this Damien of peasant stock,
rises like the sun. He is a pastor in a work and a history that is not
pastoral. And yet we see truth through his being a "simple" man.

Morris's effective portraits of the common man or woman as
hero point up the difficulties inherent in writing a heroic monodrama
centered on a ruling monarch or *Ka Lani* (The Highest). "I find it very
hard to do," Aldyth Morris writes of her Lili'uokalani monodrama; "In
Damien I seemed to be able to interpret a man, a priest, a saint, but
I find portraying a Hawaiian Queen very difficult."[19] Queen Lili'uokalani
may nevertheless prove at last to be an exception to the aloof role custom-
arily assigned to Hawaiian monarchs by commoners. Associated with
the common people by her songwriting and by her powerlessness to
halt the American takeover of all Hawai'i, Lili'uokalani seems destined
to be remembered especially for her singular role among—not above—
her subjects.

A difficult set of problems would no doubt confront a writer
wanting today to deal with Kamehameha the Great within the heroic
tradition of Hawaii's post-Cook historical literature. Kamehameha's case

tests the tradition's adequacy. Kamehameha means "The Lonely One," and nearly all portrayals of or references to him in narrative literature elevate Kamehameha above other people or set him staunchly apart from his peers: he is cast in the mold of a Greco-Roman hero, as in the grand statues of him in Honolulu and Kohala, his birthplace. Standing above all, he epitomizes the powerfully uncommon leader.

There is, however, an incident in Kamehameha's life that may one day serve as the central event for the story of the native progenitor of modern Hawai'i in the Local heroic tradition of Bushnell and Morris. That incident involves not a decisive military battle but an altercation with a group of common fishermen, where Kamehameha emerged the loser; and from it came a proclamation that may be broadly interpreted to command that no holder of authority is to bully or abuse the common folk. Samuel Kamakau tells the story:

> Kamehameha and Ka-hauku'i paddled to Papa'i and on to Kea'au in Puna where some men and women were fishing, and a little child sat on the back of one of the men. Seeing them about to go away, Kamehameha leaped from his canoe intending to catch and kill the men, but they all escaped with the women except two men who stayed to protect the man with the child. During the struggle Kamehameha caught his foot in a crevice of the rock and was stuck fast; and the fishermen beat him over the head with a paddle. Had it not been that one of the men was hampered with the child and their ignorance that this was Kamehameha with whom they were struggling, Kamehameha would have been killed that day. This quarrel was named Ka-lele-iki, and from the striking of Kamehameha's head with the paddle came the law of Mamala-hoe (Broken paddle) for Kamehameha. (*Ruling Chiefs*, 125–26)

Abraham Fornander adds to the story of Kamehameha's excursion into enemy territory that "it was one of those predatory expeditions and wild personal adventures characteristic of the times and the reckless daring of the chiefs," right in the thick of Kamehameha's enmity with Keoua, the chief of Puna whose name figures at the end of Holt's *Waimea Summer*.[20]

The outcome of this incident, where common fishermen soundly beat Kamehameha with a paddle, was a law known as the "splintered paddle." Fornander explains this law, referred to in the quotation from Kamakau as "broken paddle":

In singular commemoration of his own narrow escape from
death on the above occasion, for having wantonly attacked
peaceable and unoffending people, *Kamehameha* in after life
called one of his most stringent laws, punishing robbery and
murder with death, by the name of *Mamalahoe*, the "splintered
paddle." (*Account of the Polynesian Race*, 138)

It is the sort of story that grows through repetition even when
the storyteller sticks only to reporting historical fact—or is conjecture?
In a twentieth-century history recounting the incident, Ralph S. Kuykendall and A. Grove Day add that when the Puna fishermen who beat
him were later caught, "Kamehameha . . . admitted his fault in attacking
the innocent, and set them free with a gift of lands." One of the decrees
of the *Māmalahoe Kānāwai*, the law named after the incident, proclaimed:
"Let the aged, men and women, and little children lie down in safety
in the road."[21] Bearing values defining a main tradition of the heroic
in Hawaii's literature, this demonstration of Kamehameha's concern for
the common people is handed down to us today as one of the only reminders of his character and deeds outside of his military and political conquests and achievements and his towering feats of solitary physical and
metaphysical power.

Perhaps the single incident alone may not be enough to make
pliable and to humanize the image of Kamehameha in the way the revered
but otherwise remote Damien is brought engagingly to the stage by
Aldyth Morris. But like the imposing Kamehameha, gods and
goddesses of Hawaii's mythology may be thought poor candidates for
figuring in such realistic dramas as *Captain Cook* and *Damien*. Yet the
work of Martha Webb, a poet and playwright, exemplifies a dramatic
way of showing how the ancient mythology "persists and so alters the
lives of several modern characters," in her *He Punahele*.[22] This drama
is evidence that a "dead" Hawaiian culture and language are reborn in
successive new generations of Hawaii's children coming of age as
bearers of the local culture. Webb introduces Hiʻiaka, sister of Pele,
Pele's beloved young chief Lohiʻau, and Pele herself into a
contemporary Hawaiʻi setting. Act three opens in a Waikīkī bar. These
characters speak in all manners of Hawaii's common vernaculars today;
and it should be stressed that Webb handles pidgin without belittling
either the language or the characters who speak it.

Works such as Webb's seem inspired by the same breath that
brings Bushnell's and Morris's historical or mythological heroic characters

to life: the desire to bring forth, as Webb puts it, "older stories that persist and shape in subtle ways the way we are and what we do" (44). The tacit assumption is that Hawaii's myth and history affect and are pertinent to the very life of the common people of Hawai'i, a life tracing a winding but unbroken line from myth through history to the present day. And at the most important moments along this continuity of history and culture, the Hawai'i heroic plays its part to bind together the people and their champions.[23]

If, finally, an intuitive response to versions of the heroic in Hawaii's literature were needed to support the thesis that the main tradition is the one that values kinship with the common person in Hawai'i, I would test it against another, contrasting tradition with a different ring to it. It, too, is a popular tradition, but one which sometimes despite itself assumes an individualism peculiar to colonial power. In this tradition the hero is typically the Hawai'i landowner who controls such power that he or she does not so much rebel against as toy with, indeed exploit, the established political and social authorities for essentially individual gain. This is the tradition in which Michener frames his portraits of his Hawai'i heroes—except, however, for characters such as Kamejiro Saka-gawa, Michener's Japanese immigrant father of Golden Men, or Kelly Kanakoa, who are in any case not really royal heroes but are more like court fools, no matter how financially comfortable Kamejiro, for one, grows in spite of his limitations. This, too, is the tradition of Hawaii's missionary narratives, which, along with Asian American historical narratives of Hawai'i, constitute the bulk of two different traditions of Hawaii's immigrant sagas.

3

To be sure, the branch of Hawaii's literature on which the islands' immigrant sagas grow bears substantially more works than I shall discuss. Works already covered in previous studies, such as a number by A. Grove Day and the extensive one by Philip K. Ige, will receive only a little attention here. I refer to the stories of the heroic pioneering ventures in Hawai'i by the American missionaries who first arrived in force in 1820. Rather than these missionary narratives and others more or less directly related to them in a Colonial tradition of Hawaii's literature, I will discuss the far less recognized bases for a Local tradition: fictional histories, narratives, and chronicles of the Asian immigrant, pioneer experience in Hawai'i.

Shelley Ayame Nishimura Ota's *Upon Their Shoulders* is a realistic and yet often violent tale of the protagonist's lifelong struggle against injustice and setbacks. Following and standing in clear contrast to Ota's novel is Margaret Harada's *The Sun Shines on the Immigrant*, a success story which ends with an odd ahistorical optimism not long before Pearl Harbor is to explode. Kazuo Miyamoto's compendious *Hawaii: End of the Rainbow* is literally the biggest of these works.[24] Most recently there is Virgilio Menor Felipe's narrative based on a Filipino immigrant laborer's oral history. Felipe's work is still to be published in full. In various typescripts and partial printings over the decade, it has been titled in many ways, among which is "What You Like Know? An Oral Biography of Bonipasyo."[25]

Among these works appears no Chinese American, full-length, fictional saga of immigration in Hawai'i. This is so despite the Chinese American precedence and preeminence: the Chinese came as laborers and settled before the other Asians and, like the Filipinos, continue today to immigrate. They were the first of these peoples to publish poems, dramas, and short stories in English, which they did enthusiastically and evidently by choice and not mere assignment when writing for their yearbooks and journals in high school and at the University of Hawaii. Their mature story, however, is told in histories, among them Li Ling Ai's biography of her immigrant parents, both of them physicians.[26] Perhaps the lack of novels in this exceptional community may be explained by Li's subject: she writes her nonfictional immigrant saga about an *uncommon* Chinese American family, in this case her own. The Japanese American and Felipe's Filipino American sagas all involve the histories of at least two generations, as though without a succession of generations there is no history to be interpreted through fiction. The Filipino bachelor era in Hawai'i, glimpsed in *All I Asking for Is My Body*, had passed by the time Felipe interviewed his subject; newly immigrated Filipino American families were becoming common. For a writer even of such ambition and dedication as Li, however, it may have been difficult—somehow false or untimely—to create a fictional Chinese American family in a novel. Perhaps the genre itself requires generalizing about one's subject in ways that fiction encourages, not confined to the rehearsal of facts. But what if the subject resists generalization? In the first half of the twentieth century when Li grew up in her Hawai'i community, proliferation of Chinese American families was restricted by such U.S. laws as the Chinese Exclusion Act of 1882, which was enforced in Hawai'i when Congress approved annexation in 1898 and the Organic Act laid down the terms for Hawaii's territorial status in 1900. The Asian Exclusion Act of 1924 prolonged the Chinese American bachelor society on the mainland and its counterparts in Hawai'i. In consequence, Li and her generation of Chinese Americans born in Hawai'i may well have been affected by the uncommon status of their few families, even aside from those fewer still who achieved some eminence. Her biography of her mother Kong Tai Hueng Li, a gynecologist, and her father Khai Fai Li, gives these two exceptional immigrants who arrived from China in 1896 a recognition they deserve. A novel about the history of their group, however, is yet to be rediscovered or written.

Something must be said, too, of the Hawai'i missionary narratives usually associated with heroic pioneering in Hawai'i during the nineteenth and the present centuries. Hawaii's missionary narratives are solidly colonial; that is, a minority gains recognized power and authority over the majority, generally seen from the point of view of those empowered or who consider themselves to be. These accounts of life and history in Hawai'i distinctly contrast the Asian American immigrant stories, which were written usually by people who grew up knowing about the islands' missionary pioneers but not seeing themselves as heirs to the missionaries' power or as defined solely and centrally by their way of life or culture, however influential that culture may actually be.

In his *Books About Hawaii: Fifty Basic Authors*, A. Grove Day includes selected authors of the missionary narrative branch of Hawaii's heroic literature and summarizes each one's contribution to Hawaii's literature.[27] Day's choices include nonfictional autobiographies, journals, and histories of Hawaii's American missionaries. Among these works are *A Residence of Twenty-One Years in the Sandwich Islands* by Hiram Bingham, the grim and determined leader of the "First Company," of 1820; Lucy Goodale Thurston's *The Life and Times of Lucy G. Thurston*, the memoir of a remarkable woman, one of the longest-lived of that first group; and a modern retelling of the missionary story by Bradford Smith, *Yankees in Paradise: The New England Impact on Hawaii* (1956), which spans the period 1820–54.[28] Another nonfictional narrative is by a descendant of one of the original missionary couples: Albertine Loomis set out to write a fictional story but, perhaps like Li Ling Ai, found it impossible to better the actual history she researched. The result is Loomis's *The Grapes of Canaan: Hawaii 1820* (1951).[29]

One fictional novel in particular deserves much more attention than I am providing here, partly because this work typifies those which

Michener researched for the muscle and bone of his far more famous novel. This source is Ruth Eleanor McKee's *The Lord's Anointed: A Novel of Hawaii* (1934).[30] McKee creates a missionary couple, Jonathan and Constancy Williams, places them among the actual historical personages who constituted the 1820 missionary group and their contacts in Hawai'i, and shows through Constancy's secret journals and thoughts how she, the mission, and Hawai'i develop up to the next turn of the century, when Constancy dies, a great-grandmother nearly a hundred years old. McKee individualizes the thoughts and feelings of characters elsewhere stereotyped as inhumane in their adherence to religious dogma and discipline as well as intolerant and bigoted in their colonial treatment of the native Hawaiians, whose culture the missionaries are thought bent on eradicating. McKee's portrayal of the missionaries counteracts this rigid image by plying it with realism—though not necessarily to improve the missionary image in the way they themselves would have wanted. The central missionary character, Constancy Williams, outwardly adherent to missionary conduct and doctrine, admits in her secret diary that she faked her dramatic public conversion two weeks after first meeting the devout Jonathan—and no one but she knows the difference. Her stance is thus ironical. From her point of view she sees around her every possibility of everyone else's fakery, and she obviously does not take herself piously, while the novelist McKee demonstrates that this character's virtue lies in something other than her professed religious beliefs. Bushnell, whose own writing career was budding in the early 1930s, has told me his recollection of how McKee left Hawai'i perhaps rather discouraged—and John Dominis Holt reiterates that she was "run out of town"—shortly after publication of the *The Lord's Anointed*, which was not appreciated for its candor by descendants of the missionaries in the islands.

Among the heroic works about Hawaii's missionaries, at least one more title stands out sharply: *The White King* (1950), by Samuel B. Harrison.[31] It is a novel—Day calls it "virtually a fictionized biography"—about Dr. Gerrit Parmele Judd, the missionary "apothecary-adventurer" whom Melville reviles in his Appendix to *Typee*. Harrison's novel details Judd's decision to join the third missionary group to Hawai'i, 1828, his rise within the community, his part during the 1843 temporary cession of Hawai'i to England, and his assumption of official positions in the Hawaiian monarchy. By virtue of the power he came to wield, Judd was dubbed "The White King" of Hawai'i. The dubiousness of this title notwithstanding, Harrison is thoroughly sympathetic toward Dr.

Judd and his wife, Laura Fish Judd, whose own diary was published in 1880—*Honolulu: Sketches of the Life, Social, Political, and Religious, in the Hawaiian Islands from 1828 to 1861.*[32]

The literary treatment of these missionary characters, whether they be fictional, nonfictional, or "fictionalized," accords with a literary tradition of the heroic as I have discussed it thus far: the hero is a known historical individual, or is a character identified with an actual historical group or community generally considered to be heroic. These missionary figures impress us immediately as being strong individualists, while those more withdrawn or unprepossessing among the group still make good minor characters, consonant with and certainly part of a group that in some ways came to dominate Hawai'i, no matter how pastoral their profession. These missionaries and their successors are leaders; by their virtues and by the powers they assume, they influence Hawai'i irrevocably. In this view, each one repeats Cook's heroism and achievement of discovery and at times must suffer the hero's lonely agony. Doing their part in a worldwide pattern of colonialism, too, these missionaries prepare the ideological way for traders and companies outside the Christian world.

But in one important respect the missionaries' heroes differ significantly from the heroes of Bushnell's and Morris's works. However much they nobly and unstintingly labor for the common good through their preaching and their teaching, the missionaries and their community do not stand for the common folk: rather, they are the chosen people. "The White King" no doubt is aptly named, aptly titled; for even if Dr. Judd chafes at the nickname, and even though some utter it derisively, the title in fact fits the man's chosen function and its status, his actions and their consequences in Hawaiian society. Any resentment against Dr. Judd, for instance because of his being supposed an interloper in the monarchy, is itself confirmation of the title, which connotes the individual's solitary, heroic, superior stature and responsibility above any consideration of popularity in a mostly nonwhite Hawai'i.

But what happens when, instead of a Bingham or a Judd—whose names are inescapably familiar to Hawaii's people because, first of all, streets and neighborhoods are named after them—when instead of McKee's "Constancy Williams," Michener's "Abner Hale," an Elisha Loomis, a Damien, or a Cook, we have a protagonist named "Taro Sumida"? The individual character and his name do not carry much historical weight. Collectively, however, Sumida's community survives and grows by its *history*, according to the heroic visions underlying two out of the three major Japanese American immigrant sagas of Hawai'i.

Taro Sumida is the hero of what I find to be the first published novel in English based upon the story of Japanese American immigration.[33] Written by Shelley Ota, *Upon Their Shoulders* (1951) carried the singular burden of creating a hero in a place where none existed before in Hawaii's and America's thought, imagination, and culture, until in 1957 John Okada's novel, *No-No Boy*, was published and shared Ota's burden, so to speak.[34] The very name "Taro Sumida" connotes the unexceptional common man in Japanese, a "John Smith." In fact the surname "Sumida" happens to be one of the most common given to Japanese American characters in Hawaii's literature: among Taro's literary clan, as it were, are the nisei Saburo "Sub" Sumida, the narrator of Bob Hongo's *Hey Pineapple!* and, islands away, a Sunday School teacher Miss Sumida in one of Seiko Ogai's stories about children, "The Other Angel."[35] Added to the recognizably commonplace nature of the hero's name, what happens when the protagonist represents a nationwide community whose ethos for various reasons, including their weak position in America during and following their treatment during World War II, openly values group solidarity more than individual achievement? Still further, what if the group itself, while consisting of individuals extraordinary enough to break away from a homeland whose grip on her children was legendary, were commonly characterized not as pioneers but instead as indistinguishable parts of a labor mass somewhere at the base of Hawaii's sociopolitical pyramid? Then it would make sense that an *All I Asking for Is My Body* would result, a pastoral comedy focusing on the child and proletarian as swains—a literary form expressly allowing nimble satirical assaults against oppressive powers, a form that can make use of stereotypes to turn them against their perpetrators. But how can the Japanese immigrant story—based as it is bound to be on the common man and woman—be given heroic voice and timber when simultaneously given these social and cultural parameters?

Ota's saga is part of a heroic tradition in Asian American literature, which at the time she wrote usually sprang not out of knowledge of Asian American literary history but out of individual authors' knowledge of home communities and grassroots histories. Especially in the novels of Ota and Kazuo Miyamoto, moreover, Hawaii's heroic tradition in Asian American literature is related to the mainland in both theme and treatment, however small the direct references to the mainland may appear to be in Ota's. Like Bushnell and Morris, these are authors whose intent is to base their views and characterizations of Hawaii's peoples upon their thoughts as well of the world beyond their own shores.

Taro Sumida is representative of his community as a whole, not by any dramatic and overt heroic deed, but by virtue of a comprehensive outlook that discerns patterns and takes in contradictions and ambiguities in historical experience. In one way Sumida is, however, exceptional in the community. Like Carlos, the first person protagonist of Carlos Bulosan's *America Is in the Heart* (and like other examples of the type in American literature), Taro teaches himself to read and write in English.[36] Though he does not go on to write his community's saga, Sumida's skill allows him to read everyone's rights—in labor contracts and the law, for instance—and to detect the violations of those rights. He stands relatively undaunted when plantation bosses and other authorities try to take advantage of what they assume is the immigrants' illiteracy. Like Bulosan, Ota also treats certain cultural themes or allusions associated with the respective Asian culture not by explicating but by thoroughly implicating them in her novel's plot and structure.

Despite the vaunted military heroism of America's nisei soldiers, when Ota wrote *Upon Their Shoulders* in 1951 Japanese America was riding a seesaw with extinction. By then Ota, a nisei from Hawai'i, was a teacher in Milwaukee and evidently could see in her mainland life what the "Relocation" of Japanese Americans was still doing after the last internee had been released from a concentration camp: the Relocation was assimilating Japanese Americans into a denial of heritage, community, family, and even self. Miles Carey, the esteemed former principal of Honolulu's McKinley High School, wrote the foreword to Ota's novel. In the war's aftermath, Carey seems uncharacteristically assimilationist, for he writes about the "Americanization" of the nisei, those American-born pupils he once helped to stand up for themselves and their community on their own terms. The novel itself is not about Americanization but is in large measure a critique of America's reception of the issei, in Ota's view the first Japanese American generation. The first part of her book is set in Japan and is called "The Awakening," where it is clearly the man and woman with a vision, with ideals they hope may be fulfilled in America, who choose to emigrate from their impoverished village in Yamaguchiken, the southernmost province of the main island of Honshu. Yet though part 2 is itself titled "Hawaii—Gokuraku," a Hawai'i Heaven, that envisioned American paradise for decent work, decent living, turns out to be a *Jigoku*, a Hell, instead. In a different mode from *All I Asking for Is My Body*, Ota's novel nonetheless shares with it the issue of what is "American": is it the immigrants' ideals, or the reality they suffer on the plantation, or both of these?

The heroes of *Upon Their Shoulders* are Taro and Haruko Sumida, who leave a legacy, as the title suggests, for their child Alice and for the generations to come. In this and the other two sagas I shall go on to discuss, it is important that more than one generation be the subject, where the timeless, static, pastoral value of *'ohana* or family, in Hawaii's cultures, becomes the heroic, dynamic, historical value placed on lineage and genealogy. *Upon Their Shoulders* spans six decades, beginning with the first wave of Japanese emigration under government-negotiated contracts, 1885 to 1894, a decade when some 29,000 men and women left Japan for Hawai'i, while still others emigrated to North and South America.[37] The Sumidas are among the earliest *Kanyaku Imin*, Japanese contract laborers bound for Hawaii's sugar plantations; and their story concludes just after World War II. Time and place are the organizing principles. The titles of the novel's main parts reveal its structure, a plot, and a theme: from "The Awakening" in Japan, to the infernal Hillstone Plantation in "Hawaii—Gokuraku," the Sumidas move to the city, Nihonmachi, Honolulu's "Japanese Town," where, in parts 4 and 5 of the novel, they play out the drama of their "Honolulu" and "Onward Years." In sum, the movement is from deeply rural settings to the city, where they discover that racism is even more pernicious than on the plantation, where the open brutality had simplified such matters. The "Onward Years" wind through a very difficult time for the issei during World War II. Seeming first to map the antithesis of a Hawaii Gokuraku, Ota goes beyond showing merely the flip side of paradise, a Hawai'i hell or Jigoku. Rather, in *Upon Their Shoulders* she is ultimately not concerned with this dualistic, dialectic way of viewing experience. Her novel is about conflicts, struggles, violence, ambiguities, history, and heroism. It is a novel where the greatest joys are not material but idealistic.

The novel's most subtly powerful feature is what may be called *karma* in Buddhism. This appears in a form described by certain repetitions or cycles of violence in the novel's plot. Very early in *Upon Their Shoulders*, a Shinto priest named Noda kills with a whip a fifteen-year-old girl whom he accuses of being possessed by an animal spirit (19–22). The Yamaguchiken village is so poor that any such alleged source of their trouble is hungrily pursued. The girl is of an outcast family with a history of animal possession; and the sign of this daughter's possession is that young men seem attracted to her. Although he abhors this scapegoating, this fatal exorcism of the naked girl strapped to a plunging horse in the paper lamplight, Taro Sumida is swept up in the mob's hysteria:

> In spite of himself, Taro watched with bated breath this atavistic, barbaric spectacle. The scene which in daylight would have been abhorrent to his sensitive soul now produced within him a queer mixture of amusement, horror, and disgust. He swayed dizzily, as though he had drunk cups of *sake*. With the sleeve of his kimono he wiped the perspiration from his brow. (P. 20)

Later a similar violent beating takes place, this time in the Hawaiian sugar plantation camp (55–58). The workers, including the Sumidas, are outraged by the "fines" that have been deducted from their $12.50 monthly pay. They raise a commotion in the camp that night. Their *luna*, or foreman, Juan Quinto, staggers drunk into the camp when ordered by the manager to get everybody to bed. The Japanese workers nearly lynch him. They beat the luna with his own whip, Sumida himself stuffs a rag torn from Quinto's shirt into the luna's mouth, and they all drag Quinto and his *inu*—the "dogs" who have been tattling on their coworkers—through the foul irrigation and sewage ditch.

The triumph over the workers' immediate oppressors is predictably short lived. Quinto and the inu are themselves mere sacrificial animals, like the girl whom Noda killed in Japan. The rapacious plantation boss, Claude Merle, is unmoved by the beating his minions suffer. While earlier that day and every day he enjoys a pleasant, leisurely breakfast in his mansion up the hill, the workers are already feeling the burn of the sun. Married to Beatrice, a descendant of Hawaii's *ali'i* or royalty, Merle, the scion of a Southern family ruined by the Civil War, considers his dominion over the plantation his own "birthright" (43). Contemptuous of his laborers' prolific childbearing and obsessed with lust for those same women, to calm himself before the day's business and to "show the rats on the plantation who was master," Merle rapes a fifteen-year-old Japanese girl employed as a kimono-clad maid in his mansion (46).

This vicious characterization of the plantation master serves the purpose in Ota's novel of showing how the common laborers are viewed from the real seat of power, even while the laboring immigrants feel for a moment that they have turned the tables by beating their foreman. And frighteningly, the characterization of Claude Merle is all too plausible a portrait of some boss or another who must have gained notoriety in the secret talk of the laborers throughout the islands. It is disturbing that just such a character as Claude Merle is elsewhere in Hawaii's literature not a scoundrel but a hero. Most notably, as I have commented earlier, eight years after Ota's novel we encounter Whipple "Wild Whip" Hoxworth in Michener's *Hawaii*. As the fictional founder of Hawaii's pineapple industry, Whip also does more in many beds to father a mixed race of potentially Golden Men than any other "heroic" figure in Michener's novel. Charlton Heston plays such a role, a combination of an antebellum southern planter and a cowboy rancher, in the movie *Diamond Head*, which also includes an interracial sex theme. These "heroic" figures are also incarnated in one popular television adventure series after another set in Hawai'i. Curiously, for some of the very actions that make them heroes in that tradition, these characters are villains in Ota's, so vast is the gap between points of view. In Ota's view, it is this glorification of and acquiesence to the violence and inhumanity of the viciously powerful that kills; and scapegoating, whether Noda's killing of the girl in Japan or the workers' beating of their luna in Hawai'i, merely perpetuates self-fulfilling cycles of cruelty which miss the true sources of the community's suffering. *Upon Their Shoulders* is about seeing the larger picture; it is about not being fooled by smaller conflicts into ignoring the big ones—a lesson Milton Murayama repeats in his satiric way in *All I Asking for Is My Body*.

What is most remarkable in this pattern of scapegoating is its third karmic occurrence in the main plot of Ota's novel. It recurs as if without connection to the other two, earlier instances; but its relevance to Ota's view of issei and nisei history is profound. In the novel's second half, Jerry Noda becomes a brilliant surgeon and thus might represent the fulfillment of his immigrant parents' dreams. Young Dr. Noda is the son of the same plump and arrogant Shinto priest who whipped the girl to death in his home village, provoked the Sumidas into leaving Japan, and who, with his wife, also left that village for Hawai'i shortly after the Sumidas. Presumably the Nodas, too, were given a service for the dead when they departed, as if their Japanese lives were now entombed. But by managing their old wealth and status, the Nodas cling to a life of relative ease and refinement in Honolulu. After the Sumidas escape from the plantation to Honolulu, the lives of these two families become intertwined once more—one family, however, earning the community's respect; the other, the Nodas, continuing to be treated with the deference they demand, which means in this case the community's hatred.

In an unusual way, the elder Nodas represent the social oppression many of the issei had hoped to leave behind them in Japan. But by the same token the community perpetuates their antipathies against the kind. Jerry Noda inherits this hatred in how others in the community treat him and his family. But evidently he grows up without understanding its origins or its complexities, especially since the previous generation's emigration might be supposed to be a break from his family's decadent past, something unspoken to the child. Not knowing about the past means not coming to terms with it. Considered a prize catch for any young nisei woman, Dr. Jerry Noda marries Alice Sumida, daughter of Taro and Haruko, despite her father's direct warning to him against doing so. The story might be a comedy if it ended there, with a marriage coincidentally resolving a long-standing conflict between the two families. Jerry and Alice do marry, but the story is not a comedy. While to his colleagues and patients he is a superb physician, privately Noda is sick with doubts about his own worth. His drinking and infidelity lead Alice to discuss divorce. Haruko advises her daughter:

> "You married Jerry knowing that the strain was deep in him.
> And now—" Her face turned gray . . . .
> Haruko took a deep breath and continued, "Your marriage
> is a link between the past and the future. For you to decide
> to sever this link puts too much responsibility on your shoul-
> ders. Think of the marriages that will come later, long after
> you are gone. Think of the step you contemplate, the audacity
> of severing this link." She covered her face with her hands,
> stricken by the doom of Alice's suicidal step. (P. 183)

The talk of divorce and the "suicidal step" are reminders of still another tragedy, the earlier suicide of Taro's sister in Japan after she was divorced "solely because her husband openly displayed his affection for her . . . for love was an unwanted blessing in family life . . . something to be found in houses of pleasure" (22–23). It was this suicide, which Taro had witnessed, that finally drove him to question the way of things and to leave Japan for a better way.

Alice's and Jerry's problem, however, contrasts what happened to the aunt, about whom they perhaps have never been told. That is, Jerry shows little open affection for Alice. Moreover, she herself escapes becoming a scapegoat—or "substitute" (to use the term Murayama later draws from the same community sources as Ota's). Alice is not doomed to carry unknown burdens of her parent's past.

Jerry Noda does not escape. Shortly after Pearl Harbor the elder Noda, an outspoken Japanese jingoist, is arrested by the FBI and shipped to a concentration camp. Jerry Noda's responsibility within his family and in the community increases because of the imprisonment of his father and other issei leaders, although issei such as his in-laws, not imprisoned, also shoulder a large burden of leadership even though silenced. During the War, the nisei surgeon drinks heavily in reckless binges. One night he is arrested in a gambling raid. The newspapers make headlines of his shame. Jerry Noda commits suicide—his shattered self-worth publicly displayed and his understanding of his priestly family's lurid history more confused than ever, though it has directly affected his own upbringing and everyone's expectations of him.

Ota demonstrates a number of ideas. This scapegoating is a kind of twofold *bachi*, or retribution, we might say. Not only does Jerry punish himself for his own supposed failings, but he also substitutes for his father, who indeed returns from the concentration camp strangely altered, at peace at last with himself and the world, except for his continuing, inflamed mix of fear and contempt for those he derisively calls the *Keto*, white Americans (252–56). It is useless and even dangerous to try to bury the past when it is still alive, Ota implies, as the social implications of Noda's life in Japan persist in Hawai‘i. Whether we know it or not, we are motivated and influenced by patterns of thought and behavior passed on to us from our forebears. So, therefore, we had better know these matters, this living history, in order that we may rise upon our forebears' shoulders and not fall to untimely deaths. And while Ota thus aims to teach moral lessons about the value and necessity of understanding one's culture and history, she is not sentimental about Japan, ancestors, and the past. History for her means change. At the end of Ota's novel a deeply troubled and weary Taro Sumida dies with one consolation: he welcomes Japan's defeat in the war, for it means that Japan will have to catch up with international ideals in human rights—for the poor, for women, for the outcast. History means change, for it is a record of changes; understanding history, as Taro Sumida does and as the Noda priest tried tragically to deny, does not mean reverting to some fixed, idealized point in a time past or within traditions ever in flux.

In many ways it is remarkable that Ota wrote her novel as she did, when she did. By her underlying plot and theme—that is, by the cycle of karma she sets in motion—Ota intimates an historical vision that is indeed ancient, yet at the same time is far ahead of her intended

American readers' grasps. It is true that Ota's diction may sometimes seem cute and adolescent (for example, the verb "flounced" repeatedly occurs in the novel when nisei women, their skirts alive with movement, enter or exit rooms). But I find that the value of the novel's inner motive deserves not just acknowledgment; it deserves real thought. Ota implies, for instance, that we do indeed inherit ancestral cultures and temperaments—in new forms and manifestations—even when we think we know little or nothing about them. For good and bad, we are inheritors—despite the doctrine of assimilation which aims sharply to cut us off from our cultural descents.

With her novel, *The Sun Shines on the Immigrant*, Margaret N. Harada is Ota's direct opposite in historical perspective. Published in 1960, nine years after *Upon Their Shoulders*, at the height of a postwar rise in politics and business when the nisei gained at least a semblance of equality in Hawai'i, *The Sun Shines on the Immigrant* is as ahistorical as Ota's novel is provocative in its vision of Japanese American history. While *Upon Their Shoulders* follows a clearly didactic aim, and despite all the moralizing in *The Sun Shines on the Immigrant*, this later work does not so much embody a moral lesson as it asserts what might be called a material one: the good of the Japanese immigrant in Hawai'i consists in his or her striving to get ahead in business, and the success of family and community somehow follow naturally. Harada's sun, after all, shines from the outside, *on* the immigrant, not from within. That this idea of Japanese American success is so commonplace that its bases and assumptions go unquestioned in this novel is one indication of the lack of historical vision here.

The impoverished protagonist, Yoshio Mori, emigrates from urban Japan in May 1900. A model of filial piety, he works in Hawai'i to support himself and his poor mother back home. He marries by bringing a picture bride, Haru, to Hawai'i. From plantation laborer, to houseboy, to independent taxi driver, to laundry owner, Mori climbs from station to station in his life of increasing comfort in Honolulu. Interestingly, his various setbacks and conflicts are usually personal rather than shared by or representative of his community. His illness from typhoid fever, in the lean early years of his taxi business, is epidemic; but it is told mainly in connection with how it adversely affects his own private enterprise and disrupts the life of his individual family. "Mother," Yoshio says to his wife after his illness has broken, "God made me sick to make me think of my future more seriously. After I am completely recovered,

I shall take out life insurance" (107–8). The narrator, in one of the miniature sermons characteristic of this novel, comments that "never was there a man so thoughtful and kind to his wife and children. He thought of their happiness, for their happiness was his happiness " (108). But evidently this equation does not work the other way around: his happiness need not be theirs, since two chapters later Mori finds his happiness with a geisha from a teahouse (118–22). This may be a realistic touch, but again it is treated without irony as a personal conflict among Mori, his wife Haru, and Haru's older sister, who counsels the couple. It occurs without much testing of what such an affair would do (in fiction, where such testing may well take place) to the social and moral fabric of the issei family and community. Mori is merely "awakened" from the geisha affair as "from a bad experience" (122). Meanwhile Yoshio and Haru Mori raise a handsome family of nisei children, the husband's adultery passing by with no effect on his personal and family life.

The most startling evidence of this novel's ahistorical nature comes at the culmination of the success story. The Moris' son is elected the first nisei representative to the Territorial House (213–25). When their daughter graduates from the University of Hawaii, a dignitary at the commencement ceremony exhorts the graduates and parents to be mindful of the great potential for cooperation between the East and the West, Japan and America, in business, in diplomacy, and in culture. It is 1937. Yoshio and Haru, their children now standing tall, look forward at last to a return to Japan, this time as happy tourists. So the novel ends, literally with the Hawaiian sun shining warmly and benevolently upon this family of issei and nisei. Yet Harada writes not one word about the thunderheads that have already gathered over Asia and the Pacific on account of Japan's Manchurian invasions. Ending as the novel does in Hawai'i just prior to 7 December 1941, nothing is said about Pearl Harbor. But Harada is writing a decade after the war. She cuts short her story by a choice which makes its bright conclusion perhaps unintentionally ironic. The war and its consequences to a family such as the Moris may have been too much for Harada to face in her sunny comedy, a literary genre that makes it difficult to deal in historical terms and visions despite her obvious contravening impulse to do so.

Harada's novel, in itself, betrays as false the assumptions underlying the myth of a Japanese American success story. The political contexts not only of the novel's setting but also of the novel's writing show how conflicted and ahistorical is Harada's *way* of interpreting the past. *The*

Sun Shines on the Immigrant appeared in the era of Martin Luther King, Jr., and the great protest marches for civil rights; and Harada, in a large company of accommodationists heedless of the Japanese American internment that began less than two decades earlier, strides in the opposite direction, carrying a postwar myth that makes a stereotype of compliant Japanese Americans. However well or ill intended, the model minority, success-story myth—a political device of the late 1950s—worked against interracial unity in a certain American historical moment and afterward. Implicit in *The Sun Shines on the Immigrant* is the belief that victims of discrimination can and should raise themselves unaided, as the nisei presumably did out of their World War II imprisonment. It is precisely this imprisonment and all it implies about racism in America, however, that this novel's form, assumptions, and ahistoricity cannot face.

Harada's limiting of her novel to the prewar history of her pioneering characters is sadly understandable in the face of the great divide that World War II represents in Japanese American history. But novelists Ota and Murayama cross that divide, as also does Kazuo Miyamoto, who culminates his historical novel with the wartime experience of a sometimes forgotten group of Hawaii's Japanese Americans: those interned in American concentration camps during the war. This and other features makes Miyamoto's *Hawaii: End of the Rainbow* the most comprehensive novel yet written of the history of Hawaii's Japanese immigrants and their children. Two-thirds of the way through the novel, after Miyamoto has spent three "books" of his epic chronicling in meticulous detail the lives of two pioneering Japanese immigrant laborers and the families they have raised in Hawai'i, Miyamoto arrives at the juncture that must forever qualify the Japanese American immigrant success story. Book 4 of *Hawaii: End of the Rainbow* is starkly titled "Internment Camp." As with each of the five books, a prologue provides a present-day context for the ensuing historical narrative. The five prologues tell of the dying of Seikichi Arata, one of the pioneers who figures as a hero in the novel. Seikichi Arata, a vigorous young man when he immigrated in 1891, is stricken now with a heart attack thirteen years after his release from the American World War II concentration camp where he had been locked up for the entire war's duration, 1941 through 1945. The prologues to books 1 through 3 sketch the course of Arata's failing heart, while the chapters within these books reveal his attending physician's unlocked knowledge and reminiscences, inspired by reflections on Arata's life and significance—thoughts and memories that account for two full generations of Japanese American history. The physician himself, Minoru Murayama, the son of Arata's lifelong friend Torao, also plays an important and even heroic role in the narrative. As a doctor both in and out of the concentration camps, in his position of responsibility Minoru serves well as the novel's central intelligence, since he is generally privy to more information about the camps and his fellow inmates than most of the other internees could then know.

In the prologue to book 4, the aged family friend and fellow internee dies suddenly and peacefully, two weeks after his initial heart attack. Seikichi Arata's death suggests the demise of the entire pioneer generation. For a few years after the war, the former internees of Hawai'i held annual reunions filled with good fellowship and "tears and laughter mixed with half forgotten anecdotes" (296). "But now such get-togethers were seldom held," we are told on the occasion of Arata's funeral. With fewer and fewer alive to tell it, their history is fading:

> Only occasionally could these old-timers meet, and a funeral was a good excuse to convene. Most of them had lost heavily materially. To be deprived of freedom for four long years was not an experience relished by anyone, but after thirteen years since the end of hostilities, these men were enjoying their remaining years in peaceful Hawaii. The anguish and heartbreaking experiences were being pushed back in the foggy past and only the pleasant ones revived in such a reunion. (P. 296)

This prologue, then, foreshadows the historical events to be narrated in part 4, beginning with chapter 20, "Pearl Harbor and Confinement." The prologue and book 4 tell us of aging and death—and of the still strong urge to lighten cares by pretending to forget them. Yet book 4 also shows us how the people survived and endured their treatment to return to Hawai'i, a still-shimmering dream at the rainbow's end. Though the rainbow in the novel's title and on the cover of its many paperback reprintings seems a cliché—one which perhaps has lured countless tourists to buy the novel on their way to catch their planes home—the rainbow here becomes a complex symbol, where Hawai'i is a live, shimmering, yet somehow immaterial interplay of sun and rain, beaming smiles and veiling tears. This exactly is the image at the novel's conclusion: it belongs to the weeping former internees, returning home to behold Diamond Head from the deck of a ship. Implicitly, in his novel, the sun shines from *within* Miyamoto's characters.

Miyamoto's terms for what happened historically and imaginatively as a prelude to 7 December 1941 are the very terms of our discussion of Hawaii's pastoral and heroic. Following the prologue, book 4 returns to the historical setting immediately prior to the bombing of Pearl Harbor.

> So used to easy-going life, the people of Hawaii continued in their routine, little disturbed by the darkening clouds of uncertainty and impending catastrophe that lurked in the Far East. In spite of seeing with their own eyes the gradual increases in armaments transforming the once languid Sandwich Islands to the "Gibraltar of the Pacific," they complacently viewed these military preparations as a mere acquiescence of the Congress to the clamor for preparedness and eventual conflict voiced by the jingoists and seconded by the army and navy. (P. 297)

Reading like a history text, the novel provides details of Japan's rise to power in Asia and the Pacific. Miyamoto tells of the mounting animosities between Japan and America through the 1930s, with Hawai'i caught geographically between two contending centers of power. For the shortsighted, however, the only thing that mattered were the heady economic consequences: "People in Hawaii, in particular, were intoxicated with a boom never enjoyed in the islands' history. Millions of dollars were spent monthly in strengthening military installations" (298). The old dream of islands where there is no need to think about working, no need even to work, has been transformed into a workers' paradise: "Hundreds of civilian defense workers were arriving from the mainland to further the project. Island workers were hired by the thousands" (298). Moreover, the suddenly inflated sense of economic well-being is reinforced by faith in American ideals:

> The Japanese population of Hawaii was no exception and little realized how near the war was. Even after the freezing order of all Japanese government assets in the United States was issued, very few, if any, realized that the finale was approaching. Entrenched was the belief that the Pacific Ocean would remain forever pacific. . . .
>
> By the end of September 1941, the authorities in Honolulu began issuing statements to the effect that in the event of war in the Pacific, the Japanese aliens legally residing in the territory would be protected and that there would be no concentration camps such as existed already in the European theater of war.

This promise coming from General Short, the commanding officer of the army, helped allay the fear among the Japanese nationals. As far as the American citizens of Japanese extraction were concerned, they had implicit faith in the United States Government that they would be treated without discrimination as citizens of the United States in spite of their Japanese features. (Pp. 298–99)

The breaking of authorities' promises not to imprison Japanese alien residents in the event of war against Japan is not quite the same airy thing as the shattering of the idle dream of islands in all of that billowing dream's manifold forms. Miyamoto's narrative goes on to imply that the broken promise and the imprisonment are a worse betrayal in some ways than the Japanese attack's explosion of Hawaii's image as a timeless haven. The image is not destroyed but is merely suspended. (It seems that almost instantly after Hawai'i was the target of Japanese bombs, Hawai'i became more than ever a vacationland—for the American G.I.) Versions of that popular dream of Hawai'i still live, but the authorities' broken promises that Hawaii's Japanese Americans will not be interned because of war with Japan disillusions leaders who are not arrested, such as Ota's Taro Sumida, as well as those incarcerated, specially picked from among the issei and nisei of Hawai'i. (The FBI files used for incriminating them were already thickly prepared before the Sunday morning of 7 December 1941, as Miyamoto found upon his own arrest that very night.)

In Miyamoto's novel, among the arrested is Arata, then "spry and healthy" at sixty-nine. He spends the night before the Japanese attack and his own arrest immediately thereafter with his eldest grandson, Edward, half-Japanese, half-Hawaiian and fully an American, a soldier, much to the grandfather's pride. As a young man, Seikichi Arata was prevented by his short stature from becoming a Japanese soldier, and his disappointment over his rejection prompted his emigration to Hawai'i to find some other way through life. But in the Hawaiian Islands he considers home, American law has barred Arata along with all other Asian immigrants from becoming a naturalized American citizen. With another diabolical turn of the screw, the authorities who deny him a chance for United States citizenship now brand Arata not merely an alien but an "enemy alien," one evidence of which is popularly thought to be a continuing loyalty to the Japanese Emperor, as evidenced by a continuing to hold Japanese instead of American citizenship.

In California, a different but related broad sweep—the relocation ordered by Franklin D. Roosevelt's Executive Order 9066 of 19 February 1942—catches Dr. Minoru Murayama. Fresh out of medical school, Murayama happens to be working for a while within the order's effective zone from the West Coast to roughly a hundred miles inland. He and all other Japanese Americans within the zone are interned. In the camps he is reunited with his father and family, all of them having been yanked from Hawai'i and driven into the deserts.

Dr. Kazuo Miyamoto himself was arrested on the evening of 7 December 1941, a day he spent tending the wounded and the dying at the United States Army's Tripler Hospital on the outskirts of Honolulu and Pearl Harbor. A nisei, American-born citizen, a World War I veteran of the United States Army, Miyamoto was singled out allegedly because in the 1930s he undertook, at the behest of the Japanese government, some medical research on public health in Manchuria, and the resulting study was published in Japan. Because of this, his own American authorities considered him an enemy agent. He was arrested, imprisoned without a trial for eleven months, then freed. Miyamoto thereupon volunteered three years of his life as a doctor in the concentration camps, because he had seen firsthand the obvious medical need there. Imprisoned in the first place for publishing a book, undaunted, Miyamoto continued through those four years behind barbed wire to add to a meticulous journal the observations that would become books four and five of the novel he had already been preparing to write. The earlier story in three books might have been something like Harada's; but of course, World War II wrenched what had been, till then, the history of a still-struggling group of pioneers. Unlike Harada, Miyamoto pursued his story through the war. All told, some seventeen years of journals later became *Hawaii: End of the Rainbow*.

Miyamoto's courage in writing the story should not be taken lightly, in view of some consequences of his fellow internees' arrests in Hawai'i. The arrests swiftly divested the Japanese American community of its leadership. The nisei were generally just at the age to begin taking responsibility and control, as we see Tosh doing in *All I Asking for Is My Body*. But one pervasive effect of the arrests was a self-imposed silence among all who remained at home, almost as if they themselves had been ordered explicitly to black out their voices in order to avoid being linked with those who had once spoken up in their community. When nisei in Hawai'i today recall those arrests, it is often with a profound bewilderment. Some nisei recall the arrests with little if any knowledge of what ever became of that old man or another next door or down the street whom the FBI took away. In 1972 or so, ten years after we had gotten to know each other in high school, a friend told me that he was not born on the island of Kauaʻi. He was born in a concentration camp. His father, the Reverend Seikaku Takesono, was a Buddhist priest sought by the FBI in 1941 and arrested on Maui in 1942. His father was shipped to the mainland and, at the FBI's Santa Fe Detention Camp, was held with colleagues representing the heart of the Buddhist Sangha of America. Before the ordeal's end they were relocated to other concentration camps, in one of which Takesono was reunited with his wife Oyobu, who journeyed there from Maui with their two-year-old daughter Jane Taeko, once she could learn where her husband was and how the reunion was to be allowed. There the couple had a son they named Satoru, strictly in Japanese in case they were to be deported. Satoru grew up afterward on Kauaʻi, being nicknamed "Barbwire Baby" by his family but called "Jerald" by his friends, who over the course of nearly thirty years were generally unaware that he had been born in prison.

In an odd way, it must be some indication of the magnitude of Miyamoto's achievement that in 1964 he published the Hawaiʻi story whose underlying history has for the most part suffered burial until the mid-1980s. Patsy Sumie Saiki's nonfictional *Gambare! An Example of Japanese Spirit* (1982) comes two decades after Miyamoto's treatment of Hawaii's internees.[38] The forty-years' silence between the war and Saiki's book is broken in half by Miyamoto's own amazingly calm voice. The lull that continued despite at least nine printings of Miyamoto's novel seems mutely to testify that those arrests of the Japanese American community's leaders are still affecting us by turning silence into ignorance. Tragically, silence about one's own history may become a virtue —since the memory hurts, it seemingly must be eradicated.[39] But while he aims to bring history to life, Miyamoto also suggests in his novel's preface that his writing about the camps is not intended as an indictment of the unjust. He nowhere calls for a redress of the wrongs committed during the relocation and internment. A concerted redress movement was not to surface until ten years following Miyamoto's book. Redress is not at odds with the novel's thrust, but it does not engage Miyamoto here, though the novel surely sheds light on the issue. He is concerned instead that the history of Hawaii's Japanese Americans not be suppressed like the increasingly repressed memories—in other words, the senility that suppresses pain—of the issei at Seikichi Arata's funeral.

In the interests of history, Miyamoto offers his book as a legacy to his descendants and to all Americans:

> Having experienced this half century of travail by a minority group in America, I am sending this manuscript to press with a feeling of relief. A segment of the American people will read it and I hope a vast majority of the Japanese Americans of future generations will be reminded of the thorny years of their ancestors. In any case, had I not written this story there is perhaps no one else who could have presented to the world as it actually happened in the concentration camps and relocation centers. I may sound bombastic, but it may be the truth. I do not wish for another *Andersonville* to be written one hundred years from now by a writer highly gifted with imagination, using for his materials memoranda of the War Relocation Centers of 1942–45 found in dusty, faded files long buried in a forgotten corner in Washington. I did not write in an indictive [sic] mood and I did not materially deviate from the truth. What happened is important history and, as such, is recorded so that in the future—in handling of her minorities —America may not repeat the gross mistakes of the past. (Pp. 8–9)

It would be difficult to imagine a more serene account, on the whole, of the internment written by one who actually experienced it. If anything, Miyamoto is overly apologietic about writing his book. Impressed by the novel's equanimity of tone even in recalling the flames of violence and the victims' powerless rage, I once asked Dr. Miyamoto how he managed not to be bitter about his experience. He answered that the internment was so filled with bitterness, and was so baffling and monstrous an injustice perpetrated by one group of people upon another, that it made him finally into "a man of compassion" devoted to improving interracial understanding in America. He achieved that compassion not by burying the past, but by making history live.

The process of bringing Hawaii's history to life continues today, now much more consciously in certain respects, in that the need for recording and transmitting local history to posterity is actively recognized by more people now, it appears, than when Miyamoto and his predecessors wrote their sagas. They thought themselves to be alone in what they were doing. By contrast, an excellent example of the collaborative nature of some of the current work is Virgilio Menor Felipe's narrative on the oral history of a Filipino immigrant laborer. Completed by the mid-1970s but, regrettably, still to be published in full, Felipe's "What You Like Know? An Oral Biography of Bonipasyo" begins, like Carlos Bulosan's *America Is in the Heart*, with the protagonist's childhood in the Philippines. The English language of the narrative is sometimes rugged, sometimes lyrical—most of it is a rather close translation, Felipe says, of his informant's actual Ilocano expressions and idioms.

I quote from the narrative at length in order to provide a good taste of its language. Not so strangely at all, the oral biography is somehow reminiscent of Faulkner, as it is again reminiscent of Bulosan in some of his most ostensibly casual, most exuberant, or most lyrical moments. A published excerpt from Felipe's narrative thus begins:

> I was drenched with sweat, and so was Tata, Father. He had just taken off his squash hat and was wiping his salty lips with his short sleeves. I was already on my butt.
>
> "Don't slouch on your ass, my son. You get lazy that way," he said. And that's true, you know. When you sit and don't do anything with your hands, not moving, not talking to anyone, you get lazy. And if you don't watch out, your thoughts can go all over the place, but never get you anywhere.
>
> I squatted comfortably and opened the water pot to dip the coconut dipper for Tata to drink so I could drink. Ay, was I thirsty! But water is tastiest that way. After a few hours of continuous movement, working in the sunlight following your animal around and around, starting from the outside plowing, and circling inward, getting caught in the middle like the body of a butterfly between two wings, then taking the freedom to break through all those plow lines of life—ay, you're as hot as burning red embers. Sometimes you start in the middle— that's the best way—from the inside, churning and plowing around and around, spiraling wider and wider. And if your calculation is balanced, you finish just right, leading onto the trail for home. When the Lord Sun clears the long shade of those bamboos, your skin burns and you are winded and dry inside. You can drink like a water buffalo. If you are weak, you can get dizzy. But no matter what, you look forward to that water in the pot, cooling in the shade where the dried leaves are so thick and moist with dew.
>
> Tata gargled with the first sip then spat out the staleness and cleared his breath. "Hayhhh! Sweet is this water, ahemmm!" He swallowed the next mouthful slowly. You always do that so you taste all the sweet wetness and don't

choke. Tata handed me the water dipper, and I dripped a drop to appease the spirits of dead people and non-people, then took a long slow sip.

"Those sprouts will be good to cook over the inabraw, broth of your Nana, Mother, for our day meal my son," he said.

And I felt good and warm all the way around my ears. It would please everyone to taste it, and yes it's delicious. Ever tasted it? "Yes, Tata," I agreed.

You answer parents like that. You address people by how you are related to each other. Not like nowadays here in Hawaii where kids just say, "Yes," as if talking without salt. That's tasteless and disrespectful in our custom, and if you ever spoke out of turn in those days, you got knuckles for lunch. (Pp. 48–49)

There is much still to be said about the already published excerpts of Felipe's oral biography of Bonipasyo, and it is hoped that it will be published in its entirety so that Bonipasyo—through Felipe—will be able to speak for himself, as it were, to the general readership he deserves. The opening passage alone suggests much: Bonipasyo here is speaking about "Once in the First Times," a time and place about which he is clearly nostalgic. It is an idyllic Philippines of his distant youth, like Bulosan's, despite the fact that for both these pioneers, Bonipasyo and Carlos, wretched conditions in their homeland drove them to seek work far away. Bonipasyo journeyed with his young countrymen to Hawai'i: *Kasla glorya ti Hawaii,* "Hawai'i is like a land of glory," they spoke and dreamt of their destination. And this pastoral dream, too, was quickly stripped away in the unnatural, fruitless, womanless life awaiting the Filipino sugar-plantation laborer in Hawai'i. Nostalgia tempered by disillusionment characterizes Bonipasyo's overall outlook. It gives him a voice and a tone not merely of a factual autobiographer but also of a poet and trickster in the guise of a simple pastoralist. He characteristically and persistently compares, usually contrasts, an earthy yet pristine Philippines, idealized in memory, with the Hawai'i he and people like him helped to build—mostly for others' profit and enjoyment.

Virgilio Felipe's heroic Filipino immigrant saga reenacts the history of peoples who came before. Each group, however, has been drawn and carried onward by its own pioneers; no earlier group has, in the final analysis, fully prepared the way for the later ones. Transplanting a culture still means preparing new soil; and in any case, the already established ones in Hawai'i have all too often treated newcomers with disdain or contempt or worse. The lost dreams of a Bonipasyo, a Seikichi Arata, or a Taro Sumida recall the experience of John Forrest with his dreams and his disillusionment. Yet unlike the morose Forrest, secluded in his London rooms dreaming still and still pondering what happened fifty years earlier in his paradise, those who have stayed to work out their destinies in Hawai'i are the foundation of the pluralistic culture which today in Hawai'i is known as the "Local." Whatever their races, and beginning with the Polynesians, local peoples have come to Hawai'i not to vacation, but to work. I believe some originators of the very different "Tourist" tradition, for instance the Melvilles and Twains, knew this well. Not surprisingly, then, the Local literary tradition embodies the active life, the very essence of the heroic in literature. It most plays a part by, among, and for different peoples in common.

Hawaii's Local Literary Tradition

"To Speak of Things So Real"

I

Joining native Hawaiian oral traditions, over the course of two centuries a substantial body of literature has been created by Hawaii's polyethnic writers. Hawaii's complex pastoral and heroic represent other and larger relations among literary elements which, in concert, give whole voice to Hawaii's cultures. But in spite of the qualities (not mere existence) of Hawaii's literary works and their voices, within this literature themes of *silence* occur. By this I do not mean an aesthetically valued absence of noise as in, say, the silence within a Hawaiian forest. I mean, rather, the stifling of voices.

What is known as a "Hawaiian Renaissance" of the later twentieth century began with a deliberate breaking of a deceptive silence—a stagnant silence that seemed to envelop the ancient traditional Hawaiian arts of poetry, chant, hula, and sciences reckoned useless in the tourist trade because outsiders presumably could not "relate to" them. By the beginning of the 1960s, all these and more of the native arts were commonly but mistakenly thought dead—except to scholars, museum curators, practitioners of seemingly esoteric crafts, and oldtimers considered "elders" only of powerless memories. When George Kanahele, John Dominis Holt, and their colleagues used the term "renaissance" to describe their aim to revive knowledge and interest in the continued development of traditional Hawaiian arts—not merely its preservation—it was the voice of songs and chants that was offered again to a fortunate public as the first powerful evidence of a cultural rebirth.[1] Before these voices, in this century there had only been silence to outside ears—except for the "Hawaiian

226

music" of hapa haole songs, which were not intended to be taken seriously, removed as the lovely hula hands were from a larger, richer context.[2] At midcentury "I Want to go Back to My Little Grass Shack in Kealakekua, Hawaii" alluded neither to Captain Cook nor to Henry Opukaha'ia, a Christian convert who in 1809 journeyed from the temple of Lono at the bay to the threshold of Yale, but died before he could enter. His example inspired the missionaries to work in the Sandwich Islands. Whereas Helen Lindsey Parker's "Maunaloa" implicitly interprets the history of the visitors, including Cook and his sailors, to Kealakekua Bay, "My Little Grass Shack" effectively silences that history with a deliberately sentimental idyll.[3]

Aside from members of Hawaii's Caucasian minority group,[4] Hawaii's local people have been stereotyped as being silent or quiet, not merely reticent but deficient in verbal skills and therefore incapable of creating literature of any merit, much less a literary tradition. One of the most devoted teachers of writing to Hawaii's young adults in the 1930s and 1940s—a teacher whose students contributed immensely to Hawaii's cultural record through the dramas they wrote and he collected —was pessimistic about the growth of a Hawai'i literary tradition, even while his students were creating and furthering that very tradition.[5] However kindly and humbly intended, this widespread attitude of inferiority has helped to make the study of writing and reading almost universally disagreeable to Hawaii's students. The student who loves the written word has to struggle not only with perfecting the art, not only with scoldings and ridicule that there is no money in it, but also with the prejudice that he or she by birth and environment is "naturally" no good at it.

The following works and vignettes make a counterstatement. They indicate that silence is not inherent in Hawaii's local Polynesians and Asians, as if they embody the noble savage and the noble sage, one of them strong and silent, not possessing words; the other wise and silent, not needing words. But silence has been forced upon these people of Hawai'i by authority and circumstance, in punishment, perhaps, for someone's having spoken out in insubordination. Or the speakers simply have not been heard. To speak out is to perform a heroic deed. Silence in the following Local works and vignettes is not a virtue but an adversary.

Silence can drive one insane. In the American concentration camps, the fictional Dr. Minoru Murayama observed cases of insanity or psychoses caused or aggravated by the mass imprisonment of Japanese Americans. In Hawai'i, other symptoms were reported—psychological and spiritual problems that clawed the psyches of those who were *not* arrested.

On the island of Kaua'i, at about the time of Pearl Harbor, there occurred an outbreak—an "epidemic," some say—of a phenomenon the Japanese call *inugami no sawarimono*, possession by the dog god or spirit.[6] This is a matter handled usually by Shinto priests in the way the Noda family of priests propitiated or exorcised animal spirits in Shelley Ota's *Upon Their Shoulders*. The inugami is particularly nasty in all its stages of conception and life. The person possessed by the inugami is prone to crawling, scurrying, and hopping on all fours while barking furiously. This lunacy is said to be induced in the victim by a cruel ritual and a grisly act.

One who wishes to curse an adversary with an inugami must first leash a dog securely to a post or bury it from the neck down and then starve the animal until it is crazed from hunger. At the point where the dog is judged to be its meanest, the person thus invoking the inugami must offer the dog a generous and tempting cut of meat, taking care, however, to keep the meat just outside the animal's reach. The moment the dog makes a mad lunge at the meat, just as the animal's jaws are snapping shut on the food, the soon-to-be-master of an inugami must cut off the dog's head. The head is placed in a bag, secreted somewhere, and prayed to every day, every night. From this head the inugami will issue forth to hunt out and possess the designated victim.

Enough victims appeared on Kaua'i that they invited comparison with inugami "cults" in Japan. But one way to look at the phenomenon is to see its central moment—the beheading of the dog at the instant it expects to assuage its hunger—as indicating a grossly, permanently frustrated desire or opportunity. The essence of the belief is the meat snatched from the mouth. With Japan's occupation of Manchuria in the 1930s, the Hawai'i community could see a backlash coming. It came with World War II, when American reactions did more than merely threaten to snatch opportunity from the mouths of Japanese Americans. Put allegorically, America did the snatching and the beheading in contracting the immigrants to labor in Hawai'i, starving them with promises for a future, especially for their American-born children, then treating the immigrants as America's enemies and attempting to alienate the children not only from their parents but from their birthright of American citizenship.

I would suspect that the beheading of dogs did not happen. The story is symbolic, not actual. But for some who knew the Shinto religion, the inugami phenomenon prescribed how to behave in such a circumstance of insanely frustrated opportunity, and so, probably not by deliberate choice but by crisis-driven intuition, they behaved as they ought in order to gain the priests' and the community's help. The ravenously frustrated ones bit and barked and carried on like dogs, singly and in packs. Perhaps, far beyond this, there may have been spiritual forces at work about which I cannot speak. But it makes sense that, with a high proportion of Japanese priests and cultural leaders among the island's populace, Kauaʻi might well have been the hardest hit of all the island communities by the feared or actual arrest of its leaders—the arrests and the internment of some 1,500 Japanese Americans of Hawaiʻi—which demonstrated the snatching of opportunity from the mouths of the starving. The inugami attacks ritually anticipated or reenacted those arrests and thus externalized the fears and frustrations of the possessed.

Those possessed by the inugami were the lucky ones. At least everyone could see and hear that they were beyond suspicion of being serious threats to national security—and that they needed help, which they got. Others outside the old religion had no way even to bark.

Jo Ann Uchida, in a poem titled "Fever," retells a different sort of "purgation" in the wake of the Pearl Harbor attack.[7] Like the myth of the inugami, the poem is about a cutting off—in this case, the cutting off of history by the destruction of the Japanese immigrants' heirlooms when the FBI and United States soldiers conduct terrorizing searches. They and the fearful people themselves burn everything from letters, "my wife's lacquer dresser," and "my daughter's porcelain dolls," to "the temples, / the schools, / some houses too."

Uchida, a sansei or third-generation Japanese American, writes in the voice of her grandfather who, an immigrant from Nara at the age of seventeen, went on to earn a medical degree from Stanford. His history of seemingly fulfilled American opportunity does not protect him and his family from the searches and raids for being Japanese. But in the way typical of racism's contradictions, if anything the speaker's integration into American life makes him all the more surely a suspect, because by his race he is so visible at the time in his profession. He spends the first weeks of the war, during Hawaii's blackout and martial rule, working "In hospital wards, / In wailing half-empty / well-scrubbed houses of / wives without husbands, / mending and healing / the bodies of the jaundiced-faced people." He would find those with fevers, "the sick blanched ones / with bodies on fire / . . . who had been held" by interrogators; "And in their eyes, reflected / I saw the burnings of the shrines, / their pictures, / their tenuous links with homeland / forever charred." Ucida sharply implies that the searches of this prominent figure's home come repeatedly, until the poem ends in the silencing of the speaker's history, heritage, and self:

> They are burning my father's books of poems,
> and the silk strings of my mother's koto
> curl in the flames,
> and the red wrapped scrolls
> of my family dance
> in yellow fire.

Ucida's poem, two generations and thirty-five years later, is an attempt to restore that voice.

Silence can infuriate the one silenced. In the chapter called "Great Grandfather of the Sandalwood Mountains" of Maxine Hong Kingston's *China Men*, the sugar plantation's field laborers are strictly forbidden to talk with one another or to complain about it to the luna astride his horse. The theme of silence in many of its forms appears, too, in Kingston's *The Woman Warrior*, beginning with the narrator's necessarily made-up stories of her "No Name" aunt, a silent ghost in the well where she drowned herself and her illegitimate child. Silence about the aunt seemingly banishes her from memory and indeed from ever having existed.[8] There is the long silence, too, that comes as the narrator's punishment after she cruelly harasses a silent Chinese American girl whom she tries to force to talk. The narrator describes her own voice as nothing more than a "dried duck voice." Conversely, writing, the voice, and the word are powerful weapons for a hero. The Hawai'i Great Grandfather Bak Goong in *China Men* has a big voice, but he too is silenced by the luna. One day, unable to bear their silence any longer, the Chinese workers dig a large hole in a field, a hole they imagine to reach deep toward China. They crouch around it to call out loudly to their families back home in a thunderous outcry of emotion and curses hurled against their present conditions. Their yells break the infuriating silence: "They had dug an ear into the world, and were telling the earth their secrets" (117). Then "they buried their words, planted them 'Like cats covering shit,' they laughed" (118). They thus created a custom. Bak Goong no longer kept silent in the fields.

For Kingston, the theme of silence in these works has been troublesome beyond expectation, persisting as one of several issues that sharply conflicting critics have debated since publication of *The Woman Warrior* in 1976. Within the following year, she complained to me that much of the *praise* she was getting—and there was indeed a great deal of it—was "racist praise." It was based on abhorrent assumptions about Chinese and Chinese American exotica, in perverse contrast to presumed and unquestioned, standard and normative America, as if Chinese Americans were not American but aliens. One of the greatest bothers has been the assumption that Kingston not only breaks a silence of her own, but is the first to break the silence among all Chinese Americans, especially Chinese American women. This "praise" appalls Kingston, for it denies a Chinese American literary tradition which goes back at least to a most interesting woman fiction writer, Sui Sin Far, at the turn of the century. So indeed, there has *not* been silence through a centry-and-a-quarter of Chinese American history and culture, but there has been deafness on the outside. And if anything, *The Woman Warrior* is about its narrator's having to grow up in an American society that enforces a deafness to what she is trying to hear, learn, and say in her own noisy Chinese American home full of kids.

The University of Hawaii Ethnic Studies Program's Oral History Project has produced a slide-and-audiotape show gathered in the plantation town of Waialua, Oʻahu. At one point in the show, we hear a woman speaking vehemently: The worst thing of all, she says (and I am paraphrasing from memory), was that they never let us talk in the fields, all day long! The robust voice and distinctive accent a moment later are matched by a slide showing a good-natured grandmother; and, judging by her voice, her looks, and her name, she is a Portuguese American, a people famous for volubility even in Hawaii's noisy mix. The audience laughs at the thought of such a person—or any of us—being silenced every workday in the fields.

Unsurpassed for its insidious effect on everyday life, the *kapu* banning all talk for a designated period of time consecrated to a deity or chief must have been exceedingly taxing to the Hawaiians. The kapu system was abolished just prior to the era of the missionaries. In *The Return of Lono*, John Forrest, on the languid morning after his "wedding" to Hinahina, overhears subversive talk among the four Hawaiians on the beach. The one he calls the Poet jokes wryly about the fact that Lono's arrival cut short by two days the three-day kapu earlier ordered by the priests in observance of the Makahiki, the season dedicated to Lono. Spared from two days of deadly, enforced silence, the Poet laughs:

> "Then let us rejoice for that great comfort. . . . The one-day kapu is not beyond enduring; the two-day kapu parts a man from his good humor; but the three-day kapu—auwe! It is enough to part a man from his life. How can silence be pre-served for three days, with pigs, chicken, children—and a wife!"
>
> His jest must have been too grimly pertinent to their experi-ence, for their laughter was short and hollow. In the silence that followed it, the Worrier sighed again. "Ae—but what is there to do? Is there any other way to live?" (P. 128)

Granted, this bit of conversation is not really the talk, perhaps not even the sentiment, of a Hawaiian of Kalaniopu'u's time having no "other way to live," no perspective by which to observe and to criticize quite as Bushnell's Poet does. But the important point is that Bushnell's words about the kapu assume our own abhorrence of it. Twain expressed awe at imagining the incredible, mystifying phenomenon of days of utter ab-sence of human voices in a populated village—whether in the ancient Hawai'i he learned about from James Jarves or in King Arthur's Britain under the Church's interdict silencing all speech. Yet despite the condem-nation of the kapu by local Hawaiians and outsiders alike, despite its pro-claimed abolition by 1820, it resurfaced, smugly persistent, in such places as the sugar cane fields, where, in order to curtail dissent, management stringently imposed silence upon the workers, not for a maximum of three days but maybe even for an entire lifetime of toil, as far as the workers knew.

Silence is linked in other ways with authorities' power of life and death over the common person. Although the following example from Hawaii's literature is set in Japan at the end of its feudal era rather than modern Hawai'i, its implications are striking, almost uncanny in the con-text of this discussion.

The work is a drama by Patsy Saiki entitled *The Return of Sam Patch.*[9] It compares in interesting ways with Bushnell's tale of Lono. Saiki's drama concerns the return of a shipwrecked Japanese fisherman to his home by way of Commodore Perry's historic expedition into Yokohama Bay, an event that Americans rather proudly consider to have opened Japan to the West. As Saiki puts it, the time is July 1853, "when Commodore Matthew Perry entered Japanese waters to demand a diplomatic and trade treaty between the United States and Japan." Somewhat like the Hawaiian Makahiki, it is the season of *O-bon*, the annual Japanese festival giving thanks for the year's crops and welcoming the spirits of the deceased, who return to earth for three days to bless their living descendants with their presence.

The shipwrecked fisherman Sampachi—or "Sam Patch," as his American crewmates call him—tries to visit his mother and father and the rest of the family from whose lives he had vanished eight years earlier.[10] The play opens with Sampachi's parents watching the arrival of foreign ships. Rumors and stories have fanned their hopes that one day Sampachi might return to them thus, on a foreign vessel. But in truth, they have given up any practical hope of his being alive. Well-wishers have already presented o-bon paper lanterns to the family in memory of Sampachi, to light his spirit's way back home. They now prepare for the spiritual homecoming of a dead son, the three days and three nights of o-bon.

Meanwhile Sam Patch convinces his superiors that he be allowed to land secretly, with two American companions who beg the adventure of accompanying him, so that he can see his mother and father again. As they scramble surreptitiously toward Sampachi's old home, they encounter an ancient man making his slow way in the opposite direction to see the black ships, where already a crowd is gathering. The old man, fulfilling his last wish in his century-long life, carefully examines the Americans. He concludes that "men from A-me-ri-ca not in heaven." Sampachi interprets further for his companions:

> Old man, he say your eyes like spring sky, your skin like summer sunset, your nose like Mr. Fuji [i.e., Fuji-*san*, or Mount Fuji] . . . you look like god, but you stink like devil. He say you smell worse than night soil. He wants to know . . . how come you stink? (P. 5)

What in the course of thirteen typescript pages thus begins as something of a farce devolves into a melodrama and ends in near-tragedy with a muffled outcry against the powers that silence one's own speech and knowledge. Sampachi is reunited with his parents and even dances again in the o-bon festivities. But on the second day, the village chief, known to be a lackey for the shogun, pays a call to the household. He inquires officiously about Sampachi's supposedly unknown return. The shogunate wishes to interview Sampachi and hear of all the marvelous things the fortunate peasant must have learned in this travels—especially the knowledge he has gained of America. The village chief has somehow already learned that Sampachi even speaks and understands the language of Americans. When Sampachi, off at the festivities, is informed about the chief's visit and the shogunate's orders for him to appear, he hastily retreats to the ship. Frightened, he refuses to remain in Japan and will sail away once more.

Sampachi explains what to him is absolutely clear: the shogun wishes him to divulge all he knows about America and the West in order that the knowledge might be put to political use against the shogun's rivals. After Sampachi has disclosed all, his tongue will be cut out of his head so that his voice will be forever silenced, never to repeat to anyone else the powerful and potentially dangerous knowledge he will have told the shogun. Thus the minuscule figure of Sampachi momentarily appears and vanishes in American history and in Hawaii's literature, almost but not quite completely voiceless.

Author Patsy Saiki herself was surprised and intrigued when I suggested that *The Return of Sam Patch* in some ways parallels Bushnell's *The Return of Lono*, the publication of which preceded her play by a decade. Not a fully developed drama by any means, *The Return of Sam Patch* nevertheless floats on thematic, historical, and mythological currents and undercurrents that run strong in Hawaii's literary heritages. The theme of the emigrant's return, for instance, runs as deep as the Japanese folk tale of Urashima Taro, the man who journeys to the undersea kingdom and returns to the surface to find that three hundred years, not three days, have passed. His home has changed while he has aged and now he is but a whirl of dust in the wind. This theme is also implicitly evoked by John Okada on the opening page of his *No-No Boy*, and Washington Irving's "Rip Van Winkle" is one of Urashima Taro's analogs in world cultures.

Rather than deliberately reworking such themes that inform her drama, Saiki simply muses that they "must have been in the air" when she wrote *The Return of Sam Patch*. In any case, her work and Bushnell's make an interestingly matched and opposite pair, especially if one views the protagonists as metaphor for the writer's dilemma. (Suppose that Kailiki were, in effect, the shogun interrogating Forrest, where the latter, unlike Sampachi, is blind to this political situation even while he recalls his story.) If the tragedy of Captain Cook (and Forrest) were a Noh drama, then Saiki's brief comic melodrama of the scared and wily Sampachi might well serve as its companion Kyogen. To pursue the metaphor, the writer's decisive act is to publish words, to make characters' voices heard and known, not to keep silence, like Sampachi, out of fear. Still deeper than those impulses and inspirations by which the writer finally composes words on a page, creates and publishes them, is the risk, the very fear, central to Saiki's drama and enacted in its subtext, that the writer may be exploited or silenced after uttering his or her vision of the truth.

If the shogun's retribution seems rather too drastic to apply to our own place and time or to steadily productive writers such as Patsy Saiki, it is nonetheless still evident that speaking out in the face of power and authority is associated with anxiety. And yet silence is associated with something worse, a suffocation among Hawaii's people, when seen from the point of view of some Hawai'i writers. Dana Naone addresses this nightmarish frustration in "The Men Whose Tongues," a poem that speaks for itself:

> The men whose tongues have turned to iron
> would say water tastes like rust
> to them if they did not find it
> so hard to speak. Words pile up.
> They go through each day, their mouths full
> of unsaid words. In dreams
> they hang upside down and
> ring like bells. [11]

Then again, the "silence" of Hawaii's people may not always be a matter of their voices being stifled or stolen, but rather of simply not being heard. Hawaii's Asian American literature of this century, for example, has gone unheard until very recently—not merely unrecognized, but ignored. On occasion, to this day, it has even been denied to exist. In loud and welcome contrast, one highly verbal disruption of Hawaii's supposed silence would be difficult to ignore.

Silence has been broken by a zany crew of self-styled "Kanaka Komedians" who have come paddling into both the local and the tourist-oriented entertainment scenes, transforming nightclubs into places where the most outrageous pidgin is understood and applauded and where local audiences, too, have been standing in line. Where no one, no group, in Hawai'i is kapu from being harpooned with satire, the Kanaka Komiks have driven Hawaii's locals to laughing openly—even at themselves—and the laughter that breaks silence has made a difference in the quality of life in Hawai'i.

At times following, at times deviating from courses charted by veteran pidgin English comics (such as Kent Bowman, who calls himself "K. K. Kaumanua," and Lippy Espinda in his used-car commercials of the 1950s and 1960s), beginning in the early 1970s Rap Reiplinger, James Grant Benton, Ed Kaahea, and others who originally comprised the team called "Booga Booga" led the way in hilarious open raids, pitting local humor and comedy against sanctimoniousness and the local's own fears of "making ass" in public. At the decade's end, Andy Bumatai dazzled crowds at the Royal Hawaiian Hotel's Monarch Room with his standup comic act, where he continued his phenomenal growth in popularity and appeal among locals of all ages. Meanwhile Frank DeLima, who once devoted himself to becoming a Catholic priest, cruised majestically into Hawaii's comedy world with his outrageous "Portagee" jokes and Local ethnic humor; then DeLima lost a good many pounds and became a singer as well. Like some of his colleagues, he now also specializes in school assemblies, to his public's delight. There are others besides these, coming and going like comets from one club to another, following the vicissitudes of their rough business. But by teasing their own, local audiences into laughing, they have made a contribution to Hawaii's Local culture that the public will probably never be able fully to repay.

Regarding the silence where a voice falls dead because it is utterly unheard, many-voiced Rap Reiplinger in his first solo comedy album, the revolutionary *Poi Dog*, uses a local term to characterize the obtuseness of people who will not hear: they are "deaf ear." "I was deaf ear; I never like listen," moans one such character, crooning a farewell ballad to his beloved "Fate Yanagi," a takeoff from "Tell Laura I Love Her." He lies dying in the hospital because he ignored warnings against body-surfing in monstrous waves; so, getting what he deserves for being deaf ear, "now I stay Queen's in critical condition."[12] Through the comic bravura of *Poi Dog*, other vivid local terms have regained currency in Hawai'i, where Kanaka Komedy has helped people feel that they can hear, speak, laugh again, and be heard in the face of authorities, whether symbolical or actual, who have presumed to dictate in colonial terms what constitutes good speech, bad speech, and even fun itself in Hawai'i. And from this comic point of view, "deaf ear" nicely describes the inability to recognize the existence and the languages of Hawaii's own voices in literature.

Again in the popular mode, though on a quieter note, Robert and Roland Cazimero sing a composition of their own that implicitly carries a theme of silence, simply titled "Our Song."[13] In a spoken introduction to the song, they explain their response to "the terror of war," an extreme emotion that they glimpsed indirectly when they accompanied survivors of the 100th Infantry Battalion/442nd Regimental Combat Team to a mid-1970s reunion at Bruyeres, France. These nisei units had liberated Bruyeres from the Germans in October 1944.

> I try to speak of things so real,
> To convey with love how I act and feel.
> Turn away the hurt, turn away the pain,
> Just don't stand alone in tears of rain.
>
> But try to speak of things more real. . . .

This is admittedly a song that, in order to convey more than vague sentiment, depends on its unspecified historical context, even beyond the performer's spoken introduction. A Hawaii Public Television documentary of the reunion at Bruyeres reveals that the gathering inadvertently revived tensions and conflicts that blew an often cold breath across the gala lūʻau the Hawaiʻi veterans carried with them to France and prepared for the occasion. The reunion included not only the 100th/442nd veterans and their families but also the general populace of Bruyeres—and a German veteran and his family, the man once a prisoner of war of the Americans and the French. It was difficult for the French to accept the German's presence. Nothing overt broke the intended air of reunion and of reconciliation as well. But the Cazimeros, touring with the veterans to provide lūʻau entertainment, clearly sensed the covert mood. In their song, they try to reaffirm something ineffable, something "more real," perhaps about what Bruyeres signifies in history, including Hawaii's. It is a message of peace in the face of continuing conflict.

By virtue of its context, "Our Song" ought to be heroic. It is about "the terror of war." But though it would be very difficult to call it just that, in its gentle insistence on the need to "speak of things so real" with love and in the community of others "Our Song" is a quiet expression of the Hawaiʻi heroic today.

2

The native Hawaiian Renaissance has made possible a vision of a genuine multicultural literature of Hawai'i. Any ethnic renaissance in a place called "Hawai'i" would be a hypocrisy if it lacked recognition of the native Hawaiian and a view of how and why the newer cultures are related to the original one of this land.

In the short, very active years since the birth of a new, current generation in Hawaii's literature, what some thought to be a polyethnic literary foundling called "Local literature" has been understood further to have a lineage which, pursued far enough, connects this literary tradition with the others in their histories. But at the time it was newly celebrated in 1978, there was little more than faith—and a hunch that, in addition to Tourist and Colonial traditions, and besides a native Hawaiian tradition of literature, Hawaii's many other cultures must surely have their own literary heritages; otherwise, how could those cultures continue to exist with such obvious vigor?

In those days, not very long ago at all, it was as if a Local literary "tradition" were being created from scratch. Its authors would consider Hawai'i a home—an open idea, inclusive of all races and ethnic groups, origins and places of birth. The individual writer would identify with being of Hawai'i and would take pride in having a culture, an ethos, to draw upon to contribute to the cultural life of the islands, and would not be ashamed of his or her local or ethnic ties and place of origin. This positive understanding of oneself would include a lively respect for other individuals and their cultures.

The tradition was meant to be self-limiting: a writer who saw a local, a regional, or even a national label to be too constricting, or a writer who, say, was unaware of his or her culture as being ethnically distinct from others, could simply choose not to participate in the Talk Story conference that, in 1978, was meant in part to embody this conception of Hawaii's literatures. Nonetheless, some writers who wanted to be recognized for being actively part of a Local literary tradition still felt excluded despite their commitments to Hawai'i, the ethnic literary cause, and everyone's professed reluctance to play any role of gatekeeper; but, to their credit—by their acts, their values, ideas, and literary works —these same writers are contributing to the health of Hawaii's cultures today. This dissension, however, certainly acknowledges that the state of the art and of criticism in the Local literary tradition in Hawai'i still is imperfect and volatile, where individual misunderstanding can seem to inflame the entire tradition—that is, the living community of writers and what they together wish to stand for—or where individual deeds can do much good.

On the morning of 20 June 1978, O. A. Bushnell delivered the keynote address to open "Talk Story: Our Voices in Literature and Song; Hawaii's Ethnic American Writers' Conference." In effect, Bushnell challenged Michener's bland assumption that there is no Asian American literature of Hawai'i.[14] As he had stated before, he lamented the paucity of historical fiction of Hawai'i and cited some reasons for this lack. To suggest causes may help to suggest cures. Bushnell continues today to prod and challenge, reiterating in various guises the substance of his seminal address at Talk Story:

> In Hawaii we generate a vicious circle: lack of readers—lack of buyers of books—lack of bookstores that survive—paucity of publishers, who die for want of manuscripts, which are not produced for lack of writers. Three of our novelists had to pay to publish their own novels. In Hawaii, I sigh, writers are stifled at birth. Our geniuses with words and pen never have a chance.
>
> This sadness will be exceeded by an even greater one, a veritable horror. "Outsiders," not only from the Mainland, will be writing the novels telling us what we are and what we think. They will turn out the stuff that the rest of the world will read.
>
> "Outsiders" will be writing "the great Hawaiian novels." And shame on all our faces if we allow it to happen.

Knowing Bushnell's works and hearing him talk this way, one might think that the novelist was being ironical and harshly modest about his own works, for he had already published three important historical novels, a fourth was at that very moment released, and a fifth was probably already drafted in full, or close to it. And who but he could even guess what cobwebbed manuscripts he had been storing away? But in that morning's talk Bushnell persisted with a wonderful sarcasm to underscore the seriousness of what he was asserting: when it comes to local-born literature, Hawai'i is a sow that devours its own farrow.

Perhaps Bushnell was weary of having to explain his often delivered criticisms. Perhaps he was impatient with those who missed his point although they may have lived for years in Hawai'i, maybe even all their lives. Or perhaps he delighted in his role as local pundit who could say whatever he wanted and (sometimes to his astonishment and annoyance) still be applauded afterwards. For whatever reasons, Bushnell rarely went further in public anymore actually to document and support his scoldings. In fact, even in conversation he would maintain in those days that there was no local-born and raised writer—"of note," he might ambiguously add—until the last three decades, when a very few writers such as Jon Shirota, Bob Hongo, and Milton Murayama all too briefly appeared. Allowing a single, earlier exception to his point about a lack of local writers with long careers, he would name a lone author: Armine von Tempski, the Maui author of local novels with somewhat Biblical titles—*Dust, Fire, Lava,* and *Thunder in Heaven.*[15] There are no others, Bushnell would say, only silence.

What an assertion from Hawaii's foremost historical novelist at the start of an unprecedented Hawai'i conference called "Talk Story." A pidgin expression, "talk story" characterizes a widespread and sociable form of oral, animated exchange. "Shooting the breeze" or "chewing the fat" are the term's kin, except, of course, for the important fact that "talk story" is Hawaii's own, this verbal style being neither quaint nor "waste time." And the term could be transferred from the transient word of mouth to the durable printed page. We were already finding by mid −1978 that "talk story" also characterizes much of Hawaii's contemporary written literature: anecdotes, vignettes, sketches, short fiction, both lyrical and narrative poetry, monodramas filled with the central characters' reminiscences directly addressed to the audience, and entire novels told by a speaker whose genuine voice sounds like someone talking story. For instance, Murayama's Kiyo and Holt's Mark talk story; not only the dictions but the very structures of these works indicate so.

By chance, our group's choice of the name Talk Story, Inc., preceded by one day the 1976 release of Kingston's *The Woman Warrior,* which none of us had yet read. We soon learned that Kingston too, had chosen to use in her book the pidgin term she heard in Hawai'i, "talk story," thus naming a verbal style and form which the narrator learns from her Cantonese immigrant mother. Every connotation surrounding the title of our group, the planned conference, and the project's anthology, *Talk Story: An Anthology of Hawaii's Local Writers,* seemed to confirm the social nature of Hawaii's use of words—not the isolation, alienation, and ultimate demise of the writer. Moreover, Bushnell immediately accepted Marie Hara's invitation to join us, as did Kingston; and Bushnell in fact suggested the organization's motto: "Words bind, and words set free," a rendering of a traditional closure to Hawaiian chants. By the look he wore whenever we met, we knew Bushnell was a sly co-conspirator in a budding literary movement. He knew our faith that the relatively few writers who gathered pell-mell in Talk Story were trying to speak for many more authors, past and present, yet unknown to us. But in his keynote speech, he clearly challenged us with the insistence that too little has been done in Hawaii's own literature. Bushnell thus introduced us to our motto's more problematic implications about the power of words and the responsibilities this power incurs, if we were to go on talking story at all.

So, at this 1978 conference of Local and mainland Asian/Pacific American literatures—such as had never been held in Hawai'i—a Hawai'i novelist was reminding us that, though several hundred people had gathered and though our local project had already appeared in the national press, a river of words and books would be needed if Locals were to turn the tide of silence and misappropriation of Hawaii's cultures. Were any of us up to such a challenge? Had we been Pollyannas so far in our outlook?

That Bushnell raised these points appeared doubly ironic, and in the years after 1978 he has actively encouraged others to prove him wrong. The present book is my attempted proof that, despite the merits of his complaints, Bushnell has not only been in good company in creating Hawaii's literary traditions but has also had the odd experience of being in this company of predecessors and contemporaries without knowing that they shared these traditions. They were, in a sense, standing together in the foyer of some salon, still only about to be introduced to one another and to the public awaiting them even at the very moment Bushnell addressed the conference in 1978. These Hawai'i writers' "literary traditions" were based not so much on their shared influences from predecessors they had read in common. Rather, their culturally specific achievements were based on the living cultures of Hawaii's communities and their spoken words, their talk story. Not between bookcovers, though books turned out to be abundant, but within Hawaii's ethnic communities was the locus of the literary tradition Bushnell and many others were furthering, the one I call here the Local. Now, with the open introduction of their literary works, the locus could reside in books as well, books which Bushnell was warning may not exist.

Another irony in Bushnell's warning about a dearth of Hawai'i literature is that earlier in his own long affair with the muses, he knew quite well that he was not lacking in literary company. As president of the university's Hawaii Quill Society in the early 1930s, he helped to welcome such literary luminaries as Carl Sandburg and Hamlin Garland. The society also published a handsome journal, the *Hawaii Quill Magazine*, containing poetry, drama, and fiction—some of it rather high quality—written by student members, including Bushnell. But then again, this is to say that he himself was a veteran at seeing literary societies come and go in Hawai'i, and he was asking us if we would be any different.

Bushnell's student organization clearly recognized at least some sort of Hawai'i literary heritage. In 1931 the society presented a special evening commemorating Mark Twain, his work, and his widely appealing literary contributions to Hawai'i.[16] It appears from the printed program that Willard Wilson (drama-writing professor who was assiduously to collect his students' plays beginning in 1936) advised the production of a burlesque, "A University of Hawaii Student in King Arthur's Court." The playbill and essays on Twain, especially in his connection with Hawai'i, were published in a special issue of the *Hawaii Quill*, in which appears, for example, Mary Dillingham Frear's musical setting of Twain's famous "Prose Poem" of a Hawai'i paradise. Moreover the *Hawaii Quill* was not written by outsiders, though guests now and then contributed; it was the product of a local, polyethnic group. Alyce Chang-Tung Char served as editor-in-chief for the Twain issue. Among the contributors were Professor Charles Eugene Banks, for whom an annual literary prize would be named. Yukino Nakamura, Gladys Ling [A]i Li, Professor J. S. Donaghho, Alice Chong, and Albert Bigelow Paine, Twain's biographer, also participated. It must be noted, however, that when it came to the public program itself, those who appeared on stage were apparently exclusively Caucasians, while the Asian American committee members worked in the background, setting tables, serving, stage managing, and so forth. Still, the printed word—where the Asian Americans are named and do have a voice—lasts longer than the festive sounds of that evening in November of 1931. The banquet is over, but the Twain festschrift allows us to peek into one of the rooms in the lives of Bushnell and his generation of Hawaii's local writers. He seemed in numerous company then—and now.

In those years of the literary enthusiasm the *Hawaii Quill* exhibits, or even afterwards as those student writers matured, surely something enduring must have been created, contrary to Bushnell's claim that until recently no local writer of note had bloomed. But besides Bushnell, who eventually achieved some literary stature? What became of the others? Gladys Li, for one, continued to write, but not in the way Bushnell had in mind. Li made a career, certainly one that involved writing, as a staff member and director of the Far Eastern Department of Ripley's *Believe It or Not*. Furthermore, in 1972, as Li Ling Ai, she published *Life Is for a Long Time*, a biography and family history of her Chinese immigrant parents, who with their Canton medical educations had distinguished themselves as uniquely skilled physicians in Hawai'i.[17]

But then again, biography is not the same as fiction, and Bushnell would sharply qualify his remarks by saying that he is speaking especially of a lack of novelists who work at their interpretive art over an extended time. Hacks always abound, he might have said—but did not. Bushnell knew by 1978, as probably only a very few have known, that there have been truly talented writers in Hawai'i, not mere hacks. Across five decades he has seen the raw talent: Gladys Li, for an example; Joseph Keonona Chun Fat, for another. Fat's *The Mystery of the Ku'ula Rock*, a collection of ingenuous narratives dealing with actual encounters with metaphysical arts of the kahuna, was published in 1975 when the author was seventy-two. It reveals a man of remarkable gifts that perhaps had been ignored, denied, or refused by others but, fortunately, had not been neglected by himself during the nearly seven decades that he devoted to journal writing.[18] Bushnell was once paired with Fat in a public reading at a community library. This, their first meeting, was a lively one. Different as they were in the directions that their lives had taken, Bushnell, the retired scientist, and Fat, the self-taught recorder of underground Hawaiian cultural life, must have recognized immediately their common and deep roots. It was Bushnell who recommended that Joseph Keonona Chun Fat be asked to participate in the Talk Story Big Island Writers' Conference held in Hilo in 1979. By then, too, Bushnell and others of us had begun to ascertain that there had been, were, and are far more writers of Hawai'i through the past and present two centuries than we had even hoped when Bushnell a year earlier indicted Hawai'i—all of us—for not supporting Local literature. Why had we children of Hawai'i not heard of these writers before?

Bushnell's observations and feelings about a lack of local writers and an invasion by "outside" writers had culminated in that keynote speech. A conflict between two different views of Hawai'i and its literature was once more rife in his lifetime.

One phenomenon that has contributed at various times to a lack of a known, broadly based literary community has to do, especially in Hawai'i, with the simple pastoral itself. In this case, it is the notion of Hawai'i as a Bohemian retreat which attracts, as the historian Edward

Joesting puts it, "indolents who lived on the beach." These may live apart from but still comprise the same wave of newcomers in the 1960s and 1970s as "new kinds of missionaries" preaching beliefs the earlier Christian ones considered pagan, and "rapacious exploiters, seeking to deceive, loot and leave."[19] These types exemplify individualism—"renegades" would probably describe most of these newcomers to their own satisfaction. Typically (and I am sketching here a type, not any actual person) they do not usually have a ready relationship with a community in Hawai'i, and they are solitaries, not merely strangers in a strange land.

Historically, Hawai'i has had any number of visiting writers, some of them, such as Melville, Twain, Stevenson, and London, famous indeed in canons of male Anglo American and world literature. Whether it is accurate—and it certainly does not describe Twain—the image of the visiting writer in Hawai'i is of an artist retreating from urban, mainland America to the balm of the islands. But though Honolulu means "fair haven," its island of O'ahu, after all, means the "gathering place," with the urban congestion to prove it. To escape the crowd, the writer must retreat farther to the O'ahu North Shore, or into one of the island's valleys, or to a Kaua'i treehouse, to Maui, to tiny Lāna'i, or to the forests and the volcano expanses of the Big Island of Hawai'i, a wilderness more vast in scale than anything else actually visible in Hawai'i except for the sea and sky and heavens.

When seeking out Hawai'i writers in our research, Arnold Hiura and I heard various people name these remote places (such as a treehouse) where writers, usually in-migrants and visitors who ended up staying, were reported to have withdrawn. Directed by a pastoral impulse that sometimes goes haywire, so that the original idea of both retreat from and return to society is somewhere lost, the retreat runs toward nature and away from technology—and away from people and communities, whether of locals or of newcomers. But beneath this behavior, the retreating newcomer's deceptively simple pastoral dream is really as complex and conflicted as the centuries-old dreams of Polynesian, Asian, and European voyagers, explorers, and pioneers who crossed the trackless Pacific. To fulfill it, the visiting writer seeks solitude, maybe mistaking the solitude essential to writing—in a room of one's own—for the very different, unbroken solitude of one's life spent as if forever outside the regular company of and immediate responsibility to others in cultural, intellectual, and artistic matters, as he or she sets up a study in the damp of an isolated tropical forest. The example becomes impressive to a child of Hawai'i when the child is falsely taught in any manner of instances that only mainland haoles, but not locals, have written Hawaii's modern literature: You like be one writer? Try look at the haole writer living in the treehouse out in the sticks.

With such a display of individualism, the writer in retreat poses a difficult model for local aspiring writers to follow. A youth in a Hawaiʻi community would be torn between becoming like the visiting writer without a local community, on the one hand, and conforming with community and family standards of propriety, on the other. What is worse, the writer by definition is outspoken, a dealer in words. But to the contrary, the community ethos strongly emphasizes the "virtue" of silence, a continuing legacy of cane field rules against talking while working, condemnations of the vernacular, Pearl Harbor, World War II, blackouts, and the arrests of those issei and nisei who had voices in the pre-war Japanese American community.

Somehow the manifest virtues of being an imaginative writer have clashed stubbornly with the idea of a local writer's remaining in Hawaiʻi and continuing to write about Hawaiʻi and its peoples. This concern of course is not only a local one. On one level it is economic, and this too is far more complicated by such factors as racism than hot emotions can explain. In the postwar flowering of Local literature which saw the emergence of Charles Kong, Patsy Saiki, Philip Ige, Clara Kubojiri, Seiko Ogai, and quite a few others whose works for a brief time consistently appeared in a handful of local literary journals and other periodicals, one rather prolific writer expressed his agony over what he loved doing —writing. In his drama *Sunao*, James Mishima seems to rehearse his own conflict when that title character tries to justify to his father his decision to major in English and become a writer.[20] The father objects, disappointed that Sunao is not thinking of a career in business. Besides the poverty that the father is convinced his son as a writer will gain for his efforts, one of the most painful issues raised is the "novelty" of aspiring to be a "Japanese English writer" at all. In other words, because of his race and circumstances, Sunao's ambition is considered out of line. The drama is sketchy and blunt, and it ends in a standoff: Sunao remains stubborn, and Otʻsan lets him go his own way without approval. As for James Mishima himself, Philip Ige, who remembers him as a fellow writer at the university, vaguely recalls that the talented student writer might have become an interior designer, those writings perhaps indeed being his last.

To write honestly about Hawaiʻi in the way Bushnell called for, it has seemed that one must leave Hawaiʻi—or must like Bushnell himself have a peculiar fortitude that I include in my use of the term "heroic" to speak of Hawaii's resident local writers today. Or perhaps it means having a job not in an English department, but at a place where hiring, pay, and promotion have nothing to do with literary merit. Bushnell researched and taught in a medical school. Darrell Lum is a counselor for special students at the University of Hawaii. Wing Tek Lum is a businessman. To some it means having a living not dependent upon Hawaiʻi and its politics. Some clear cases of "expatriates" suggest themselves even now: Jon Shirota lives and writes in Los Angeles, as does Edward Sakamoto, who is the most performed playwright at East West Players, the most firmly established Asian American theater in our time. In a sense more known to Los Angelenos than to Honolulu's peoples, Sakamoto's dramas are about Hawaiʻi subjects.[21] Milton Murayama lives and writes in San Francisco. Today, students and scholars of Hawaii's cultures are sometimes choosing not only to see the world but also to retreat, as it were, to the mainland and elsewhere to learn humanistic disciplines, preparing themselves to interpret Hawaiʻi in ways the individual considers honest and true to her or his vision as a student, scholar, critic, and member still of a Hawaiʻi community—because, as Bushnell charged, in matters literary, Hawaiʻi up close seems a devouring sow.

But while one image of the writer in Hawaiʻi during the later 1960s and 1970s drew the aspiring local away from his or her community, away from the established middle-class value on silence, literary interests at the University of Hawaii revived after what appears to have been a slight hiatus in the late 1950s and just into the 1960s. As had been the case in the earlier surges of literary activity on campus—beginning not only with the *Hawaii Quill* but, even earlier, with the Chinese Students' Alliance and the Japanese Students' Association yearbooks, replete with literary sections—the revival since the sixties of the university's literary journal was characterized by the formation of a literary society in one form or another. This time it was nurtured by an active faculty in creative writing. The core consisted of William Huntsberry, a fiction writer and himself the author of Hawaiʻi thrillers and mysteries; the poet Phyllis Thompson, originator of the Hawaiʻi Poets-in-the-Schools Program and in recent years a devoted student of native Hawaiian language and culture; and Helen Topham, a successor to Willard Wilson in the teaching of drama writing. They and the colleagues who joined them since the late 1960s have obviously played educational and social roles diametrically opposite the image of a writer in indefinite retreat.

The growth of this university branch of Hawaii's literary activity was boosted further with the creation of the Hawaii Literary Arts Council (HLAC), thanks to the efforts of Phyllis Thompson, Frank Stewart, Warren Iwasa, and others. Made official in 1974, HLAC became shaped by its president of two years, the late poet and critic John Unterecker. The inception of HLAC, in what some members besides Bushnell even today might say is an environment not especially hospitable to literary endeavors, was quite a vision for Unterecker to begin filling. His selfless dedication and his own literary talents brought to him unsolicited recognition and respect in Hawai'i, where, after resigning from his position at Columbia University, he joined the faculty of the University of Hawaii and literally devoted his life thereafter to the arts. The Hawaii Literary Arts Council's programs consisted of readings by visiting and local writers and literary scholars. The council also assumed sponsorship and administration of the Poets-in-the-Schools Program as well as conferences and writers' retreats. Funded largely by the Hawaii State Foundation on Culture and the Arts, the National Endowment for the Arts, and the Hawaii State Legislature, HLAC in the mid-1970s was obviously to be looked to for broad public sponsorship of literary programs and cultural leadership.

The naturally changing character of this leadership, however is open to public applause and criticism, for HLAC and the university are public institutions. I associate HLAC with the university here because, although membership to HLAC is unrestricted, the organization began with a membership that consisted largely of university and college teachers and their most serious and dedicated literature students. Seemingly, every member was a writer and a scholar or was aspiring to both. It seemed at once natural yet unfortunate that a literary society must be elite, the term "literature" itself connoting high culture (such that its use in the subtitle of the Talk Story Conference, "Our Voices in *Literature* and Song" drew questions and criticism). But despite no one's conscious desire to be elitist, with such internationally noted writers and scholars as Unterecker and, later, Leon Edel at HLAC's helm in its early years, and with HLAC having the honor and responsibility of making an annual Hawaii Award for Literature, the council, like the university, seemed an arbiter of taste as well as quality. An early impression, that is, was that HLAC represented an established American canon and those new works and writers who fit into it. It would have appeared to an interested and critical observer that this judgment did not include a taste for Local literature of certain kinds. For instance, in the mid-1970s HLAC lacked pidgin English in any of its dealings. The visiting writers' series in the 1970s was called "Major Writers," while the other series was called "Local Writers." The inference that "Local" thus meant "minor" was a fairly widespread source of discomfort, for these program titles maintained those very attitudes that some, including Unterecker, Thompson, and Stewart, had hoped HLAC would change for all Hawai'i.

To the overlapping group called Talk Story, the overt response typically was strained once the first smiles were exchanged over the novel idea of studying Local literature in regular classes or basing major projects on it.[22] But at the university and in HLAC some individuals responded enthusiastically and began to work on the numerous Talk Story projects involved in the research and creation of the literature; so HLAC itself felt the strain of a potentially ugly split separating two of the parts of Hawaii's total literary body. One had a name: the Local, the forever here and now, but paradoxically a newcomer to the visible and audible Hawai'i literary scene. The other, having long been presumed to be "universal," had no particular name of the kind, though the easily recognizable names of, say, those "Major Writers" who had written occasional pieces about Hawai'i would comprise the established canon opposing the Local, even though there appeared to some to be no literary reasons why the two different traditions should be thought competitors.

Those of us working on various literary projects in Hawai'i soon entered a time of ferment and conflict while on the surface we worked enthusiastically among ourselves to get many projects done. Much was achieved by organizations both from the general community and from the university in cosponsoring the Talk Story Conference. But the split evidenced within HLAC ran deep; it was indeed the racial issue itself which Talk Story in part was meant to raise and not evade yet once more in Hawaii's fallacious "melting pot." Against the Talk Story projects, an HLAC member charged that Talk Story excluded haole writers, whites, though these projects were claimed to be open to anyone contributing to Hawaii's cultures, unrestricted by race or origin. The complaint went so far as to note that Bushnell and Holt, both of them prominent in Talk Story, could not be counted even as token haole because the former is part-Portuguese and the latter, of course, part-Hawaiian—while other haole writers in Talk Story, such as Martha Webb, Stewart, and Thompson, were considered merely the tokens proving the complaint. On the other side were charges that the establishment itself had excluded locals for generations from the colonial cultural hegemony, so it was time for now to hear Local literature, not the canon already heard and indeed taught and studied. And the claim was being raised from both sides, for opposite reasons, that the very appearance now of local voices in Hawaii's literature made the usual haole canon seem relatively shrunken in comparison to its formerly exclusive place in Hawaii's English-language literature.

The ideas of cultural values and society—pluralism rather than assimilation, class consciousness versus its lack—were and are on the local side radically different from the colonial. There are some opponents of recognizing Local literature who, in an attempt to deny the intellectual merit of viewing Hawai'i as a pluralistic, multicultural, and multiracial society with sharp class distinctions, insist on lumping all Hawaii's locals except native Hawaiians under the category of colonizer, the same as the whites in power, as though owning the plantation and laboring in its fields were the same thing.[23] Fearful of and quite possibly deaf ear to the postcolonial world that local literature and, truly, the Hawaiian Renaissance has evidenced a hundred years ago and today, such a view replays the plantation politics of interethnic conflicts based on the exploitation of racial and ethnic prejudices. It divides in presumed rivalry native Hawaiians (in this view, supposedly the only truly colonized ones in the state) from all other locals, then sets Asian American ethnic groups against one another as expediency dictates for the maintenance of colonial power, just as effectively as differential pay scales by race and by gender divide and conquer any group of workers. In this colonial view, in some ways unchanged since the nineteenth century, to attempt to write literature in English is to submit to its assumption of the Anglo colonizer's cultural supremacy, which means the colonized can never make the grade.

The very notion of a "Local literature" was indeed a contradiction in terms to those who could not comprehend pluralism, a diversity within a whole based on racial equality and not hierarchy, or the idea of anything "local" being so distinguished as to have a "literature." Such "ethnic" writing is "political" rather than "literary," one critic advised, while another equated it with what in those days was the fad of "found poetry," ingenuous or clever graffiti, and many again considered any local particulars to be constricting whereas somehow the same was not considered true of the particulars found in literature of any other locales in the world. But in spite of the myriad entanglements of a "universalist" point of view dubious of "Local literature," beginning with the term itself, the importance of the term and concepts it represents—and the terms and concepts "Local literature" is therefore distinguished from—became all the more surely felt. To paraphrase Mark Twain, the use of the term "Local" (like "native Hawaiian," "Colonial," and its offshoot, "Tourist") to label one of Hawaii's literary traditions was increasingly understood to be necessary, from a local point of view, to discourage people from making the mistake of thinking that writers in these three literary traditions of Hawai'i are all trying to sound alike but failing at it.

Yet the very idea of Local literatures's being taken seriously enough to be compared with Twain and the Tourist and Colonial canon must have seemed both ludicrous and appalling to some. Perhaps confirming these criticisms against the new tide, the support for the swiftly aroused movement in Local culture and literature grew not from academia but from the "community." It included large parts of Hawaii's society that previously appeared to have been untouched by literature outside of formal education, but who were now rediscovering or disclosing literary interests that no one had cared to ask about, much less awaken. Baffling to the movement's critics, Talk Story must have seemed literally a bastard in contrast to the Colonial, so established as to be taken for granted, and to the native Hawaiian, so ancient as to need a revival, when Talk Story's audiences and activities included writers and teachers, to be sure, and also laborers, fishermen and fisherwomen, politicians, a drama group of the deaf, lawyers, garage mechanics, insurance sellers, nightclub entertainers, homemakers, shopkeepers, store clerks, military personnel, farmers, secretaries, dentists, meetings disguised as parties, literary readings with very heavy *pūpū* or refreshments, a rummage sale, and benefit sales of such island delicacies and innovations for the occasion as smoked marlin, kālua chicken, and boiled peanuts. As for the critics' serious questions about the size of Local literature in addition to its merits, it took a year beyond the 1978 conference to give any measured response other than pointing out the presence of some three dozen local writers at the event. The next major task would be the comprehensive collecting and reading of works from the past: the researching of a literary history.

I must stress that despite the ignorance Bushnell and the rest of us shared of that literary history, many of the disputants as well as the mediators in these critical issues sincerely felt that somewhere in our Hawai'i there must be a cultural treasure chest full of already written yet unknown works and the live talent needed to create further works of Hawaii's Local literature. And so we set out to find it, unearth it, work with its contents, and rededicate it to Hawaii's literature and culture in such a way as to end the colonial era at last. For how could anyone —in whichever of the Talk Story Conference's contrasting, polarized, but polite and still cosponsoring groups—work to educate Hawaii's public about literature, without a belief that literature should live among and in people, that it should not simply be imported from the outside for only a moment of study in the classroom?

3

Though it may be true, as Bushnell urged, that it takes the writing of full-length novels most powerfully to swell the several currents of Hawaii's literary traditions today, of equal importance to the growth and recognition of the Local—in other words, to break the deafness— is the upsurge of Hawaii's local poetry in the 1970s and 1980s. When we think of new voices in poetry of Hawai'i today, we at last recognize Asian American poets among an ethnically diverse group. But one response is as if, again, Hawaii's Asian Americans had not until recently begun to develop a poetic voice or a poetry of any significance. The notion that descendants of Asian immigrants have special linguistic difficulties discouraging their writing of poetry, the most demanding literary use of language, has seemed to be validated by the bare history of Hawaii's Asian American poetry of the first three-quarters of this century. But the interesting history of this scarcity of poetry applies to all aspiring poets since the 1930s, regardless of race.

In the introduction to *Poetry Hawaii: A Contemporary Anthology* (1979), Frank Stewart remarks that poetry in twentieth-century Hawai'i appears to have been squelched the moment it raised its voice.[24] For example, the first winner of the Charles Eugene Banks Memorial Prize for creative writing at the University of Hawaii was Richard Fujii, who won twenty dollars and publication of his 22–line poem, "Caravan," in the *Honolulu Advertiser*, 21 April 1934. A pessimistic depiction of humanity's groping "trek through this / Yet unknown and ever unknowable / Immanent and boundless firmament," Fujii's poem marked a great, global departure from the kind of light verse and doggerel his contemporaries, with few exceptions, had been writing about Waikīkī, palm trees, the beach, and other breezy delights. Yet Fujii's portentous poem was swiftly overwhelmed by criticism from *Advertiser* readers, one of whom wrote that "Here is stupid stuff indeed . . . merely a dead level of foetid pessimism. . . . And not even a sweet jingle of rhyme to tickle the ear." Needless to say, this reader and others following behind would not buy a ticket on Fujii's caravan, considering the direction in which it was headed. The shocked reader, who signed his letter "Psychiatrist," was utterly dismayed at what such an outlook as the Hilo sophomore's revealed about "the future destiny of the world" in the hands of youths such as Fujii, the would-be poet.

More letters followed, both for and against Fujii's "Caravan." As Stewart puts it, "Before long, the damage had been done." Possibly because of the poem's stormy reception, among a number of other factors, poetry of Hawai'i in English—except for light verse jingling about Hawaii's charms—rarely found its way into print, and it never again won any prizes until 1972, when Banks Prizes were awarded to poems once more, this time because poetry and fiction awards were split that year into separate categories.

A survey of Asian American literature of Hawai'i certainly confirms Stewart's observation. From the mid–1930s until the mid–1960s, when the university brought a poetry-writing teacher aboard, almost no poems by Hawaii's Asian Americans were published in English, while extant collections and publications of dramas, short fiction, and novels were plentiful. For part of the 1930–60 period, meanwhile, poetry written and published by Hawaii's Japanese immigrants, in Japanese, continued to flourish as it had from at least as far back as the start of the century; but, of course, this activity too, grew quiet among the issei when publications were suspended during World War II, the Japanese language in Hawai'i then being suppressed.[25] But starting from the three dozen or so Hawai'i Asian American writers whose poems in English appeared in the 1930s, a comparable number having appeared in the 1920s as well, only six poets were published in the 1940s, and still fewer than a dozen in the following decade.[26] Since then, the output has virtually erupted with a dramatic increase and growth in both the quantity and the quality of poetry of Hawai'i written by locals.

In another, related development in the Hawaiian Renaissance, among the new voices to be heard in the 1960s was Larry Lindsey Kimura's. Drawing upon his native Hawaiian heritage—and often upon his Waimea, Hawai'i homeland—Kimura is a recognized scholar and creator of contemporary mele in which he uses traditional and modern techniques. As early as 1967 the young poet published his work, beginning with "He Manawa Wale No." The accompanying English translation reveals the use of a "braided wreath" as a dominant motif or image, in the way the image would be used in traditional Hawaiian mele.[27]

Strong in undertones, Kimura's next published poem, "Kapalaoa," is preceded by an English narrative with Hawaiian dialogue in prose telling "The Legend of Kapalaoa."[28] The story is of Pele. Disguised as an old woman wandering the north Kona coast of Hawai'i, she is refused food by one at Kapalaoa who denies her requests for any scrap to eat by scolding her gruffly, "Everything is for the king!" Pele, "the three legged," the old woman walking with her cane, withdraws up Maunaloa and afterward destroys the royal family and those who denied her food: "She merely appears, merely disappears / Fiery blanket without corners / The devastating flow of Pele," Kimura writes, drawing a stunning image of the lava flow. Going also by his Hawaiian name, Kauanoe, Larry Lindsey Kimura has since the 1960s steadily developed his distinctive, traditional yet innovative composition and performance of Hawaiian poetry; and with the consistent growth of his creativity through this time, the poet and his poetry have already achieved an enduring quality.

One of Kimura's best-known poems might even be called a Hawai'i classic. Asked by Eddie Kamae in the mid–1970s to provide lyrics for a melody that had come to Kamae in a dream, Kimura after a month of thought composed "E Ku'u Morning Dew," spontaneously inspired, he says, by the sight of dew glistening on the grasses at sunrise in Waimea, Hawai'i, his birthplace.[29] The poem's theme is the dew's transience, which can be interpreted as the transience of a romance. Roughly paraphrased, in the poem the speaker calls out to the dew to wait, to linger a little while longer with him. When the dawn breaks red and gold, making cheeks rosy with the morning chill of Waimea, the speaker wishes there could be a place where he and the dew could remain together forever, fresh and cool. In many respects "E Ku'u Morning Dew" exemplifies the pastoral in native Hawaiian mele today.

As the *Kipu'upu'u*, the chilly wind and rain, the chicken-skin or goosebump-raising rain, is distinctive to Waimea, placing any song that mentions it immediately in that cool highland region, the chill that makes cheeks rosy in the dawn identifies "E Ku'u Morning Dew" as being of Waimea. The poem's dawn setting also elicited comment at the Talk Story Big Island Writers' Conference in 1979. Rather than painting sunsets, someone noted, Hawaiian poets more often greet the sunrise. The songs discussed at the conference reminded the audience that the usual Hawai'i resident's workaday world begins at sunrise, with its "plantation time" bred into two or more generations by the shrill call of the sugar mill's morning whistle. This rude local hour of awakening is perpetuated in the predawn rush-hour of traffic to work in Honolulu. By contrast, the sunset appears in Hawai'i travel posters, a red-orange visual convention crossed by palm trees and a lone sail. Ironically, this sunset convention is more "universally" recognized and associated with Hawai'i than the sunrise that connotes a kind of birth, freshness, and early morning labor —which together with the universal symbolism of the dew in Kimura's poem evidently is closer than the sunset to evoking a Hawaiian sensibility. Mark Twain, too, perceived this, it may be said, when he balked at the clichés by describing a sunset peeping through the coconut trees at Kealakekua as a "blooming whiskey bloat through the bars of a city prison," while the Haleakalā sunrise awed him as the most sublime spectacle he had ever witnessed.[30]

Contemporary poetry such as Kimura's has the distinction in Hawai'i of being immediately identifiable by nearly everyone as being rooted in the islands' native soil yet being understood only by a relatively small number of people who know the Hawaiian language. For the general public in Hawai'i, the identification of the song with the Hawaiian culture is so predominant that Kimura's poem is probably thought to be anonymous, like a traditional folk song. It would appear, then, that the kind of individual criticism or praise directed at Richard Fujii's 1934 poem, "Caravan," would not likely be aimed at Kimura's Hawaiian works, except in the stringent test of whether his lyrics set to Eddie Kamae's music were to gain favor in the popular Hawaiian entertainment business and record album sales. And here the Kamae / Kimura composition, "E Ku'u Morning Dew," has succeeded eminently.

The burgeoning poetry of Hawaii's Asian American writers today results from a distinctive set of circumstances, a different kind of pressure for public, community, family, and self-recognition from the more established place of the native Hawaiian poet, weaver of words or *haku mele*, in the culture's arts. By comparison, the Asian American poet seemed an oddity in his or her own culture at the time Kimura began publishing successfully in Hawaiian. But in 1976 Eric Chock won a City and County of Honolulu Poetry Prize with his "Poem for My Father," an achievement that brought serious local poetry once more into public attention and recognition for the first time since Fujii's ignominy in 1934.[31] Chock's theme is similar to James Mishima's in the dramatic sketch *Sunao*, from twenty-five years before Chock won his prize. A disdain —or discomfort—over writing as a serious endeavor continued from Fujii's time through Mishima's and into the 1970s, until Eric Chock wrote "Poem for My Father," won a prize, and showed his award to his father with a grin:

I lie dreaming
when my father comes to me and says,
I hope you write a book someday.
He thinks I waste my time,
but outside, he spends hours over stones,
gauging the size and shape a rock will take
to fill a space,
to make a wall of dreams around our home.
In the house he built with his own hands
I wish for the lure that catches all fish
or girls with hair like long moss in the river.
His thoughts are just as far and old
as the lava chips like flint off the hammer,
and he sees the mold of dreams
taking shape in his hands.
His eyes see across orchids on the wall,
into black rock, down to the sea,
and he remembers the harbor full of fish,
orchids in the hair of women thirty years before
he thought of me, this home, of stone walls.
Some rocks fit perfectly, slipping into place
with light taps of his hammer.
He thinks of me inside
and takes a big slice of stone,
pounds it into the ground
to make the corner of the wall.
I cannot wake until I bring
the fish and the girl home.

Although it is true enough that the act of writing has been compared elsewhere with building a masonry wall, in Chock's poem the
point of the comparison has a distinctive sound when the father clinks
his stones home, never dreaming that his son sleeping inside the house
might think his wall-building as much a useless, aesthetic, and creative
an activity as poem-writing. In the years following 1976, without explicit
fanfare outside of what Chock would say and read to his audiences on
numerous occasions, his "Poem for My Father" implicitly stood as a proclamation of a newly recognized value of poetry in Hawai'i. Most important, it brought attention to a poet who actually lived in the community,
who was strengthening rather than undermining or severing family ties
and community values, and who was doing so without treating these
matters uncritically, lightly, and easily. It came as no small pleasure, too,

that in Chock's description of his father's hefting stones and building a lava moss-rock wall, local readers in their imagining could touch something of what Chock through his poem was talking about. In style and subject the poem is "concrete" in a way that has come to typify much local poetry for now.

Another kind of poem brings the family's generations even closer together. In writing "Manoa Cemetery, for Moi Lum Chock," Chock was among the first local poets besides native Hawaiians to turn expressly to his pioneering ancestral heritage for a poetic subject and, in doing so, to relate it to the poet's own life and times.[32] This poem's first line is evocative, though its suggestions will not be known until one rereads the entire poem: "I am late as usual," the poet begins, "but no one makes an issue of my coming." The poet enters Mānoa Cemetery, where Chinese immigrants and pioneers lie buried. Stone after stone, one plot above another on the hillside is bright with offerings in the observance of Bai San in honor of the ancestors buried there:

> Candles are lit and incense burns
> around the stone.
> The rituals have begun.
> We offer five bowls of food;
> bamboo shoots and mushrooms
> we've cooked for you today.
> And there are five cups of tea
> and five of whiskey
> to nourish and comfort you
> on your journey.

The poet addresses his grandmother, dead now "a long year." He begins "to wonder who you are" and wishes to say things left unsaid at their parting. Everyone follows the prescribed ritual of offering and bowing, rites perhaps changed by faulty memory and further altered by actual practice, "Chinese" custom thus made local on that Mānoa hillside. Uniform rituals cannot fit every individual being honored that day. The poet feels "silly / to think I follow custom / pouring you a sip of whiskey / I never saw you drink." But he does remember his grandmother's prayers, and so the poet prays as she used to for their forebears. The hillside was given to a "Chinaman" by "an old Hawaiian king," who offered an immense wedge from the sea to the cleft of Mānoa Valley, the poet explains; and the Chinaman accepted only "enough / to bury my people." And now there must be thouasnds crowded on the hill, some of them the descendants of immigrants. "Even you, two generations before me, / were not born in China / but I think Hanalei," the poet wonders; "So what is it gains a place / among these laborers, merchants, tailors?"

The question is central to the poem. What ties these generations together, within generations and between generations? "The repetition of names" that "sprawls across the hillside," is one tie, the poet answers himself. The Chinese surnames are few, though the graves are many. He then sinks into a reverie about once seeing in himself the yearning for a child, "a baby in my lover's eyes":

> Now I keep an endless pain
> regretting great-grandchildren
> that were lost.
> I forget what I tried to save
> when I had to get on that plane
> and fly away. Forgive me.
> I cannot name the reasons.
> And if you
> who put your earthly life
> in taro and sugarcane
> deserve a burial and worship on this hill,
> surely I should have my ashes scattered from an airplane!

At some critical moment the poet must have flown off, straining the generational bonds between the grandmother's expectations and the grandson's inability or unwillingness to fulfill them. The poet has fostered regrets rather than the great-grandchildren the grandmother wanted but never got. Now the poet wonders about what ties these generations of his own family together, and he regrets something still, still childless, here again too late.

These thoughts and the grandmother's spirit living in the poet's memory are put to rest by the ritual of washing the gravestone, trimming the plot, offering food and drink, exploding firecrackers to drive evil spirits away, and burning paper money to ensure the grandmother's spiritual prosperity and good fortune. That done, "it's as if you were always dead," the poet says with rich irony, passions quieted by these yearly "rituals of fire."

While writing like Chock on themes such as heritage, family, and childhood, Jody Manabe is one of the most stylistically innovative of the local Hawai'i poets. Among her works, one is especially appropriate to this discussion: "Hadaka De Hanasu (talking nakedly), for Kiyoko."[33] It is dedicated to the poet's mother, with whom the poet would take long soaks in the household o-furo, their Japanese-style bath. There her mother once discussed the topic of having babies, and "Hadaka De Hanasu" is the poet's response to that frank talk:

> Tell me, water,
> Of this power you have over me.
> The sound of your voice
>   fills my mouth with honey,
>   my throat with a difficult roar.
>
> It is ours, Lioness,
> This madness we share
>   so deep in our blood
>   that we speak of babies
> As if they could hear?
>
> Filament breath of you,
> Tell me how they cling to the sides of your womb
>   pink eyeless things that steal your blood
>   while I lie here breathing beside you
>   easily your bulk, your water,
> It is ours?
>
> I have gathered the cloth together
>   in both hands I have made an octopus
>   out of air! Listen to the sound of it
> Against your lips.

Manabe and some other Hawaii's poets have been experimenting with and developing an abstract use of objects and images in poems like the one above. Elsewhere, however, when Manabe reminisces about certain memorable incidents and probes them with her poetry, she writes in a straightforward manner that nevertheless gets its power from its compactness, its snugly held visual elements, as in "Omiyage," the fifth and last part of a sequence of reminiscences called "Dear Reiko: 1968 / 1978."[34] The poem is a version of the childhood idyll; its title signifies a reciprocity, a giving of a gift in recognition of kindnesses shared in a relationship. The view of nature in the poem is anthropomorphic, in this case not a merging, but a deliberate paralleling of nature and people that comes to the poet from many cultural sources, including the native Hawaiian and romantic:

Your grandmother takes us
to her garden for the last time:
we squat among flat, wet leaves,
afraid of worms and centipedes
and potatoes that will not let go.
But she finds them easily—
her fingers emerge,
brown as the earth she has taken them from.
We turn to where the loquats dangle,
already the size of a man's thumb.
We pluck them from the trees
and poke them into egg cartons
where each pale fruit glistens
in its own moist compartment,
waiting.

Reluctant to leave,
we race the length of the field,
the cabbages clumsy and mute around us—
our brothers' heads! No arms to hurt us!
So we kick them toward the dim lines
of the mountains.
And there I see
our grandmothers,
their backs bent,
carrying the sky.

Still another variety of Hawaii's contemporary local poetry is epitomized by the work of Wing Tek Lum, who writes with a style so filled with intensity and so precisely cutting that it slices like a laser. Lum's "Grateful Here" is a good example of an aspect of his poetry that led during the 1970s to his being the most widely published Hawai'i poet to be found in nationwide Asian American poetry collections.[35] In "Grateful Here" he focuses each of five stanzas on a memory that reveals something about this poet's felt place or identity in America; the poem spans his entire native land, from Hawai'i to New York.

The first of the tight, seven-line stanzas describes how the poet, "Emerging from the subway station / then lost among the orange signs on Nedick's snackbars," would seek out "the thick rice soup and dumplings" of a lunch counter in New York City Chinatown by following his "Chinese nose." We can assume the food satisfies him. He is at home here where he eats. In the second stanza, two rites are juxtaposed that would seen incompatible if it were not for the plain fact that Lum and many others in Hawai'i and the rest of Asian America and, for that matter, throughout America live and perform some such combination of rites without fragmenting the wholeness of their full identities. First, the poet takes part in Bai San, the Chinese gravesite ritual as in Chock's "Manoa Cemetery." Indeed, Lum's observance is held at the same hillside. Second, immediately following the Bai San ceremonies on a Sunday morning, the poet participates in a Christian church service where he "sang in the choir and would carry, that day, / fragile lilies to the altar of my risen Lord." The child experienced that Sunday as an especially busy one which produced in him a unified impression the stanza evokes; the adult poet, recalling the coincidence of rites which makes the day thus memorable, implies, mainly by the control of understatement, that he knows how the experience of growing up in a multicultural world is misinterpreted to be a confusion of identities.

For the third stanza of "Grateful Here" begins to tighten the tension, still only undercurrent, of the poet's being misjudged, prejudged, and misunderstood on racist grounds, where he is seen by others either as an alien or as a product of two contradictory cultures, a dual personality and identity. The poet describes how, when he and "a Caucasian girl" would walk holding hands past "teenage hangouts, / overhearing insults. They would always pick on the girl, / as though she were a lesbian" —that is, as if he, a Chinese American man, were a woman. The couple pretends not to notice, "avoiding embarrassment / for the other, tightening our grips." The complex of racist issues and conflicts laid upon him and contained by Lum's understatements continues into the fourth stanza, where this time the poet remembers how, in the deliberately perpetrated sexual confusion of such racism,

> Observing two gay Negroes, powdered gray,
> and strutting regally in their high-heeled boots,
> I followed them half-enviously with my eyes,
> understanding, for the first time, that dark allure
> of nighttime caresses.

Then he proceeds to describe how he himself has similarly been stared at and described in terms alien to his own view of himself, in a rural Pennsylvania grocery store where housewives brought children—innocent of racism, we would ourselves be naive to think—"with small, craning necks to whisper about me" while they gawked.

The final stanza cuts through the bone: "After a sit-in at the

Pentagon, / the arresting marshal misspelt my name," it begins, with this detail about a misspelled name that every Asian American who has traveled outside his or her community in America must experience. Reminded thus that he is no doubt in one way or another seen as a foreigner, the poet adds with his icy irony, "Actually, though, I know I should feel grateful here." Perhaps he was even told that if he did not like it in America, he should "go back" to China—as so many were told regardless of race during those demonstrations of the 1960s, and as Asian Americans especially have been told throughout their history. The final lines of Lum's poem, however, with their highly refined tone of mock deference and their obliqueness, would probably further baffle the marshal attempting to process the arrested demonstrator—would baffle him, that is, if he even detected the sharp edge of what the poet says. The ending is a put-on, a diversion, a verbal triumph not by dispelling ignorance, but by placidly rising above it:

> Actually, though, I know I should feel grateful here.
> In fact, just last week on the radio, I heard
> that the Red Guards had broken the wrists
> of a most promising young pianist. Among other things,
> he once journeyed to Manila for a recital of Brahms.

Thus the poet pretends humbly and graciously to agree with those who say that he should be "grateful here," and his interrogator stands yet unaware that he has been cut through the bone with the poet's sarcasm. The poet knows some, like the marshal, would hear in these lines a comparison between two "Chinese" artists, the poet and the pianist. At the poem's core, however, inside a test Lum presents of false comparisons and false readings versus the true, is the similarity he draws between the Red Guards and the guardians of the Pentagon.

By virtue of his language, tone, voice, and subjects, Lum is an outstanding example of the poet in Hawai'i writing in an Asian American literary tradition which he himself sees articulated by Frank Chin and others, based on a distinct literary heritage reaching back into the nineteenth century in America, further back in China. Like native Hawaiians working within traditions they have studied, Murayama, Holt, and Saiki in their complex pastorals, the local authors of heroic narratives who also researched their subjects, and—in a strongly intuitive as well as researched way—Chock in his poetry and other literary activities, Wing Tek Lum in 1978 was rare among local writers in his informing his poetry with Asian American history however deeply subsumed within his understatement. This history, historiography, and historicity is a basis for the "Asian American literary tradition" and sensibility to which I am referring. Whether or not anyone is capable of perfecting it, the concept of history in this sensibility demands that a writer work interpretively with already known or researched historical facts in mind. This idea has been ridiculed for being the antithesis of what should be "literary," "creative," and "imaginative," but I for one am not persuaded by the ridicule.

Lum's historicity means, for a simple example, that since there were American laws forbidding the immigration of Chinese women from 1882 to World War II (when China became an ally and immigration was still nonetheless difficult, to say the least), a writer working within that epoch and with its consequences thereafter should know that the society of chauvinistic, aging bachelors in America's Chinatowns themselves did not live apart from Chinese women by their own preference. Simply to blame the Chinese immigrant pioneers of misogyny is false, in this reading of history, because the United States had and still has a great deal to do with the differential treatment of Chinese women and men by sheer force of American law, custom, and prejudice. And still Chinese American men and women survive, even while antagonism against them from some other Americans continues, based on fear of the yellow peril. Historical parameters tighten impassioned literary works such as Lum's, cold in mere appearance like an incandescent light, and can significantly result in an artists' insight into the human condition in America at a given setting which is further assumed to have consequences in current times. The tone of "Grateful Here" tells us that the poem is informed not by Lum's own discovery that he is mistaken for an alien on the mainland, but by a knowledge that this awareness is undercurrent and commonplace throughout his community: the poem is based upon Lum's knowing the development, dominance, and meaning of a "dual identity" theory about Asian Americans and the theory's historical consequences, for instance, in the Japanese American internment. Lum's ready example for this Asian American sensibility in the form of a novel is Louis Chu's *Eat a Bowl of Tea*, about a young Chinese American couple, their life together in New York City made possible by the tiny window open to her immigration between the end of World War II and the Communist takeover. With great will, Ben Loy and Mei Oi accomplish in their generation what was inconceivable until now: they begin to transform a bachelor society into one of children and families.[36] With outrageous fun, Chu tells the story. This version of an Asian American sensibility in literary works (though not often in the heated critical arguments about them) is characterized by a valuing of the heroic yet, interestingly, a continual satirizing, trickery, and play that are reminiscent of the pastoral, including that sense—born out of study, contemplation, and the solo act of writing —that history itself is a kind of continual transience.

No doubt it was my own distaste for the ahistorical, simplistic pastoral in Hawai'i that opened me to studying Asian American and Hawaii's Local literatures in my way; but I myself saw the participation of Asian American writers from the mainland in the Talk Story Conference of 1978 as a means to introduce an awareness and a questioning of literary, cultural, and social history into the development of Local literature and the reading of it in Hawaii's own terms, yet to be discovered.[37] Wing Tek Lum would not simply do this alone through his poetry, outside of which he was usually reticent, and neither could I by trying as I did to deliver this same message in the conference.

In a sense Lum's poetry brings us full circle, to before Richard Fujii's rather unfortunate experience in 1934. By the 1920s Hawaii's Chinese Students' Alliance, whose very name connotes political action, the agreement to join several parties each in power, was regularly publishing a yearbook, every volume of which contained poetry, short stories, sketches, essays, oratory, and now and then a drama, in what appears to have been a well-developed spirit of literary endeavor aiming to serve the Chinese American community. In the early years, poets of this group would sometimes cry out in impassioned exhortations that all Chinese worldwide should take up the revolutionary battles against warlords and provide overseas relief for disasters in China. The Chinese Students' Alliance's political fervor naturally applied to their Hawai'i home and circumstances as well.[38] The purpose of their own writing, wrote Lawrence Lit Lau in 1923, was to "interpret the romance and tragedy of our own people—their passions, sentiments, desires . . . to overthrow such misconceptions as others sometimes so stupidly bring on our heritage," and to "share in bringing about a mutual goodwill throughout the world."[39] The exhortative tone of the overtly political poems and esasys in those days perhaps has not had to be refined but has been replaced by the ironical tone of Wing Tek Lum, whose message today about our misunderstandings of one another is as pertinent as it was in the era of the Chinese Students' Alliance.

Recognition of a Hawai'i poet—a local, Asian American one— has clearly gone beyond the limitations those categories have often been mistakenly thought to entail. Cathy Song in 1982 won the Yale Series of

Younger Poets Award for her first volume, assuring the national reading and readership her work deserves. Song's work includes poems having to do with a local setting and poems inspired by pictures—for instance photographs, home movies, woodblock prints, and paintings—which often serve to remind the poet of Asian and Asian American heritage, of childhood, and of forebears. Like Eric Chock, Wing Tek Lum, Jody Manabe, and Diane Mei Lin Mark, another contemporary in Hawaii's Asian American poetry of the early and mid–1970s, Song is a pioneer among a generation reexamining its heritage and furthering rather than merely preserving a literary tradition in doing so.

Her two poems appearing in *Talk Story: An Anthology of Hawaii's Local Writers*, and published again five years later in her *Picture Bride*, are rather conspicuous in the Talk Story collection for several of their qualities. One, "Lost Sister," focuses first squarely on China.[40] Song's voice resonates with a confidence rare among her generation when trying to speak of a perhaps never visited or otherwise distant ancestral land. "In China," the poet asserts, "even the peasants / named their first daughter, Jade—." She proceeds to tell us how the stone for which the daughters are named could cause men to work miracles, moving entire mountains in mining it, "the healing green of the inner hills, / glistening like slices of winter melon." She tells, then, with an irony like Wing Tek Lum's, of how the "grateful" daughters never left home, their feet bound to rob them of movement: "But they travelled far / in surviving, / learning to stretch the family rice, / to quiet the demons / the noisy stomachs" of all those they fed. The poem's second part tells of the one considered the "Lost Sister," the one who crossed the ocean, "who relinquished her name, / diluting jade green / with the blue of the Pacific." Locustlike, she swarmed with other Chinese "to innundate another shore," where, "In America, / there are many roads / and women can stride along with men."

The apparent freedom of unbound feet, however, is a delusion, for America is "another wilderness" where "the possibilities, / the loneliness, / can strangulate like jungle vines." Fears and terrors crowd around the newcomer to the land, to its cities, where

> A giant snake rattles above,
> spewing black clouds into your kitchen.
> Dough-faced landlords
> slip in and out of your keyholes,

making claims you don't understand,
tapping into your communication systems
of laundry lines and restaurant chains.

The poet addresses the sister lost in America: "You find you need China: / your one fragile identification / a jade link / handcuffed to your wrist." But whatever was the cause for the sister's departure from China—the desire perhaps to break those links, to unbind her feet—her steps are irrevocable:

You remember your mother
who walked for centuries,
footless—
and like her,
you have left no footprints,
but only because
there is an ocean in between,
the unremitting space of your rebellion.

Song's other poem in the *Talk Story* anthology incorporates neither an Asian, Asian American, nor local Hawai'i speaker but rather a visitor placed in a local setting nicely fitting this particular individual. The poem is titled "from A Georgia O'Keeffe Portfolio: Flower Series, No. 3, An Orchid (Makena Beach, Maui)"[41] In it O'Keeffe the painter is pictured sitting at the beach and trying to protect herself from the sun as she scans the scene around her. Wearing a hat like a halo and "sensible shoes" she dislikes having to wear but must in order to protect her feet from the heat, in mock ceremony she crosses herself with ti leaves, "a gesture they [the local people on the beach] do not understand," while the native fishermen launch their canoes at dawn. The portrait Song paints of the painter is of a self-possessed observer studying the scene with a great deal of patience, for nothing much happens at all, all day long, except the coming of children who, "Strung along the beach like cowrie shells, / . . . / squat and brood for hours," and the beckoning of the Filipino women who chatter in the shade of ironwoods as they shred coconuts "for the noon fire. Their bird language / rises with the smoke / that spirals up in the blue air. . . . "

But her self-possession may really be just a diminished thing, an isolation, an alienation, from all the other elements in the scene. Resourcefully, in deliberate acts of self-sufficiency, the painter takes her colors from what she calls her "side of the beach": "I comb the tidepools for algae, / pound the blue organs of jelly fish / into pulps for seagreen pastels," as though she wanted somehow to make her painting and its subject and object into one, indivisible thing. She finds herself in a paradoxical world—or rather finds herself to be a paradox in that setting. The painter echoes Keats's knight in "La Belle Dame sans Merci": "These islands have swollen my appetite; / still, each fish, fruit and flower / diminishes me." Her appetite for something more than any earthly paradise can possibly supply causes her to yearn for more as she sits there alone in the shade with her easel. The poem ends with the painter wishing the bright sun would allow her to "crawl out of my sensible shoes / and wear the humid stillness / like the young wahines / running to meet the first canoes" that return now from fishing. Distant from ever experiencing what those native wahine surely take for granted in running to the water and greeting the returning fishermen day after day, the painter draws suddenly close and intimate to them in her imagination, and only in her imagination: "They bear the sweet sour / odor of mangoes / that rises from welcoming limbs." In Hawaii's local literature, next to Bushnell's creation of John Forrest, Song's creation of Georgia O'Keeffe as this poem's speaker is the best example of the rendering of the viewpoint of the visitor to Hawaii's shores, the visitor as seen by the local writer.

I would like to think it somehow fitting that this entire discussion of Hawaii's literature, the pastoral and the heroic, should draw to a close with the poem above demonstrating Cathy Song's achievement especially in "from Georgia O'Keeffe . . . An Orchid." The poem suggests a kind of catholicity and range that help to break the critical stranglehold that threatened to choke Local literature again, just as it was reborn in the 1970s. No sooner had the literature reappeared, this time with more public acknowledgment and open readings and discussions than ever before, than some voices rained down on the event, once more criticizing the literature of Hawai'i for being insular, provincial, not univerasl, and so forth. I hope this discussion may serve in some way to dispel such false criticism, which in the final analysis speaks of Hawaii's people as if they were not human beings at all, but were meaningful and meaningless only as figments of others' dreams of islands.

4

For six chapters I have been analyzing but one aspect, the "literary" as I understand the term, of a sweeping Hawaiian cultural renaissance which, while based in part on the teachings and heritage of the islands' ancients, encompasses all of Hawaii's peoples and brings with it political and economic ramifications as well. The first Talk Story Conference was certainly energetic. But beyond that step, a year later some of us came at last to begin perceiving this energy as power based on an accumulating knowledge.

By midsummer of 1979, barely a year after Bushnell seemed in his keynote address all but to announce even his own retirement from writing, a note was sounded that was wholly different from the many-mouthed first Talk Story Conference. This was the Talk Story Big Island Writers' Conference. A new knowledge and confidence in a Local literary history was evident, for instance, when midway through the Big Island Conference Harvey Hess, a teacher and poet, introduced his teachers and fellow writers among the issei haiku poets of Hilo. He carefully noted that the issei, too, along with native Hawaiians, play a vital role in the *paideia* or literary foundation of the current Hawaiian Renaissance.[42] And even so, this literary material published by the issei is relatively young —not locally conceived until the late nineteenth century with the arrivals of Japanese immigrants, and not born until issei founded the Hilo haiku club in 1903—compared with the centuries-old native Hawaiian oral traditions and the great literary traditions of the East and the West, both with currents that run also through Hawai'i.

At the 1979 Talk Story Big Island Writer's Conference a copy of Arnold Hiura's and my *Asian American Literature of Hawaii* was displayed.[43] We had begun our full-time work on this annotated bibliography a year earlier, when Bushnell worried for all of us about who else in history had been writing among us. Joking and fretting that Bushnell may have been right, what we had then thought might result in a two-, ten-, or twelve-page publication became, even to our own surprise (we were sometimes treated patronizingly for being "promoters" of Local literature), a bibliography with 740 entries in a book of 210 pages. An update today, some ten years later, would increase it perhaps by another third, because activities on behalf of Hawaii's literatures have indeed made a difference. With knowledge in hand, we had the power to change some mistaken ideas and introduce some new ones, thereby disrupting certain cycles of reinventing the literary wheels that had already been spinning for a while with their tires flat. But some problems do not change. Flush with foolish optimism, and with indignation as well, in 1979 I felt that the bibliography would disprove forever Michener's erroneous claim about the lack of (and not the discouragement of, which Bushnell really charged) literature by Hawaii's Asian Americans and other peoples; yet to this day, as Bushnell warned, Michener is ignorant of or simply ignores any other novels of Hawai'i but his own, and he seems able to get away with stating such falsehoods even today in Hawai'i.[44]

But as serious as it is, that aggravation and its source are trivial compared with what I witnessed at the time of the 1979 Talk Story Conference in Hilo. The conference was dedicated to Edith Kanaka'ole, the *kupuna* or elder in chant and hula from Ka'ū, the southernmost shores of the island and of the United States, and the first place where Pele, followed afterwards by the Polynesian people, landed at the end of the journey from Bora Bora.[45] Kanaka'ole had passed away shortly before the conference; still it was evident, in the polyethnic programs and in our feelings, that the traditions she represented were the bedrock of this gathering in a way that no single tradition had or could have been a year earlier.

Our daily seminar on the literature of the island of Hawai'i turned one morning to the subject of the pastoral, where Patsy Saiki and John Dominis Holt were among the featured participants. At sunrise on that Friday in July 1979, the seminal idea for this book—and a fresh awareness of a need for serious reading and criticism of Hawaii's literature—occurred to me, and I was very lucky to be able to return to the conference and begin tentatively to discuss the light and the dark sides of the Big Island setting with my elders and colleagues. That night, members of the Hilo Bon Dance Club demonstrated with drums, dance, and song the astonishing, profoundly moving fact that since World War II the issei of Hilo have been composing and performing live, during their annual o-bon festival held that very weekend in July, an epic story of their sons who went to war for their country, America, in one of the seasons the sugar cane tasseled in its two-year cycle of growth in a certain Big Island field. It was certainly not a difficulty with English, but perhaps a difficulty with Japanese—the archaic, local poetic diction of the issei wailing high up in the *yagura* around which the dancers circle to the delirious skirl of *fue* and boom of *taiko*—that caused nisei and sansei to neglect this continuing local and American epic poem for thirty years while yet they danced to what they thought was the imported *Iwakuni Ondo* folksong of Yamaguchiken. That night, too, I saw a long, silent look I hesitate to interpret on the face of Saburo Higa, a Hilo *tanka* (31-syllable verse) poet of the Gin-u Shi Sha or Silver Rain [Tanka] Society, an Okinawan immigrant, and a 1935 graduate in English of the University of Washington as he held our bibliography in his hands. I like to think that as a person spending a lifetime in the love of literature, he was at that moment gauging the weight of a work of scholarship long overdue in Hawaii's literary history. And I had to apologize that our bibliography did not even include works such as his, written in other languages than English. Shortly after the Talk Story Big Island Writers' Conference, back in Honolulu, I rushed to see Bushnell. When I gave him a copy of the bibliography, he, too, had that look on his face for a long moment: "Who would have thought so much has been written, so much?" he said quietly. And when in that hour he heard my plans to write a broader critical study he urged me not to mention his name so much in it, because there is no need to.[46]

Following upon the Big Island conference, that moment with Bushnell represents to me a recognition that our "deaf ear" as readers was now by rights all *pau*, finished. His target was not really the Talk Story writers listening to him, but it was readers and critics whom Bushnell had indicted in his keynote address for not having done their part. Until 1979, writers of Hawai'i had been anxious enough about silence or deafness that the instances (including Bushnell's speech) of the theme I tell earlier in this chapter were once rather common. To say, however, that silence is now "broken" is a misleading cliché, since even the expressions of the theme of silence have been published in full voice for years.

Their voices long neglected or unempowered as "forgotten pages" (as Gerald W. Haslam wryly put it) of American literature, portions of Hawaii's literature are hardly unique in how they have been and, in contrast, how they ought to be treated. But where is the state of the art and criticism now? Challenges to the American literary canon have been raised nearly everywhere in the 1980s, and one would think that this challenge should apply strongly to Hawaii's contemporary literatures. Canonical issues are nevertheless largely the responsibility of critics and scholars, who in Hawaii's and, in general, ethnic American literary studies have been far more scarce than writers, it seems—the reverse of the boast or the complaint that in any year thousands study and may attempt to publish articles on, say, one Shakespeare, one Melville, one Dickinson, or one Twain. Whatever the heightened activity among local writers of Hawai'i in the recent decade, it is criticism that has lacked the extent, kind, and quality needed to reverse the spiral Bushnell indicated—lack of readers leads to lack of publishers' interest in the literature, and lack of readers and publishers discourages writers, which leads to a further diminution of interest, making it possible for *outside* writers to visit and claim the territory because it is thought to be empty.[47] Among the readers

Bushnell challenged are critics and scholars whose honest job it may well be to interest readers at large in Hawaii's literary works and traditions, if it is at all true that critics mediate in some ways between authors and audiences. It is simply a tautology, only another closed circle, to say that fresh interest cannot come from criticism based on reinventing the already canonical wheel. When examined anew from the points of view of literary works and sensibilities that have till now been denied a voice in it, the literary canon and the canonized assumptions that are its counterparts in historiography themselves become part of the renaissance: and this refreshing and renewing, this reborn attempt even, for instance, to understand mere fragments of the "novel" Twain announced he had written about Hawai'i, is what "renaissance" means. It does not mean the resurrection, preservation of, or addition to any canon, which implies the existence of saints in a religion, so to speak—when the very exclusiveness of any single "religion" or mythology is precisely in question, and not in my first chapter or in this entire study alone. The roles awaited of criticism are many. Milton Murayama and Dawn Pyne were able to prove virtually on their own that the localism of his novel does not prevent widespread reading of it. But publishing, publicizing, marketing, and criticizing his own pidgin discourse should not be mainly his responsibility while we "critics" add to the burden by asking him to explain himself and his work to us even as we anxiously await his most valued literary part: further fictive words from him, the artist. Not only the literature of Hawai'i but also the criticism of that literature have yet to be recognized for what they both contain and express: a cultural criticism through literary creation and study that no society, whether its verbal arts are oral or written (and Hawai'i is fortunate to have both), can afford for long to go without.

The fact is that great Hawaiian novels and their counterparts in short fiction, poetry, and drama have already been written. They very possibly will be surpassed when the extant literature, literary history, theory, and criticism are themselves taken critically and seriously and are comprehended by authors, some of them already active, of works yet to come. These authors of Hawai'i, of diverse ethnicities and places of birth (and, I might as well add, regardless of whether everything they write is about Hawai'i) have dared to intuit beyond the entrenched *simple* pastoral notions of Hawai'i; they have thus made it possible to challenge the sentimentalized, false, and meaningless past that is formidable, but only for being ensconced as a smartly commercial commodity in the tourist paradise that Hawai'i has become dependent upon mimicking. The balmy dreams of these islands deny the local writer a voice because they reduce the local to less than human, and they render the natural Hawaiian social setting unrecognizable and truly unspeakable, whether in reality or in conception to the resident. Local writers of Hawaii's complex pastoral and heroic traditions—among them one "whose name I forget," Ozzy Bushnell says, after naming all others he can think of except himself —and their books, too, have been around for at least a lifetime, their ways prepared by predecessors whose identities and roles are only now being recognized.

It is time again, as it was for Melville, Jarves, Twain, and of course more immediately for native Hawaiian and other local writers, to be blunt about how vital this recognition and its consequences are. In spite of longstanding boasts of cultural diversity and racial tolerance, Hawai'i—perhaps still vending the image of life without a care in the world—may continue to be patronized as being insular, "a paradise of fools," when in the twenty-first century the rest of the United States will have to awaken to the colliding facts of cultural pluralism and social (particularly racial) inequalities, because "minorities" will be perceived, however belatedly, to be a majority presence everywhere. If it really is true that Hawai'i (or America as a whole) has already been experiencing such pluralism *and* has been learning from it, the contrary image of a Hawai'i vacant of life's complexities would mean a loss to Hawai'i, the nation, the world; for the need to understand and not merely boast about pluralism is already immensely complex indeed, but *awareness* of the need is not yet widespread at all. Diversity, even when recognized and celebrated, does not automatically mean equality in anything. There is a lesson and a warning to be learned about the deepening complexion of America in the currents of how Hawaii's literary traditions have arisen and fared, and in the insights and treatments Hawaii's writers have achieved by their explorations of these very themes of a multiracial world.

We perhaps cannot, and most of us ultimately would not want to return to the system of self-sufficiency Polynesians developed on high volcanic islands by establishing and following strict measures governing every act, where I know I would have to become a taro farmer with soles blackened permanently by the mud ground into my cracked and splitting skin during most of my waking hours, all devoted to feeding our community. In Hawai'i the system was called the *ahupua'a*, symbolized by what the word literally means: a trussed pig placed on a pile of stones at a place where the *konohiki* (the manager in charge of maintaining the sufficiency of that particular pie-shaped wedge of land from the shore to the crotch of the valley and higher) would collect his pay, in the form of that pig, from the common people. Singapore, in our time, comes to mind as an island nation where, with laws many outsiders consider Draconian, the government and the people seem successful in keeping things clean, all trussed up, ready to be hefted away, cooked, eaten, and somehow recycled. And yet—even in the centuries of the *ahupua'a*, when from the point of view of the *maka'āinana* or commoner there was no excess but one, and that was the material exaction of the chiefs and priests, whose productivity was metaphysical at most—even then, the Hawaiian culture was rich in chants, dance, poetry, history, myth, legend, and countless other arts. It seems to me that in this is a recognition —from a people's actual hard experience of living on islands—that the arts, too, are absolutely necessary for survival. I was told this, explicitly and beautifully, on a very small island where I too was stranded without a boat once in my life. And the lesson I was told—that together we shall eat stones and drink seawater should we run out of rice and sweetwater, but without our sharing of stories and jokes, words and laughs, we go crazy and die—is meant not merely for that island called Marore, but for this island we call "the world." There is the possibility that understandings of the polyethnic literatures of Hawai'i in particular, in a microcosmic, paradigmatic way, may improve what always needs improvement: the quality of imagination, the intellect, values, art, and life in the communities where writers and readers must actively cultivate views by their interpretive and expressive use of words from their shores.

Lawa

Notes

PREFACE

1. Toni Morrison, "Unspeakable Things Unspoken: The Afro-American Presence in American Literature," *Michigan Quarterly Review* 28.1 (1989):1–34.

2. The titles of my book and Ronald Takaki's resemble each other purely by coincidence (*Strangers from a Different Shore: A History of Asian Americans.* Boston: Little, Brown, 1989). Takaki and I, being locals, both grew up on Hawaii's shores. The term, the idiom, the metaphor of the shore as margin would occur to us—and others—in common (e.g., Stewart's *Passage to the Dream Shore*). But the situation and point of view implied by Takaki's title differ from mine. "And the view from the shore" almost chose itself. Various readers and hearers of one version or another of my manuscript from 1982 to 1985 remarked to me about the moment in chapter 1 where a shift in point of view occurs. This inspired my title.

3. Because of racism such a "choice" is not everyone's. I know of an interesting case in Washington State where a Japanese immigrant father, angry and frustrated at the racism that denied him the privilege of becoming a naturalized citizen of the United States, changed the family's name from Nishimura to its English equivalent, "Weston," the name he had already given his son, who then became known legally as Weston Weston. Despite this clever trick the family was not spared from the internment of Japanese Americans during World War II; and Weston Weston later regained his prewar Japanese American name. The father's act was perhaps a parody of suicide: his story makes a deliberate mockery of choosing one's fate when there is no choice—whether of one's birth, one's race, or the fact of one's death.

4. For a discussion of "recognition" versus "acceptance"—pluralism versus assimilation, as contrasted in these terms—see Jeffery Chan et al., "Resources for Chinese and Japanese American Literary Traditions," in *Amerasia* 8, no. 1 (1981):19–31.

273

MYTHS AT FIRST SIGHT

1. From Nathaniel B. Emerson, ed. and trans., *The Unwritten Literature of Hawaii: The Sacred Songs of the Hula* (Washington, D.C.: Bureau of American Ethnology, 1909; rpt. Rutland, VT: Charles E. Tuttle, 1965), 187.

2. For another discussion of Western dreams of Pacific islands and islanders, see Gavan Daws, *A Dream of Islands: Voyages of Self-Discovery in the South Seas* (New York: W. W. Norton, 1980).

3. For a concise yet wide-ranging discussion of Europeans' first direct contact with "Indians" and Asians around the world, including the Native Americans Columbus encountered living in what he proclaimed to be Edenic conditions, see Arthur E. Christy, "The Sense of the Past," in *The Asian Legacy and American Life* (New York: John Day, 1945), 1–55. Because Christy's essay and the other essays collected in this volume are concerned primarily with Asia, the discussions are especially pertinent to views expressed of Asians in Hawai'i, in Hawaii's literature.

4. John Winthrop, "A Modell of Christian Charity," in *Winthrop Papers*, 1623–1630, vol. 2 (n.p.: Massachusetts Historical Society, 1931), 295, 293. I have modernized the spelling in the quoted passages.

5. James Cook, *The Journals of Captain James Cook on His Voyage of Discovery*, vol. 3., pt. 1, *The Voyage of the Resolution and Discovery 1776–1780*, ed. J. C. Beaglehole, Hakluyt Society Series (Cambridge: Cambridge University Press, 1967), 264. Unless otherwise specified, further quotations of Cook's journals are from Beaglehole's authoritative, modern edition. References to page numbers are hereafter provided in the text of this study.

6. See Leo Marx's interpretation of the *Pequod*, in his *The Machine in the Garden: Technology and the Pastoral Ideal in America* (New York: Oxford University Press, 1967), 285–87. In the "fictive world" of *Moby Dick*, Marx points out, "the ship occupies a place like that of 'Concord' in *Walden*."

7. The idea of the "complex pastoral" which Marx discusses includes the observation that a pastoral retreat is an end in itself in the simple pastoral, but not in the complex. Heroes in complex literary pastorals, like Henry David Thoreau upon his "return" to Concord society after his "retreat" at Walden Pond, put into practice what their contemplations have taught them of life and society. Thoreau's purposeful actions gave life to certain literary pastoral ideas, such that his civil disobedience following the experiences recounted in *Walden* has served as nothing less than a guide for social and political activism admired by Gandhi. As in Milton's *Paradise Regained*, the hero's strength and ambition mature into moral and spiritual power through his or her wilderness sojourn—where the complex pastoral figure experiences not merely contemplation but also the tests and conflicts that narrative and dramatic genres require.

8. See Robert C. Suggs, *The Island Civilizations of Polynesia* (New York: New American Library, 1960), 86ff.

9. For a fine commentary on Cook's development of a plain and functional writing style through his journal writing on three Pacific voyages, see J.C. Beaglehole, *Cook, the Writer* (Sydney: Sydney University Press, 1970).

10. Daws, *A Dream of Islands*, 3.

11. See, for instance, the 1784 edition of Cook's journals in *A Journal to the Pacific Ocean Undertaken, by the Command of His Majesty, for Making Discoveries in the Northern Hemisphere to Determine the Position and Extent of the West of North America; its Distance from Asia, and the Practicability of a Northern Passage to Europe*, vol. 2 (London: W. and A. Strahan, 1784), 192, where Hawaii's natives are described as having "visages not . . . very unlike those of Europeans" and as being evidently innocent of knowing iron's use as the material for weapons. Perhaps using the hindsight that, of course, Cook could never have on his entire Hawai'i experience, the 1784 editor wanted to prepare the way for the ensuing tragedy of Cook's death at the Hawaiians' hands by showing the natives first to pose no threat or danger to the European visitors. In our own time, O. A. Bushnell's novel, *The Return of Lono* (1956; rpt. Honolulu: University of Hawaii Press, 1979), and Aldyth Morris's monodrama, *Captain Cook* (1977), continue the tradition of interpretation of Cook and his significance through Hawaii's imaginative historical literature. Bushnell's and Morris's works are discussed in chapter 5 of my book.

12. See J. C. Beaglehole's introduction to his edition of Cook's *Journals*, clxi–ccx. According to Beaglehole, John Douglas was closest to Cook in the plain style of his editing, but other editors' embellishments of the journals of the Pacific explorers helped to launch Western mythological views of the Pacific islands. Beaglehole elsewhere recounts how editor John Hawkesworth, a playwright, transformed the journals of British explorers Byron, Wallis, Carteret, and Cook for consumption by the "polite world" (*Cook, the Writer*, 9–12). Beaglehole relates Hawkesworth's version of Cook's first voyage, when Cook "sighted a party of Maori women collecting shellfish, how instantaneously he was reminded of the chaste Diana and her nymphs" (*Cook, the Writer*, 10–11). The captains, when they returned again from sea and read the published version of their journals, did not appreciate what Hawkesworth had done. The editor in turn was mortified by the criticism leveled at his work by those who had actually lived the adventures he rewrote. Beaglehole adds a final comment that whether Hawkesworth shortly thereafter "died of chagrin, as was widely noised about, we have no real means of knowing" (*Cook, the Writer*, 11). For King's and Clerke's journals of Cook's fateful third voyage to the Pacific, see Beaglehole's edition of *The Journal of Captain James Cook*, vol. 3.

13. Samuel M. Kamakau, *Ruling Chiefs of Hawaii* (Honolulu: Kamehameha Schools Press, 1961). Originally written and published as Hawaiian newspaper columns in and around the 1860s, Kamakau's history is presented here in an English translation by various Hawaiian scholars. See Malcolm Naea Chun, "He Mo'olelo No S. M. Kamakau, He Mo'oku'auhau: A Biographical Essay

of S. M. Kamakau, Historian," in *I ka Wa o Kamehameha: In the Time of Kamehameha, Selected Essays by Samuel M. Kamakau*, ed. Malcolm Naea Chun (Honolulu: Folk Press, Kapiolani Community College, 1988), 11–22. Citing *Kuokoa*, a nineteenth-century Hawaiian newspaper, Chun notes that Kaneakahoowaha, a *kupunakane* (grandparent or granduncle) of Kamakau, was with the priest Ku-'ohu and the chief Ki'ikiki at that first meeting with Cook (12). This elder may well have been one of Kamakau's prime eyewitness sources for the events reported and discussed here; Kamakau's prose has the verve of being drawn directly from such sources within a Hawaiian oral tradition.

14. The editors of Kamakau's history note that "Moa-'ula-nui-akea is the land of Raiatea of the Society Islands from which Moikeha migrated to Hawaii" (93n). Raiatea neighbors Tahiti; both are of the Society group, from which Hawaii's Polynesians are said to originate. Migratory waves, which included return voyages to Tahiti, began as early as the third century A.D., according to archaeological data, and continued through some two centuries thereafter. See Eleanor C. Nordyke, *The Peopling of Hawaii* (Honolulu: University of Hawaii Press, 1977), 5–11.

15. David[a] Malo, *Hawaiian Antiquities (Moolelo Hawaii)* (ca. 1838; trans. Nathaniel B. Emerson, 1898 [Honolulu: Bernice P. Bishop Museum, 1951]), 144–45. Malo's manuscript, in Hawaiian, dates back to the late 1830s or early 1840s, according to Malcolm Naea Chun, editor of a Hawaiian text of *Ka Mo'olelo Hawai'i* (Hawaiian Antiquities), by Davida Malo (Honolulu: Folk Press, Kapiolani Community College, 1987).

16. Abraham Fornander, *An Account of the Polynesian Race, Its Origin and Migrations and the Ancient History of the Hawaiian People to the Times of Kamehameha I*, vol. 2 (1879; rpt. Rutland, VT: Charles E. Tuttle, 1969), 158, 165–67.

17. Although Fornander cites Malo's *Moolelo Hawaii* as the source from which he quotes, I am unable to find any passages there resembling what Fornander provides. Fornander, however, has been taken as an authoritative source for Malo's narrative of Cook's arrival. J. C. Beaglehole, for instance, turns to Fornander in order to quote the Malo narrative in full (Cook, *Journals*, 266 n. 1). Malcolm Naea Chun, current translator and editor of Malo, speculates that perhaps Fornander not only quoted from a version of Kamakau for one source but also misattributed another version of Kamakau's narrative to Malo. Malo wrote very little that survives about Cook because in the Hawaiian historical society to which both Malo and Kamakau belonged the members were assigned different subjects. Kamakau dealt mainly with the relatively modern times to which Cook belonged, while Malo drew the work of compiling the ancient traditions. My own interest, meanwhile, is in the differing interpretations of events told in various published versions drawn from native Hawaiian sources in the nineteenth century. These versions were then current and were evidently not perceived to be unanimous.

18. Beaglehole adds his own succinct comment: "Whatever the success

the young lady might have had with Lono, it is very certain she could not have had much with Cook" (Cook, *Journals*, 266 n.1).

19. Such a "Self Discovery" is a theme in Gavan Daws's biographies of Westerners who deeply experienced the Pacific and its islanders, in *A Dream of Islands*.

PARADISE OF THE PACIFIC?

1. James Fenimore Cooper, *The Crater: Or, Vulcan's Peak; a Tale of the Pacific*, 2 vols. (New York: Burgess, Stringer, 1847).

2. Daws, *A Dream of Islands*, 76.

3. Howard Mumford Jones, *The Age of Energy: Varieties of American Experience 1865–1915* (New York: Viking Press, 1971), 285. Harrison Hayford notes that Melville was known in his day as the author and hero of *Typee* more than as the creator of *Moby Dick*, in Hayford's Afterword to *Typee: A Peep at Polynesian Life During a Four Month's Residence in a Valley of the Marquesas*, by Herman Melville (New York: New American Library, 1964), 309.

4. See Daws's *A Dream of Islands* for a facsimile of La Farge's painting, "Fayaway Sails Her Boat," n.p.n. Jones calls Fayaway "perhaps the most perfect representation of sensuous female loveliness in the American nineteenth century" (*The Age of Energy*, 285). The character who mirrors the protagonist's preconceptions is a recurrent type in literature. For instance, David Henry Hwang's *M. Butterfly*, the 1988 Tony Award–winning Broadway hit, features just such a theme as Melville tries to expose through the inherently narcissistic relationship of Tommo with Fayaway and thus with the Typee generally. Interestingly, *M. Butterfly* also shares with *Typee* a peculiar fate: despite the authors' overt condemnations of the Western male protagonist's misreading of the presumed Asian or Pacific female, their audiences, too, fall in love with the illusion in a way Bertholt Brecht, for example, tried to avoid by distancing rather than merging audience and work. In the nineteenth century, adventurous American tourists actually searched for Melville's fictitious, blue-eyed Fayaway in Taipivai. Today the sheer theatrical spectacle of a "Chinese woman" stripping to reveal a Chinese man is a lasting image from Hwang's play. The vivid central tricksterism of sexual disguise tends to be confused for the theme itself, which, baldly stated in the play, is that the French male protagonist tricks himself into believing the Chinese actor to be an actress with whom he has a long love affair, for in "her" he sees only and exactly what he wants to.

5. This sense of the appropriateness, decorum, and sufficiency of a human dwelling is much admired in the Western pastoral tradition, even from rustic to the "civilized." See, for example, an upper-class treatment in Andrew Marvell's "Upon Appleton House."

6. A. O. Lovejoy points out that the basic element of "cultural primitivism" is "the discontent of the civilized with civilization, or with some conspicuous and characteristic feature of it. It is the belief of men living in a relatively highly evolved and complex cultural condition that a life far simpler and less sophisticated in some or in all respects is a more desirable life." In addition to being America's first full-length rendition of the "actual exotic," *Typee* is the nation's first full-length expression of cultural primitivism applied to Pacific islands and peoples. This American cultural primitivism itself, however, does not originate with Melville. Rather, it is in part transferred to a new, Oceanic setting from earlier and contemporary American ones: the frontiers and the plains where our Natty Bumppos and Chingachgooks stalk their game and spurn the American civilization that creeps upon them. It is no wonder that Cooper wrote of a primitivist Pacific frontier in *The Crater*. See Arthur O. Lovejoy et al., eds., *A Documentary History of Primitivism and Related Ideas* (Baltimore: Johns Hopkins Press, 1935), 1:7.

7. Melville in his underlying assumptions again departs from classical forms of cultural primitivism, where, Lovejoy observes, "The individual in primitive society has often—by those who have known little of the complexity and terrible force of primitive tabus—been pictured as relatively exempt from constraint by the social group, more free to do as he pleases" (Lovejoy, 9). Probably because he observed firsthand the Typee culture, including its tabus, Melville questions and subverts the naive views of the "primitive," such as Lovejoy describes.

8. A. Grove Day, *Books about Hawaii: Fifty Basic Authors* (Honolulu: University of Hawaii Press, 1977), 10–12. For further background on Jarves, see the *DAB*.

9. James J. Jarves, *Kiana: A Tradition of Hawaii* (Boston: James Munroe, 1857).

10. Philip K. Ige, "Paradise and Melting Pot in the Fiction and Non-Fiction of Hawaii: A Study of Cross-Cultural Record" (Ph.D. diss., Columbia University, 1968), 40. As far as I know, Ige's was the only available comprehensive study of Hawaii's literature when I began my work on the topic. By "comprehensive" I mean that Ige discusses works and authors of a widely representative variety of cultures, races, and origins.

11. On the question of European "discovery" of Hawai'i predating Cook's, see E. W. Dahlgren, *The Discovery of the Hawaiian Islands* (New York: AMS Press, 1917), originally published as *Were the Hawaiian Islands Visited by the Spaniards Before Their Discovery by Captain Cook in 1778?* (Stockholm: Almquist and Wiksells, 1916). Dahlgren disputes the idea of Spanish discovery, usually associated with the sailor Juan Gaytan of Kiana's time. Writing of "Roman Catholicism in Hawaii," however, in his *Ruling Chiefs of Hawaii*, Samuel Kamakau identifies not only early Spanish arrivals, but also Jewish ones, long predating Cook (*Ruling Chiefs*, 324–25).

12. The Hawaiians' prior acquaintance with iron when Cook arrived has often prompted speculations about who introduced such materials before 1778. See Dennis M. Ogawa, *Kodomo no Tame Ni, For the Sake of the Children: The Japanese American Experience in Hawaii* (Honolulu: University of Hawaii Press, 1978), 1–2, for a narrative sketch of shipwrecks of Japanese on Hawaii's shores in ancient times. These Japanese are supposed also to have introduced certain cultural artifacts and motifs to Hawai'i. Ogawa echoes a 1933 study by John F. G. Stokes on "Japanese Cultural Influence in Hawaii," which Ogawa cites, and Ernest K. Wakukawa, *A History of the Japanese People in Hawaii* (Honolulu: Toyo Shoin, 1938). *A History of Japanese in Hawaii*, ed. by the Publication Committee (Honolulu: United Japanese Society of Hawaii, 1971), 5–7, contains the years and conjectured names involved in thirteenth-century arrivals of Japanese in Hawai'i, with the introduction of sugar cane attributed to one such group.

13. On Kapi'olani the chiefess, not Kalākaua's consort later in the nineteenth century, see Ralph S. Kuykendall and A. Grove Day, *Hawaii: A History from Polynesian Kingdom to American State*, rev. ed. (Englewood Cliffs: Prentice-Hall, 1948), 46. Although the Kapi'olani who defied Pele is not commonly remembered in Hawai'i today, in 1937 Margaret C. Kwon (now known as poet and educator Margaret Pai) was drawn to the story. She scripted a drama based on the incident at Kīlauea, *I Fear Not Pele*, a scene from which survives in *College Plays* (University of Hawaii, 1937), 47–54.

14. See, for instance, A. Grove Day's introduction to Day's edition of *Mark Twain's Letters from Hawaii* (London: Chatto & Windus, 1967), especially where Day discusses Twain's effulgent praise of Hawai'i, the "Prose Poem" delivered in an 1889 speech in New York City, with which Day climaxes his own introductory remarks (xvi–xvii). See also Walter Francis Frear, *Mark Twain and Hawaii* (Chicago: Privately printed, 1947), passim. Albert Bigelow Paine, in *Mark Twain: A Biography* (New York: Harper, 1912), 1:283; Paul Fatout, in *Mark Twain on the Lecture Circuit* (Bloomington: Indiana University Press, 1960), 34; and Frederick Anderson et al., eds., in *Mark Twain's Notebooks and Journals* (Berkeley and London: University of California Press, 1975), 1:192, by their simply titling the disparate materials of March to April 1866 "The Loveliest Fleet of Islands," are among an array of commentators who provide the impression that Twain's view was sentimental and idyllic. Among the few serious looks at Twain's interest in Hawai'i are Louis J. Budd's, in *Mark Twain: Social Philosopher* (Bloomington: Indiana University Press, 1962), 20–22, and Philip Ige's in his dissertation, "Paradise and Melting Pot in the Fiction and Non-Fiction of Hawaii: A Study of Cross-Cultural Record," 159, 203–11. Budd places the subject within social and political contexts that were important to Twain himself; Ige structures his extensive reading of Hawaii's literature by differentiating the positive and the negative, the idyllic and the hellish in the non-Native literature of Hawai'i dating from Captain Cook's arrival in 1778 to statehood in 1959. Also, my present study of Twain's novel—or, more accurately, its fragments—appears in slightly different form as

"Reevaluating Mark Twain's Novel of Hawaii," in *American Literature* 61, no. 4 (December 1989):580–609.

15. Twain's words about Hawai'i are most meticulously identified—and many of them published—in Walter Francis Frear's extensive volume, *Mark Twain and Hawaii*. Frear, governor of Hawai'i from 1907 to 1913, avidly and uncritically followed the course of Twain's involvement with Hawai'i. The darker aspects that Twain recorded appear in Frear's primary documents, but they lie there unexamined.

16. Day, *Mark Twain's Letters from Hawaii*, 3.

17. *Mark Twain–Howells Letters*, ed. Henry Nash Smith and William M. Gibson (Cambridge: Harvard University Press, 1960), 2:460–61. Paine, *Biography*, 2:739–40, is the only source giving Bill Ragsdale's age as eleven just prior to the missionaries' arrival. Other texts, including Paine's edition of *Mark Twain's Letters* (New York: Harper, 1917), 2:439–40, give Ragsdale's age as twelve. Introducing the letter, Paine voices the usual opinion that Twain's months in Hawai'i were "golden," idyllic ones, despite the reference in the letter to leprosy.

18. Paine, *Mark Twain's Letters*, 2:440.

19. Twain's lively description of Ragsdale interpreting on the floor of the legislature occurs in *Mark Twain's Letters from Hawaii*, 110–11. For other historical accounts of Ragsdale (always told in connection with both his leprosy and his politics), see W. Storrs Lee, *The Islands* (New York: Holt, Rinehart and Winston, 1966), 191–92; Gavan Daws, *Shoal of Time: A History of the Hawaiian Islands* (Toronto: Macmillan, 1968), 186–87; and, especially, *News from Molokai: Letters Between Peter Kaeo and Queen Emma 1873–1876,* ed. Alfons L. Korn (Honolulu: University of Hawaii Press, 1976), passim. The Board of Health appointed Ragsdale resident assistant supervisor of the leper settlement at Kalawao, on the remote, wet peninsula of Kalaupapa, Moloka'i, during his first year of voluntary exile in 1873. He became known as "Governor Ragsdale," the *luna* or foreman of the colony.

20. *Mark Twain to Mrs. Fairbanks*, ed. Dixon Wecter (San Marino: Huntington Library, 1949), 255.

21. In his parodic opening fragment, Twain imitates so perfectly the clichés touting the paradise of the Pacific that his words have often been taken as an expression of his own sentiments. Ironically, it remains one of the best examples of the conventional manner. Gavan Daws, in *Shoal of Time*, provides an illustration of "The beginnings of tourism, 1870s," an advertisement of the Hawaiian Hotel at "Honolulu, Sandwich Islands, The Famed Paradise of the Pacific," a wording that indicates the nickname was already a cliché, as is suggested too by Melville's ballyhooing of the exotic splendors of the tropics when Tommo anticipates his escape into Nukuhiva. In this connection it is significant that, unlike visiting authors to the Pacific who mainly came after him, Twain—along with Melville and Jarves before him—was what Daniel J. Boorstin calls a "traveler" and not a "tourist," in *The Image: A Guide to Pseudo-Events in America*

(1961: rpt. New York: Atheneum, 1977), 91–92. "The traveler used to go about the world to encounter the natives. A function of travel agencies now is to prevent this encounter. They are always devising efficient new ways [such as air-conditioned buses with tinted glass] of insulating the tourist from the travel world." Boorstin sees the shift from traveling to touring as having occurred in the late nineteenth century with the advent, for instance, of Cook's Tours in Britain.

22. The manuscript of the fragments is in the Bancroft Library of the University of California at Berkeley: The Mark Twain Papers, DV 111. All previously unpublished words by Mark Twain quoted in this book and my earlier published article adapted from it (see note 14, above) are copyright 1989 by Edward J. Willis and Manufacturers Hanover Trust Company as trustees of the Mark Twain Foundation, which reserves all reproduction or dramatization rights in every medium. They are published here with the permission of the University of California Press and Robert H. Hirst, General Editor of the Mark Twain Project at Berkeley.

23. *Mark Twain–Howells Letters*, 2:462 n. 4.

24. The historical sketch that follows is drawn mainly from Daws, *Shoal of Time*, and Edward Joesting, *Hawaii: An Uncommon History* (New York: W. W. Norton, 1972).

25. James Jackson Jarves, *History of the Hawaiian or Sandwich Islands* (Boston: Tappan & Dennet, 1843).

26. See, for instance, Fred W. Lorch, "Hawaiian Feudalism and Mark Twain's *A Connecticut Yankee in King Arthur's Court*" in *American Literature* 30 (1958): 64, n. 38; and Day, *Mark Twain's Letters from Hawaii*, vii.

27. *Mark Twain Speaking*, ed. Paul Fatout (Iowa City: University of Iowa Press, 1976), 4.

28. Lorch, "Hawaiian Feudalism . . . in *King Arthur's Court*," 61–63.

29. *Mark Twain's Letters from Hawaii*, 110–11.

30. Lorch, "Hawaiian Feudalism . . . in *King Arthur's Court*," 52–60.

31. *Roughing It*, ed. Franklin R. Rogers and Paul Baender (Berkeley: Iowa Center for Textual Studies and University of California Press, 1972), 411.

32. Lorch, "Hawaiian Feudalism . . . in *King Arthur's Court*," 58.

33. *Mark Twain Speaking*, 14. Fred W. Lorch's edition of the speech, in *The Trouble Begins at Eight: Mark Twain's Lecture Tours* (Ames: Iowa State University Press, 1968), includes neither the opening passage describing Twain's sight of leprosy in Hawai'i nor the idyllic closing passage quoted here, both of which Fatout provides.

34. *A Connecticut Yankee in King Arthur's Court*, ed. Bernard L. Stein (Berkeley and London: University of California Press, 1979), 10. The Sunday stillness also signals the beginning of Huck Finn's final escapade at the Phelps farm: "When I got there it was all still and Sunday-like, and hot and sunshiny." The undertones to Huck's entrance into the farm, away from the "Arcadian per-

fection of life aboard the raft," are somber, even mournful and ominous (Marx, *The Machine in the Garden*, 338–39). While Twain's idiosyncratic phrasing by itself may link these works in only a slight way, his later repetitions of his words about Hawai'i as a "Sunday land" remind us that they and the subject of Hawai'i were not simply adrift somewhere in his reveries but remained in many ways consonant with his overall style and thinking.

35. *Following the Equator* (Hartford: American Publishing, 1897), 25.

36. During the horrid spread of leprosy, mainly among those of Hawaiian blood, Ragsdale became something of a popular hero for exiling himself before anyone else knew he bore signs of the disease. Lee, in *The Islands*, 191–92, quoting an eyewitness, offers a sketch of the colorful character taking leave of his hometown and people of Hilo with a tearful and gallant flourish.

37. Twain coined the much-quoted expression on the occasion of the completion of his final residence ("Stormfield") and his seventy-third birthday, in a 30 November 1908 letter of thanks to the Hawaii Promotion Committee for the gift of a mantelpiece and wall decoration carved out of Hawaiian koa wood to grace his new home. A facsimile of the letter appears in Frear, *Mark Twain and Hawaii*, facing page 243. Frear was at that time governor of the Territory of Hawaii.

38. Bushnell models his Caleb Forrest, a main character in *Molokai* (Honolulu: University of Hawaii Press, 1963), on Ragsdale. In a letter of 20 November 1984 he states, however, that he had no knowledge of Twain's Hawai'i novel when writing his own. But because law would have been the only career open to a part-Hawaiian, part-white Caleb Forrest "in that period in Hawaii's social history," Bushnell "consciously chose Ragsdale for a model of sorts" and went further to make his Caleb "much more 'sassy' a fellow" to "explain" and to heighten the character's delight in verbal wit and in "the beauties of the English language." Ragsdale arrived at Kalaupapa at the end of June 1873, less than two months after the coming of the celebrated Father Damien, who in 1889 died of leprosy among the sufferers to whom he had devoted his life.

HAWAII'S PASTORAL

1. Charles Warren Stoddard, "The Night Dancers of Waipio," in his *South-Sea Idylls* (1873; rpt. New York: Charles Scribner's Sons, 1909), 113–31, esp. 124–29. Judging from Stoddard's unstudied, candid impression of the hula on serious themes, even if these, too, were publicly allowed and performed through that century, their basically narrative nature, telling of events among gods and humans in their natural Hawaiian settings, may well have been misinterpreted as being demonic. Stoddard voices his impression that certain of the movements apparently made "in violence and fear" seem aimed "to repulse a host of devils that hovered invisibly about" the dancers (126–27). With the mounting

cadence of the gourd, drum, and chant, Stoddard sees the dancers to be motioning as if "embracing. . . the airy forms that haunted" them (127). Stoddard is a little closer to the mark, though, in seeing what was probably a love song and its hula for what they were (128–29). Curiously, Stoddard's narrative of the night dancers of Waipiʻo Valley ends with his memory of the most passionate hula he had ever known—the dance of death by the inhabitants of the leper settlement on Molokaʻi. They held a grand ball, the joyousness and "unnatural gaiety" of which were in direct measure to the bitterness of the lepers' condition.

2. Today the authoritative, comprehensive work of scholarship on the subject of mele, and far more, is George S. Kanahele, ed., *Hawaiian Music and Musicians: An Illustrated History* (Honolulu: University of Hawaii Press, 1979).

3. Samuel H. Elbert and Noelani Mahoe, comps., *Nā Mele o Hawaiʻi Nei: 101 Hawaiian Songs* (Honolulu: University of Hawaii Press, 1970), 35–36. References hereafter to "Elbert and Mahoe" and their song collection are provided parenthetically.

4. Gavan Daws, *Shoal of Time: A History of the Hawaiian Islands* (Toronto: Macmillan, 1968), 264.

5. "Lyrics of Hawaii Today," panel discussion at Talk Story: Our Voices in Literature and Song: Hawaii's Ethnic American Writers' Conference, Mid-Pacific Institute, Honolulu, 20 June 1978.

6. On pre- and post-contact Hawaiian song types available for study, see Amy K. Stillman, "Published Hawaiian Songbooks," in *M[usic] L[ibrary] A[ssociation] Notes* (Dec. 1987):221–39, which includes a very good bibliography, more thorough and recent than I provide through my own discussion of mele. Aside from the works of scholarship Stillman cites in her article, S. E. Solberg also briefly surveys published studies of mele in his "Hawaiian Lyrics, Chant, and Dance: An Introductory Note with Bibliography," *MELUS* 6:2 (Summer 1979):41–45.

7. Diana Aki, "Lā ʻElima," in *Eddie Kamae Presents the Sons of Hawaii*, Hawaii Sons, HS–2002, 1976.

8. Daws, *Shoal of Time*, 263.

9. Queen Kapiʻolani, "Ipo Lei Manu," lyrics provided on record liner of *The Gabby Pahinui Hawaiian Band*, Panini Records, PS–1007, 1975. Palani Vaughan performs a longer version of "Ipo Lei Manu," in *Iaʻoe E Ka Lā: Palani Vaughan Sings the Music of Hawaiʻi's King David Kalākaua*, Nakahili Productions, NP–CAS–300, 1977. This version, too, ends with the elegiac phrase, "No ka lani hele loa."

10. See Lily Leialoha Apo Mark Perkins, "The Aesthetics of Stress in ʻOlelo and Oli: Notes Toward a Theory of Hawaiian Oral Arts," Ph.D. dissertation, University of Pennsylvania, 1978. On 102–3 Perkins raises a question, based on her analyses of the musical tones and the poetic themes of various *oli*: "In what sense are both the *kanikau* and *hoʻouwēuwē* [dirges and lamentations] . . . different from . . . *hoʻāeāe* intended for a 'happy' occasion, if both 'sad' and

'happy' reflect the same source of inspiration, namely *aloha*?" She goes on to hypothesize that while the sad and the happy types of oli alike share a similar *tonus*, the traditional categories differ by context, theme, or function. I would suggest that the emphasis therefore is on the poetry, or words, rather than on the musical performance as the element distinguishing one category from another. This is consonant with other evidence that the words, poetry, or lyrics are the essence of the traditional oli, mele hula, and other modes of performance—and that the essential sentiment whether in joy or in grief is a complex—not a reduction—of thoughts and emotions that Perkins calls "aloha."

11. Robert and Roland Cazimero, Jacket Notes, "Maunaloa," *The Brothers Cazimero*, Music of Polynesia, MOP 3800,n.d.

12. The Peter Moon Band has recorded a strong modern rendition of "Maunaloa" in *Cane Fire!*, Pānini Records, PS1012, 1982; lyrics are provided in Hawaiian and English on the record liner of *Cane Fire!* The guess that Helen Lindsey Parker composed "Maunaloa" in the 1920s was told to me by the native Hawaiian scholar and poet Larry Lindsey Kimura, her nephew.

13. Eddie Kamae and the Sons of Hawaii, "Kela Mea Whiffa," *Eddie Kamae Presents the Sons of Hawaii*, Hawaii Sons, 1001, n.d.

14. Robert and Roland Cazimero, Jacket Notes, "Ku'u Ipo I ka He'e Pu'e One," *The Brothers Cazimero*. I am indebted to Larry Lindsey Kimura for his criticism of this mele's diction.

15. Alfons L. Korn, "Preface," in *The Echo of Our Song: Chants and Poems of the Hawaiians*, tr. and ed. Mary Kawena Pukui and Alfons L. Korn (Honolulu: University of Hawaii Press, 1973), xv–xvi.

16. Katherine Newman, "Hawaiian-American Literature: The Cultivation of Mangoes," *MELUS: The Journal of the Society for the Study of the Multi-Ethnic Literature of the United States*, 6:2 (Summer 1979):71. In a 1977 meeting on the grounds of Kawaiaha'o Church in Honolulu, Michener and his wife Mari unambiguously declined Marie Hara's invitation for him to take part in the Talk Story Conference. Understandably, judging by his statements denying Local literature before and since that meeting, the larger subject of the conference has meant nothing to him. Also understandably, as Newman knows, locals were thus free of any desire to mention him.

17. T. S. Eliot, *Sweeney Agonistes: Fragments of an Aristophanic Melodrama* (London: Faber & Faber Limited, 1932), 25–26.

18. James A. Michener, *Hawaii* (New York: Random House, 1959).

19. Ibid., disclaimer between dedication page and table of contents.

20. A. Grove Day, *Books About Hawaii: Fifty Basic Authors* (Honolulu: University of Hawaii Press, 1977), 31.

21. A. Grove Day, *James A. Michener* (New York: Twayne, 1964), 112.

22. James A. Michener, "Povenaaa's Daughter," in his *Return to Paradise* (New York: Bantam Books, 1951), 63–104. Page citations are to this edition.

23. Day, *Michener*, 119. Day uses the metaphor of a "stage" to describe

what Michener sees Hawai'i ever to have been: "Erecting this empty stage is a basic part of Michener's plan, for one strand of his theme is that the 'Paradise of the Pacific' was never originally an Eden but merely a place where one could possibly be built by human hands."

24. Milton Murayama, *All I Asking for Is My Body* (San Francisco: Supa Press, 1975), 95–96.

25. Earl Miner, *The Japanese Tradition in British and American Literature* (Princeton: Princeton University Press, 1958), 46–49.

26. In commenting as I do about Michener's explicit versus his implicit views on race relations, I am aware of a fact well known to those who remember Michener's experience in Hawai'i, where he was allegedly refused residence in a white neighborhood because his wife Mari is a Japanese American. See Day, *Michener*, 27–28.

27. This judgment is voiced by the Hawai'i poet Phyllis Thompson, for instance, as quoted by Newman in "Hawaiian-American Literature: The Cultivation of Mangoes," 71.

28. A. Grove Day and Carl Stroven, eds., *A Hawaiian Reader* (New York: Appleton-Century-Crofts, 1959). Page references are to this edition.

29. Jerry Santos, "Ku'u Home 'o Kahalu'u," in *Olomana*, Seabird Productions/Seabird Sound, SS 1001, 1976. The lyrics quoted in the text of this chapter are transcribed from the recording. On the album's jacket, lyrics are provided which vary slightly from what is sung in the recording; namely, in the sung lyrics the second stanza's line, "But I fear I am not as I left you," appears instead as a repetition of the one in the first stanza, "But I fear you won't be like I left you." In the sung lyric, this acknowledgment of change in the singer as well as in the setting saves "Ku'u Home 'o Kahalul'u" from being simplistic and sentimental. For another kind of reflection on a Hawai'i once left behind, see Gail Harada's "away poems," written while she was studying in Iowa: for example, her "7 O'Clock," "Hearing a Train Whistle at Night," and "First Winter," in *Talk Story: An Anthology of Hawaii's Local Writers*, ed. Eric Chock et al., (Honolulu: Petronium Press and Talk Story, 1978), 96–97.

30. In Elbert and Mahoe, *Nā Mele o Hawai'i Nei*, see three patriotic mele: "Hawai'i Aloha," by the Reverend Lorenzo Lyons (42); the former national, now state anthem, "Hawai'i Pono'ī," by King David Kalākaua and Henry Berger (43–44); and "Nā Ali'i," by Samuel Kuahiwi (no date of composition suggested in the text, 79–80). The first two of these are especially well known in Hawai'i today and generally taken to be expressions of the strength of Hawaiian pride. Their composition in the 1870s and 1880s, however, suggests that their purpose was to rally a people whose strength was steeply in decline, as is also paradoxically evident in "Nā Ali'i," which means "the chiefs" who, in effect, are summoned forth from Hawaii's history, as in "Kaulana nā Pua," for needed strength in the present. S.E. Solberg, quoting a relevant passage from Nathaniel Emerson's *Unwritten Literature*, also comments on these motives behind the patriotic mele, in

"Hawaiian Music, Poetry, and Dance: Reflections on Protection, Preservation, and Pride," *MELUS* 10:1 (Spring 1983):62 n. 33.

31. Armine von Tempski, *Born in Paradise* (New York: Duell, Sloan and Pearce, 1940), 3. Her dozen books include seven works of fiction which von Tempski sometimes subtitles as novels, romances, or sagas; three others written mainly for teen-aged readers; and an autobiographical sequel to *Born in Paradise* (*Aloha, My Love to You: The Story of One Who Was Born in Paradise* [New York: Duell, Sloane, 1946]).

32. On the development of Asian American literary traditions and with them a "sensibility" neither unchangingly "Asian" nor assimilatively "American," see the "Preface" and "Introduction: Fifty Years of Our Whole Voice" by Frank Chin, Jeffery Paul Chan, Lawson Fusao Inada, and Shawn Hsu Wong, eds., in their *Aiiieeeee! An Anthology of Asian-American Writers* (1974; rev. ed., Washington, D.C.: Howard University Press, 1983), vii–xlvii, and S. E. Solberg's "An Introduction to Filipino-American Literature," xlix–lxiv of the same edition.

33. Garrett Kaoru Hongo, "The Hongo Store / 29 Miles Volcano / Hilo, Hawaii," in *Hawaii Review* 7 (1977):42; rpt. in the *Talk Story Big Island Anthology*, ed. Arnold Hiura, Stephen Sumida, and Martha Webb (Honolulu: Bamboo Ridge Press and Talk Story, 1979), 22; and in Hongo's *Yellow Light* (Middletown: Wesleyan University Press, 1982), 65.

34. Patsy Sumie Saiki, *Sachie: A Daughter of Hawaii* (Honolulu: Kisaku, 1977). Portions of the summary that follows in my discussion are adapted from the volume I authored with Arnold T. Hiura, *Asian American Literature of Hawaii: An Annotated Bibliography* (Honolulu: Japanese American Research Center and Talk Story, 1979), 107–8.

35. Malcolm Naea Chun, "S. M. Kamakau: A Biographical Essay," 13. The telling of time, or remembering, by event or person occurs also in part I of Milton Murayama's *All I Asking for Is My Body*, discussed in the following chapter.

36. Patsy Saiki, "The Unwilling Bride," in *Talk Story Big Island Anthology*, 60–63; originally published in *The Lit* 1 (April 1951):22–25, a University of Hawaii literary journal.

37. Patsy Saiki, "The Return," TS, in *University of Hawaii Plays* (University of Hawaii Department of Drama, 1959), 97–111.

38. Clara Mitsuko Jelsma, *Teapot Tales and Other Stories* (Honolulu: Bamboo Ridge Press, 1981).

39. Milton Murayama, "Yoshitsune," TS, 1977.

40. Philip K. Ige, "The Forgotten Flea Powder," *Bamboo Ridge* 1 (December 1978):56–59; originally published in *Paradise of the Pacific* 58 (November 1946):24–25.

41. Philip K. Ige, "The New Road," *The Lit* 1 (January 1951):26–27.

42. *Paradise of the Pacific* 58 (November 1946):24.

43. Darrell H. Y. Lum, "Beer Can Hat," in his *Sun: Short Stories and*

Drama by Darrell H. Y. Lum a special issue of *Bamboo Ridge* 8 (September—November 1980):10–19; originally published in *Bamboo Ridge* 4 (September 1979):67–71, without a second part.

44. Literary workshop with Frank Chin, Honolulu, November 1979. This was the first of the regular monthly meetings, continuing today without a break, of the "Study Group" consisting of a dozen or so Hawai'i writers, literary scholars, and their occasional guests and devoted to the reading and criticism of mainly contemporary and new works of polyethnic American literature. Each member of the Study Group also contributes pieces of his or her writing for criticism at the meetings.

45. Sheldon Hershinow, "Coming of Age? The Literature of Contemporary Hawaii," in *Bamboo Ridge* 13 (December 1981–February 1982);9–10.

46. William Empson, *Some Versions of Pastoral* (Norfolk, Conn.: New Directions, n.d.).

47. Carey McWilliams, "Introduction" to Carlos Bulosan, *America Is in the Heart* (1946; rpt. Seattle: University of Washington Press, 1973), xx.

48. Darrell H. Y. Lum, "Primo Doesn't Take Back Bottles Anymore," in *Kapa* (Spring 1972):51–53; rpt. *Talk Story: An Anthology of Hawaii's Local Writers,* 33–38; and in *Sun,* 20–25.

49. See *A Pacific Islands Collection,* for editor Richard Hamasaki's broadened interest in the Pacific which, rather oddly to the contrary, some critics seem to see as a narrowing of view.

50. See Arthur E. Christy, "The Sense of the Past," in *The Asian Legacy and American Life,* 17ff., for a discussion of Confucius as noble sage in the same eighteenth-century, European Enlightenment way of thought where Rousseau conceived the noble savage. Confucius had the reputation of being eminently rational, a prime virtue in the Age of Reason; and, according to Christy's study, Enlightenment philosophers, whether of Europe or of the American colonies, were rationally and purposefully interested in Confucius's social and political philosophy, where the Revolutionaries could, after all, find venerable precedents for both the popular overthrowing of an unjust aristocracy and the establishment of a meritocracy.

51. For titles and summaries of stories by Seiko Ogai and Charles Kong, as well as for citations and summaries by the nisei-generation writers already discussed, see their entries in Sumida and Hiura, *Asian American Literature of Hawaii: An Annotated Bibliography.* The younger generation of writers named here (Jody Masako Manabe [Kobayashi], Gary Tachiyama, Susan Nunes, Juliet Kono, and Vinnie [Wini] Terada) are among many contemporaries published in *Bamboo Ridge: The Hawaii Writers' Quarterly* since its inception in 1978.

52. For meanings of Hawaiian words and terms beyond what is found in a literary text I am discussing, my source is mainly Mary Kawena Pukui and Samuel H. Elbert, *Hawaiian Dictionary* (Honolulu: University of Hawaii Press, 1971). I have thus consulted this authoritative work in discussing the term

'*ohā* and its ramifications, but I also acknowledge that my observations are commonplace and self-evident to those who speak the Hawaiian language.

53. As Frank Chin and others have been pointing out for years, the ordinal numbering of generations is the issei's acknowledgment that they, like their descendants to come, are the first *Japanese Americans*, not the last *Japanese*. The issei's own terminology actively contradicts the stubbornly held view that they migrated to America mainly to get rich and then to return to Japan without rooting themselves in the land of their sojourn and without contributing permanently to America. The local Hawai'i writers discussed throughout my present work are aware that they themselves and their neighbors simply would not exist if that sojourner theory were true. Like the laws forbidding Asian naturalization, the sojourner theory was really meant to discourage Asians from staying after Americans no longer needed their labor. Issei obviously remained in Hawai'i: the subsequent use of nisei, born to labor on Hawaii's plantations with their parents, systematically bound to that class and situation, is another matter. It lies at the heart of Murayama's novel, discussed in the following chapter. Cf. the different history of Chinese American names for their community—terms at times seeming to support a sojourner theory—in Sau-ling C. Wong's "What's in a Name? Defining Chinese American Literature of the Immigrant Generation," in *Frontiers of Asian American Studies: Writing, Research, and Criticism*, ed. Gail M. Nomura et al. (Pullman: Washington State University Press, 1989), 159–67.

HAWAII'S COMPLEX IDYLL

1. Milton Murayama, *All I Asking for Is My Body* (San Francisco: Supa Press, 1975; rpt., with an afterword by Franklin S. Odo, Honolulu: University of Hawaii Press, 1988); John Dominis Holt, *Waimea Summer: A Novel* (Honolulu: Topgallant Publishing, 1976). In slightly different form this discussion of the two authors and their works is previously published as *Two Novels of Hawaii*: Waimea Summer *by John Dominis Holt [and]* All I Asking for Is My Body *by Milton Murayama: A Critique* (Honolulu: Ku Pa'a [formerly Topgallant Publishing], 1989).

2. A. Grove Day and Carl Stroven, eds., *The Spell of Hawaii* (New York: Meredith Press, 1968), 323.

3. Philip K. Ige, "The Forgotten Flea Powder," discussed in chapter 3, above.

4. For Murayama's own comments about his use of pidgin and mixed languages in *All I Asking for Is My Body*, see his "Problems of Writing in Dialect and Mixed Languages," in *Bamboo Ridge* 5 (December 1979): 8–10, a paper originally delivered at the Pacific Northwest Asian American Writers' Conference, University of Washington, 29 June–2 July 1976. See also his letter to editor Darrell

Lum, in the same issue of *Bamboo Ridge*, 6–7; an article by Jimmy Shimabukuro, "As Close As Possible to Experience," in *The Hawaii Herald* [Honolulu], 21 November 1980, n.p.n., where Murayama discusses his ties to the Japanese language and culture; and Murayama's comments in *Writers of Hawaii: A Focus on Our Literary Heritage*, ed. Eric Chock and Jody Manabe (Honolulu: Bamboo Ridge Press, 1981), 59–61. Remarks by others about Murayama's uses of language and literary devices include Rob Wilson, "Review: *All I Asking for Is My Body*," *Bamboo Ridge* 5 (December 1979):4; his expanded version of that essay, "The Languages of Confinement and Liberation in Milton Murayama's *All I Asking for Is My Body*," in *Writers of Hawaii*, 62–65; and Arnold Hiura, "Comments on Milton Murayama," in *Writers of Hawaii*, 65–67, where Hiura stresses the literary qualities of the novel suggesting how Murayama, through fiction, provides readers what sociological studies of Hawaii's plantations cannot. *Writers of Hawaii* resulted from a 1980 conference by that name, directed by Eric Chock. It featured Murayama, John Dominis Holt, Maxine Hong Kingston, and two of the authors of Hawaii's heroic literature, O. A. Bushnell and Aldyth Morris, all of whom are represented in the published proceedings.

5. Bob Nobuyuki Hongo, *Hey, Pineapple!* (Tokyo: Hokuseido Press, 1958). I remember the excitement, especially of Hawaii's Korean War veterans, when Hongo's novel was released.

6. Jon Shirota, *Lucky Come Hawaii* (New York: Bantam Books, 1965; rpt. Honolulu: Bess Press, 1988); and *Pineapple White* (Los Angeles: Ohara Publication, 1972). *All I Asking for Is My Body* overlaps Shirota's earlier story in both place and time, Maui at the time of Pearl Harbor. Shirota's later *Pineapple White* concerns an issei who retires from labor on a sugar plantation by joining his son in Los Angeles (where Shirota lives); but in a variation on the Hawai'i pastoral, the issei returns to his rural Hawai'i home when he finds that urban Los Angeles life does not agree with him.

7. Darrell H. Y. Lum, "Primo Doesn't Take Back Bottles Anymore," discussed in chapter 3, above.

8. See Ronald Takaki, *Pau Hana: Plantation Life and Labor in Hawaii 1835–1920* (Honolulu: University of Hawaii Press, 1983). By 1920, "Hawaiians and part-Hawaiians made up only 16.3 percent of the population, while Caucasians represented 7.7 percent, Chinese 9.2 percent, Japanese 42.7 percent, Portuguese 10.6 percent, Puerto Ricans 2.2 percent, Koreans 1.9 percent, and Filipinos 8.2 percent" (28). Historically the Japanese laborers imported to Hawai'i were preceded by the Chinese, who came from a civilization that had developed the technology of refining sugar and so served as very early pioneers, if not the earliest after the native Hawaiians who grew sugar cane since long before Cook's arrival, in the refined-sugar industry in Hawai'i (see chap. 2, n. 4).

9. John Okada, *No-No Boy* (Tokyo and Rutland, VT: Tuttle, 1957; rpt. San Francisco: C.A.R.P., 1976; and Seattle: University of Washington Press, 1979). For a comparison of Okada's and Murayama's novels, including their naive

and unreliable fictional narrators, see my article, "Japanese American Moral Dilemmas in John Okada's *No-No Boy* and Milton Murayama's *All I Asking for Is My Body,*" in *Frontiers of Asian American Studies: Writing, Research, and Criticism,* ed. Gail M. Nomura et al. (Pullman: Washington State University Press, 1989).

10. Elaine H. Kim, *Asian American Literature: An Introduction to the Writings and Their Social Context* (Philadelphia: Temple University Press, 1982), 146. Kim comments that in Murayama's and in some other strong examples of nisei literature, "community traditions" and "race discrimination"—the issei family on the one hand, the plantation on the other—constitute a "double tyranny." She focuses her discussion of *All I Asking* on the oppressiveness of the Japanese immigrant family and community, and she assumes that the parents are rigidly enforcing rather than violating their professed traditions. Kim, in effect, blames them for their own oppressed condition on the plantation.

11. Milton Murayama, "Problems of Writing in Dialect and Mixed Languages," 10.

12. This device of the naive narrator, particularly in Japanese American literature, is reminiscent of works by Murayama's peers: Hisaye Yamamoto, "Yoneko's Earthquake," in *Aiiieeeee! An Anthology of Asian American Writers,* 178–90; and, less obviously so, Wakako Yamauchi, "And the Soul Shall Dance," both the original short story in *Aiiieeeee!,* 193–200, and the two-act drama based upon it, where the central point of view is that of the child Masako, who observes and imagines what must be happening among the adults in her world.

13. See the *Proceedings of the Second Annual Conference of New Americans* (Honolulu: n.p., 1928). At the"New Americans" conferences, the sugar planters promoted an "Americanization" aimed at persuading nisei youth to return to or remain on the plantations. Contradicting the speakers who urged that the nisei do their "American" duty of serving them, Miles Carey, the principal of McKinley High School, said that his students aspired to something better: white-collar jobs (6–7). It appears that with his striking message on behalf of the nisei, Carey was never invited back to speak in later "New Americans" conferences. The conferences ran annually until 1941, when Pearl Harbor and the war made them patently absurd, whether in the United States or Canada, because despite their being Americans, the nisei of the continent's West Coast were imprisoned in North American concentration camps. See also Gail M. Nomura, "The Debate over the Prewar Role of Nisei in Hawaii: The New Americans Conference, 1927–1941," *Journal of Ethnic Studies* 15, no. 1 (Spring 1987):95–115.

14. Murayama, in *Writers of Hawaii,* 61.

15. Snooky is an *eiron,* a critic from the outside who appears again and again in Hawaii's modern literature and history. Three contemporary authors who themselves play or otherwise resemble the type are Lawrence H. Fuchs, *Hawaii Pono: A Social History* (New York: Harcourt, Brace and World, 1961), Francine du Plessix Gray, *Hawaii: The Sugar-Coated Fortress* (New York: Vintage Books, 1973), and Richard L. Rapson, *Fairly Lucky You Live Hawaii! Cultural*

Pluralism in the Fiftieth State, (Washington, D.C.: University Press of America, 1980). For an indication of how controversial Fuch's socio-political history was considered by an old guard of Hawai'i, despite the recognitions of excellence it was accorded, see A. Grove Day, *Books about Hawaii: Fifty Basic Authors* (Honolulu: University of Hawaii Press: 1977), 87–88, where Day's own assessment of Fuchs is apparently mixed and vigilant. Rapson opens his book with an essay titled "Coming to Eden" and an introduction to the writer's "Outside Perspectives," in this case the haole's perspective on a Hawaiian localism that can be "galling" (1–3). Among the writers Rapson cites and discusses is the novelist Francine du Plessix Gray and her deeply critical examination of the military complex entrenched in the islands and, on an ironically contrary note, the simplistic paradise image promoted by tourism. Gray herself acknowledges John Dominis Holt as "the spiritual mentor of this book" (xi); yet again ironically, James A. Michener supplies one of the laudatory remarks gracing the paperback's back cover, where Michener applauds Gray's championing of the native Hawaiians and criticizing of the Japanese, the Chinese, and the descendants of the haole missionaries of the islands, the same three groups Michener himself aggrandizes in his novel at the expense of the native Hawaiians. A somehow haunting figure of an *eiron* appears in Molly Tani Shell's "Where Dwells the Heart," TS, in *Theater Group Plays,* University of Hawaii Theater Group, 1953–54/1954–55, where he is an itinerant who enters the deeply rural, isolated setting of the drama and the lives of the main characters, a mother and daughter. A theoretical discussion of the *eiron* type and its kin, applicable to Murayama's Kiyo as well as to his Snooky, may be found in Northrop Frye, *Anatomy of Criticism: Four Essays* (New York: Atheneum, 1967), 172–75 and elsewhere.

16. Murayama, letter in *Bamboo Ridge* 5 (December 1979):6. For a preview of an ambitious work in progress by Murayama, where he greatly expands upon the story of the Oyamas in Japan and Hawai'i, see his "A Novel, Untitled, Part I: Five Years on a Rock," in *The Seattle Review: Blue Funnel Line* [ed. Shawn Wong] 9 (Spring/Summer 1988):150–55. The first performance of a stage version of *All I Asking for Is My Body* occurred in San Francisco in 1989.

17. The ranchlands of Waimea are nowadays nicknamed "Paniolo Country" after Hawaii's cowboys, whose history dates back to the Spanish and Mexican cowboys, the *Español* whom the Hawaiians called "Paniolo," brought to Waimea in the early nineteenth century to tend the herds first introduced by Captain George Vancouver in 1793. See Ralph S. Kuykendall and A. Grove Day, *Hawaii: A History,* rev. ed. (Englewood Cliffs: Prentice-Hall, 1961), 96. Armine von Tempski also provides facts on her family's business of cattle ranching in Hawai'i in her autobiography *Born in Paradise,* 7 et passim.

18. For thoughts quite different from mine on how an interracial, *hapa haole* conflict of identities within Mark Hull and Holt himself may be central to *Waimea Summer,* see Sheldon Hershinow, "John Dominis Holt and Hawaiian-American Literature," in *Writers of Hawaii: A Focus on Our Literary Heritage,*

7–12, and "John Dominis Holt: Hawaiian-American Traditionalist," *MELUS* 7 (Summer 1980): 61–72. Hershinow's reading of Holt's fiction and nonfiction is based on assumptions about what absolutely, racially and culturally, is presumed to be "Hawaiian" and what "American," (e.g., "A rural, traditional, superstitious Hawaii" versus the high European airs of Aunt Nita Warrington in *Waimea Summer*). These assumptions and this approach, however, I do not find borne out by Holt's novel. Hershinow sees as further evidence of conflict and contradiction of identities the fact that each Holt character, regardless of race or races, lives by or else values the elements derived from several cultures which overlap in the contemporary local Hawaiian culture. While Mark may at moments seem conflicted by race, I find that ethnic identities in this novel are givens, not issues (one has no choice about being born into a race or races), and that Holt as the author of a work of fiction (in this case neither an autobiography nor an *a priori* endorsement of the protagonist's views) critically examines young Mark's inclination to fall into such conflict because of the way Mark sees Hawaiian culture to be exclusively of the past, a dead thing he wishes to revive, but not renew. Views of *hapa haole* (half-whites) as conflicted by dual cultures and races tend to be precisely that: versions of an assimilationist notion of "dual identities" of "marginal" individuals. To apply this same point to the previous novel discussed, I might add that this view of a "dual identity" was germane to the ideology that rationalized the internment of Japanese American citizens in concentration camps during World War II on the presumption of their being at least partly "Japanese" and therefore the enemy.

19. Regarding Laka, goddess or god of the hula, see Nathaniel B. Emerson, *Unwritten Literature of Hawaii: The Sacred Songs of the Hula* (Bureau of American Ethnology, 1909; rpt. Charles E. Tuttle, 1964), esp. 23–24. Emerson identifies Laka as seeming "to have been a friend, but not a relative, of the numerous Pele family," that is, the family of the fire and volcano goddess. Martha Beckwith, however, in *Hawaiian Mythology* (Folklore Foundation of Vassar College, 1940; rpt. Honolulu: University of Hawaii Press, 1967), 185–86, identifies Laka as a sister of Pele and as the goddess of forest growth. For a modern poem in English evoking the icy yet arid, rarified air of Poli'ahu, at the summit of Mauna Kea, see Martha Webb, "Mauna Kea," in *Talk Story Big Island Anthology*, ed. Arnold T. Hiura, Stephen H. Sumida, and Martha Webb (Honolulu: Bamboo Ridge Press and Talk Story, 1979), 64.

20. According to Holt, these lands on the island of O'ahu would actually be at and adjoining the estate called Manulani, Makaha Valley, in the district of Wai'anae, and at Waialua.

21. Leslie Marmon Silko, *Ceremony* (New York: Viking, 1977).

22. On Keoua Kuahu'ula, chief of Puna on the island of Hawai'i, see *Ruling Chiefs of Hawaii*, esp. 156–58, where Samuel Kamakau tells of Keoua's defeat by Kamehameha's warriors at Pu'u-koholá heiau at Kawaihae, in 1791. Kamakau discounts a belief held at the time of Keoua's defeat that, when his

body was laid on the altar of Puʻu-koholá, a prophecy was fulfilled. This prophecy, however, in very real military and political terms, required Kamehameha to build the heiau, consolidate control of his home island Hawaiʻi, and proceed from there to snatch the other islands and create a unified kingdom. These deeds Kamehameha accomplished. Why Keoua accepted his hostile cousin's invitation to attend the dedication of the heiau, the occasion when he was slain, is a question that has engendered wonderful stories, I believe yet to be written, about his motives and behavior in that event. There is Kamakau's widely shared report, for instance, that Keoua mutilated himself before arriving at Kawaihae, perhaps in order that Kamehameha might be punished for offering Keoua's body, now an imperfect sacrifice, on the altar. Puʻu-koholá (possibly meaning a"whale-shaped hill") is today a national historic site; and its lofty ramparts and interior are kapu, with entrance forbidden to anyone except its keepers and native Hawaiians visiting the heiau for religious purposes. See also Edward Joesting, *Hawaii: An Uncommon History*, 49–50.

23. Gavan Daws, *Shoal of Time: A History of the Hawaiian Islands*, 219–20. One of Kalākaua's advisors was a wild and passionate white man, Walter Murray Gibson, who reportedly coined the slogan "Hawaiʻi for Hawaiians" in accordance with his monarch's Hawaiian Renaissance; for a biographical essay, see Daws, *A Dream of Islands*, 128–61. Though of a very different temper, Gibson is reminiscent of Gerrit P. Judd, of the reign of Kamehameha III, in exemplifying why and how white advisors committed to the betterment of Hawaiʻi and Hawaiians exerted their influences.

24. John Dominis Holt, *Kaulana Na Pua, Famous Are the Flowers: Queen Liliuokalani and the Throne of Hawaii; A Play in Three Acts* (Honolulu: Topgallant Publishing, 1974). See also Holt's five-part poem and its accompanying glossary and "Hanauna" (ancestry, birth, generation, or, in such a sense, history), *Hanai: A Poem for Queen Liliuokalani* (Honolulu: Topgallant Publishing, 1986).

25. John Dominis Holt. *Princess of the Night Rides and Other Tales* (Honolulu: Topgallant Publishing, 1977).

26. *On Being Hawaiian* (1964; rpt. Honolulu: Topgallant Publishing, 1974). For an example of Holt's historical writings, see his *Monarchy in Hawaii* (Honolulu: Topgallant Publishing, 1971). Also see Carol Silva's "Remarks on John Dominis Holt" in *Writers of Hawaii: A Focus on Our Literary Heritage*, 12–15, an examination of Holt's historicism and its vibrancy in his fiction and nonfiction.

27. 13 July 1979, University of Hawaii at Hilo.

HAWAII'S HEROIC LITERATURE

1. Information on the genesis of Bushnell's work on Captain Cook is from a conversation, 8 July 1979. All of my references to his *Return of Lono* (1956; rpt. Honolulu: University of Hawaii Press, 1971) are from the 1971 edition.

2. For these readings of Camoën's epic I am indebted to the late Professor Joan Webber, who expressed these ideas in her 1975 University of Washington seminar. See Luis Vaz de Camoëns, *The Lusiads*, tr. William C. Atkinson (Harmondsworth: Penguin Books, 1952).

3. For an authoritative version and discussion of the *Kumulipo*, technically a genealogy chant, see *The Kumulipo: A Hawaiian Creation Chant*, tr. Martha Beckwith (Chicago: University of Chicago Press, 1951). Bushnell quotes from this text, in *The Return of Lono*, 90. Another fine scholarly treatment is Rubellite Kawena Johnson's *Kumulipo: The Hawaiian Hymn of Creation* (Honolulu: Topgallant Publishing, 1981).

4. Cook's *Journals*, vol. 3, pt. 1 (Cambridge: Cambridge University Press, 1967), 473–74.

5. Philip K. Ige, in "Paradise and Melting Pot," demonstrates that a paradise-and-hell "duality of vision" is assumed and expressed in nearly every work he documents of Hawaii's fiction and nonfiction, beginning with Cook's journal.

6. Charles M. Newell, *Kamehameha, the Conquering King* (New York: Putnam, 1884). Cf. S. N. Haleole, *Ke Kaao o Laieikawai: Ka Hiwahiwa o Paliuli, Kawahineokaliula* (Honolulu: Henry M. Whitney, 1863), a native Hawaiian romance by a colleague of Samuel Kamakau and Davida Malo. This tale of a sacred princess, born at Lā'ie-in-the-water, and her journey to a mythical paradise is translated by Martha Beckwith as *The Hawaiian Romance of Laieikawai*, in the *The Annual Report of the United States Bureau of American Ethnology, 1911–12* 33 (1919): 285–666. In full, the title of Haleole's novel may be translated, "the legend (or fiction) of Lā'ieikawai: the precious one of Paliuli (according to Pukui and Elbert in their *Hawaiian Dictionary*, 'a legendary land of plenty and joy, said to be on Hawaii, where chief's children were raised'; literally 'a green cliff'), the woman of the twilight (or the mirage)."

7. O. A. Bushnell, *Molokai* (1963; rpt. Honolulu: University of Hawaii Press, 1975).

8. Bushnell writes in a letter of 20 November 1984 that while he did not know of Twain's unpublished novel, it was only natural that as a novelist himself he would be drawn to Ragsdale. See my discussion of Twain's novel about Ragsdale in chapter 2 above.

9. O. A. Bushnell, *Ka'a'awa: A Novel about Hawaii in the 1850s* (Honolulu: University of Hawaii Press, 1972). In 1973, Popular Library, New York, published a paperback edition, oddly retitled *The Valley of Love and Delight*.

10. O. A. Bushnell, *The Stone of Kannon* (Honolulu: University of Hawaii Press, 1979); *The Water of Kane* (Honolulu: University of Hawaii Press, 1980).

11. Aldyth Morris, *The Fourth Son* (1959), TS provided by the author.

12. Information from page following the title page of *The Fourth Son* TS.

13. Aldyth Morris, *The Secret Concubine* (revised for the New York production, June 1959), TS provided by the author.

14. Aldyth Morris, personal letter, 26 February 1982.

15. Gavan Daws, *Shoal of Time*, 218–20.

16. Aldyth Morris, *Captain Cook* (1977), TS provided by the author. Page references throughout my book are to the typescript.

17. Aldyth Morris, *Damien* (Honolulu: University of Hawaii Press, 1980).

18. Aldyth Morris, *Robert Louis Stevenson* (1977), TS provided by the author.

19. Aldyth Morris, personal letter, 26 February 1982.

20. Abraham Fornander, *An Account of the Polynesian Race,* 2: 318.

21. Ralph S. Kuykendall and A. Grove Day, *Hawaii: A History, From Polynesian Kingdom to American State*, rev. ed. (Englewood Cliffs: Prentice-Hall, 1961), 24.

22. Martha Webb, "He Punahele," *Bamboo Ridge: The Hawaii Writers' Quarterly* 10 (March–May 1981):44–60.

23. In a major work entitled *Māui the Demigod: An Epic Novel of Mythical Hawai'i* (1984; rpt. Honolulu: University of Hawaii Press, 1989) Steven Goldsberry studiously adapts heroic Hawaiian oral sources to a modern literary form. Goldsberry's novel is like works of Webb and others who compose two centuries of the artistic experimentation that is an inherent challenge in transforming the oral into the written.

24. Shelley Ayame Nishimura Ota, *Upon Their Shoulders* (New York: Exposition Press, 1951); Margaret N. Harada, *The Sun Shines on the Immigrant* (New York: Vantage Press, 1960); Kazuo Miyamoto, *Hawaii: End of the Rainbow*, First Tut Book ed. (Rutland, Vt.: Charles E. Tuttle, 1968), originally published by Tuttle in 1964. Page references are to these respective publications or editions of these works.

25. Virgilio Menor Felipe, "Chapter I. Once In the First Times from *What You Like Know? An Oral Biography of Bonipasyo,*" in *Bamboo Ridge: The Hawaii Writers' Quarterly* 11 (June–August 1981): 48–58; rpt. in *The Best of Bamboo Ridge*, 122–30. Other published excerpts from Felipe's *Oral Biography of Bonipasyo* include "Hawaii: A Filipino Dream," in *Searching for the Promised Land —Filipinos and Samoans in Hawaii* ed. Nancy F. Young (Honolulu: General Assistance Center of the Pacific, 1974), 22–37; "Hawaii: Plantation of Destiny," in *Manna-Mana*, ed. Leonard Lueras (Honolulu: privately printed, 1973), 3–20; and "from *Hawaii, Plantation of Destiny*," in *Talk Story Big Island Anthology*, ed. Arnold Hiura, Stephen Sumida, and Martha Webb (Honolulu: Bamboo Ridge Press and Talk Story, 1979), 26–31. For a study of Filipino Americans in Hawai'i, see Ruben R. Alcantara, *Sakada: Filipino Adaptation in Hawaii* (Washington, D.C.: University Press of America, 1981).

26. Li Ling Ai, *Life is for a Long Time: A Chinese Hawaiian Memoir*

(New York: Hastings House, 1972). The many works of Hawaii's Chinese American studies include the useful compilation and edition by Tin-Yuke Char, *The Sandalwood Mountains: Readings and Stories of the Early Chinese in Hawaii* (Honolulu: University of Hawaii Press, 1975), and the commemorative pictorial collection of essays and articles by Arlene Lum, ed., *Sailing for the Sun: The Chinese in Hawaii 1789–1989* (Honolulu: University of Hawaii Center for Chinese Studies, Three Heroes, 1988). Tin-Yuke Char and Wai Jane Char, at the core of the Hawaii Chinese History Society, like their friend Li Ling Ai, write nonfictional accounts that not only interpret the historical record but also aim to articulate a cultural criticism—for instance, of immigrants' songs. From the Korean American community of Hawai'i, author Margaret Pai (nee Margaret C. Kwon) has published a biography of her immigrant parents, *The Dreams of Two Yi-Min* (Honolulu: University of Hawaii Press, 1989). This community has yet to publish a fictional saga in English despite the strength of literary, artistic, and other cultural values historically demonstrated by its members, including Pai (see chap. 2, n. 13). It is not merely hoped but expected that these gaps will soon be filled by the completion and publication of novels based upon Chinese American, Korean American, and other histories of Hawai'i as yet unrepresented in this form.

27. A. Grove Day, *Books about Hawaii: Fifty Basic Authors* (Honolulu: University of Hawaii Press, 1977).

28. Hiram Bingham, *A Residence of Twenty-One Years in the Sandwich Islands* . . . (New York: Sherman Converse, 1847); Lucy Goodale Thurston, *The Life and Times of Lucy G. Thurston* (Ann Arbor: S. C. Andrews, 1882); Bradford Smith, *Yankees in Paradise: The New England Impact on Hawaii* (New York: Lippincott, 1956).

29. Albertine Loomis, *Grapes of Canaan: Hawaii 1820* (1951); rpt. Honolulu: Hawaii Mission Children's Society, 1966).

30. Ruth Eleanor McKee, *The Lord's Anointed* (Garden City: Doubleday, 1934). McKee went on to write a sequel, *After a Hundred Years*, which Day summarizes: "Constancy's great-grandson . . . returns to the islands in 1920 to take part in the centennial celebration of her arrival. Along with his bitterly cynical wife . . . [he] works out his destiny on a sugar plantation" (Day, *Books about Hawaii*, 104). McKee also went on to write *Christopher Strange: A Novel* (Garden City: Doubleday, Doran, 1941) about the westward saga of pioneers starting out from Concord, Massachusetts, in the mid–1800s and crossing the Great Plains, as did McKee's mother at age six, to whom McKee dedicates her novel.

31. Samuel B. Harrison, *The White King* (Garden City: Doubleday, 1950).

32. Laura Fish Judd, *Honolulu: Sketches of the Life, Social, Political, and Religious, in the Hawaiian Islands from 1828 to 1861* (New York: Anson D. F. Randolph, 1880).

33. The first Japanese American novel in English is, to my knowledge, James T. Hamada's *Don't Give Up the Ship* (Boston: Meador, 1933). The plot

and characters of this novel, however, concern not Japanese American history but the shipping industry and its contemporary place in Hawai'i. See my article, "Waiting for the Big Fish: Recent Research in the Asian American Literature of Hawaii," in *The Best of Bamboo Ridge: The Hawaii Writers' Quarterly*, ed. Eric Chock and Darrell H. Y. Lum (Honolulu: Bamboo Ridge Press, 1986), 311.

34. In the preceding chapter I note a comparison of Okada's novel with Murayama's later one. Though stating these comparisons, I still do not suppose that either Okada or Murayama knew Ota's novel, or that Okada influenced Murayama's writing of his. Their shared connection is indirect in a way I try to suggest in my discussion below.

35. Bob Nobuyuki Hongo, *Hey, Pineapple!*; Seiko Ogai, "The Other Angel," in *Nisei: In Hawaii and the Pacific* 6 (Holiday Issue 1952): 1, 18, 20.

36. Carlos Bulosan's *America Is in the Heart* (1946; rpt. Seattle: University of Washington Press, 1973) is the story of a lone protagonist's experiences through boyhood and youth in the Philippines, emigration to Seattle, migrations through fields and canneries up and down the West coast, and travails as a *Pinoy* (a Filipino American laborer) and a labor organizer. Though narrated in the first person by a character named "Carlos," "Allos," or "Carl"—obviously like Bulosan himself—the narrative is not strictly autobiographical but instead conflates the stories of many Pinoys. The book, in both characterization and plot, comes to stand for the heroism of the entire class and group of people. The protagonist Carlos is typical, yet is distinguished by his ability to read and to write his observations with honesty and passion, determined to tell his people's story. As for Bulosan himself and his own Philippine culture, literary backgrounds in a sense are so familiar as not to need explicit allusions (Ota is rather like this, except her silent allusions are to Buddhism). Three hundred and fifty years of Spanish colonialism in the Philippines by Bulosan's own time had established *Don Quixote* as a classic in his contemporary culture; *America Is in the Heart*, though it is realistic rather than romantic, is literally a picaresque narrative about a man who tilts against giants. According to the fiction-writer and scholar N. V. M. Gonzalez, in a conversation with me (November 1986), this literary undercurrent in Bulosan's sensibility supplements Filipino myths of the people's origins, such that the Pinoy's traveling east to America completes the circle begun by the primordial mythical beings who sailed westward originally to populate the islands—ages later named the Philippines by the Spanish. The earlier comparison of Ota with Bulosan is cogent yet evocative. Both authors are concerned with Asian immigrants' shared visions. They exemplify one of the connections (and distinctions) among the polyethnic Asian American literatures of Hawai'i and the mainland.

37. Publication Committee, ed., *A History of Japanese in Hawaii* (Honolulu: United Japanese Society of Hawaii, 1971), 110. In 1985 the centennial of Japanese contract labor immigration to Hawai'i was celebrated, accompanied by the publication of histories, including Roland Kotani, *The Japanese in Hawaii: A Century of Struggle* (Honolulu: Hawaii Hochi, 1985); Alan Takeo Moriyama,

Imingaisha: Japanese Emigration Companies and Hawaii 1894–1908 (Honolulu: University of Hawaii Press, 1985); and Franklin Odo and Kazuko Sinoto, *A Pictorial History of the Japanese in Hawai'i 1885–1924* (Honolulu: Hawai'i Immigrant Heritage Preservation Center, Bishop Museum, 1985). See also Ronald Takaki, *Pau Hana: Plantation Life and Labor in Hawaii 1835–1920* (Honolulu: University of Hawaii Press, 1983); Edward D. Beechert, *Working in Hawaii: A Labor History* (Honolulu: University of Hawaii Press, 1985); Dorothy Ochiai Hazama and Jane Okamoto Komeiji, *Okage Sama De: The Japanese in Hawai'i 1885–1985* (Honolulu: Bess Press, 1986); Patsy Sumie Saiki, *Japanese Women in Hawaii: The First 100 Years* (Honolulu: Kisaku, 1985); and Yukiko Kimura, *Issei: Japanese Immigrants in Hawaii* (Honolulu: University of Hawaii Press, 1988). The coincidence of the 1985 centennial of Japanese contract laborer immigration to Hawai'i and the ripening of these scholars' work over many years has obviously brought much attention in the decade to the history of the Japanese American segment, now about 30 percent of the total population of roughly a million.

38. Patsy Sumie Saiki, *Gambare! An Example of Japanese Spirit* (Honolulu: Kisaku, 1982).

39. I am reminded of Joy Kogawa's sounding of themes of silence and the word—the attempt to manage painful historical memory in the World War II and subsequent experience of Japanese Canadians—in her novel, *Obasan* (Boston: David R. Godine, 1982).

HAWAII'S LOCAL LITERARY TRADITIONS

1. See "The Sound of (Hawaiian) Music," *East-West Perspectives*, vol. 1, no. 4 (Fall 1980): 32–36, for an interview with George Kanahele on music, song, and the Hawaiian Renaissance. In 1971 Kanahele helped found and was elected president of the Hawaiian Music Foundation. In 1976 the foundation sponsored a scholarly encyclopedia of Hawaiian music with Kanahele as editor, resulting in the 1979 publication of *Hawaiian Music and Musicians: An Illustrated History*. Music is but one aspect of a total cultural movement. While Kanahele has assumed a central role in writing about this effort, he bases his publications on broad support, consultation, and research shared with other scholars and their constituencies. *Hawaiian Renaissance* (Honolulu: Project WAIAHA, 1982) is a chapbook containing three of Kanahele's lectures from 1977 to 1982. *Ku Kanaka, Stand Tall: A Search for Hawaiian Values* (Honolulu: University of Hawaii Press and WAIAHA Foundation, 1986) is a major philosophical work reflecting the efforts of Polynesians to cultivate the *mana* of experts—as in the spirit of Hanohano in Holt's *Waimea Summer*. Kanahele's purpose is like Malo's and Kamakau's when they compiled their respective *mo'olelo Hawai'i*, gatherings of traditions, yet his own often reflective and abstract inquiry is shaped distinctly in the style of a personal essay.

2. I do not mean that hapa haole (mixed English-Hawaiian) music and lyrics, widely popular in the 1930s to the 1960s, are outside of what may be considered "Hawaiian." I do mean, however, that hapa haole music is certainly not the only music Hawai'i has produced, traditional or contemporary, and that it indeed is itself most meaningful within a far more comprehensive context such as is provided in Kanahele's *Hawaiian Music and Musicians*. See pp. xxv–xvi of that encyclopedia, where Elizabeth Tatar characterizes 1930 to 1960 as "a golden age to many people" in Hawaiian music, when "hapa haole music had become Big Business," with full orchestras playing it around the world. An example of a "classic hapa haole hula tune" is "Little Brown Gal" (1935) by Don McDiarmid and Lee Wood; another is "Lovely Hula Hands" (1939), by R. Alex Anderson.

3. On Henry Opukaha'ia (Obookiah), see Gavan Daws, *Shoal of Time*, 61–63, and Edward Joesting, *Hawaii: An Uncommon History*, 68–69. Opukaha'ia's memoirs were published after his death in Connecticut in 1818. Today, Cecily H. Kikukawa's *Ka Mea Ho'ala, the Awakener: The Story of Henry Obookiah, Once Called Opukaha'ia* (Honolulu: Bess Press, 1982) retells for Hawaii's youngsters the moral tale once used to inspire New Englanders.

4. Counting nonwhites by their different ethnicities, there is no majority group in late twentieth-century Hawai'i. Caucasians, at one-third of the population, are by this reckoning more numerous than members of any of the other groups. If Caucasians in Hawai'i (or in all of America) were counted by different European ethnicities, however, it would be all the more obvious that Hawaii's society is ethnically pluralistic, with no majority, no group numbering more than 50 percent of the population.

5. See *College Plays* (1936–1955), TS, University of Hawaii Department of English, Hamilton Library, Hawaii Pacific Collection, in which Willard Wilson, the drama-writing professor who compiled his students' works, comments on each year's efforts.

6. See Diane Matsunga, "Inu-gami: The Spirit of the Dog," in *Kodomo no tame ni, For the Sake of the Children: The Japanese American Experience in Hawaii*, 73–75. Matsunaga's account of the *inu-gami no sawarimono* that "used to be very prevalent on the island of Kauai in the late 1930s and immediately preceding World War II" is said there to be based on interviews with her father, the late United States Senator Spark Matsunaga, who, "as an Ikibotoke, or living saint, . . . was recognized on Kauai as a sort of a spiritual healer," his powers enabling him to deal with the inugami. My information on how an inugami is invoked comes from Glen Grant, who writes and lectures on the supernatural in Hawaii's cultures. The interpretation I provide of the phenomenon, and its particular application to the historical context, however, are my own.

7. Jo Ann Uchida, "Fever," *Bamboo Ridge: The Hawaii Writers' Quarterly* 1 (December 1978):20–23, rpt. *The Best of Bamboo Ridge*, 103–5).

8. Maxine Hong Kingston, *China Men* (New York: Alfred A. Knopf,

1980); and "No Name Woman," in her *The Woman Warrior: Memoirs of a Girlhood Among Ghosts* (New York: Vintage Books, 1977), 1–19.

9. Patsy Saiki, *The Return of Sam Patch*, TS *Theatre Group Plays* (1966–67), University of Hawaii Theatre Group, Hamilton Library, Hawaii Pacific Collection.

10. For the early nonfictional report on the return to Japan of this historical figure, Sampachi or "Sam Patch," see the edition of the expedition's journals authorized by Commodore Matthew C. Perry, edited by Francis L. Hawkes, *Narrative of the Expedition of an American Squadron to the China Seas and Japan, Performed in the Years 1852, 1853, and 1854* . . . (Washington, D.C.: Publ. by order of the Congress of the United States, A. O. P. Nicholson, 1856), 340–42, 485–86. The Americans report that Sam Patch was astonishingly fearful of Japanese officials who requested interviews.

11. Dana Naone, "The Men Whose Tongues," in *Talk Story: An Anthology of Hawaii's Local Writers*, 100; also in *Poetry Hawaii: A Contemporary Anthology*, ed. Frank Stewart and John Unterecker (Honolulu: University of Hawaii Press, 1979), 74.

12. Rap Reiplinger, "Fate Yanagi," *Poi Dog*, Mountain Apple Company, MAC 1002, 1978.

13. Robert and Roland Cazimero, "Our Song, "*The Brothers Cazimero*, vol. 2, Music of Polynesia, MOP 41000, n.d.

14. O. A. Bushnell, "Hawaii's writers stifled at birth, one of them says," in the Honolulu *Sunday Star-Bulletin and Advertiser*, 25 June 1978, F–3. See also an interview in *Honolulu* 14 (September 1979):93–100. Asked about his Talk Story reference to "predatory journalists" who appropriate Hawaii's literary materials, Bushnell said he was "talking primarily about raiders like Michener" (100).

15. Armine von Tempski, *Dust: A Novel of Hawaii* (New York: Frederick A. Stokes, 1928); *Fire: A Novel of Hawaii* (New York: A. L. Burt, 1929); *Lava: A Saga of Hawaii* (New York, Frederick A. Stokes, 1930); *Thunder in Heaven* (New York, Duell, Sloan and Pearce, 1942). Others of von Tempski's, novels soften the Old Testament ring of those titles; e.g., *Hula: A Romance of Hawaii* (New York: Frederick A. Stokes, 1927) and *Ripe Breadfruit* (New York: Dodd, Mead, 1935).

16. See *Hawaii Quill Magazine*, vol. 5, no. 1 (30 November 1931), an issue devoted to the event.

17. Li Ling Ai, *Life Is for a Long Time: A Chinese Hawaiian Memoir* (see chap. 5, above).

18. Joseph Keonona Chun Fat, *The Mystery of the Ku'ula Rock: A True-to-Life Novel Based on the Life and Legends of the People Living in Kalapana, Hawaii, and the Surrounding Area and the Unraveling of the Mystery of the Ku'ula Rock* (Hicksville, NY: Exposition Press, 1975).

19. Joesting, *Hawaii: An Uncommon History* (New York: W. W. Norton, 1972), 330.

20. James Mishima, *Sunao*, TS, in *Theatre Group Plays* (1951–52/1952–53), University of Hawaii Theatre Group, Hamilton Library, Hawaii Pacific Collection.

21. Jon Shirota is the author of *Lucky Come Hawaii* and *Pineapple White* (see chap. 4, above). For an early example of Edward Sakamoto's dramas, see his *In the Alley*, in *Talk Story: An Anthology*, 156–67; and on his work as a playwright in Los Angeles, see Lawrence Christon,"Life's Roads: *Fast Lane, Pilgrimage, Los Angeles Times*, 25 July 1982, "Calendar," 42.

22. Talk Story, Inc.: The Hawaii Ethnic Resources Center was the principal sponsor of "Talk Story: Our Voices in Literature and Song," Hawaii's Ethnic American Writers' Conference, held 19–24 June 1978 at Mid-Pacific Institute in Honolulu. Co-sponsors of the conference were HLAC; the Japanese American Research Center; the Hawaii Multi-Cultural Center; and the Departments of English and of American Studies, the Ethnic Studies Oral History Project, and the Campus Center Board of the University of Hawaii at Manoa, with funding in part from the Hawaii Committee for the Humanities and the State Foundation on Culture and the Arts. Because quite a few individuals were active in several of these organizations at the same time, any achievements or misunderstandings in the project affected every group, though with distinctive emphases and consequences in any one organization. My comments implying differences between, say HLAC and Talk Story, Inc., are made with respect for distinctions and indeed cooperation among these supporters.

23. For an expression of this idea, see the letter by Gay Sibley (*Honolulu Advertiser*, 11 February 1988, A–23) in response to mine (*Advertiser*, 28 January 1988, A–15). I had taken issue with Hawai'i critic, editor, and scholar A. Grove Day, who with his latest book, *Mad About Islands*, had been the subject of an *Advertiser* feature, 31 December 1987, B-2. In her letter Sibley defends Day's limiting his subjects in Hawaii's literature to authors, all expressly "outsiders" to Hawai'i, who constitute an almost exclusively white male canon. Sibley in effect maintains that Asian Americans born in Hawai'i themselves cannot be considered indigenous to Hawai'i, but are colonizers. As such, they are colonials like the whites whom Day's authors represent. Yet no response is made to the question of why Day's work (titled, for instance, *A Hawaiian Reader* and *Books about Hawaii: Fifty Basic Authors*) do not include local Asian American authors, whether immigrants, Hawai'i-born, outsiders, peasants, or colonials of whatever kind Sibley may have had in mind. In my view, the dispossession from their homeland of locals of any race is cruel. In a letter of 17 February 1988, A–11 a reader questions my use of the term"nesomaniac." The reader assails the term as being so obscure he could not find its meaning. The *Advertiser's* editor replies, however, that "nesomaniac," meaning "mad about islands," is Michener's coinage, not mine (repeated by Day in his book and in the article prompting this series of exchanges). Since I welcome criticism that questions rather than takes matters for granted, I should be grateful that the reader questioned me, even

though no one had criticized the term "nesomaniac" when it came first from the mouths of Michener and Day. In "Conversations with a Nesomaniac: An Interview with A. Grove Day," in *Literary Arts Hawaii* (Spring/Summer 1988): 22–26, when asked to respond to my charge that he is colonial in his view —and to my question of why—Day expressed satisfaction that Asian American literature by "Chinese" and "Japanese" was at last appearing in the Pacific basin, but he betrayed his evident assumption that it is written entirely in languages other than English and needs still to be translated (24).

24. Frank Stewart, Introduction to *Poetry Hawaii: A Contemporary Anthology*, ed. Frank Stewart and John Unterecker (Honolulu: University of Hawaii Press, 1979), xi–xii. My discussion is from Stewart's longer account of Richard Fujii and the brief brush of his "Caravan" with public opinion.

25. According to Jiro Nakano of the Hilo Shou Kai, founded by issei in 1903, the group is the oldest active haiku club in the world. The diction of this poetry is as distinctive to the locale as Hawaii's seasons. Since the Japanese language had no readymade terms, or *ki-go*, to note the local Hawaiian season in each poem, as the genre requires, the issei poets of Hawai'i created their own ki-go. See my "Hawaii, the Northwest, and Asia: Localism and Local Literary Developments in the Creation of an Asian Immigrants' Sensibility," in *Blue Funnel Line*, an Asian American issue of *The Seattle Review* 11 (Spring/Summer 1988):9–18, esp. 11–12. See also my "Waiting for the Big Fish: Recent Research in the Asian American Literature of Hawaii," in *The Best of Bamboo Ridge*, 302–21, esp. 305–8.

26. See Arnold T. Hiura and Stephen H. Sumida, *Asian American Literature of Hawaii: An Annotated Bibliography*, for lists, by decades, of Hawaii's Asian American poets.

27. Larry L. Kimura, "Any Time Now," in *Mele: International Poetry Letter* (December 1967): n.p.n. This is an English translation of Kimura's "He Manawa Wale No."

28. Larry L. Kimura, "Kapalaoa," in *Mele: International Poetry Letter* (July 1968): n.p.n.; rpt. in *Forgotten Pages of American Literature*, ed. Gerald W. Haslam (Boston: Houghton Mifflin, 1970), 139–41; and in *Talk Story Big Island Anthology*, 41–43.

29. Eddie Kamae and Larry Kimura, "Morning Dew," in *Eddie Kamae Presents the Sons of Hawaii*, Hawaii Sons, 1001, n.d.

30. *Mark Twain's Letters from Hawaii*, 215.

31. Eric Chock, "Poem for My Father," in his *Ten Thousand Wishes* (Honolulu: Bamboo Ridge Press, 1978), n.p.n.; rpt. in *Talk Story: An Anthology*, 95.

32. Eric Chock, "Manoa Cemetery, for Moi Lum Chock," in his *Ten Thousand Wishes*, (Honolulu: Bamboo Ridge Press, 1978), n.p.n.; rpt. in *Talk Story: An Anthology*, 92–94.

33. Jody Masako Manabe, "Hadaka De Hanasu (talking nakedly), for Kiyoko," in *Hanai* (1977):11; rpt. in *Talk Story, An Anthology*, 89.

34. Jody Masako Manabe, "Dear Reiko: 1968/1978," *Bamboo Ridge: The Hawaii Writers' Quarterly* 1 (December 1978):16–18; rpt. in *The Best of Bamboo Ridge*, 46–48.

35. Wing Tek Lum, "Grateful Here," in his *Expounding the Doubtful Points* (Honolulu: Bamboo Ridge Press, 1987), 89–90; originally published in *Bulletin of Concerned Asian Scholars* 4 (Fall 1972):56; also published in *Yardbird Reader Volume III*, ed. Shawn Wong and Frank Chin (Berkeley: Yardbird Publishing, 1974), 243; rpt. in *Poetry Hawaii*, 56–57.

36. Louis Chu, *Eat a Bowl of Tea* (1961; rpt. Seattle: University of Washington Press, 1979; rpt. New York: Carol Publishing Group, 1986).

37. At times the rationale for inviting mainlanders to speak alongside locals has been questioned, both in Hawai'i and on the mainland. In Talk Story we tried to neutralize, with play, the prejudices standing in the way of understanding between locals and mainlanders. We sponsored a softball game—local vs. mainland, "mokes" vs. "katonks"—and "Honorary Local Boy" and "Honorary Tita" awards given by noisy popular vote to Bienvenido Santos and Jessica Tarahata Hagedorn. Superficially, there would be no problem at all. But we expected a great deal more than superficiality, and I believe we got what we expected: the opportunity to address real issues. Conference participants and registrants from the mainland included the following writers, performers, and scholars, a few of them originally from Hawai'i: Nikki Bridges, Jeffery Chan, N. V. M. Gonzalez, Jessica Hagedorn, Garrett Kaoru Hongo, Momoko Iko, Lawson Inada, Norman Kaneko, Elaine Kim, Bea Kiyohara, Laureen Mar, Dorothy Yoshimori McDonald, Toshio Mori, Milton Murayama, Katharine Newman, Priscilla Oakes, Oscar Penaranda, Bienvenido Santos, S. E. Solberg, Ronald Takaki, Nellie Wong, Shawn Wong, Mitsuye Yamada, Hisaye Yamamoto, and Wakako Yamauchi. Nearly all the writers of Hawai'i who participated in the conference appear in my present study, while many other local "resource persons" in the arts, humanities, social sciences, education, and journalism are impossible to name individually here, for the entire project was not merely groundbreaking but also rather hugely gregarious. The mainland participants were not invited to take over Hawaii's local literary scene, and certainly the local participants would not have allowed them to do so even if that were an aim. In protest Frank Chin—himself hardly representative of all the mainland participants—declined to participate, pointedly refusing to risk being used as just such a "mainland" imposition only to stir up trouble he judged inevitable because of his strong views against Maxine Hong Kingston, on what was then her home ground. He believed Kingston's position in central events of the entire project, including her team-teaching a university course in Asian American literature with Inada and Santos that summer, compromised its intellectual integrity. His criticism of Kingston, whom he consid-

ers ahistorical and therefore a propagator of what is "fake," however, was heard from others at the conference, where Kingston herself rebutted her critics' charges that she misrepresents Chinese and Chinese Americans in "racist," stereotypic ways. Kingston explained that she intended the narrator of *The Woman Warrior* to be as affected as any white American by the stereotypes impressed upon her by "the silver screen" where historicity ought always to be doubted. Kingston was fascinated with imaginative effects she found she could produce with her verbal style, so she created a naive and unreliable narrator who is not a direct representative of herself, and through whom she could try out verbal (as distinct from her own "real-life") effects and "realities." At the time, several critics argued that *The Woman Warrior* had been mislabled "memoirs," to bad effect. Though it has taken a toll, the fighting that has continued since the 1976 publication of *The Woman Warrior* and Chin's attacks on it (attacks misleadingly thought by some at the conference to come only from an outsider against an insider) has been salutary for the development of Asian American literature and literary studies of Hawai'i and the mainland. Today some views developed by Asian American writers, among them Chin and Kingston, appear to oppose diametrically their original views. The authors themselves have been profoundly motivated by critical and literary controversy to pursue over great distances matters that were already implied in their beginnings. At the Talk Story Conference in 1978, it was clear that discussing the literatures of Hawai'i and the mainland did more than merely showcase them. It created a realization, in both harmony and discord, that the literatures and their historical contexts matter so vitally to the life of "America" and its peoples, that writers and audience alike would stand up to voice their hearts and minds.

38. James Chun is exemplary. He appears first with "Fate?" in the *Chinese Students' Alliance Annual* 3 (May 1920):43–48, 50, a fanciful, intricate romance involving mistaken identities and a forbidden marriage, like a (rather cleverly written) plot summary of a Shakespearean comedy set in a timeless China. Chun next appears with a poem, "China," in *Chinese Students' Alliance Annual* 4 (1921): inside cover, where he extolls the past and exhorts Chinese to throw off all bonds in order to create a righteous future. The crowning achievement of his published writings of his student years, however, is not about China, but Hawai'i: "In the Camp," in *Chinese Students' Alliance Annual* 6 (May 1923):27, 29–31, is a naturalistic story of the tragedy of an immigrant laborer on a sugar plantation. See my "Waiting for the Big Fish," 309–11.

39. "Literary Lethargy," *Chinese Students' Alliance Annual*, 6 (May 1923):5.

40. Cathy Song, "Lost Sister," in *Talk Story: An Anthology*, 80–81. My comments have been adapted for and published in a review article, "Pictures of Art and Life," in *Contact II* 7.38–40 (1986):52–55.

41. Cathy Song, "from a Georgia O'Keeffe Portfolio: Flower Series, No. 3, An Orchid (Makena Beach, Maui)," in *Talk Story: An Anthology*, 82–

83. This poem and "Lost Sister," above, are also in Cathy Song's award-winning *Picture Bride* (New Haven: Yale University Press, 1983).

42. Harvey Hess, introduction to "Issei Poets of Hawaii," Talk Story Big Island Writers' Conference, University of Hawaii at Hilo, 13 July 1979.

43. My article, "Waiting for the Big Fish," is an account of Hiura's and my work on *Asian American Literature of Hawaii*, and it therefore overlaps what I say in the present chapter about that crucial period, 1978 to 1979. There is scant duplication, however, between one account and another of the research and subsequent projects, since what we observed and learned does not fit into any single book, article, or report.

44. See Jeanne Ambrose, "Michener—in His Own Words," *Honolulu Star-Bulletin*, 9 November 1988, D–1, where Michener laments that in the thirty years since publication of his *Hawaii* "no new version of [it] has come out" from another writer's pen. Not to be faulted for modesty, Michener disingenuously complains that "Chinese," "Japanese," and "Hawaiians" have yet to do what he did in and for the literature of Hawai'i.

45. Aunty Edith Kanaka'ole recorded two albums I know of, *Ha'aku'i Pele i Hawai'i! Pele Prevails in Hawai'i!* (Hula Records, 1978), and *Hi'ipoi i ka 'Āina Aloha: Cherish the Beloved Land* (Hawaii Calls Music Group, 1979). The former mainly but not exclusively voices a heroic Hawaiian tradition in chants about gods and goddesses, Lono and Pele, and on serious and somber themes. These same chants also convey such vigor and energy that their very seriousness erupts in exhilaration. See—hear—Kanaka'ole's "Halema'uma'u," a chant about the exploding sexual parts of Pele, the "flirtatious one," based on a parallelism linking the acts of deities, humans, and nature in a way distinctively different from what we usually mean by anthropomorphism and the "pathetic fallacy" (recorded on the *Pele* album and published in *Talk Story Big Island Anthology*, 23). On a pastoral note, hear her "Ka'ū, ke One Hānau" (*Pele* album and *TS Big Island* 24). For a traditional chant perhaps once performed for Captain Cook in the heiau or temple of Lono, Hikiau on Kealakekua Bay, hear "Hula Kōlani" on that same album. The second album, recorded very shortly before Aunty Edith's death, is complementary: its jacket is green; its title and mele are richly pastoral in the Hawaiian idiom.

46. At this time, too, Katharine Newman was completing her article, "Hawaiian-American Literature: The Cultivation of Mangoes," in which she states that one of the "obstacles to future growth" of the literature is "the lack of a developed esthetic"; in other words, the lack of "a formalized esthetic statement—that may never be made" (72). Somewhat like Bushnell's keynote speech at the first Talk Story conference, Newman's words distinctly challenged some writers and readers in Hawai'i to ponder and debate *what* was lacking and *how*, as far as "a developed esthetic" is concerned. My feeling is that, for the ongoing articulation of an "esthetic statement," literary works do not suffice *in* themselves to speak *for* themselves—the partnership of literary criticism is needed. In order

to free writers to further their arts by continually transforming their intuitive truths into the known, criticism needs to be based on scholarship both broad and specific, not simply on impressions of what the writers themselves already understand about their works. And no one critical point of view constitutes a "correct" formal esthetic statement, because no one person or study alone can possibly supply the needed scholarship, analyses, and judgments to achieve such a thing. By its very nature the contribution of criticism to "an esthetic" must come dynamically from interactions of different points of view, approaches to literature, and specific topics of study.

47. However obviously and intentionally provocative, the view Bushnell stated in 1978 is not xenophobic because, it ought to be recognized, the appropriation of the local and the native primarily for profoundly *outside* purposes, such as the promotion of stereotypes already familiar to Hawaii's millions of visitors —as the noble savage is to John Forrest and Tommo—occurs powerfully *inside* Hawaiʻi as well. (It is curious that, to the contrary, we Americans do not typically tour Europe, or, say, Japan with the prejudice that the inhabitants of these places have no meaningful cultures of their own and that they are meant by nature to be of service to us. Might not a shift in expectations about Hawaiʻi—to views from the shore informed by Hawaii's histories and literatures—be healthy for the tourist industry, which is vulnerable to any news of endemic violence, disease, or bad service in Hawaiʻi, as well as healthy for Hawaii's cultures?) Meanwhile writers from the "outside" who have come to settle in Hawaiʻi include a good many who have not misappropriated these cultures. Indeed, they have added to them—and some have been met with the deafness to which Hawaii's native-born literary voices have been treated.

Bibliography

PRIMARY WORKS

Abe, Keith S. *Hawaii Aloha*. Honolulu: Topgallant Publishing, 1986.

Aki, Diana. "Lā 'Elima." *Eddie Kamae Presents the Sons of Hawaii*. Hawaii Sons, HS–2002, 1976.

Altizer, Nell. *The Man Who Died En Route*. Amherst: University of Massachusetts Press, 1989.

Balaz, Joseph. *After the Drought*. Honolulu: Topgallant Publishing, 1985.

Beckwith, Martha, trans. and ed. *The Kumulipo: A Hawaiian Creation Chant*. Chicago: University of Chicago Press, 1951; rpt. Honolulu: University of Hawaii Press, 1972.

————, trans. *The Hawaiian Romance of Laieikawai*. In *Annual Report of the United States Bureau of American Ethnology, 1911–12* 33 (1919):285–666.

Bingham, Hiram. *A Residence of Twenty-one Years in the Sandwich Islands; or the Civil, Religious, and Political History of Those Islands: Comprising a Particular View of the Missionary Operations Connected with the Introduction and Progress of Christianity and Civilization Among the Hawaiian People*. New York: Sherman Converse, 1847.

Bulosan, Carlos. *America Is in the Heart*. 1946; rpt. Seattle: University of Washington Press, 1973.

Bushnell, O. A. *Ka'a'awa: A Novel about Hawaii in the 1850's*. Pacific Classics Series, No. 7. Honolulu: University of Hawaii Press, 1972.

————. *Molokai*. 1963; rpt. Pacific Classics Series, No. 4. Honolulu: University of Hawaii Press, 1975.

————. *The Return of Lono*. 1956; rpt. Pacific Classics Series, No. 1. Honolulu: University of Hawaii Press, 1971.

————. *The Stone of Kannon*. Friends of the Library of Hawaii Publications. Honolulu, University of Hawaii Press, 1979.

————. *The Water of Kane*. Friends of the Library of Hawaii Publications. Honolulu: University of Hawaii Press , 1980.

Cazimero, Robert, and Roland Cazimero. "Our Song." In *The Brothers Cazimero*. Vol. 2. Music of Polynesia, MOP 41000, n.d.

Chock, Eric. "Manoa Cemetery, for Moi Lum Chock." In *Talk Story: An Anthology of Hawaii's Local Writers*, 92–94. Edited by Eric Chock et al. Honolulu: Petronium Press and Talk Story, 1978

———. "Poem for My Father." In *Talk Story: An Anthology of Hawaii's Local Writers*, 95. Edited by Eric Chock et al. Honolulu: Petronium Press and Talk Story, 1978.

———. *Ten Thousand Wishes*. Honolulu: Bamboo Ridge Press, 1978.

Chock, Eric, and Darrell H. Y. Lum, eds. *The Best of Bamboo Ridge: The Hawaii Writers' Quarterly*. Honolulu: Bamboo Ridge Press, 1986.

Chock, Eric, Darrell H. Y. Lum, Gail Miyasaki, Dave Robb, Frank Stewart, and Kathy Uchida, eds. *Talk Story: An Anthology of Hawaii's Local Writers*. Foreword by Maxine Hong Kingston. Honolulu: Petronium Press and Talk Story, 1978.

Chu, Louis. *Eat A Bowl of Tea*. 1961; rpt., Seattle: University of Washington Press 1979; New York: Carol Publishing Group, 1986.

Chun, James. "China." In *Chinese Students' Alliance Annual* 4 (1921):inside cover.

———. "Fate?" In *Chinese Students' Alliance Annual* 3 (May 1920):43–48, 50.

———. "In the Camp." In *Chinese Students' Alliance Annual* 6 (May 1923):27, 29–31.

Chun, Wai Chee. "For You a Lei." In *College Plays*, 1937. TS. Hawaiian Pacific Collection. Hamilton Library. University of Hawaii.

Clemens, Samuel L. *A Connecticut Yankee in King Arthur's Court*. 1889; rpt. New York: Harper and Brothers, 1899.

———. *Following the Equator*. Hartford: American Publishing, 1897.

———. *Mark Twain–Howells Letters*. Edited by Henry Nash Smith and William M. Gibson. 2 vols. Cambridge: Harvard University Press, 1960.

———. The Mark Twain Papers. DV 111. Bancroft Library. University of California at Berkeley.

———. *Mark Twain's Letters*. Edited by Albert Bigelow Paine. 2 vols. New York: Harper and Brothers, 1917.

———. *Mark Twain's Letters from Hawaii*. Edited by A. Grove Day. London: Chatto & Windus, 1967.

———. *Mark Twain's Notebooks and Journals, 1855–1873*. Vol. 1 of *Mark Twain*. Edited by Frederick Anderson, Michael B. Frank, and Kenneth M. Sanderson (Mark Twain Papers No. 8). Berkeley and London: University of California Press, 1975.

———. *Mark Twain Speaking*. Edited by Paul Fatout. Iowa City: University of Iowa Press, 1976.

———. *Mark Twain to Mrs. Fairbanks*. Edited by Dixon Wecter. San Marino: Huntington Library, 1949.

————. *Roughing It.* 1872; rpt. Hartford: American Publishing, 1897.

Cook, James. *The Journals of Captain Cook on His Voyage of Discovery.* Vol. 3, pt. 1. Edited by J. C. Beaglehole. *The Voyage of the Resolution and Discovery, 1776–1780. Hakluyt Society Series.* Cambridge: Cambridge University Press, 1967.

————. *A Voyage to the Pacific Ocean Undertaken, by the Command of His Majesty, for Making Discoveries in the Northern Hemisphere to Determine the Position and Extent of the West Side of North America; its Distance from Asia; and the Practicability of a Northern Passage to Europe.* Vol. 2. London: Published by Order of the Lords Commissioners of the Admiralty, W. and A. Strahan, 1784.

Cooper, James Fenimore. *The Crater: or, Vulcan's Peak; a Tale of the Pacific.* 2 vols. New York: Burgess, Stringer, 1847.

Day, A. Grove, and Carl Stroven, eds. *A Hawaiian Reader.* Introduction by James A. Michener. New York: Appleton-Century Crofts, 1959. [rpt. Honolulu: Mutual Publishing, 1985].

————, eds. *The Spell of Hawaii.* New York: Meredith Press, 1968.

de Camoëns, Luis Vaz. *The Lusiads.* Translated by William C. Atkinson. Harmondsworth: Penguin Books, 1952.

Elbert, Samuel H., and Noelani Mahoe, eds. *Na Mele o Hawai'i Nei: 101 Hawaiian Songs.* Honolulu: University of Hawaii Press, 1970.

Eliot, T. S. *Sweeney Agonistes: Fragments of an Aristophanic Melodrama.* London: Faber & Faber, 1932.

Emerson, Nathaniel B., ed. and trans. *Unwritten Literature of Hawaii: The Sacred Songs of the Hula.* Washington, D.C.: Bureau of American Ethnology, 1909; rpt. Rutland, VT: Charles E. Tuttle, 1965.

Fat, Joseph Keonona Chun. *The Mystery of the Ku'ula Rock: A True-to-Life Novel Based on the Life and Legends of the People Living in Kalapana, Hawaii, and the Surrounding Area and the Unraveling of the Mystery of the Ku'ula Rock.* Hicksville, NY: Exposition Press, 1975.

Felipe, Virgilio Menor. "'Chapter 1. Once In the First Times' from *What You Like Know? An Oral Biography of Bonipasyo.*" In *Bamboo Ridge: The Hawaii Writers' Quarterly* 11 (June–August 1981):45–58.

————. "From 'Hawaii, Plantation of Destiny.'" In *Talk Story Big Island Anthology,* 26–31. Edited by Stephen Sumida, Arnold Hiura, and Martha Webb.

————. "Hawaii: A Pilipino Dream." In *Searching for the Promised Land—Filipinos and Samoans in Hawaii,* 22–37. Edited by Nancy F. Young. Honolulu: General Assistance Center of the Pacific, 1974.

————. "Hawaii: Plantation of Destiny." In *Manna-Mana,* 2–20. Edited by Leonard Lueras. Honolulu: By the editor, 1973.

Fornander, Abraham. *An Account of the Polynesian Race, Its Origin and Migrations and the Ancient History of the Hawaiian People to the Times of Kamehameha I.* 2 vols. 1897; rpt. Rutland, VT: Charles E. Tuttle, 1969.

Frear, Mary Dillingham. "Hawaii." *Hawaii Quill Magazine* 5 (30 November 1931):n.p.n.

Goldsberry, Steven. *Māui the Demigod: An Epic Novel of Mythical Hawai'i.* New York: Poseidon Press, 1984; rpt. Honolulu: University of Hawaii Press, 1989.

Goring, Ken. *Gone to Maui.* N.p.: Puna Publishing, 1983.

Haleole, S. N. *Ke Kaao o Laieikawai: Ka Hiwahiwa o Paliuli, Kawahineokaliula.* Honolulu: Henry M. Whitney, 1863.

Hamada, James T. *Don't Give Up the Ship.* Boston: Meador, 1933.

Hamasaki, Richard, and Wayne K. Westlake, eds. *A Pacific Islands Collection: Seaweeds and Constructions* 7 (1983).

Harada, Gail. "First Winter." In *Talk Story: An Anthology of Hawaii's Local Writers,* 97. Edited by Eric Chock et al. Honolulu: Petronium Press and Talk Story, 1978.

———. "Hearing a Train Whistle at Night." In *Talk Story: An Anthology of Hawaii's Local Writers.* 96–97. Edited by Eric Chock et al. Honolulu: Petronium Press and Talk Story, 1978.

———. "7 O'Clock." In Talk Story: An Anthology of Hawaii's Local Writers, 96. Edited by Eric Chock et al. Honolulu: Petronium Press and Talk Story, 1978.

Harada, Margaret N. *The Sun Shines on the Immigrant.* New York: Vantage Press, 1960.

Harrison, Samuel B. *The White King.* Garden City: Doubleday, 1950.

Hawkes, Francis L., ed. *Narrative of the Expedition of an American Squadron to the China Seas and Japan Performed in the Years 1852, 1853, and 1854, under the Command of Commodore M. C. Perry, United States Navy, by Order of the United States.* Washington, D.C.: Published by order of the Congress of the United States, A. O. P. Nicholson, 1856.

Hawkesworth, John, ed. *An Account of the Voyages Undertaken by the Order of His Present Majesty for Making discoveries in the Southern Hemisphere and Successively Performed by Commodore Byron, Captain Wallis, Captain Carteret, and Captain Cook, in the Dolphin, the Swallow, and the Endeavor: Drawn up from the Journals Which Were Kept by the Several Commanders, and from the Papers of Sir Joseph Banks, Bart.* Fourth Edition. Perth: R. Morrison, 1789.

Hiura, Arnold, Stephen Sumida, and Martha Webb, eds. *Talk Story Big Island Anthology.* Honolulu: Bamboo Ridge Press and Talk Story, 1979.

Holt, John Dominis. *Hanai: A Poem for Queen Liliuokalani.* Honolulu: Topgallant Publishing, 1986.

———. *Kaulana Na Pua, Famous Are the Flowers: Queen Liliuokalani and the*

Throne of Hawaii: A Play in Three Acts. Honolulu: Topgallant Publishing, 1974.

――――. *Princess of the Night Rides and Other Tales.* Honolulu: Topgallant Publishing, 1977.

――――. *Waimea Summer: A Novel.* Honolulu: Topgallant Publishing, 1976.

Hongo, Bob Nobuyuki. *Hey Pineapple!* Tokyo: Hokuseido Press, 1958.

Hongo, Garrett. *The River of Heaven.* New York: Alfred A. Knopf, 1988.

――――. *Yellow Light.* Middletown: Wesleyan University Press, 1982.

Honma, Dean. *Night Dive.* Honolulu: Petronium Press, 1985.

Ige, Philip K. "The Forgotten Flea Powder." *Paradise of the Pacific* 58 (November 1946):24–25.

――――. "The New Road." *The Lit* 1 (January 1951):26–27.

Jarves, James J. *History of the Hawaiian or Sandwich Islands, Embracing Their Antiquities, Mythology, Legends, Discovery by Europeans in the Sixteenth Century, Re-Discovery by Cook, with Their Civil, Religious, and Political History, from the Earliest Traditionary Period to the Present Time.* Boston: Tappan & Dennett, 1843. Second edition, Boston: James Munroe, 1844.

――――. *Kiana: A Tradition of Hawaii.* Boston: James Munroe, 1857.

Jelsma, Clara [Mitsuko Kubojiri]. *Teapot Tales and Other Stories.* Honolulu: Bamboo Ridge Press, 1981.

Judd, Laura Fish. *Honolulu: Sketches of the Life, Social, Political, and Religious, in the Hawaiian Islands from 1828 to 1861.* New York: Anson D. F. Randolph, 1880.

Kaeo, Peter, and Queen Emma. *News from Molokai: Letters Between Peter Kaeo and Queen Emma 1873–1876.* Edited by Alfons L. Korn. Honolulu: University of Hawaii Press, 1976.

Kalākaua, King David, and Harry Berger. "Hawai'i Pono'i." In *Nā Mele o Hawai'i Nei: 101 Hawaiian Songs,* 43–44. Edited by Samuel H. Elbert and Noelani Mahoe. Honolulu: University of Hawaii Press, 1970.

Kamae, Eddie. "Kela Mea Whiffa." *Eddie Kamae Presents the Sons of Hawaii.* Hawaii Sons, 1001, n.d.

Kamae, Eddie and Larry Lindsey Kimura. "Morning Dew." *Eddie Kamae Presents the Sons Of Hawaii.* Hawaii Sons, 1001, n.d.

Kamakau, Samuel M. *I ka Wā o Kamehameha: In the Time of Kamehameha, Selected Essays by Samuel M. Kamakau.* Edited by Malcolm Naea Chun. Honolulu: Folk Press, Kapiolani Community College, 1988.

――――. *Ruling Chiefs of Hawaii.* Honolulu: 1866; rpt. Honolulu: Kamehameha Schools Press, 1961.

Kanaka'ole, Edith. *Ha'aku'i Pele i Hawai'i! Pele Prevails in Hawai'i!* Hula Records, 1978.

――――. "Halema'uma'u." Translated by Kalani Meinecke. In *Talk Story Big Is-*

land Anthology, 23. Edited by Arnold Hiura, Stephen Sumida, and Martha Webb. Honolulu: Bamboo Ridge Press and Talk Story, 1979.

———. *Hiʻipo i ka ʻĀina Aloha: Cherish the Beloved Land.* Hawaii Calls Music Group, HS–568, 1979.

———. "Kaʻū ke One Hānau." Translated by Kalani Meinecke. In *Talk Story Big Island Anthology*, 24. Edited by Arnold Hiura, Stephen Sumida, and Martha Webb. Honolulu: Bamboo Ridge Press and Talk Story, 1979.

Kapiʻolani. "Ipo Lei Manu." *Iaʻoe E Ka Lā: Palani Vaughan Sings the Music of Hawaiʻiʻs King David Kalākaua.* Nakahili Productions, NP–CAS–300, 1977.

———. "Ipo Lei Manu." Liner notes. *The Gabby Pahinui Hawaiian Band.* Panini Records, PS–1007, 1975.

Kawano, Doris Kimie. *Harue, Child of Hawaii.* Honolulu: Topgallant Publishing, 1984.

Kikukawa, Cecily H. *Ka Mea Hoʻala, the Awakener: The Story of Henry Obookiah, Once Called Opukahaʻia.* Honolulu: Bess Press, 1982.

Kimura, Larry Lindsey. "Any Time Now." *Mele: International Poetry Letter* (December 1967):n.p.n.

———. "Kapalaoa." *Mele: International Poetry Letter* (July 1968): n.p.n.

———. "Kapalaoa." In *Forgotten Pages of American Literature*, 139–41. Edited by Gerald W. Haslam. Boston: Houghton Mifflin, 1970.

Kingston, Maxine Hong. *China Men.* New York: Alfred A. Knopf, 1980.

———. *The Woman Warrior: Memoirs of a Girlhood Among Ghosts.* New York: Alfred A. Knopf, 1976; rpt. New York: Vintage Books, 1977.

Kogawa, Joy. *Obasan.* Boston: David R. Godine, 1982.

Kono, Juliet S. *Hilo Rains.* Honolulu: Bamboo Ridge Press, 1988.

Kuahiwi, Samuel. "Nā Aliʻi." In *Nā Mele o Hawaiʻi Nei: 101 Hawaiian Songs*, 79–80. Edited by Samuel H. Elbert and Noelani Mahoe. Honolulu: University of Hawaii Press, 1970.

Kwon [Pai], Margaret C. *I Fear Not Pele.* TS. In *College Plays*, 1937. University of Hawaii Department of English. Hawaii Pacific Collection. Hamilton Library. University of Hawaii.

Li Ling Ai [Gladys Li]. *Life is for a Long Time: A Chinese Hawaiian Memoir.* New York: Hastings House, 1972.

Likelike. "Kuʻu Ipo i ka Heʻe Puʻe One." Translated by Ruth Leilani Tyau and S. H. Elbert. In *Nā Mele o Hawaiʻi Nei: 101 Hawaaian Songs.* Edited by Samuel H. Elbert and Noelani Mahoe. Honolulu: University of Hawaii Press, 1970.

Liliʻuokalani. "Aloha ʻOe." In *Nā Mele o Hawaiʻi Nei: 101 Hawaiian Songs*, 35–36. Edited by Samuel H. Elbert and Noelani Mahoe. Honolulu: University of Hawaii Press, 1970.

Loomis, Albertine. *Grapes of Canaan: Hawaii 1820.* 1951; rpt. Honolulu: Hawaii Mission Children's Society, 1966.

Lum, Darrell H. Y. "Beer Can Hat." *Bamboo Ridge: The Hawaii Writer's Quarterly* 8 (September–November 1979):10–19.

———. "Primo Doesn't Take Back Bottles Anymore." *Kapa* (Spring 1972):51–53.

———. "Sun: Short Stories and Drama by Darrell H. Y. Lum." *Bamboo Ridge: The Hawaii Writers' Quarterly* 8 (September–November 1979).

Lum, Wing Tek. *Expounding the Doubtful Points.* Honolulu: Bamboo Ridge Press, 1987.

Lyons, Lorenzo. "Hawai'i Aloha." In *Nā Mele o Hawai'i Nei: 101 Hawaiian Songs*, 42. Edited by Samuel H. Elbert and Noelani Mahoe. Honolulu: University of Hawaii Press, 1970.

McKee, Ruth Eleanor. *Christopher Strange: A Novel.* Garden City: Doubleday, Doran, 1941.

———. *The Lord's Anointed.* Garden City: Doubleday, 1934.

McPherson, Michael. *Singing with the Owls.* Honolulu: Petronium Press, 1982.

Malo, David[a]. *Hawaiian Anitquities (Moolelo Hawaii).* Translated by Nathaniel B. Emerson. Honolulu: 1838; rpt. Honolulu: Bernice P. Bishop Museum, 1951.

———. *Ka Mo'olelo Hawai'i* (Hawaiian Antiquities). Edited by Malcolm Naea Chun. Honolulu: Folk Press, Kapiolani Coummunity College, 1987.

Manabe, Jody Masako. "Dear Reiko: 1968/1978." *Bamboo Ridge: The Hawaii Writers' Quarterly* 1 (December 1978):16–18.

———. "Hadaka De Hanasu (talking nakedly), for Kiyoko." *Hanai* (1977):11.

Matsueda, Pat. *The Fish Catcher.* Honolulu: Petronium Press, 1985.

Melville, Herman. *Typee: A Peep at Polynesian Life During a Four Months' Residence in a Valley of the Marquesas.* Edited by Harrison Hayford, Herschel Parker, and G. Thomas Tanselle. Newberry Library Series. Evanston: Northwestern University Press, 1968.

Merwin, W. S. *Finding the Islands.* San Francisco: North Point Press, 1982.

———. *The Rain in the Trees.* New York: Alfred A. Knopf, 1988.

Michener, James A. *Hawaii.* New York: Random House, 1959.

———. "Povenaaa's Daughter." In his *Return to Paradise.* New York: Bantam Books, 1951.

Mishima, James. *Sunao.* TS. In *Theatre Group Plays*, 1951–52/1952–53. University of Hawaii Theatre Group. Hawaii Pacific Collection. Hamilton Library. University of Hawaii.

Miyamoto, Kazuo. *Hawaii: End of the Rainbow.* Rutland, VT: Charles E. Tuttle, 1964; First Tut Book ed., 1968.

Morales, Rodney. *The Speed of Darkness.* Honolulu: Bamboo Ridge Press, 1988.

Morris, Aldyth. *Captain Cook.* TS. 1977.

———. *Damien.* Honolulu: University of Hawaii Press, 1980.

———. *The Fourth Son.* TS. 1959.

———. *Robert Louis Stevenson.* TS. 1977.

———. *The Secret Concubine*. TS. Revised for the New York production, June 1959.

Murayama, Milton. *All I Asking for Is My Body*. San Francisco: Supa Press, 1975; rpt. Honolulu: University of Hawaii Press, 1988.

———. "I'll Crack Your Head *Kotsun*." *Arizona Quarterly* 15 (Summer 1959):137–49.

———. "A Novel, Untitled, Part I: Five Years on a Rock." *The Seattle Review: Blue Funnel Line* 9 (Spring/Summer 1988):150–55.

———. "Yoshitsune." TS. 1977.

Naone, Dana. "The Men Whose Tongues." In *Talk Story: An Anthology of Hawaii's Local Writers*, 100. Edited by Eric Chock et al. Honolulu: Petronium Press and Talk Story, 1978.

Newell, Charles M. *Kalani of Oahu: An Historical Romance of Hawaii*. Boston: By the author, 1881.

———. *Kamehameha, the Conquering King*. New York: Putnam, 1885.

Nunes, Susan. *A Small Obligation and Other Stories of Hilo*. Honolulu: Bamboo Ridge Press, 1982.

Ogai, Seiko. "The Other Angel." *Nisei: In Hawaii and the Pacific* 6 (Holiday Issue 1952):1, 18, 20.

Okada, John. *No-No Boy*. Rutland, VT: Charles E. Tuttle, 1957; rpt. San Francisco: Combined Asian American Resources Project, 1977; Seattle: University of Washington Press, 1979.

Ota, Shelley Ayame Nishimura. *Upon Their Shoulders*. New York: Exposition Press, 1951.

Pai, Margaret K[won]. *The Dreams of Two Yi-Min*. Honolulu: University of Hawaii Press, 1989. (*See also* Kwon[Pai], Margaret C.)

Parker, Helen Lindsey. "Maunaloa." *Cane Fire! With the Peter Moon Band*. Panini Records, PS1012, 1982.

Perkins, Leialoha Apo. *Kamaka of Mamala Bay*. Honolulu: Kamaluʻuluolele, 1980.

———. *Kingdoms of the Heart: Odyssey of a Hawaiian Woman from Lahaina to Boston and Back, Before Tonga*. Honolulu: Kamaluʻuluolele, 1980.

———. *Natural and Other Stories about Contemporary Hawaiians*. Honolulu: Kamaluʻuluolele, 1979.

Pukui, Mary Kawena, and Alfons L. Korn, eds. and trans. *The Echo of Our Song: Chants & Poems of the Hawaiians*. Honolulu: University of Hawaii Press, 1973.

Quagliano, Tony. *Fierce Meadows*. Honolulu: Petronium Press, 1981.

Reiplinger, Rap. "Fate Yanagi." *Poi Dog*. Mountain Apple Company, MAC 1002, 1978.

———. "Hawaii Haiku." *Poi Dog*. Mountain Apple Company, MAC 1002, 1978.

Saiki, Patsy. *The Return*. TS. In *University of Hawaii Plays*, 1959. University of Hawaii Department of Drama. Hawaii Pacific Collection. Hamilton Library. University of Hawaii.

———. *The Return of Sam Patch*. TS. In *Theatre Group Plays*, 1966–67. University of Hawaii Theatre Group. Hawaii Pacific Collection. Hamilton Library. University of Hawaii.

———. *Sachie: A Daughter of Hawaii*. Honolulu: Kisaku, 1977.

———. "The Unwilling Bride," 1951; rpt. in *Talk Story Big Island Anthology*, 60–63. Edited by Arnold Hiura, Stephen Sumida, and Martha Webb. Honolulu: Bamboo Ridge Press and Talk Story, 1979.

Sakamoto, Edward. *In the Alley*. In *Talk Story: An Anthology of Hawaii's Local Writers*, 157–67. Edited by Eric Chock et al. Honolulu: Petronium Press and Talk Story, 1978.

Santos, Jerry. Jacket Notes. "Ku'u Home 'o Kahalu'u." *Olomana*. Seabird Productions/Seabird Sound, SS 1001, 1976.

Shell, Molly Tani. *Where Dwells the Heart*. TS. In *Theatre Group Plays*, 1953–54/1954–55. University of Hawaii Theatre Group. Hawaii Pacific Collection. Hamilton Library. University of Hawaii.

Shirota, Jon. *Lucky Come Hawaii*. New York: Bantam Books, 1965; rpt. Honolulu: Bess Press, 1988.

———. *Pineapple White*. Los Angeles: Ohara Publication, 1972.

Sinclair, Marjorie. *Kona: A Novel*. Honolulu: Mutual Publishing, 1986.

———. *The Wild Wind: A Novel*. 1950; rpt. Honolulu: Mutual Publishing, 1987.

Skinner, Michelle Cruz. *Balikbayan: A Filipino Homecoming*. Honolulu: Bess Press, 1988.

Song, Cathy. *Frameless Windows, Squares of Light*. New York: W. W. Norton, 1988.

———. "from A Georgia O'Keefe Portfolio: Flower Series, No. 3, An Orchid (Makena Beach, Maui)." In *Talk Story: An Anthology of Hawaii's Local Writers*, 82–83. Edited by Eric Chock et al. Honolulu: Petronium Press and Talk Story, 1978.

———. "Lost Sister." In *Talk Story: An Anthology of Hawaii's Local Writers*, 80–81. Edited by Eric Chock et al. Honolulu: Petronium Press and Talk Story, 1978.

———. *Picture Bride*. New Haven: Yale University Press, 1983.

Stewart, Frank. *Flying the Red Eye*. Point Reyes Station, CA: Floating Island Publications, 1986.

———. *The Open Water*. Point Reyes Station, CA: Floating Island Publications, 1982.

———. *Reunion*. Honolulu: Paper Press, 1986.

Stewart, Frank, ed. *Passages to the Dream Shore: Short Stories of Contemporary Hawaii*. Honolulu: University of Hawaii Press, 1987.

Stewart, Frank, and John Unterecker, eds. *Poetry Hawaii: A Contemporary Anthology*. Honolulu: University of Hawaii Press, 1979.

Stoddard, Charles Warren. *South-Sea Idylls*. 1873; rpt. New York: Charles Scribner's Sons, 1909.

Terada, Vinnie. "Intermediate School Hapai." *Bamboo Ridge: The Hawaii Writers' Quarterly* 5 (December 1979): 28–45.

Thompson, Hunter S., and Ralph Steadman. *The Curse of Lono*. Toronto: Bantam Books, 1983.

Thurston, Lucy Goodale. *The Life and Times of Lucy G. Thurston*. Ann Arbor: S. C. Andrews, 1882.

Uchida, Jo Ann. "Fever." *Bamboo Ridge: The Hawaii Writers' Quarterly* 1 (December 1978): 20–23.

von Tempski, Armine. *Aloha, My Love to You: The Story of One Who Was Born in Paradise*. New York: Duell, Sloan, 1946.

———. *Born in Paradise*. New York: Duell, Sloan and Pearce, 1940.

———. *Dust: A Novel of Hawaii*. New York: Frederick A. Stokes, 1928.

———. *Fire: A Novel of Hawaii*. New York: A. L. Burt, 1929.

———. *Hula: A Romance of Hawaii*. New York: Frederick A. Stokes, 1927.

———. *Lava: A Saga of Hawaii*. New York: Frederick A. Stokes, 1930.

———. *Ripe Breadfruit*. New York: Dodd, Mead, 1935.

———. *Thunder in Heaven*. New York: Duell, Sloan and Pearce, 1942.

Webb, Martha. *He Punahele*. In *Bamboo Ridge: The Hawaii Writers' Quarterly* 10(March–May 1981):44–60.

———. "Mauna Kea." In *Talk Story Big Island Anthology*, 64. Edited by Arnold Hiura, Stephen Sumida, and Martha Webb. Honolulu: Bamboo Ridge Press and Talk Story, 1979.

Winthrop, John. "A Modell of Christian Charity." In *Winthrop Papers, 1623–1630*. Vol. 2. N.p.: Massachusetts Historical Society, 1931.

Yamamoto, Hisaye. "Yoneko's Earthquake." In *Aiiieeeee! An Anthology of Asian-American Writers*, 178–90. Edited by Frank Chin et al. 1974; rev. ed. Washington, D. C.: Howard University Press, 1983.

Yamauchi, Wakako. "And the Soul Shall Dance." In *Aiiieeeee! An Anthology of Asian-American Writers*, 193–200. Edited by Frank Chin et al. 1974; rev. ed. Washington, D.C.: Howard University Press, 1983.

SECONDARY WORKS

Ambrose, Jeanne. "Michener—In His Own Words." *Honolulu Star-Bulletin*, 9 November 1988, D-1.

Beaglehole, J. C. *Cook the Writer*. Sydney: Sydney University Press, 1970.

Beckwith, Martha. *Hawaiian Mythology*. Folklore Foundation of Vassar College, 1940; rpt. Honolulu: University of Hawaii Press, 1970.

Beechert, Edward D. *Working in Hawaii: A Labor History*. Honolulu: University of Hawaii Press, 1985.

Bernardino, Haunani, Darryl Keola Cabacungan, John Charlot, Larry Kimura,

Peter Moon, and Leon Siu. "Lyrics of Hawaii Today." Panel presentation at Talk Story: Our Voices in Literature and Song. Hawaii's Ethnic American Writers' Conference. Honolulu, Hawai'i, 20 June 1978.

Boorstin, Daniel J. *The Image: A Guide to Pseudo-Events in America.* 1961; rpt. New York: Atheneum, 1977.

Budd, Louis J. *Mark Twain: Social Philosopher.* Bloomington: Indiana University Press, 1962.

Bushnell, O. A. "Hawaii's writers stifled at birth, one of them says." [*Honolulu*] *Sunday Star-Bulletin and Advertiser,* 25 June 1978, F–3.

———. [Interview.] *Honolulu* 14 (September 1979): 93–100.

Cazimero, Robert, and Roland Cazimero. Jacket Notes. *The Brothers Cazimero.* Music of Polynesia, MOP 3800, n.d.

Char, Tin-Yuke, ed. *The Sandalwood Mountains: Readings and Stories of the Early Chinese in Hawaii.* Honolulu: University of Hawaii Press, 1975.

Charlot, John. *Chanting the Universe: Hawaiian Religious Culture.* Hong Kong and Honolulu: Emphasis International, 1983.

———. *The Hawaiian Poetry of Religion and Politics: Some Religio-Political Concepts in Postcontact Literature* [Lā'ie:] Institute for Polynesian Studies, 1985.

———. *The Kamapua'a Literature: The Classical Traditions of the Hawaiian Pig God as a Body of Literature* Lā'ie: Institute for Polynesian Studies, Brigham Young University–Hawai'i Campus, 1987.

Chin, Frank, Jeffrey Paul Chan, Lawson Fusao Inada, and Shawn Hsu Wong, eds. *Aiiieeeee! An Anthology of Asian-American Writers.* Washington, D.C.: Howard University Press, 1974; rpt. Garden City, NY: Anchor Press/Doubleday, 1975; rev. ed. Washington, D.C.: Howard University Press, 1983.

Chock, Eric, and Jody Manabe, eds. *Writers of Hawaii: A Focus on Our Literary Heritage.* Honolulu: Bamboo Ridge Press, 1981.

Christon, Lawrence. "Life's Roads: *Fast Lane, Pilgrimage.*" *Los Angeles Times,* 25 July 1982, "Calendar," 42.

Christy, Arthur E. "The Sense of the Past." In *The Asian Legacy and American Life.* Edited by Arthur E. Christy. New York: John Day, 1945; rpt. Westport, CT: Greenwood Press, 1968.

Chun, Malcolm Naea. "He Mo'olelo No S. M. Kamakau, He Mo'okū'auhau: A Biographical Essay of S. M. Kamakau, Historian." In *I ka Wā o Kamehameha: In the Time of Kamehameha, Selected Essays by Samuel M. Kamakau.* Edited by Malcolm Naea Chun. Honolulu: Folk Press, Kapiolani Community College, 1988.

Dahlgren, E. W. *The Discovery of the Hawaiian Islands: Were the Hawaiian Islands Visited by the Spaniards Before Their Discovery by Captain Cook in 1778?* Stockholm: Almquist and Wiksells, 1916; rpt. New York: AMS Press, 1917.

Daws, Gavan. *A Dream of Islands: Voyages of Self-Discovery in the South Seas.* New York: Norton, 1980.

————. *Shoal of Time: A History of the Hawaiian Islands.* Toronto: Macmillan, 1968, rpt. Honolulu: University of Hawaii Press, 1974.

Day, A. Grove. *Books about Hawaii: Fifty Basic Authors.* Honolulu: University of Hawaii Press, 1977.

————. "Conversations with a Nesomaniac: An Interview with A. Grove Day." Interviewed by Gay Sibley. *Literary Arts Hawaii* (Spring/Summer 1988):22–26.

————. *James A. Michener.* New York: Twayne Publishers, 1964.

————. *Mad About Islands: Novelists of a Vanished Pacific.* Honolulu: Mutual Publishing, 1987.

Empson, William. *Some Versions of Pastoral.* Norfolk, CT: New Directions, 1960.

Fatout, Paul. *Mark Twain on the Lecture Circuit.* Bloomington: Indiana University Press, 1960.

Frear, Walter Francis. *Mark Twain and Hawaii.* Chicago: Privately printed, 1947.

Frye, Northrop. *Anatomy of Criticism: Four Essays.* New York: Atheneum 1967.

Fuchs, Lawrence H. *Hawaii Pono: A Social History.* New York: Harcourt, Brace and World, 1961.

Gray, Francine du Plessix. *Hawaii: The Sugar-Coated Fortress.* New York: Vintage Books, 1973.

Hawaii Quill Magazine. Vol. 5, no. 1 (30 November 1931).

Hayford, Harrison. Afterword to *Typee: A Peep at Polynesian Life During a Four Months' Residence in a Valley of the Marquesas,* by Herman Melville. New York: New American Library, 1964.

Hazama, Dororthy Ochiai, and Jane Okamoto Komeiji. *Okage Sama De: The Japanese in Hawai'i 1885–1985.* Honolulu: Bess Press, 1986.

Hershinow, Sheldon. "Coming of Age? The Literature of Contemporary Hawaii." *Bamboo Ridge: The Hawaii Writers' Quarterly* 13 (December 1981–February 1982): 5–10.

————. "John Dominis Holt and Hawaiian-American Literature." In *Writers of Hawaii: A focus on Our Literary Heritage,* 7–12. Edited by Eric Chock and Jody Manabe. Honolulu: Bamboo Ridge Press, 1981.

————. "John Dominis Holt: Hawaiian-American Traditionalist." *MELUS* 7 (Summer 1980):61–72.

Hess, Harvey. "Issei Poets of Hawaii." [Introduction to panel presentation.] Talk Story Big Island Writers' Conference. Hilo, Hawai'i, 13 July 1979.

Higa, Saburo. Hilo Gin-u Shi Sha (Silver Rain Society, Tanka Club). Interview. 13 July 1979.

Hiura, Arnold. "Comments on Milton Murayama." In *Writers of Hawaii: A Focus on Our Literary Heritage,* 65–67. Edited by Eric Chock and Jody Manabe. Honolulu: Bamboo Ridge Press, 1981.

Hiura, Arnold T., and Stephen H. Sumida. *Asian American Literature of Hawaii: An Annotated Bibliography*. Honolulu: Japanese American Research Center and Talk Story, 1979.

Holt, John Dominis. "The Big Island in Literature." Panel discussion. Talk Story Big Island Writers' Conference. Hilo, Hawai'i, 13 July 1979.

———. *Monarchy in Hawaii*. Honolulu: Topgallant Publishing, 1971.

———. *On Being Hawaiian*. 1964; rpt. Honolulu: Topgallant Publishing, 1974.

Ige, Phillip K. "Paradise and Melting Pot in the Fiction and Non-fiction of Hawaii: A Study of Cross-Cultural Record." Ph.D. dissertation, Columbia University, 1968.

Joesting, Edward. *Hawaii: An Uncommon History*. New York: W. W. Norton, 1972.

Johnson, Rubellite Kawena. *Kumulipo: The Hawaiian Hymn of Creation*. Honolulu: Topgallant Publishing, 1981.

Jones, Howard Mumford. *The Age of Energy: Varieties of American Experience 1865–1915*. New York: Viking Press, 1971.

Kanahele, George S., ed. *Hawaiian Music and Musicians: An Illustrated History*. Honolulu: University of Hawaii Press, 1979.

———. *Hawaiian Renaissance*. Honolulu: Project WAIAHA, 1982.

———. *Ku Kanaka, Stand Tall: A Search for Hawaiian Values*. Honolulu: University of Hawaii Press and WAIAHA Foundation, 1986.

Kimura, Yukiko. *Issei: Japanese Immigrants in Hawaii*. Honolulu: University of Hawaii Press, 1988.

Korn, Alfons L. Preface to *The Echo of Our Song: Chants & Poems of the Hawaiians*. Translated and edited by Mary Kawena Pukui and Alfons L. Korn. Honolulu: University of Hawaii Press, 1973.

Kotani, Roland. *The Japanese in Hawaii: A Century of Struggle*. Honolulu: Hawaii Hochi, 1985.

Kuykendall, Ralph S., and A. Grove Day. *Hawaii: A History from Polynesian Kingdom to American State*. Rev. ed. Englewood Cliffs: Prentice-Hall, 1948; rpt. 1961.

Lau, Lawrence Lit. "Literary Lethargy." *Chinese Students' Alliance Annual* 6 (May 1923):5.

Lee, W. Storrs. *The Islands*. New York: Holt, Rinehart and Winston, 1966.

Lorch, Fred W. "Hawaiian Feudalism and Mark Twain's *A Connecticut Yankee in King Arthur's Court*." *American Literature* 30 (March 1958):50–66.

———. *The Trouble Begins at Eight: Mark Twain's Lecture Tours*. Ames: Iowa State University Press, 1968.

Lovejoy, Arthur O., Gilbert Chinard, George Boas, and Ronald S. Crane, eds. *A Dictionary History of Primitivism and Related Ideas*. Vol. 1. Baltimore: Johns Hopkins Press, 1935.

Lum, Arlene, ed. *Sailing for the Sun: The Chinese in Hawaii 1789–1989*. Honolulu: University of Hawaii Center for Chinese Studies, Three Heroes, 1988.

McWilliams, Carey. "Introduction." In *America Is in the Heart*, by Carlos Bulosan. Seattle: University of Washington Press, 1973.

Marx, Leo. *The Machine in the Garden: Technology and the Pastoral Ideal in America*. A Galaxy Book. New York: Oxford University Press, 1967.

Matsunaga, Diane. "Inu-gami: The Spirit of the Dog." In *Kodomo no Tame Ni, For the Sake of the Children: The Japanese American Experience in Hawaii*. Edited by Dennis M. Ogawa. Honolulu: University of Hawaii Press, 1978.

Miner, Earl. *The Japanese Tradition in British and American Literature*. Princeton: Princeton University Press, 1958.

Moriyama, Alan Takeo. *Imingaisha: Japanese Emigration Companies and Hawaii 1894–1908*. Honolulu: University of Hawaii Press, 1985.

Morrison, Toni. "Unspeakable Things Unspoken: The Afro-American Presence in American Literature." *Michigan Quarterly Review* 28.1 (1989):1–34.

Murayama, Milton. [Letter to Darrell H. Y. Lum] *Bamboo Ridge: The Hawaii Writers' Quarterly* 5 (December 1979):6–7.

———. "Problems of Writing in Dialect and Mixed Languages." *Bamboo Ridge: The Hawaii Writers' Quarterly* 5 (December 1979):8–10.

Nakano, Jiro. "Issei Poets of Hawaii." Panel presentation. Talk Story Big Island Writers' Conference. Hilo, Hawai'i, 13 July 1979.

Newman, Katharine. "Hawaiian-American Literature: The Cultivation of Mangoes." *MELUS: The Journal of the Society for the Study of the Multi-Ethnic Literature of the United States* 6 (Summer 1979):44–47.

Nomura, Gail M. "The Debate over the Prewar Role of Nisei in Hawaii: The New Americans Conference, 1927–1941." *Journal of Ethnic Studies* 15, no.1 (Spring 1987):95–115.

———. et al., eds. *Frontiers of Asian American Studies*. Pullman: Washington State University Press, 1989.

Nordyke, Eleanor C. *The Peopling of Hawaii*. East-West Population Institute Publication. Honolulu: University of Hawaii Press, 1977.

Odo, Franklin, and Kazuko Sinoto. *A Pictorial History of the Japanese in Hawai'i 1885–1924*. Honolulu: Hawai'i Immigrant Heritage Preservation Center, Bishop Museum, 1985.

Ogawa, Dennis M. *Kodomo no Tame Ni, For the Sake of the Children: The Japanese American Experience in Hawaii*. With the assistance of Glen Grant. Foreword by Lawrence H. Fuchs. Honolulu: University of Hawaii Press, 1978.

Okimoto, Ken. "Issei Poets of Hawaii: Hilo Bon Dance Club." Panel presentation. Talk Story Big Island Writers' Conference. Hilo, Hawai'i, 13 July 1979.

Paine, Albert Bigelow. *Mark Twain: A Biography*. 2 vols. New York: Harper and Brothers, 1912.

Perkins, Lily Leialoha Apo Mark. "The Aesthetics of Stress in 'Ōlelo and Oli:

Notes Toward a Theory of Hawaiian Oral Arts." Ph.D. dissertation, University of Pennsylvania, 1978.

Proceedings of the Second Annual Conference of New Americans. Honolulu: n.p., 1928.

Publication Committee of the United Japanese Society of Hawaii, eds. *A History of Japanese in Hawaii.* Honolulu: United Japanese Society of Hawaii, 1971.

Pukui, Mary Kawena and Samuel H. Elbert. *Hawaiian Dictionary.* Honolulu: University of Hawaii Press, 1971.

Rapson, Richard L. *Fairly Lucky You Live Hawaii! Cultural Pluralism in the Fiftieth State.* Washington D.C.: University Press of America, 1980.

Saiki, Patsy Sumie. *Gambare! An Example of Japanese Spirit.* Honolulu: Kisaku, 1982.

―――. *Japanese Women in Hawaii: The First 100 Years.* Honolulu: Kisaku, 1985.

Shimabukuro, Jimmy. "As Close as Possible to Experience." *Hawaii Herald* [Honolulu], 21 November 1980, n.p.n.

Sibley, Gay. [Letter.] *Honolulu Advertiser*, 11 February 1988, A–23.

Silva, Carol. "Remarks on John Dominis Holt." In *Writers of Hawaii: A Focus on Our Literary Heritage*, 12–15. Edited by Eric Chock and Jody Manabe. Honolulu: Bamboo Ridge Press, 1981.

Smith, Bradford. *Yankees in Paradise: The New England Impact on Hawaii.* New York: Lippincott, 1956.

Solberg, S. E. "Hawaiian Lyrics, Chant, and Dance: An Introductory Note with Bibliography." *MELUS* 6.2 (Summer 1979): 41–45.

―――. "Hawaiian Music, Poetry, and Dance: Reflections on Protection, Preservation, and Pride." *MELUS* 10.1 (Spring 1983):39–63.

―――. "An Introduction to Filipino-American Literature." In *Aiiieeeee! An Anthology of Asian-American Writers*, xlvix–lxiv. Edited by Frank Chin et al. Rev. ed. Washington, D.C.: Howard University Press, 1983.

"The Sound of (Hawaiian) Music." *East-West Perspectives* 1 no. 4 (Fall 1980): 32–36.

Stillman, Amy K. "Published Hawaiian Songbooks." *M[usic] L[ibrary] A[ssociation] Notes* (December 1987):221–39.

Suggs, Robert C. *The Island Civilizations of Polynesia.* New York: New American Library, 1960.

Sumida, Stephen H. "Hawaii, the Northwest, and Asia: Localism and Local Literary Developments in the Creation of an Asian Immigrants' Sensibility." *The Seattle Review: Blue Funnel Line* 11(Spring/Summer 1988):9–18.

―――. "Japanese American Moral Dilemmas in John Okada's *No-No Boy* and Milton Murayama's *All I Asking for Is My Body*." In *Frontiers of Asian American Studies: Writing, Research, and Criticism*, pp.222–33. Edited by Gail M. Nomura, Russell Endo, Stephen H. Sumida, and Russell Leong. Pullman: Washington State University Press, 1989.

————. [Letter.] *Honolulu Advertiser*, 28 January 1988, A-15.

————. "Reevaluating Mark Twain's Novel of Hawaii." *American Literature* (December 1989): 586–609.

————. *Two Novels of Hawaii*: Waimea Summer *by John Dominis Holt [and]* All I Asking for Is My Body *by Milton Murayama: A Critique.* Honolulu: Ku Pa'a, 1989.

————. "Waiting for the Big Fish: Recent Research in the Asian American Literature of Hawaii." In *The Best of Bamboo Ridge: The Hawaii Writers' Quarterly*, 302–21. Edited by Eric Chock and Darrell H. Y. Lum. Honolulu: Bamboo Ridge Press, 1986.

Takaki, Ronald. *Pau Hana: Plantation Life and Labor in Hawaii 1835–1920.* Honolulu: University of Hawaii Press, 1983.

————. *Strangers from a Different Shore: A History of Asian Americans.* Boston: Little, Brown, 1989.

Wakukawa, Ernest K. *A History of the Japanese People in Hawaii.* Honolulu: Toyo Shoin, 1938.

Wilson, Rob. "The Language of Confinement and Liberation in Milton Murayama's *All I Asking for Is My Body.*" In *Writers of Hawaii: A Focus on Our Literary Heritage*, 62–65. Edited by Eric Chock and Jody Manabe. Honolulu: Bamboo Ridge Press, 1981.

————. "Review: *All I Asking for Is My Body.*" *Bamboo Ridge: The Hawaii Writers' Quarterly* 5 (December 1979):2–5.

Wilson, Willard, ed. *College Plays* (1936–1955). TS. University of Hawaii Department of Englsih. Hawaii Pacific Collection. Hamilton Library. University of Hawaii.

Wong, Sau-ling C. "What's in a Name? Defining Chinese American Literature of the Immigrant Generation." In *Frontiers of Asian American Studies: Writing, Research, and Criticism*, 159–67. Edited by Gail M. Nomura et al. Pullman: Washington State University Press, 1989.

Yaggi, Albert S., Jr. [Letter.] *Honolulu Advertiser*, 17 Februrary 1988, A–11.

Index

Native Americans, xxii, 83, 154, 274n3
Native Hawaiians. *See* Hawaiians
"New Americans" (conferences), 290n13
Newell, Charles M.: *Kamehameha,* 190–91
New England, 55, 192, 299n3; and Puritans 4–5. *See also* Missionaries (Christian)
Newman, Katherine, 68, 305n46
Noble sage, 83, 107, 156
Noble savage, 24, 34, 80, 83, 166, 172, 178, 306n47
Nomura, Gail M., 290n13
Nordyke, Eleanor C., 276n14
Northwest Passage, 18, 168, 179, 197, 198
Norwegian Americans, 164
Nukuhiva *(Typee),* 20–31 passim, 160
Nunes, Susan, 108

Odo, Franklin, 298n37
Ogai, Seiko, 108, 207, 245
Ogawa, Dennis M., 279n12
'Ohana, 96; in pastoral, 106, 209; derivation of, 108–9
Okada, John: *No-No Boy,* 116, 234, 297n34
O'Keeffe, Georgia, 265–66
Oliveira, Paul L., 107
Olomana, 89–90
Omai, 179
Opukaha'ia, Henry, 227
Oral History Project (University of Hawaii Ethnic Studies Program), 231
Organic Act (1900), 203
Ota, Shelley Ayame Nishimura: *Upon Their Shoulders,* 203, 206–14, 228

Pahinui, Gabby (Gabby Pahinui Hawaiian Band), 283n9
Pai, Margaret (Margaret C. Kwon), 279n13, 296n26
Paine, Albert Bigelow, 242, 279n14
Paradise (image of Hawai'i). *See* Pastoral, simple
Paradise of the Pacific (magazine), 98, 112
Parker, Helen Lindsey: "Maunaloa," 64–65, 227
Pastoral, 3, 54, 100, 104, 105, 107, 108, 110, 127, 141, 163, 172, 184, 218, 244, 263, 268; defined, 4–7; Acadia (Arcadia), 5, 281–82n34
—, simple, 5, 56, 57–58, 67, 87, 92, 104, 180–81, 227, 263, 270, 271; in *Typee,* 24–26, 28–29; Twain and, 38, 39–40, 41,

43–44; Michener and, 68–69, 70, 72, 75, 78, 82; as parodied by Eliot, 68–69
—, complex, 6, 40, 67, 75, 109, 146, 160, 226, 261, 271, 274n7; Murayama and, 124, 136. *See also* Exoticism; Primitivism; Tourism
Paulet, George, 30–31
Pearl Harbor. *See* World War II
Pele (goddess of fire), 201, 253, 268, 279n13, 305n45; and hula, 3–4, 8; worship of, 35
Perkins, Leialoha Apo Mark, 283–84n10
Perry, Matthew C., 232–33
Pidgin and creole, 60, 97–99, 103–4, 106, 108, 236–37, 240, 247; and Michener, 79–80, 81, 82; criticism of, 101–3; and Murayama, 112–14, 270; and Holt, 152, 159
Plantation (sugar), 111, 114–37, 209–11, 231, 232, 245 passim
Pluralism, xvii–xviii, 88, 122, 225, 249, 259–61, 271, 299n4; in *All I Asking for Is My Body,* 135
Portuguese Americans, 164–65, 231, 236
Prendergast, Ellen Wright: "Kaulana nā Pua," 62–63, 109, 285n30
Primitivism, 25–26, 27, 28, 54, 278n6
"Princess of Kauai." *See* Lelemahoalani
Prometheus, 178; and Cook, 179, 182. *See also* Heroic literature
Puccini, Giacomo: *Madama Butterfly,* 76
Puerto Rican Americans, 114
Pukui, Mary Kawena, 287n52
Pyne, Dawn, 112, 270

Racism. *See* Mixed cultures and racism
Ragsdale, Bill, 41–42, 46–47, 48–49, 53–55, 191–92, 282n38
Raiatea, 8, 276n14
Ranching, 91, 111, 291n17; in *Waimea Summer,* 110–12, 137–59, 162, 178, 240, 261
Rapson, Richard L., 290–91n15
Reiplinger, Rap, 236–37
Renaissance: European, 70; Hawaiian, 60, 90, 160–61, 226, 238, 249, 266–67, 270

Saiki, Patsy, 108, 221, 245, 261, 268, 298n37; *Sachie,* 93–94, 96; "The Unwilling Bride," 94–96, 109; *The Return,* 96; *The Return of Sam Patch,* 232–35